THE PRIDE OF LUCIFER

THE
PRIDE
OF
LUCIFER

Morgan Grenfell 1838–1988:
The Unauthorized Biography of
a Merchant Bank

Dominic Hobson

HAMISH HAMILTON
LONDON

HAMISH HAMILTON LTD

Published by the Penguin Group
27 Wrights Lane, London w8 5tz, England
Viking Penguin Inc., 40 West 23rd Street, New York, New York 10010, USA
Penguin Books Australia Ltd, Ringwood, Victoria, Australia
Penguin Books Canada Ltd, 2801 John Street, Markham, Ontario,
Canada l3r 1b4
Penguin Books (NZ) Ltd, 182–190 Wairau Road, Auckland 10, New Zealand

Penguin Books Ltd, Registered Offices: Harmondsworth, Middlesex, England

First published in Great Britain by Hamish Hamilton Ltd, 1990

Filmset in Monophoto Baskerville

Printed in Great Britain by
Richard Clay Ltd, Bungay, Suffolk

A CIP catalogue record for this book is available from the British Library

ISBN 0-241-127793

Contents

For Jamanda

List of Illustrations

Roger Seelig (*Times Newspapers*)
Tony Parnes (*Times Newspapers*)
Dr Arthur Furer (*Times Newspapers*)
Patrick Spens (*Times Newspapers*)
David Mayhew (*Times Newspapers*)
Dr Ashraf Marwan (*Times Newspapers*)
Ephraim Margulies (*Times Newspapers*)
Alistair Buchanan (*Times Newspapers*)
Sir Peter Carey (*Times Newspapers*)
John Craven (*Times Newspapers*)
John Craven (*Times Newspapers*)

Preface

The omissions in this book are involuntary. Many stem from a libel law whose generosity to the plaintiff now stretches even to the excision of jokes which are made at his expense. Other erasures were made on the grounds that the events with which they deal are currently matters of judicial consideration. But a number of episodes were excluded solely because of contractual obligations to Morgan Grenfell into which I entered during the course of my employment by the bank between October 1983 and April 1988. Since a mischievous intent may be ascribed to a man who publishes a book about his former employer, I should like to dispel that misconception. Though I cannot pretend to have enjoyed the work of a merchant banker, or to have been conspicuously successful at it, during the course of my four and a half years with the bank I encountered much happiness, generosity and companionship. I was paid far larger sums than my efforts could possibly have warranted, and I forged many friendships which remain strong today. I left in the spring of last year both happy and generously compensated, with much goodwill on the part both of employer and of employee.

Sadly, this concord has not survived the writing of this book. Though I made every effort to involve the bank in its production, and gave undertakings that I would not publish confidential material which came to my attention during the course of my employment, Morgan Grenfell have sought, through their solicitors, Slaughter & May, to prevent its publication. My decision to proceed with the book, irrespective of the misgivings of the bank, is not, I hope, a dishonourable one. My lowly capacity within the bank meant that I was left untouched by almost all of the events described in it, but I have learnt that there are others whose lives and careers they changed irrevocably, and it is them who are owed this glimpse at the truth.

Those who are familiar with the story of Morgan Grenfell will recognize my indebtedness to those writers and journalists who have already traversed the eventful history of the bank. During the preparation of the book I read countless newspapers and magazines spanning a period of over fifty years. I owe an enormous debt of gratitude to the financial journalists, past and present, from whose work on the story of Morgan Grenfell I have drawn so freely. I owe much also to the assistance of the staff at Companies House, the City Business Library, the Senate House Library, the Library of the London School of Economics, the Guildhall Library, the London Library, the Peabody Trust, the Pierpont Morgan Library in New York, and the Peabody Archives in Baltimore.

I am grateful also for access to a large number of books on the Morgan banks, especially Vincent P. Carosso's monumental *The Morgans: Private International Bankers*, whose range and detail is unlikely ever to be surpassed. I have drawn on the published work of the official historian of Morgan Grenfell, Dr Kathleen Burk, and especially on *Morgan Grenfell 1838–1988: The Biography of a Merchant Bank* and *Britain, America and the Sinews of War*. Much of the material on the Guinness affair has already been published, in *Takeovers*, by Ivan Fallon and James Srodes; *The Guinness Affair*, by Nick Kochan and Hugh Pym; and in Peter Pugh's *Is Guinness Good For You?* Margaret Reid's pioneering study of Big Bang and its immediate aftermath, *All-Change in the City*, is indispensable to any student of that period. I am embarrassed to record my thanks to Andrew Sinclair for pointing out to me, on a train to Cumbria, that his *Corsair: The Life of J. Pierpont Morgan*, contained some pleasing sexual anecdotes. Many other works are acknowledged in the footnotes. Most importantly, I would like to thank all of those, many of them leading characters in this drama, who gave me so freely of their time. I fear that none of them would thank me for naming them here, but my debt to them is evident in the pages that follow.

I can, however, freely thank Susanna Burgess, whose idea the book was, her sister Kate, for her researches, my father Dick Hobson for editing early drafts and preparing an index, my agent, Caroline Dawnay, for her enthusiasm, and most of all my editor, Christopher Sinclair-Stevenson, for his humour, and especially for the faith and courage lacking in others.

January 1990

ONE

The Immortal Part

'No, sir. The first thing is character.' John Pierpont Morgan's aphorism is more readily associated in English minds with preparatory school masters or retired majors than with the lending criteria of modern merchant bankers, but for the greatest Gentile banker of his age it came before 'money or anything else . . . because a man I do not trust could not get money from me on all the bonds in Christendom'.[1] The statement was businesslike rather than pious; J. P. Morgan understood that for the private banker an unsullied reputation for plain dealing is the only guarantee of continued prosperity. He had learned it from his father, the London banker Junius Spencer Morgan,[2] and passed it to his son, John ('Jack') Pierpont Morgan, Jnr, who told the United States Senate twenty years later that 'at all times the idea of doing only first-class business, and that in a first-class way, has been before our minds . . . Since we have no more power of telling the future than other men, we have made mistakes . . . but our mistakes have been errors of judgement and not of principle.'[3] In private banking, the house of Morgan is a dynasty comparable with Fugger, Medici, Rothschild, Hambro or Baring. The name alone is sufficient to gain entry to any palace, parliament, banking parlour or boardroom in any of the six continents, giving its bearers enormous scope to enrich themselves as well as their reputations. For this reason, successive generations of Morgan bankers have been steeped in a code of ethics and customs designed, as Jack Morgan put it, 'to justify the confidence of his clients in him and thus preserve it for his successors'. To the founders of Morgan Grenfell, the paramountcy of the reputation of the house over personal enrichment was

I

beyond question. Their successors in the 1980s were less scrupulous in their dealings and so made errors of principle as well as of judgement.

Jack Morgan's powerful exposition of the ethics of the business of moneylending seemed anachronistic to the group of men who took charge of Morgan Grenfell at the end of the 1970s. To them, it was pure nostalgia, richly redolent of the heroic age of merchant banking in nineteenth-century London, when British, rather than American or Japanese, capital and industrial power seemed to be dictating the course of history. Dwelling upon it had retarded the adaptations necessary to survival in a more competitive world than that of the early Morgans, when the entire pattern of world trade – to say nothing of the outcome of wars and the might of princes and potentates – hinged on the deliberations of a small group of private bankers living within yards of each other in the City of London. They felt that Jack Morgan, already in possession of a very considerable fortune, could afford his virtuous hypocrisy. His code was naive in the age of Ivan Boesky and Michael Milken, Guinness and Hanson Trust and all the other industrialists, financiers and Stock Market gamblers who shaped rather than adhered to the ethics of corporate warfare. His scrupulousness was irrelevant amid the magnitude and complexity of the political, economic, commercial, technological and moral changes that assailed the City of London in the 1980s. Merchant bankers, they said, must not just adapt more often and more quickly to change, but initiate, grasp and direct it. Unfortunately, in shedding the incubus of the past, they imperilled all that their forebears had built. A banker's credit, warned Jack Morgan, is 'the result of years of fair and honourable dealing and, while it may be quickly lost, once lost cannot be restored for a long time, if ever'.[4]

City gentlemen hurrying past the back of the Royal Exchange will rarely glance at the seated bronze figure unveiled by the Prince of Wales on 23 July 1869 and they are still less likely to read the inscription on the pedestal, or to make a better association with the name George Peabody than the barrack blocks of flats they pass on their way to play squash in the lunch hour. It is hard now to recapture the esteem in which George Peabody was held by his contemporaries, but the accolades he received in his lifetime are ample testimony to it. During the course of his life George Peabody received a Congressional Resolution of Praise and a Congressional Gold Medal. After he gracefully declined her offer of a knighthood or a baronetcy, Queen Victoria sent him a private letter of thanks and a priceless miniature of herself. He was offered the post of Secretary of the Treasury under President Andrew Johnson and was asked to run for President in 1867. His birthplace, the Massachusetts town of Danvers, renamed itself Peabody in his honour in 1866. On 18 February 1895 the state of Tennessee declared the centenary of his birth a public holiday. In the New York University Hall of Fame a bust of him was unveiled in 1926. He was in 1862 the first American to receive the Freedom of the City of London, and was granted honorary membership of both the Clothworkers' Company and the Fishmongers' Company, honorary degrees from Harvard and Oxford (in 1867) and a private audience with Pope Pius IX.[5]

After his death in London on 4 November 1869, at the Belgravia home of his friend, Sir Curtis Lampson, his body lay in state in Westminster Abbey for thirty days as the people of London came to pay him homage. His granite memorial is next to the Tomb of the Unknown Soldier. On hearing the news of his death, the United States Congress, state legislatures and a wide variety of religious and philanthropic bodies passed resolutions of sorrow. His body was returned to the United States aboard HMS *Monarch*, accompanied by the pride of the United States Navy, USS *Plymouth*. These ships, which accompanied him on his final journey across the Atlantic from Portsmouth Harbour on 11 December 1869, had been made available at the express request of Queen Victoria and President Grant. In the stern of the *Monarch* a mortuary chapel was

3

created, in which the coffin was draped with black cloth, on which the initials 'G.P.' were picked out in white satin. On reaching Portland Harbor, Maine, on 26 January 1870, the coffin remained on board for three days before being removed to City Hall, where it lay in state again until 1 February. It was not finally interred until 8 February 1870, after a final week on display at the Peabody Institute in Peabody. Queen Victoria sent her son, Prince Arthur, to the funeral.[6] The dying Robert E. Lee, the former Confederate commander, had to be restrained from attending. The funeral was arranged by John Pierpont Morgan, the son of Peabody's first partner and a man destined to become the greatest financier of his age. It was he who suggested that American and British marines march together behind the coffin.[7] Two days after Peabody's body was despatched to the United States, Victor Hugo wrote in the London *Times* that

On this earth there are men of hate and men of love. Peabody was one of the latter. It is on the face of these men that we see the smile of God.[8]

This was a panegyric fit for a saint rather than a merchant banker and he earned it as a pioneer of modern capitalist philanthropy.

His philanthropy was munificent and unprecedented, setting an example of private generosity which spawned a host of imitators like Guinness, Sutton and Lewis. Initially, much of his giving was sentimental, endowing worthy institutions in the towns and cities where he grew up and learned his trade. In 1857 he gave $1.5 million to found a Peabody Institute at Baltimore in Maryland, which included a library, a lecture hall, an academy of music and an art gallery. A gift of $250,000 funded a second Peabody Institute at Peabody, his birthplace. Like many clever men denied a formal education, Peabody had an exaggerated regard for academic achievement, giving $150,000 to establish the Peabody Museum of Natural History at Yale; $150,000 to establish the Peabody Museum of

Archaeology and Ethnology at Harvard; and $140,000 to found the Peabody Academy of Science at Salem, Massachusetts. He also endowed the Phillips Academy at Andover and two state historical societies. Four public libraries were built at his expense, at Georgetown and Newburyport in Massachusetts and Georgetown, a suburb of Washington DC – all places where he had worked as a young man – and at Thetford in Vermont, where his uncle and aunt lived. His donations to his nephew, Othniel C. Marsh, enabled him to become one of the leading palaeontologists of the day.[9]

Occasionally his wealth was deployed in eccentric causes, pioneering a mannerism now common among reclusive millionaires. When in 1851 the United States Congress failed to appropriate money for a display at the Great Exhibition at Crystal Palace, Peabody gave $15,000 to make it possible to display American inventions and products. In 1852 he gave £2,000 to equip the *Advance* for an expedition under Dr Elisha Kent Kane to scour the Arctic for the missing Dr John Franklin, the navigator who died searching for the North-West Passage. Greenland still has a Peabody Bay. He even built a church. But he craved immortality, and reasoned that giving to the poor was the means of ensuring it. A friend of the Utopian Socialist and businessman, Robert Owen, Peabody first considered the idea after a visit to industrial Lancashire in the 1830s, but did not commit himself wholeheartedly to poor relief until he had largely withdrawn from the management of his merchant-banking partnership in the late 1850s. At first, he wanted to equip London with drinking fountains. Then he proposed to fund the Ragged School Movement, founded by Lord Shaftesbury in 1843, to give destitute children shelter and education, but Shaftesbury asked him to provide better housing for the working class instead. This he resolved to do, though the outbreak of the American Civil War delayed the gift for a year.

Peabody explained his decision to become a philanthropist as a simple desire to be remembered as a good man:

5

When aches and pains came upon me, I realised I was not immortal. I became anxious to use my millions for the greatest good of humanity. I found that there were men in life just as anxious to help the poor and destitute as I was to make money. I called in friends in whom I had confidence and asked them to be trustees for my first gift. They accepted. For the first time I felt a higher pleasure and a greater happiness than making money – that of giving it away for good purposes.[10]

In March 1862 the Peabody Donation Fund was established with a gift of £150,000. The trustees were his friends Lord Stanley, Sir Curtis Lampson, Sir James Emmerson Tennant and his partner J. S. Morgan. The first scheme, the Spitalfields estate, was opened two years later. It provided sixty-two flats at a cost of £22,000. Estates followed at Chelsea, Bermondsey, Islington and Hammersmith. A second gift of £250,000 in 1866 was followed by a third of £100,000 in 1868 and he left the fund another £150,000 in his will. By 1914 there were over 6,000 Peabody Homes throughout London and, by 1939, over 8,000, each with gas, electricity and hot water. Today the Peabody Housing Association – which supplanted the trust in 1975 – runs some 12,000 homes around London. Peabody insisted that nobody was excluded from a home on grounds of sectarian religion or party politics.

The scale of Peabody's liberality in an age of unfettered capitalism startled his contemporaries. It won him the admiration of Queen Victoria who, when he refused her offer of either a baronetcy or the Grand Cross of the Order of the Bath, sent him on 28 March 1866 a letter of appreciation written in her own hand:

The Queen hears that Mr Peabody intends shortly to return to America & she would be sorry that he should leave England without being assured by herself how deeply she appreciates the noble act of more than princely munificence by which he has sought to relieve the wants of the poorer class of her subjects residing in London. It is an act as the Queen believes wholly without parallel, & which will carry its best reward in the consciousness of having contributed so largely to the assistance of those who can little help themselves.

The Queen would not however have been satisfied without giving Mr Peabody some public mark of her sense of his munificence, & she would gladly have conferred upon him either a baronetcy or The Grand Cross of the Order of the Bath, but that she understands Mr Peabody to feel himself debarred from accepting such distinctions.

It only remains therefore for the Queen to give Mr Peabody this assurance of her personal feelings which she would further wish to mark by asking him to accept a Miniature Portrait of herself which she will desire to have painted for him & which when finished can either be sent to him in America or given to him on the return, which she rejoices to hear he meditates, to the country that owes him so much.[11]

Though he replied to the Queen's letter, Peabody shunned most other forms of approbation, appearing in public only once, to distribute prizes at the Working Classes' Exhibition at the Guildhall in 1866. He composed his own verdict on his life:

I have prayed my Heavenly Father day by day that I might be enabled before I died to show my gratitude by doing some great good to my fellow men.

It is inscribed on his memorial in Westminster Abbey.

Peabody seems to have valued mankind only in the abstract. At close quarters generosity of spirit seems to have eluded him. He had few interests outside business. One contemporary described him as

One of the dullest men in the world: he had positively no gift except that of making money.[12]

This gift he had in full measure -- his fortune may have reached the Victorian equivalent of $100 million.[13] Like many millionaires, George Peabody was a bore. A hagiographical monograph published in 1914 described him as follows:

Although a bachelor, living plainly and quietly, he could enjoy unselfish sociability. He was a total abstainer from liquors and tobacco, and was very fond of fruit, and preferred plain, well-cooked food to luxuries. Angling seems to have been his only gratification.[14]

And, like a caricature, he combined public largesse with personal meanness. He often sent his office boy out to buy him a bag of apples, giving him tuppence to pay for them. The apples cost a penny ha'penny, but he always asked for the change. Similarly, he would stand in the rain to wait for a ha'penny bus rather than hail a cab. Once, he insisted that a railway ticket clerk should be sacked after overcharging him a shilling, explaining himself priggishly:

Not that I could not afford to pay the shilling, but the man was cheating many travellers to whom the swindle would be oppressive.[15]

While in New York in 1866 he received 4,000 private applications for financial help. He burned them all. His personal expenses in the last ten years of his life rarely exceeded £600 per annum and he never owned a house, keeping rooms for a time in Hampton Court, before moving eventually to Richmond. He was almost teetotal. J. P. Morgan, who worked as his assistant in 1856[16] and helped him pack for his first return visit to the United States that summer, suggests that he was something of an old woman:

Ue is a very agreeable gentleman and very full of wit, but a regular old bachelor. If you could have seen the quantity of nic-nacs which he carried with him to America and which were stored away in his trunks ... you ... would have thought he was going ... to some unexplored regions.[17]

His one indulgence was a mistress in Brighton, who bore him a daughter. He told those who asked why he had never married that he had been betrothed to a young woman from Maryland who had been sent to London to escape an unsuitable association, but that he had eventually lost her to her former lover.[18] His staff were not fooled by this explanation; J. P. Morgan claimed to have been told of the mistress by one of the London firm's older clerks. Though Peabody's daughter married poorly, and lost her inheritance, her two sons inherited some of Peabody's gift, one becoming a barrister at the Parliamentary bar and the other a professor of geology.[19]

*

George Peabody was born on 18 February 1795, in the middle of George Washington's second term as President, into a family which could claim direct descent from Francis Peabody, a Leicestershire Puritan who landed in America in 1635, only fifteen years after the *Mayflower*. Despite this valuable pedigree, George's father was no more than a small farmer and leather-worker who could afford his son only four years' schooling. At the age of eleven, George was apprenticed to a grocer in Danvers where, it is recorded, he demonstrated a precocious addiction to hard and repetitive work by making eight dozen whips in a day, easily breaking the record of six dozen.[20] From April 1811 he was a clerk at his brother's store at Newburyport in Massachusetts. On 13 May 1811 their father died. Two weeks later a fire raged through the town, destroying their business. Worse, an English trade embargo depressed trade in New England and George, now a penniless orphan, was obliged to leave Massachusetts with his bankrupt uncle, John Peabody, to peddle goods from door to door in George-town, DC.[21] The business seems to have prospered; an advert-isement placed in a Georgetown newspaper of the time gives a flavour of it:

Just Received and for Sale by George Peabody, Budge St . . . 30 pair Rose Blankets . . . 20 dozen Gentlemen's leather gloves . . . 1,000 pair Ladies Morocco shoes . . . 200 pieces India cottons . . . 1 case Nun's Thread . . . 20 cases Men's fine hats.[22]

At seventeen George served in the war of 1812, leaving the artillery in 1813 to assume the management of Elisha Riggs's warehouse in Georgetown. He was soon admitted to a junior partnership. In 1815 Peabody Riggs & Co. moved to Baltimore and, within seven years, established branches in New York and Philadelphia. In 1829 Elisha Riggs retired and George became senior partner, traversing Maryland and Virginia on horseback collecting merchandise for the firm. He visited London for the first time in 1827, trading Southern cotton for English manufac-tured goods. He found the business profitable and returned four times before 1837, when he decided to settle there permanently the following year. He did not return to the United States again for twenty years.

The story of Morgan Grenfell begins with the establishment by George Peabody of 'a counting-house, with desks, chairs, a mahogany counter and a safe' at No. 31 Moorgate in the City of London in 1838.[23] He seems, initially at least, to have traded under the names of both Peabody, Riggs & Co. and plain George Peabody, Merchant. By 1843 he had withdrawn his capital from Peabody, Riggs & Co. but the Baltimore connection was not finally severed until 1845, when he moved to No. 6, Warnford Court, Throgmorton Street and began to trade solely under the name of George Peabody & Co. There was no great change of direction. His principal business was importing cotton and tobacco from the southern United States, exporting in return English textiles and steel rails for the rapidly growing American railway system. Even his involvement in trade was not unusual. All the historic names in merchant banking – Hambro's, Baring Brothers, N. M. Rothschild – have their roots in merchanting of much the same kind. John and Francis Baring, founders of the Baring banking dynasty, initially established a merchanting business in London in 1763. Nathan Rothschild came to England in 1798 to sell English cotton for his family in Germany. Carl Joachim Hambro, who moved to London in the same year as George Peabody, was descended from a long line of Jewish merchants. Initially they competed little. Hambro's Bank grew out of Baltic trade; Baring Brothers and N. M. Rothschild out of Continental trade; and Morgan Grenfell out of trade between Britain and the United States. In time they began to intrude upon each other's markets and the animosities and rivalries which this sparked still animate their successors today.

Britain in 1838 was, economically, the most advanced country on earth. No society, either before or since, so dominated the world economy as Britain did during the first half of the nineteenth century. As the only industrialized nation, Britain had for a few decades no competition at all in any of the markets of the world for manufactured goods. The British economy assumed the shape it retained until the First World War. Nine-tenths of Britain's imports were raw materials and food; an equal proportion of its exports were manufactured goods. Although Britain maintained a surplus on trade throughout the nineteenth century the import of commodities continuously exceeded the export of manufactured goods; exports never paid for imports. The deficit was covered instead by Britain's domination of the shipping and financing of world trade, much expanded by peace and a political establishment favourable to it. As the ideas of free trade took root, duties on imports of all kinds were progressively removed during the 1840s, culminating in the repeal of the Corn Laws in 1846. More than half of Britain's burgeoning trade, both imports and exports, was shipped, serviced and financed in London.[24] The City of London grew wealthy from this business and a surplus of capital accumulated in relatively sophisticated hands. Oddly, it was not reinvested in the manufacturing towns of the north of England, where the entrepreneurs largely funded themselves. It was applied instead to the financing of the processes of trade. With goods often taking months to reach their destination, the greatest need in international trade was to plug the gap between buyers and sellers. This was the role that Peabody, in common with his illustrious contemporaries, fulfilled.

The steel-makers of England knew that there was a profitable market for their steel in the American railway industry. What they could not know was how, when or even if they would be paid for it. Similarly, the American railway companies did not want to part with their cash until the steel had arrived. The missing ingredient was a middleman confident in the creditworthiness of both parties, who could advance money to the supplier, knowing that he could rely on the buyer to meet the bill when it became due. Peabody, who knew both buyers and sellers, performed this function. The tool he used was the bill of exchange, or the 'bill on London', which had been invented in the late eighteenth century. Originally this was no more than a bill sent by the supplier to the customer requesting payment by a certain date; then merchant bankers like George Peabody found that if they used their reputation and creditworthiness to guarantee the payment of these bills – 'accepted' them – their exporting clients were prepared to forego a modest proportion of the proceeds. By selling their bills at a discount to a merchant bank, suppliers received most of their cash but still left the customer a period of grace in which to pay. For his trouble, the merchant received a fee and enjoyed the 'interest' reflected in the discount. Sometimes, he sold the bills for profit to others, allowing the entire transaction to be financed by the surplus cash of outside investors. Once the bill became due for payment, the customer sent funds to the merchant bank, which then repaid the investors the face value of the bills.

Britain's surplus of capital was also invested abroad, at first in securing the governments of Europe bankrupted by the French Wars of 1793 to 1815. As the burden of debt of the Napoleonic Wars receded, the higher returns available from financing (often speculative) projects abroad attracted investors in London. Large sums were invested in Latin American mines, railways and sewerage systems. Naturally enough, Peabody sold in London the bonds of American states, collecting commissions and taking a 'turn' on the difference between the prices at which the bonds were bought and sold. By 1843 he was probably the major dealer in American bonds in London. As early as 1837 Peabody arranged in London a loan of $8 million for the then bankrupt state of Maryland, using his associates in Baltimore to secure the business. The funds were used to build the Chesapeake and Ohio canal. Peabody returned his commission of $60,000 to the state of Maryland, earning its eternal gratitude. In 1848 he helped the United States Government sell the Mexican War Loan to London investors. In common with most nineteenth-century merchant bankers, he abjured industrial finance, preferring the less speculative arts of funding railways and foreign governments, where reputation counted for more than creditworthiness. In this the network of agents and informants he maintained abroad – for spotting new business opportunities and paying local traders –

were an invaluable source of intelligence. Foreign investment was a characteristic of the British economy in the nineteenth century from which Peabody and his successors profited greatly. By the outbreak of the First World War, Britain had invested some £4 billion abroad in the bonds and shares of various foreign governments, municipalities, provincial administrations and commercial enterprises. Until these holdings of foreign, and especially American, securities were severely reduced to repay the debts incurred in two world wars, the interest and dividends received from abroad more than compensated for Britain's chronic deficit in physical trade, keeping the pound strong and transforming the workshop of the world into an international *rentier*.[25]

By 1843 Peabody's business had prospered sufficiently for him to take on a book-keeper, G. C. Gooch, paying him a salary of £150 a year.[26] In 1852 Gooch became his first partner but, although he was reliable and diligent, keeping the books and writing letters with iterative efficiency, Gooch was no substitute for Peabody, whose gout, rheumatism and intestinal complaints led to increasingly lengthy absences from Warnford Court. During the first four months of 1853 he was unable to work at all. Reports of his ill health disturbed his American clientele and Peabody's transatlantic business began to suffer. Peabody himself had not visited the United States since May 1836 and his connections were growing rusty. Gooch, an Englishman and a clerk, was a poor makeweight. Peabody needed an able and respected American partner. In May 1853 he found just such a man, Junius Spencer Morgan, then a partner in a firm of dry-goods importers in Boston.[27]

Like Peabody's, J. S. Morgan's early life was scarcely vivid. Unlike Peabody, his family was wealthy. He was born at West Springfield, Connecticut, on 14 April 1813, the third and last son of Joseph Morgan, a New England farmer and land dealer of Welsh descent who had branched out into banking and insurance. He was educated at Captain Alden Partridge's American Literary, Scientific and Military Academy in Middletown and at a private school in East Windsor, and was apprenticed in 1829 to Alfred Welles, a merchant and banker in Boston. He stayed five years, stacking shelves and selling watches and lamps on the streets as far south as Philadelphia. Travel gave him his first experience of banking, since he also arranged for Welles's invoices and those of his clients to be discounted (sold at less than face value, the difference representing interest) with local finance houses. In 1833, against his father's advice, he accepted a partnership from Welles, who was by then over-trading. In 1834 Joseph Morgan had to guarantee his son's debts and lend the partnership money. Chastened, Junius was moved by his father to a partnership at a private bank in New York City run by a Connecticut business colleague, Morris Ketchum. Morgan, Ketchum & Co. was a fully fledged private banking house, selling stocks and bonds, but Junius disliked New York and left Ketchum in January 1836 to return to Connecticut, settling for a partnership with Howe, Mather & Co. in Hartford. He invested $10,000, on which he received an income of 6 per cent plus a quarter of the profits. He was also drawn back to Connecticut by Juliet Pierpont, the 20-year-old daughter of a Boston Unitarian pastor, whom he married in May of the same year. Her father, the Reverend John Pierpont, was an outspoken man, whose homilies from the pulpit on the evils of slavery and strong drink very nearly led to his deposition by an outraged congregation. This may explain the fierce Episcopalian allegiances of his son-in-law and grandson, John Pierpont Morgan, the first of the five children borne by Juliet.

Young John, who was born on 17 April 1837, was brought up in a household that valued thrift. His command of decimal calculation was prodigious and he formed his first company at the age of twelve, with a friend called Jim Goodwin, maintaining a cash account at the back of his diary.[28] Unlike his father, he received a cosmopolitan education, at the local dame school, the English High School in Boston, the Institute Sillig on Lake Geneva and at the University of Göttingen. Junius, however, remained in Hartford for the first fifteen years of his son's life, travelling widely throughout the southern states of

Virginia, South Carolina, Georgia and Florida, buying cotton and wool and collecting debts which were often paid in cotton rather than cash. He became a pillar of the local business establishment, collecting directorships at the Hartford Fire Insurance Company, the New Haven and Hartford Railroad and the Phoenix Bank. He became a vestryman at the Hartford Episcopal Church, was active in charity work for orphans and juveniles and endowed the Wadsworth Athenaeum, Hartford's library, museum and art gallery. When his father died on 23 July 1847 he was left a sizeable fortune in stocks, bonds and real estate. In February 1850 he was elevated to senior partner and the firm's name was changed to Mather, Morgan & Co.[29]

In the autumn of 1850 Junius decided to go into partnership with James M. Beebe, a Boston importer. Beebe, Morgan started business in January 1851 and, since the firm's turnover rose from $2 million in 1849 to $7 million in 1853, his appointment must have been a success. Like most of Boston's leading merchants, the firm relied heavily on sterling credits from Baring Brothers in London, and it was business of this nature that took him to Warnford Court in May 1853 for his first meeting with Peabody. Morgan impressed Peabody, who praised his 'high moral and business character', and he was invited to a dinner at the Star and Garter Hotel in Richmond, hosted by Peabody in honour of the American Minister in London, Joseph R. Ingersoll.[30] Despite his distaste for alcohol and a frugal appetite, Peabody understood well the value of dining in business. His Independence Day banquets on 4 July were a legendary feature of the London social calendar, attended not only by business associates but also by members of the aristocracy and the diplomatic community, at least one being graced by the Duke of Wellington. During one week in 1855 Peabody entertained eighty guests at dinner and another thirty-five at the opera, but the purpose of such engagements was never frivolous. Relations between Britain and the United States were tense for much of the nineteenth century. Peabody himself had fought the British in 1812 and the *Trent* affair in 1861 nearly led to war again. The submission to arbitration of the *Alabama* claims in 1868 led to much popular resentment against the United States in Britain.[31] With this mutual suspicion a constant threat to his business, Peabody's dinners were intended to engender the national goodwill on which his earnings depended. This was not always forthcoming. At the 1854 dinner James Buchanan, later President but then the American Minister in London, refused to rise during the loyal toast; and one member of his delegation simply walked out.

Morgan was sufficiently interested to return to London in February 1854, spending several weeks examining Peabody's books before returning to Boston and deciding to accept the offer of a partnership from 1 October 1854. 'I hope ultimately to raise the character and standing of my house so that it will prove creditable to myself and to our country,' he wrote to a Boston merchant in May,[32] while in August Peabody wrote to Morgan urging him to

Visit the principal cities as far south as Charleston, and west as Cincinnati, for the purpose of gaining information and establishing business correspondence with the best houses connected with the business of Europe, China & India.[33]

Peabody's advice to Morgan in July 1854 on how to win an account expressed perfectly the unwritten code by which Morgan bankers sought business for the next 120 years. 'It would not do for Morgan to solicit them a second time,' Peabody cautioned, but a friendly visit 'so as to be favourably remembered' was entirely acceptable. Despite this gentlemanly approach, Peabody's appointment of Morgan alarmed the competition. Samuel Ward, who in 1852 succeeded his father Thomas as American agent for Baring Brothers, wrote to London that

Mr Morgan is highly thought of as a man of talent, energy and labour. If Mr Peabody was safe before he will be much safer now with Mr Morgan at his side ... [He] has a hold on this side which will make the competition more formidable than before.[34]

Junius Morgan and his wife sailed for Liverpool on the *Europa* on 13 September 1854, arriving in London thirteen days later and dining with Peabody that night. On 30 September a ten-year partnership agreement was signed. Peabody supplied £400,000 of the total capital of £450,000, Morgan £40,000 and Gooch £10,000.[35] Peabody did not retain the near nine-tenths of the profits to which this arrangement entitled him, yielding Morgan 28 per cent and Gooch 7 per cent. Morgan was also allowed entertainment expenses of £2,500 a year. At the end of October Peabody wrote to a colleague in the United States:

Mr Morgan, my new partner, has been with us about a month, and I begin to find him useful, and I trust when we get into our new counting house in Broad Street (which will be one of the best in London) and get proper assistance around us, I shall begin to experience the good results of my late arrangements.[36]

They moved to new premises at 22 Old Broad Street at the beginning of 1855 but left the name of the partnership – George Peabody & Co. – unchanged. Morgan himself acquired two houses, a town house at 13 Princes Gate and a large Georgian residence at Roehampton, Dover House, whose lawns rolled down to the Thames. By careful acquisition he eventually surrounded Dover House with ninety-two acres, on which he reared prize cattle; from its upper floors could be seen the spires of Harrow School.[37] By the standards of the day, Morgan and Peabody worked exceptionally hard. They were usually at their desks in Old Broad Street by 10 a.m., supervising the staff of three until midday, when they received visitors. From 1 p.m. until 2 p.m. they were in the banking-office, before spending an hour at the Stock Exchange. They did not leave the office until 4 p.m. In the summer J. S. Morgan would live at Roehampton rather than Princes Gate, taking a carriage daily to the City, but most summers were punctuated by long spells touring Europe.

It is impossible to overestimate the importance of the American connection to the business of the firm, especially during the 1850s. 'My own house is engaged more as American bankers than as Merchants,' Peabody wrote to a friend at this time.[38] 'Steamer nights', the nights before the twice-weekly steamships from New York and Boston docked in London, were times of intense activity at 22 Old Broad Street. Britain exported iron and manufactured goods in exchange for wheat and cotton, all of which Peabody and Morgan helped to finance. Their commission from credits to American exporters rose from £30,000 in 1855 to over £55,000 two years later.[39] American railways, which expanded enormously at this time, were almost exclusively built with British iron and funded with British capital. American imports of iron rails averaged 200,000 tons a year throughout the 1850s as the United States spent $838 million adding 22,000 miles of new track to its rail network.[40] George Peabody & Co. bought the rails, insured them, shipped them and and extended credits to the British manufacturers. Vanderbilt, the greatest of the American railway magnates, used Peabody and J. S. Morgan to arrange the import of iron rails for his expanding network.[41] Eventually they began to raise finance directly for the railway companies. George Peabody had dealt in US federal, state and municipal bonds since the 1840s, buying them cheap in London and selling them dear in New York, where the credit was better understood. This introduced him to potential investors in railway bonds in the 1850s, allowing him in April 1853 to sponsor the first issue of US railway bonds on the London market: $1.89 million of 7 per cent convertible first-mortgage bonds of the Ohio and Mississippi Railroad Company. In an inauspicious start, the company failed to complete the railway on time and defaulted twice. By the close of the 1850s Peabody & Co. counted among its clients the railways of New York Central, Michigan Central, Illinois Central, the Ohio & Mississippi and the Baltimore & Ohio, and business was sufficiently voluminous to occupy Peabody's friend, Sir Curtis Lampson, full time.[42] Lampson, born in Vermont in 1806, was a Cheapside fur merchant who became a naturalized British subject in 1849. Though he never joined Peabody's partnership, they were close friends as well as business associates. Both became directors and shareholders of the Atlantic Telegraph Company, formed in 1856 by the American paper millionaire, Cyrus W. Field, to lay a cable across the North Atlantic. Within two years, Queen Victoria and President James Buchanan were able to exchange messages of congratulation but the cable soon snapped and it was not reconnected for several years.[43]

In 1857 the American connection almost broke Peabody. Excessive lending to the railways and shrinkage in European wheat markets, coupled with speculation in western farm prices, led to a panic in New York. Five of Peabody's principal debtors were unable to pay. English investors, sensing a crisis, sold their American securities back to Peabody & Co., further reducing available cash. By November, with immediate liabilities of £2.3 million, Peabody had to ask the Bank of England for a loan. On November 25 the Bank advanced £800,000, with guarantees from thirteen other City institutions, several of which had earlier offered to support Peabody privately if he undertook to withdraw from the market within a year. This is said to have goaded Peabody to anger. One report said he 'went into a rage, like a wounded lion' and 'told Mr Morgan that he *dared them* to cause his failure'.[44] Baring Brothers had pressed so hard for immediate settlement of their outstanding bills that Peabody refused to allow them to act as a guarantor.[45] The *New York Herald* opined that to have allowed the firm to fail would have been a 'national calamity'.[46] 'Rather mortifying to the pride,' said J. P. Morgan of the loan from the Bank of England,[47] but in the event only £300,000 of the advance was used and it was repaid in full in March 1858. By November 1858 the firm had recovered and profits from commercial lending and the securities business were growing steadily. The profits available for division among the partners grew from £43,043 in 1858 to £60,000 in 1859 and £76,437 in 1860. 'Everything regarding my business goes on as satisfactory and profitable as ever,' said Peabody in December 1859.[48] Concluding that the crisis had been sparked by over-zealous solicitation of new accounts, Peabody left for the Continent in the summer of 1858 for his first holiday in twenty-one years.

That autumn and winter were his last extended spells of work at the firm.

In April 1862 Peabody cut his share of the profits from 65 per cent to 30 per cent and on 1 October 1864, when the partnership agreement expired, he withdrew altogether. Since he was unwilling to lend his name to a firm over which he had no control, George Peabody & Co. ceased to exist and was succeeded the same day by J. S. Morgan & Co., from which Junius received 82.5 per cent of the profits and G. C. Gooch, the £150-a-year clerk of 1843, the remaining 17.5 per cent. Otherwise, nothing changed. The staff of three clerks and the office at 22 Old Broad Street were retained. Day-to-day control of the firm had passed increasingly to J. S. Morgan after the crisis of 1857. His son, John Pierpont Morgan, who had started work in New York that year with Duncan, Sherman & Co., Peabody's largest client in the United States, managed the New York accounts. It was while working at Duncan, Sherman that J. P. Morgan closed his first deal, buying a consignment of coffee with a draft drawn on the firm and selling it in lots at a handsome profit.[49] It was an act of independence which cost him a partnership and in early 1861 he started his own business in New York, J. Pierpont Morgan & Co. He took the Peabody accounts with him. Fearful of a repetition of the 1857 panic, Junius took an intense personal interest in the bank's American clients and, recognizing his son's inexperience, he asked the 57-year-old Charles Dabney, a partner at Duncan, Sherman & Co., to join J. P. Morgan & Co. and teach his son bookkeeping. John lived largely on an allowance from his father, and Dabney, Morgan & Co. operated more or less as the New York office of J. S. Morgan & Co. in London.[50] Dabney, Morgan & Co. was wound up in July 1871, when J. P. Morgan was joined by Anthony Drexel, the second son of Francis Drexel, founder of the Philadelphia banking family with operations in New York and Paris. This too was at the behest of his father. 'It is possible that he may want to see you about a certain matter and, if he does, I hope you will go to see him,' he had written to his son.[51] The formation of Drexel,

Morgan & Co. gave the house of Morgan its first outlet in Paris, Drexel, Harjes & Cie. This powerful triad – New York, London and Paris was still at work in the 1970s.[52]

It took J. S. Morgan until 1870 to earn the respect of his contemporaries. Brown Shipley, his principal rivals for transatlantic business, restricted his credit on the grounds that he was 'an undoubtedly speculative turn'.[53] and one or two accounts defected to them. The outbreak of the American Civil War in April 1861 brought into sharp focus the firm's dependence on United States business, and not solely because Peabody was a lifelong Republican and Unionist. The house had hardly penetrated Europe, making no attempt to dislodge the houses of Baring, Hambro and Rothschild from their dominant position there. When the Union blockade of Southern ports disrupted the cotton and iron trade, Morgan was reduced to little more than dealing in Union bonds, a hair-raising business, one issue dropping to only 40 per cent of its face value. They never regained par throughout the war and lost 4 per cent when Lincoln was assassinated, but Morgan's nerve in backing the Union bonds paid handsomely in the end. Unlike most British banks, whose interests in the cotton trade had obliged them to back the Confederacy, Morgan lost virtually nothing. When the war was over he took the lead in restoring confidence, negotiating the sale of £800,000 worth of convertible bonds for the Erie Railway Company in September 1865, only five months after Lee's surrender. In a foretaste of the close relationship that developed between the British Government and the Morgan houses during the First World War, J. S. Morgan played a key role in the payment of $15 million in settlement of the *Alabama* claims.

Not all of the dealings of the House of Morgan during the Civil War were so commendable. The London house was later accused of being a 'funk hole' for American capital fleeing the vicissitudes of war, and of supporting the blockade runners that brought Southern cotton to English mills. J. P. Morgan installed the first telegraph on Wall Street in order to be first with the news from the front, using his advance information to speculate against Abraham Lincoln's treasury policy. Like most young men of his class, J. P. Morgan also evaded the draft introduced after Gettysburg by paying for a substitute to serve in his place. His attempt, with Edward Ketchum, to corner the gold market was only partially successful, but resulted in a profit of $160,000. The 'Gold Room' affair scandalized Wall Street, and Ketchum ended in jail for forging gold certificates. Congress later passed legislation outlawing gold speculation. In 1861 J. P. Morgan derived a profit of 50 per cent from his involvement in the sale to the Union army of a consignment of obsolescent carbines at six times their real value, in a transaction subsequently described by a Congressional committee as 'utterly indefensible' and a 'crime against the public policy'.[54] The Hall Carbine scandal, as it became known, was rehearsed as late as the 1930s as evidence of the House of Morgan's voracious cupidity. J. P. Morgan salved his conscience by renting a pew in St George's church and giving generously to charities for the wounded and those widowed by the war. These were accompanied by an act of inexplicable selflessness. In October 1861 he married Mimi Sturges, the daughter of a well-established Manhattan family, even though he knew she was doomed by tuberculosis. She was too ill to attend the wedding breakfast, and Morgan had to carry her to the carriage in which they embarked on a European honeymoon. She died in Nice in February 1862.[55]

The lesson of the Civil War was that J. S. Morgan had to look for business beyond the United States. He syndicated bonds for Canadian and Chilean railways, sold and traded debts for several European governments, became a director of the International Financial Society, a prototype investment vehicle to finance Continental industry, and managed a large bond issue for Spain. Morgan financed the import of tobacco from the Philippines, coffee from Brazil and guano from Peru. The gross earnings of the partnership rose from £50,794 in 1865 to £374,362 in 1871, a figure not matched until the end of the century.[56] Junius's own share rose from £37,462 to £264,206. It was quintessential merchant banking, developing entirely new areas of business as older markets dried up, became crowded or ruinously expensive. But his greatest coup, giving the house of Morgan a reputation to compare with that of Rothschild or Baring, was the £10 million French Government loan of 1870.

On 2 September 1870 the French Emperor Louis Napoleon lost the battle of Sedan to Wilhelm of Prussia. Two days later, a crowd invaded the Legislative Assembly in Paris, the Empire was dissolved and a republic was declared from the Hotel de Ville, the traditional location of Paris revolutions. To forestall a seizure of power by revolutionaries and to protect the city against the approaching Prussian armies, a Provisional Government of National Defence was formed by republican parliamentarians. Cattle, grain, salt, hay and food were brought into the city and stored. Within a fortnight two Prussian armies, a quarter of a million strong, had surrounded Paris. The fifty-one gates of the city were closed and the siege began. Several of the older members of the Government of National Defence had earlier decamped to Tours, where they had formed a 'Delegation' of the new Provisional Government safe from both the Prussians and the Parisian revolutionaries. They were charged with organizing fresh elections to a national assembly. In the first week of October they were joined by Leon Gambetta, a member of the Provisional Government in Paris who opposed the plans of his colleagues to sue for peace with Prussia. He left Paris on 7 October in a balloon filled with highly inflammable coal gas, with the additional danger of crossing the fire of the enemy lines.[57] Once safely at Tours Gambetta took charge, appointing himself Minister of War and Minister of the Interior, and attempted to raise a loan in London to buy men and arms to fight the invaders. He was refused by both Baring's and Rothschild's, who had previously financed the Prussians. So the two London envoys of the delegation at Tours, Clement Laurier of the Ministry of the Interior and Count André de Germiny of the Ministry of Finance, turned instead to J. S. Morgan, hoping his American connections would prove more fruitful. Unflinching, Morgan agreed on 24 October to provide £10 million at 6 per cent interest, far below the $8\frac{3}{4}$ to 9 per cent the two envoys had expected to pay. He charged an initial commission of $3\frac{1}{4}$ per cent (£325,000), though this was later reduced, and within a week had safely placed £4.9 million of the loan with British and French investors. Gambetta, who had returned to Paris, did not learn of the success for several days because the pigeons carrying the good news from Tours were shot down and eaten by the starving Parisians, who had already consumed the inmates of the zoo, stripped the Bois de Boulogne for firewood and developed a new cuisine using rats and horses.

Although Morgan later boasted that there had been no risk – 'There was no gamble. I thought it a safe operation,' he told a journalist – he was almost alone in this view.[58] When news of the loan reached Bismarck – through a Prussian spy – the Iron Chancellor exploded:

The loan contracted by the Tours Government will not be recognised by the one with which we shall make peace, and we may even place that amongst the conditions of peace.

A torrent of subscriptions became a flood of sales. Issued at £85 the price sank quickly under relentless Prussian threats. Worse, the plight of the Provisional Government deteriorated rapidly. Though Gambetta raised two armies with the proceeds, the unexpected surrender of General Bazaine at Metz released another 150,000 Prussian troops and Paris fell after only four months, on 27 January 1871. An armistice was signed the following day. On 18 March an insurrection broke out in Paris. The armistice with Prussia fuelled the resentment of Parisians and after elections on 26 March the Government was overthrown in favour of a bloody Commune, characterized by summary executions, the murder of the Archbishop of Paris and five other hostages and the burning of the Tuileries.[59] But Morgan kept his nerve admirably. As the price sank to £55, he began to buy back the bonds.[60] After a siege lasting several weeks Government troops occupied the city in May and suppressed the Commune. He was triumphantly vindicated. In

1873, three years after the Peace of Versailles, the French
Government redeemed the bonds at £100, giving Morgan an
astonishing profit of £1.5 million on the transaction. Curiously,
it did not mark the start of a profitable relationship. After 1870
Morgan was supplanted in the affections of the Third Republic
by Baring's and Rothschild's, who thereafter handled most of
France's debt operations until the turn of the century. The
république des ducs did not regard the house of Morgan as being
of the first rank. It was a snobbery shared by most of Europe's
governments. Morgan did not lead a single loan for a European
government throughout the 1880s and 1890s, though he participated in many led by Baring's, Rothschild's and Hambro's.
This failure to penetrate Europe made indelible the Anglo-
American character of the bank.

Here, change was occurring. By the 1870s the United States
had begun to industrialize, producing its own iron, steel and
textiles, often behind protective tariffs. American steel production surpassed Britain's for the first time in 1886. Tariffs on
imported manufactures were first introduced in 1861 and were
raised to 50 per cent by the McKinley tariff of 1890. Similar
tariffs on British goods erupted across Europe from the 1870s,
as industrialists became a significant political force. This hit
J. S. Morgan's traditional franchises: financing the import of
cotton and the export of manufactured goods like rails and
textiles. Competition with Baring's and Brown Shipley to
finance diminishing transatlantic trade was fierce. Britain's own
adherence to free trade abruptly reversed the terms of trade
with the United States. By 1910 Britain was running a trade
deficit with the United States of £50 million, offset by mounting surpluses on trade with India, Australia, China and Japan,
where Morgan was not traditionally strong.[61] The American
surplus with Britain made it possible for American industry to
finance its investments at least partially in New York. The
British economy was already developing the feature – deficits
with advanced economies – that undermined the market for
capital in London and so weakened the pound after the
1914–18 war that it toppled the merchant bankers of the City

of London from their leadership in international finance. It obliged Morgan partially to abandon the financing of trade in favour of financing big business and the United States Government. McCormick Harvesting Machines, the manufacturer of Cyrus McCormick's famous 'mechanical reaper' and Thomas Edison's Electric Light Company, the principal industrial vehicle of a man whose name is also linked with devices as diverse as the telephone, the typewriter, the gramophone and the moving-picture camera, became clients of the house.

But big business during these years primarily meant railways.[62] Between 1870 and 1890 the United States railway network grew from 53,000 miles to 166,700 miles and the volume of railway stocks and bonds outstanding multiplied fourfold, from $2.5 billion to $10 billion.[63] In this business J. S. Morgan grew close to Andrew Carnegie, the Scottish-American steel magnate, who negotiated several of Morgan's bond issues for the Pennsylvania Railroad. It was an important alliance at a time when the business was becoming increasingly disreputable, with bankers starting railways, selling stock in them and then forcing competitors to buy them out. The use of different gauges made the network impossibly complex, a traveller from New York to Buffalo having to change trains ten times. During the 1860s the battle for control of the railways sparked violent clashes between rival gangs fuelled with alcohol and armed with bottles, knives and revolvers. In 1869, amid scenes of this kind, J. P. Morgan outmanoeuvred Jim Fisk and Jay Gould to win control of the Albany and Susquehanna Railroad in the first of his railway coups.[64] Union Pacific became a client and in January 1874 Morgan's replaced Baring's as bankers to the Baltimore & Ohio Railroad, providing a platform on which the house of Morgan built a position of great – even dangerous – influence in the American railroad industry. In 1879 a syndicate organized by Junius and J. P. Morgan placed in London $18 million of shares in the Baltimore & Ohio Railroad sold by William Henry Vanderbilt – the son of Cornelius Vanderbilt, founder of the New York Central Railroad – which netted the firms a profit of $2.25 million.[65]

Subsequent transactions demonstrated for the first time J. P. Morgan's contempt for legal obstacles to the rationalization of the American railways. In 1885 he merged the Pennsylvania and New York Central railways, though the alliance was against State laws. 'I hire him to tell me how to do what I want to do,' he said of his lawyer's objections. In 1888 he assembled all the railway magnates at his house on Madison Avenue to secure their agreement to bypass federal competition legislation. When he failed to secure it, he resumed the process of 'Morganizing' the railways, recapitalizing insolvent lines at lower rates of interest, tapping stockholders for additional capital and charging a large fee – rarely less than $500,000 – for his trouble. Where Morgan did not take a majority shareholding, shareholders were persuaded to cede voting rights to his nominees on the board or to exchange their voting shares for shares in a holding company he controlled.[66] When the merger of the Great Northern Railroad with the Northern Pacific Railroad was struck down by the Supreme Court in 1895, Morgan simply arranged for the stock of the Great Northern to be held by individuals like himself rather than by the Great Northern Railroad.[67] After masterminding a bewildering series of railway mergers, J. P. Morgan emerged after the Panic of 1893 as the single most important influence in the American railway industry. John D. Rockefeller achieved power of similar magnitude in the oil industry. By 1880 his Standard Oil trust controlled 95 per cent of the oil produced in America. Though merchant bankers had long assumed responsibility for the rehabilitation of clients who defaulted on bonds they had sold, they had not hitherto reshaped the corporate structures of industrial capitalism. In 1890 their efforts provoked the first legislative backlash, the Sherman Anti-Trust Act. In coercing companies into the monopolistic 'trusts' that preoccupied American politicians from the Civil War to the First World War, Morgan, Rockefeller and others were unwittingly pioneering the art of the takeover.

The Morgans wielded great influence over American railways but it was in refinancing the Civil War debts of the

United States Government that J. S. Morgan made best use of the affection and respect of his fellow countrymen. No other business could compare with it in terms of sheer size: between 1871 and 1879 the United States refinanced some $1.4 billion of war debts.[68] To absorb sums of this magnitude, Morgan syndicated the loans among a number of houses in London and New York. It was heady business. The August 1876 syndicate to sell $200 million of federal government bonds netted the Morgan houses on both sides of the Atlantic a profit of £109,334, but still won plaudits for its ingenuity. The reliance of the government on the Morgans was starkly apparent in 1877, when J. P. Morgan guaranteed the army's pay while it was fighting the last of the Indian wars, advancing $2.5 million when Congress refused the appropriation.[69] J. S. Morgan's role in mobilizing British capital on behalf of the federal government and big business was celebrated at a dinner at Delmonico's in New York on 8 November 1877, where he was fêted by such members of the American political and business establishments as Theodore Roosevelt and Cyrus Field.[70]

To administer the syndicates, Morgan took on help. In May 1871 S. Endicott Peabody, a 46-year-old Bostonian distantly related to George Peabody, was admitted to a partnership, replacing Gooch, who retired in September 1873 after thirty years' continuous service with the firm. Partnerships were never proffered lightly, and they were usually kept within the family. Three – Gooch, Robert Gordon and Frederick Lawrence – of the six partners who served J. S. Morgan between 1864 and 1890 were British, the rest American. Two of the Americans, Endicott Peabody and Jacob C. Rogers (Endicott Peabody's brother-in-law) were undistinguished but family, and Rogers served until 1900 as the firm's representative in Boston. Walter Hayes Burns, who joined in January 1879, was J. S. Morgan's son-in-law. Burns had lived in Paris and had – at Morgan's insistence – acted as official translator during negotiations over the French Government loan in 1870. Morgan himself spoke no French (though he was a frequent visitor to the south coast of France) and did not trust his translators. He had wanted Burns to join the partnership then, but Burns had refused.

These were prosperous years. Earnings were still primarily from commissions and lending at interest. In only eight of the twenty-five years that J. S. Morgan ran the firm did income from securities sales and trading exceed that from commissions and interest. This partly reflected J. S. Morgan's distaste for investment rather than merchant banking; he always considered himself a merchant rather than a banker. It was a sound assessment. Commission income never failed to post a profit, but the securities business made losses six times during his tenure. It reflected his tight personal control of the partnership. Under J. S. Morgan's regime, access to the profits of the firm was only grudgingly conceded to outsiders. Junius kept over four-fifths of the profit for himself in the early years and was still collecting two-fifths at his death in 1890. Unlike the other partners he was unrestricted in the amount he could take out of the partnership. His share of the profits rarely dipped below £80,000 and his personal account showed a balance of £1.5 million.[71] The debate between the excitements, risks and rewards of investment banking, the sober skills of merchant banking and the concentration of profits in a few hands are continuous themes in the history of the house of Morgan. To the modern mind, the nepotism and asymmetries of power and reward are scarcely justifiable, but in a small Victorian partnership, where those who stood to gain most also stood to lose most, they made sense. Their persistence long into the twentieth century, when the partnership was gradually supplanted by a company employing hundreds of salaried staff, did not.

By the late 1880s Junius Morgan was old and tired. He was now in his mid-seventies and spent much of the English winter in Monte Carlo. His visits became more frequent and his stays longer after the death in 1884 of his wife Juliet, the Pierpont girl he had married in Hartford forty-eight years before.[72] Though he entertained rich and illustrious American friends like Tony Drexel and James Roosevelt, he was undoubtedly lonely and relied heavily on his family to visit him. 'Pierpont & family left today – house very lonely – miss them dreadfully,' he confided to his diary in 1889.[73] Much of his time was passed alone, except for servants, writing letters, reading and being driven in his coach. It was on just such an outing, on 3 April 1890, that he was fatally injured. Between Beaulieu and Eze the road ran beside a railway line. As his coach passed, the horses were frightened by a passing train and bolted. Morgan, anxious to see what the coachman was doing, stood up just as the wheels went over a pile of stones. He was thrown from the coach against a wall, striking his head. He was rushed to Monte Carlo but he never regained consciousness and died on 8 April 1890, a week short of his 77th birthday. John Pierpont and his daughter Louisa, hurrying from a holiday in Ireland, were unable to reach him in time. His body was returned to Hartford, Connecticut, where he had laid the foundations of his career, married Juliet Pierpont and lived for fifteen years. His funeral on 6 May was attended by 200 mourners and his pallbearers included Levi P. Morton, the Vice-President of the United States, and Cornelius Vanderbilt II. On the day after his death, the *New York Tribune* paid him this tribute:

Probably no other foreign banker was so well and widely known and liked, or exerted so great an influence in the United States as he did.[74]

Immediate estimates of the size of his estate varied between $30 million and $70 million, but more recent estimates suggest that he was worth only $12 million or so, of which fully four-fifths represented his (unobtainable) capital in the firm.[75] Of more lasting value than his wealth and achievements was his legacy to future generations of Morgan bankers. This was aptly summarized by his friend and business associate, Andrew Carnegie, who was once repaid $10,000 by Morgan after a mistake was discovered:

A great business is seldom if ever built up, except on lines of the strictest integrity. A reputation for 'cuteness' and sharp dealing is fatal in great affairs. Not the letter of the law, but the spirit, must be the rule. The standard of commercial morality is now very high. A mistake by anyone made in favour of the firm is corrected as promptly as if the error were in favour of the other party. It is essential to permanent successes that a house should obtain a reputation for being governed by what is fair rather than what is merely legal. A rule which we adopted and adhered to has given greater returns than one would believe possible, namely: always give the other party the benefit of the doubt. This, of course, does not apply to the speculative class. An entirely different atmosphere pervades that world. Men are only gamblers there. Stock gambling and honorable business are incompatible. In recent years it must be admitted that the old-fashioned 'banker' like Junius S. Morgan of London has become rare.[76]

In December 1890 J. P. Morgan received Dover House, Princes Gate and $1.5 million from his father's estate and became, for the first time, a partner of the London house. He was 53 years of age.

NOTES

[1] Statement to a sub-committee of the Banking and Currency Committee of the House of Representatives (the 'Pujo Committee'), *Money Trust Investigation Report*, 1913, cited in Vincent P. Carosso, *The Morgans: Private International Bankers, 1854–1913*, Harvard University Press, 1987.

[2] On 25 March 1858 J. S. Morgan wrote to J. P. Morgan, then embarking on his career in private banking in New York, as follows:

Never under any circumstances do an act which could be called in question if known to the whole world. Remember that there is an Eye above that is ever upon you and that for every act, word & deed you will one day be called to account. Act in every transaction of your life under this solemn responsibility and all will be well. Without it and altho you may acquire wealth it is worse than useless when you consider the awful cost at which it has been accomplished.

Carosso, *op. cit.*

In a subsequent letter, dated 16 April 1858, he reinforced the point:

Do not let the desire of success or of accumulating induce
you ever to do a single action which will cause you regret.
Self-approbation and a feeling that God approves will bring a
far greater happiness than all the wealth the world can
give.

Cited in Andrew Sinclair, *Corsair: The Life of J. Pierpont Morgan*,
Weidenfeld & Nicolson, 1981.
[3] Official Statement submitted to a Committee of the United States
Senate by J. P. Morgan Jnr on 23 May 1933.
[4] *ibid.*
[5] Franklin Parker, *George Peabody: Founder of Modern Philanthropy*,
George Peabody College for Teachers, Nashville Tennessee,
1955.
[6] J. S. Bryant, *The Life of the Late George Peabody*, 1914.
[7] Sinclair, *op. cit.*
[8] *The Times*, 13 December 1869.
[9] Parker, *op. cit.*
[10] *ibid.*
[11] *George Peabody & Co., J. S. Morgan & Co., Morgan Grenfell &
Co., Morgan Grenfell & Co. Ltd, 1838–1958*, printed for private circulation
by Oxford University Press, 1958; hereafter cited as *George Peabody
& Co.*
[12] Augustus Hare, cited in Parker, *op. cit.*
[13] Parker, *op. cit.* Parker estimated that his fortune was worth
between $14 million and $20 million at 1958 prices, roughly
between $70 million and $100 million at today's prices. Andrew
Sinclair, *op. cit.*, estimated it at $20 million. Kathleen Burk, in
Morgan Grenfell 1838–1988: The Biography of a Merchant Bank,
(Oxford University Press, 1989), estimated it at $10 million.
[14] Bryant, *op. cit.*
[15] *ibid.*
[16] Sinclair, *op. cit.*
[17] Parker, *op. cit.*
[18] Edwin Hoyt, *House of Morgan*, Muller, 1968.
[19] Carosso, *op. cit.* Burk, *op. cit.*
[20] Bryant, *op. cit.*
[21] *ibid.*
[22] Parker, *op. cit.*
[23] *George Peabody & Co., op. cit.*

[24] Peter Mathias, *The First Industrial Revolution, An Economic History of Britain, 1700–1914*, Methuen, 1976.

[25] *ibid.*

[26] *George Peabody & Co., op. cit.*

[27] Hoyt, *op. cit.*

[28] Sinclair, *op. cit.*

[29] Carosso, *op. cit.*

[30] *ibid.*

[31] The American Civil War, by starving industrial Lancashire of cotton, polarized opinion in Britain. On the outbreak of the war Canada became the scene of activity by Confederate agents. The kidnapping of two Confederate agents from the SS *Trent* in November 1861 produced a diplomatic crisis which nearly developed into war between Britain and the Union. After the Civil War, the Americans claimed compensation for the damage caused by British-built and -manned ironclads such as the *Alabama*, which had preyed on Union commerce during the war, when Britain allegedly failed to prevent them sailing to the Confederate States. After Disraeli agreed to submit the claims to arbitration in 1868, £3.25 million was awarded to the United States by the arbitrators. This was popularly judged an affront to British prestige.

[32] To Abbott Lawrence, 7 May 1854, cited in Carosso, *op. cit.*

[33] *ibid.*

[34] Samuel G. Ward to Baring Brothers, 11 April and 27 October 1854, Baring Brothers & Co. manuscripts, Ottawa, Canada, cited in *ibid.*

[35] *ibid.*

[36] George Peabody to Charles MacAlester, 31 October 1854, cited in *George Peabody & Co., op. cit.*

[37] Hoyt, *op. cit.*

[38] Carosso, *op. cit.*

[39] *ibid.*

[40] *ibid.*

[41] Sinclair, *op. cit.*

[42] Carosso, *op. cit.*

[43] *ibid.*

[44] *ibid.*

[45] Philip Ziegler, *The Sixth Great Power: Barings, 1762–1929*, Collins, 1988.

[46] Carosso, *op. cit.*

[47] Sinclair, *op. cit.*

[48] Carosso, *op. cit.*

[49] Sinclair, *op. cit.*

[50] Carosso, *op. cit.*

[51] Bunk, *op. cit.*; *ibid.*

[52] Carosso, *op. cit.*

[53] *ibid.*

[54] *ibid.*

[55] *ibid.*

[56] Carosso, *op. cit.*

[57] Stewart Edwards, *The Paris Commune 1871*, Eyre & Spottiswoode, 1971.

[58] Morgan found that, despite 'a dozen' governments since the revolution, 'not one of these governments had ever repudiated or questioned the validity of any financial obligation contracted by the other'. To George Smalley, London correspondent of the *New York Tribune*, cited in Carosso, *op. cit.* and Burk *op. cit.*

[59] Edwards, *op. cit.*

[60] *George Peabody & Co.*, *op. cit.*

[61] Mathias, *op. cit.*

[62] John Pierpont Morgan took the association with Edison sufficiently seriously to install primitive electric lighting at his house in Madison Avenue, alarming the neighbours with the noise and on one occasion singeing his desk with live wires. He also bought one of Edison's phonographs, which he used to play hymns.

[63] Carosso, *op. cit.*

[64] Sinclair, *op. cit.*

[65] Carosso, *op. cit.*; Hoyt, *op. cit.*

[66] Sinclair, *op. cit.*

[67] *ibid.*

[68] Carosso, *op. cit.*

[69] Sinclair, *op. cit.*

[70] Carosso *op. cit.*; Hoyt, *op. cit.*

[71] Carosso, *op. cit.*

[72] Hoyt, *op. cit.*

[73] Carosso, *op. cit.*

[74] *New York Tribune*, 9 April 1890, cited in *ibid.*

[75] Carosso, *op. cit.*

[76] Excerpt from Carnegie's autobiography, published in 1920. Cited in Hoyt, *op. cit.*

TWO

The Great Financial Gorgon

John Pierpont Morgan had assumed the senior partnership of a firm about which he knew little. Until his father's death, Pierpont had no official association with the London firm, having concentrated since 1871 on making Drexel, Morgan & Co. the predominant source of finance for the United States Government. Schooled in the United States, his arrival shifted irreversibly the weight of the house of Morgan from his father's walnut-panelled office at 22 Old Broad Street in London to his own roll-top desk on the Broad Street side of 23 Wall Street, New York. Increasingly, triumphs became associated with the New York house rather than London, and with Pierpont Morgan himself rather than the houses which bore his name. After Anthony Drexel died in June 1893, the New York house bore his name alone, becoming J. P. Morgan & Co. The Paris house of Drexel, Harjes was renamed Morgan, Harjes & Cie and J. P. Morgan became senior partner in Paris and London as well as New York.[1]

  J. P. Morgan was a big, rugged man with a huge nose which grew more bulbous with age, 'No nose in caricature ever assumed such gigantic proportions or presented such appalling excrescences,' said James Henry Duveen, an art dealer who knew him.[2] 'It is part of the American business structure,' quipped Morgan in later life, but it undeniably caused him much anxiety and sexual diffidence in his youth. Caused by the *acne rosacea* inherited from his mother and which had afflicted him since childhood, it gave him an increasingly frightful appearance and his formidable reputation a palpable form. This was based as much upon his egregious poses as the fact that he was, to liberal Americans in the decades before the

35

First World War, the 'money trust' made flesh. He lived luxuriously, with a house on Madison Avenue, an estate on the Hudson River (Cragston, at Highland Falls) and a series of yachts, all called *Corsair*. As the commodore of the New York Yacht Club, he revelled in the reputation of his namesake, the pirate Henry Morgan, and flew his personal pennant, a white crescent and a star on a red background, with conviction. Morgan once told an acquaintance who asked how much his yachts cost to operate that 'if it is any consequence to you, keep out of it'.[3] He maintained a steamer, the *Kargeh*, solely for the purpose of cruising the Nile, which he visited every year from 1871 to the end of his life. Morgan indulged unstintingly a passion for fine art first stimulated on a visit to Egypt in 1871, ostentatiously buying rare works – like the Gothenburg Bible – and acquiring manuscripts by Byron, Keats, Thackeray and Dickens. He was a generous patron of the Metropolitan Museum of Art in New York, and bought the two houses next to his own on Madison Avenue, which he razed to make way for the Morgan Library.

These were not attributes he displayed at work, where he cultivated the fearsome taciturnity and certitude which he knew attracted men of business and of means by their very lack of ostentation. 'I am not in Wall Street for my health,' he would say.[4] At the office he sat in his glass booth, brooding. Though the door was always open, the staff were too terrified to approach him. 'If he thought the price right, he'd say "I'll take it"; nothing more. It was always "yes" or "no"; no other talk at all,' said one broker who dealt with him. In the panic of 1893 he wrote a cheque for $1 million to the beleaguered Colgate Hoyt, spurning the offer of collateral: 'I am lending you the money on your business record in Wall Street and upon what I know your character to be.'[5] In the panic of 1907, he tamed the crisis, almost by the force of his reputation alone. The overspeculation which followed the bumper harvest of that year had led to a flight of foreign capital, putting at risk the adventurous 'chain banks' (banks acquired with the stock of another bank) which had mushroomed during the bull market, like the fancifully titled Knickerbocker Trust. With depositors queueing to withdraw their money, J. P. Morgan convened a meeting of New York financiers in his library on Sunday, 20 October 1907. 'If people will keep their money in the bank, everything will be all right,' he advised.[6] He then left the bankers alone in the east wing, amid tapestries and illuminated medieval manuscripts, while he repaired to the west wing to play solitaire until they had devised a workable solution. The Knickerbocker Trust was allowed to collapse but Morgan chose to save the Trust Company of America, which was down to its last $180,000, with a $3 million infusion, on the grounds that 'this is the place to stop the trouble'.[7] He persuaded the trust-company presidents to put up the balance required to save the Trust Company of America and the bank presidents to supply $25 million to the New York Stock Exchange, where fifty firms were at risk, warning that any member of the New York Stock Exchange who exacerbated the panic would be 'properly attended to' after the crisis was over. He even called together the rabbis and Protestant clergymen of New York and advised them to tell their congregations to leave their money in the bank.[8] Striding down Nassau Street he was, in the words of his son-in-law Herbert Satterlee, 'the embodiment of power and purpose'.[9] As he rode to work in his brougham, drawn by a single white horse, onlookers cheered, crying 'There goes the old man, the big chief.'[10] Though eight banks and trust companies failed before the crisis was over, it was Morgan who staunched the flood of withdrawals. Afterwards, Senator Aldrich said, 'Something must be done. We may not always have Pierpont Morgan with us to meet a banking crisis.'[11]

His confessor, W. S. Rainsford, the rector of St George's, never doubted the power of his personality. 'When he said a thing, and looked full at you as he said it, to doubt him was impossible,' he said.[12] The two clearly never discussed adultery eye-to-eye for, although he was a founder of the New York Society for the Suppression of Vice, which took a prurient interest in the erotica of the day, J. P. Morgan had a formidable sexual appetite. In May 1865 he remarried, to Frances Tracy, the daughter of a New York lawyer, who bore him his successor, John Pierpont Morgan Junior, two years later. However, the pathos of his first marriage seems to have been forgotten in the subsequent drive to prove that his nose was not a handicap to further sexual conquest. He was notorious for his habit of cruising the eastern seaboard in *Corsair* or travelling by private rail car in the company of New York actresses like Lillian Russell, or society beauties like Mrs John Markoe, while his wife stayed at home. The high street at Bar Harbor, Maine, was dubbed 'Rotten Row' in popular parlance on account of his periodic visits to the houses of two elderly actresses he maintained there. 'Morgan not only collects old masters, he collects old mistresses,' observed a painter who enjoyed his patronage, A. E. Gallatin. There was considerable mirth when he endowed the lying-in ward at Manhattan General Hospital, where several doctors were said to have wooed mistresses of his during their confinements there. He shared one actress, Maxine Elliott, with Edward VII, but nursed a genuine affection for Lady Victoria Sackville, whom he seduced when buying £65,000 of tapestries from her collection at Knole. The feeling was reciprocated. 'That man has such marvellous personality and attraction for me,' she confided to her diary after he had 'crushed' her between meetings in London.[13]

Morgan was also vehemently anti-Semitic. Lord Revelstoke, the head of Baring's, spoke to J. P. Morgan in New York in 1904 and reported that

he inveighed bitterly against the growing power of the Jews and of the Rockefeller crowd, and said more than once that our firm and his were the only two composed of white men in New York.[14]

On another occasion he refused to meet the senior partner of Goldman Sachs simply for being Jewish. Yet Revelstoke also thought Morgan 'a great, big, large-hearted generous man . . . with a character which is remarkable for straight dealing'. Though he was reportedly kind, tender and thoughtful in his personal dealings, and relied hugely on 'character' in his business, Morgan brought much the same contempt he reserved for Jews to bear upon his business opponents in the great restructuring of American capitalism which he wrought between 1885 and his death in 1913.

'When Pierpont Morgan was around the banker had the whip hand,' a young investment banker told Paul Ferris in 1984.[15] It is hard to grasp now the enormous concentrations of economic and political power wielded by private interests like J. P. Morgan in the two decades before war broke out in 1914. Contemporary cartoons depicted him as a big-bellied, swollen plutocrat, arm-in-arm with Andrew Carnegie, whose fingers dripped with the blood of the Homestead steel strikers shot by Pinkerton's men hired by Carnegie during a strike in 1892. Morgan financed successive election campaigns by the big-business Republican Party. In 1896 he bedecked 23 Wall Street with a Republican banner six storeys high, and gave his staff the day off to demonstrate in McKinley's favour. Morgan money was used adroitly by Roosevelt and Taft in the 'dollar diplomacy' of the pre-war years, being used to purchase the Panama Canal Zone (for $50 million) and to build railways in Russia and China. In 1895 J. P. Morgan averted a Treasury crisis by forming a syndicate to replenish the Federal Government's depleted gold reserves, in what amounted to a private deal with President Grover Cleveland. Cleveland had believed that Congress would authorize a popular loan to halt the run on gold. It did not, but Morgan's syndicate provided $65 million in gold to be paid for by a subsequent issue of bonds. $18 million of gold, awaiting shipment to America's European creditors, was unloaded from ships in New York harbour. J. P. Morgan counted it the greatest accomplishment of his career.[16] 'Everything depended on my changing Mr Cleveland's mind. When I went into the room, I had an unlighted cigar in my hand; as I arose from the chair to go, I had no cigar, but saw on the floor a little pile of snuff,' he said of the crucial encounter later.[17] When, in 1895, political considerations obliged Cleveland – a Democrat – to shun a second offer of help, Morgan bought most of the bonds anyway, solely to demonstrate his power.[18]

The great reorganizations of the railways of the eastern United States, in which, from 1869, J. P. Morgan stabilized ownership and crushed the overly chaotic competition that had developed, was achieved largely through control of the shares of the companies involved. By 1898 he was financing giant industrial agglomerations, which reached their peak in February 1901 with the merger of eight separate companies to form United States Steel, based on the Pittsburgh steel mills of his father's friend, Andrew Carnegie. It eliminated competition in the American steel industry and created what was then the biggest company in the world. To achieve it, Morgan raised the unprecedented sum of $1.4 billion; Carnegie alone received $300 million in bonds. 'Mr Carnegie, I want to congratulate you on becoming the richest man in the world,' Morgan told his client, after a fifteen-minute meeting to finalize the transaction. Morgan's itself earned a profit of $11.5 million on the merger.[19] In 1902 he created International Harvester and the International Mercantile Marine Company, an amalgamation of the transatlantic shipping lines more commonly known as the Morgan shipping trust. It was in his capacity as head of this trust that he attended the launching of the *Titanic*, the pride of the British White Star line, at Belfast in 1911.[20] It alarmed the British government sufficiently to prompt them to subsidize the building of two new liners, the *Lusitania* and the *Mauretania*.

These mergers pushed J. P. Morgan's influence way beyond that of the banker. By the beginning of 1903 there were four hundred trusts or combinations collectively worth around $20 billion, which were ultimately controlled by perhaps twenty men.[21] They were intended to reduce production costs, stimulate management and impose economies of scale. They in fact aroused deep political anxieties and turned J. P. Morgan & Co., in the words of a popular song of 1900, into 'Morgan's, Morgan's, the Great Financial Gorgon'.[22] In the belief that the way to check these 'trusts' or monopolies was to make their formation a legal offence, Congress in 1890 passed the Sherman

Anti-trust Act, but no significant prosecution was attempted until 1903, when the government successfully dissolved Edward H. Harriman's North-Western Railroad Trust. It presaged increasing government regulation of the railways and other industries during the 'trust-busting' administration of President Theodore Roosevelt, which eventually made unfettered capitalism of the kind personified by Morgan, Carnegie, Rockefeller and Vanderbilt impossible to practise. Despite increasing government interference in industry, J. P. Morgan remained convinced that combination was essential to the maintenance of stability and efficiency in business. His contempt for the political and judicial processes that assailed him was evident in his response to Roosevelt's threat of litigation to dissolve Morgan's Northern Securities Corporation Trust: 'If we have done anything wrong, send your man [meaning the Attorney-General] to my man [naming one of his lawyers] and they can fix it up.'[23] Roosevelt eventually won the Northern Securities case in the Supreme Court in 1904, but a nine-year suit against United States Steel was ejected by the same body. Though publicly distant from Morgan, Roosevelt was privately close to him, and his heart was not in it. His successor, Taft, initiated twice as many anti-trust suits – over fifty – in four years as Roosevelt did in seven. And with popular agitation against the capitalist plutocrats increasing, Morgan received death-threats from anarchist groups, and was given police protection.

In most cases, J. S. Morgan & Co.'s only role was to sell any securities that resulted from the reorganizations. It had also helped to sell the treasury bonds for the loan agreed with Grover Cleveland. This earned $18,400 but they lost $440,000 on underwriting shares in the unpopular sale of the Morgan shipping trust, the International Mercantile Marine Company.[24] By the end of 1903 J. P. Morgan in New York employed 150 people, perhaps ten times the number employed in London. The shift not just of people and business, but of emphasis and ideas, from London to New York was unmistakable and reflected the waning of English economic power. It was appreciated by Robert Gordon, a partner in London since 1884:

We are essentially an American firm, our business relations lying almost exclusively with the United States.[25]

Though J. P. Morgan was not much interested in London – his brother-in-law, Walter Burns, was not replaced as senior partner for two years after he died – it also testified to a certain atrophy in London. The bank's services in the 1890s – the financing of transatlantic trade, gold and currency dealing, deposit-taking and highly selective lending – were almost indistinguishable from those that were offered in the 1840s. Yet in the United States Morgan was pioneering mergers and acquisitions, riskless and fee-related business of exactly the kind at which the London merchant banks had once excelled. London stuck throughout the 1890s to its traditional franchises, issuing bonds for Turkey, Russia, Spain, Norway, Romania and Germany. Most were undertaken for reasons of prestige rather than profit and only four issues yielded any gain at all. The ambience of the London house, which remained conservative and patrician, was untouched by the aggressive approach across the water. J. P. Morgan left the London partnership agreement entirely separate, with no participation in the profits of the New York operation. He did not even change the name of the London house, which remained J. S. Morgan & Co., until 1910.

Not all was decay, however. The foundations of the London house's long domination of the financing of trade with Russia and South America were laid during these years. A £20 million bond issue for Russia in September 1891 opened new opportunities in a country planning rapid industrialization. Robert Gordon became a trusted figure among the financiers of St Petersburg, forging a relationship which survived the Revolution of 1917 and which, through Morgan Grenfell, still dominates the financing of Anglo-Soviet trade. But a century ago Latin America was the most important area of growth. Here Junius Morgan had established the first contacts, using commercial clients to effect introductions to South American politicians. Here too the pattern of development in the north was being repeated, especially in railway construction. Bond issues followed during the 1890s for Uruguay, Brazil, Costa Rica and Peru. Chile was initially lost to Rothschild but Argentina was won. Though he had to wait until September 1884 before snatching a £6 million loan mandate from Baring's – sparking a rivalry that blew exceedingly hot in the decades ahead – Argentina became J. S. Morgan & Co.'s most important Latin American client for the next twenty years.[26]

It became even more important after the Baring's crisis of November 1890. Baring's had become deeply involved in financing the booming Argentinian economy until worries about unemployment, inflation and defaults turned private investors against Argentinian bonds, obliging the merchant banks which had underwritten the issues to buy them instead. Baring's was most exposed to this change in sentiment. By the end of October 1890 the bank had liabilities of £20.96 million and was unable to discharge them as they fell due.[27] As the word spread that Baring's was in difficulty, depositors began to withdraw their money. Bankruptcy loomed. 'The name and the glory and the position and everything is gone . . . Verily a great Nemesis overtook Croesus,' wrote Tom Baring to Evelyn Baring on 14 November.[28] Baring's was saved by William Lidderdale, Governor of the Bank of England, who set up a guarantee fund which eventually topped £17 million and averted a failure of the bank, but the family had to dispose of property and furnishings. Unlike Baring's in 1857, who had willed Peabody to fail, J. S. Morgan & Co. and Drexel, Morgan & Co. contributed £100,000 each.[29] The old Baring partnership was liquidated and replaced with a limited liability company, Baring Brothers & Co. Limited. Baring's was not free of repayments on the fund until 1895 but the very idea of it, let alone its success – which today would be taken for granted – was greeted at the time with astonished relief. It prompted the Chancellor of the Exchequer, George Goschen, to recommend Lidderdale for a GCB, explaining that 'he is not rich enough for a Baronetcy'.[30]

After the crisis had passed, a Bank of England committee

was set up under the chairmanship of Nathan Rothschild to reschedule Argentina's debts. In March 1891 this committee completed the humiliation of Baring's by appointing J. S. Morgan & Co. as financial managers for Baring's holdings of Argentinian bonds. In March 1891 the committee approved Argentina's appointment of Morgan's as agents for a $75 million loan to Argentina. On 5 March 1891 the firm cabled J. P. Morgan in New York to test his reaction:

Pure commission business. Our acting at the request of Bank of England Committee relieves us of all moral responsibility. We think good business.[31]

It was. The firm earned £28,700 in commissions from the issue and over the next two years and for the rest of the decade Morgan's either led or co-led all major Argentinian financing in London. The bank effectively ran the Argentina Great Western Railway, which ran into financial difficulties in 1891. Throughout these years Baring's strove to regain the account. They got their chance in 1899 when, with war between Argentina and Chile apparently imminent, Morgan's rejected an Argentinian request to raise £6 million in London. Baring's, poaching a client in a manner then approaching the unthinkable, took advantage of Morgan's caution and arranged a £2 million two-year loan of their own, in which they invited Morgan's to participate. This broached a delicate matter of protocol, of a type still familiar to modern merchant bankers: would Baring Brothers & Co. Limited place their name above that of J. S. Morgan & Co. on the offering document? The partners of Morgan's were flabbergasted when Baring's suggested that they would. An appeal for advice was cabled to J. P. Morgan in New York, in the curious jargon of Victorian telegrams:

We have taken the position you will not allow J.S.M. & Co.'s name to be second in any business here: they [Baring Brothers] appeal to precedent 1886 and other loans and their larger connection Argentina Confederation affairs, and while very polite decline recede. Our personal feelings for them makes us most unwilling hurt them, but we fear that our yielding will establish a bad precedent, though [Lord] Revelstoke [told J. P. M., jr.] in any other business but Argentina Baring would be quite willing. Cable your views as soon as possible as business depends settlement this difficulty.[32]

Morgan's advice was to yield to the arbitration of Everard Hambro, head of the house of C. J. Hambro & Son. He advised submission, but that the name of J. S. Morgan & Co. should not appear on the document at all, so denying Baring's the support of the house. It rankled with both houses for years, surfacing in periodic battles for supremacy in Argentina well into the twentieth century.

Rivalry with Baring's dominated events during the Edwardian era. In 1900 Cecil Baring suspected J. P. Morgan of building up his London house 'without regard to expenditure of money, to make the position of said firm unrivalled for the next generation'.[33] Revelstoke considered his house in 'constant and active competition' with Morgan's and that 'a real community of interests with them is impossible'.[34] Cecil Baring's alarm was sparked by an unusual appointment to the senior partnership at J. S. Morgan & Co. in July 1899. The firm had lacked a permanent senior partner since the death of Walter Burns, J. P. Morgan's brother-in-law, in November 1897. Morgan's twenty-year-old son, John Pierpont Morgan, Jnr ('Jack'), was posted to London as acting senior partner while his father scoured the City for a replacement of suitable stature. In this he failed, settling eventually for Clinton Dawkins, a senior civil servant, instead. Dawkins was a forty-two-year-old Balliol graduate who had enjoyed a distinguished career in the Civil Service, acting as Principal Private Secretary to Lord Cross, the Secretary of State for India, and George Goschen, the Chancellor of the Exchequer. He was working for Lord Curzon, the Viceroy of India, at the time of his appointment. The go-between appears to have been J. P. Morgan's friend, Everard Hambro, who had met Dawkins while serving on the Royal Commission on the Indian Currency.[35] It was then an unusual migration to abandon a successful career in government service for the City and the move attracted considerable press speculation. *The Times* thought the Bank of England anxious to 'see an Englishman for the first time in the position of a partner in Messrs Morgan & Company'.[36] Of course, Gooch, Gordon and Lawrence had all been Englishmen, but Dawkins was the first partner to join the firm from outside. Dawkins's motive was probably money. Morgan gave him a 25 per cent interest in the firm, a proportion which ranked behind only his own half share. The balance of the partnership was split between Jack Morgan and the son of J. S. Morgan's son-in-law, Walter Burns. He was called, as if to parody the blatant nepotism, Walter Spencer Morgan Burns.[37] Dawkins started work in April 1900, three months after returning from India.

Morgan hoped that Dawkins's contacts in the Foreign Service, India and the Far East would yield new areas of business and to some extent they did. In the early years of the twentieth century Morgan's participated in loans to Indian railways, the Royal Government of Siam, the Dominion of New Zealand, the Electric Lighting and Traction Company of Australia and the Malacca Rubber Plantations.[38] Dawkins's political connections were impeccable. In 1902, amid mounting British opposition to J. P. Morgan's incorporation of two British shipping lines, Leyland & Co., and White Star Line, into the International Mercantile Marine Company, he arranged meetings with both the Colonial Secretary, Joseph Chamberlain, the Prime Minister, Arthur Balfour (a Baring's client) and King Edward VII. As a public servant, Dawkins himself considered the merger a 'disagreeable business' and his appointment was not a conspicuous success. He disliked the work and had little aptitude for it, complaining to his friend Lord Milner that the City was a 'jealous mistress':

The City does not involve long hours or much fatigue. But it means incessant presence and attention. You never know when you may be called upon . . . I am happy enough in the City, but there is not enough to do there, and I feel the want of handling big questions again.[39]

Dawkins was frequently absent on government business, earning a knighthood for helping to reorganize the War Office. The firm was really run by Jack Morgan, who now spent at least half the year in London rather than New York, and Edward ('Teddy') Grenfell, a salaried partner who joined J. S. Morgan & Co. as manager at the same time as Dawkins. For much of the first quarter of the twentieth century these two men governed the house of Morgan.

It fell to Dawkins, however, to handle an almost immediate rekindling of the conflict with Baring's, occasioned by the mounting costs of the Boer War. Britain's growing financial weakness in relation to the United States was first exposed by the costs of financing the Boer War, which broke out in October 1899. With the pound then on the gold standard – until 1919 anybody could, in theory, go to the Bank of England and demand gold in exchange for bank notes – and all international debts settled in gold, the costs of fighting the war had severely diminished the Bank of England's gold reserves. Ironically, because the new gold fields of the Witwatersrand were in the Boer Republic of the Transvaal, the war was arguably being fought largely to secure Britain's principal source of gold. The lack of gold had restricted the Bank's ability to increase the supply of money, for fear that it would have insufficient reserves of gold to meet its liabilities. The consequent shortage of money had sharply increased interest rates in London. In January 1900, the Chancellor of the Exchequer, Sir Michael Hicks-Beach, consulted J. S. Morgan & Co. on the feasibility of a bond offering in New York, the proceeds of which could be used to replenish the Bank of England's gold reserves and so ease the mounting pressure on the London money markets. This followed an initial approach to Dawkins by his friend, Sir Alfred Milner, High Commissioner in South Africa and a passionate imperialist who provoked the war in the interests of English-speaking dominance of southern Africa. It was certainly a remarkable suggestion, and characteristic of Milner's determination to surmount obstacles. Britain had not borrowed abroad since the Seven

Years War (1756–63). More importantly, most industrialized nations were then vehemently pro-Boer, and J. P. Morgan initially demurred when Hicks-Beach asked if it was feasible to raise £5 million in New York. For this timidity he was obliged to accept the involvement in the loan of Baring Brothers, who had been more bullish. It infuriated Morgan's. Hicks-Beach was 'notoriously stupid and most unbusinesslike' wrote Clinton Dawkins, who negotiated with the Chancellor and the Governor of the Bank of England, but rather than lose the business he accepted the imposition.[40]

This sparked a fresh round of insults between Baring's and Morgan's in London. The head of the house, Lord Revelstoke, sensed that the house of Morgan's greater strength in the United States might yield them ultimate victory in this contest, since New York was rapidly becoming the financial centre of the world. Baring's performed a modicum of American business through Kidder Peabody in Boston and Baring Magoun in New York – the partnership of Tom and Cecil Baring and George Magoun, who had once been with Kidder – but neither was conspicuously successful. In March 1901 Clinton Dawkins wrote to Milner:

In London, the resuscitated Baring's are the only people nearly in the same rank with us. In the US they are nowhere now, a mere cipher, and the US is going to dominate in most ways. The Barings have nobody but Revelstoke, a man commonly reported to be strong, but a strange mixture of occasional strength and sheer timidity. He has no nerve to fall back on . . . He has greatly irritated the Morgans once or twice by want of tact and by talking loosely (after they helped Baring's largely in 1891) and it cost me a good deal of difficulty this summer to patch up the old alliance between the two houses.[41]

The contempt was mutual. Revelstoke said Dawkins 'is not, and never will be, a success in City circles' but, being unaware of his limitations, might be 'unwilling to retire'.[42] Vincent Carosso, in his history of the Morgans, intimates that J. P. Morgan shared this view and regretted his appointment of

Dawkins, the only partner he ever appointed from outside the world of banking.[43] It would certainly explain his receptivity to Lord Revelstoke's daring suggestion in 1904 that the two houses pool their resources.[44] By October 1904 the two men were discussing a merger of their activities, under which Baring's would close Baring, Magoun in New York and Morgan's would close J. S. Morgan & Co. in London. Morgan said this would cause him no anguish and that J. S. Morgan 'ought to be liquidated and could not exist without him as a partner'.[45] Nothing came of it, doubtless because of J. P. Morgan's reluctance to sacrifice his protégé, Dawkins, and his son, Jack. Certainly Baring's was keen enough, and pursued other possibilities with Kidder Peabody after the Morgan deal collapsed in early 1905. Revelstoke was unforgiving:

The London lot, as at present constituted, are so entirely useless and so out of touch with anything which is of value in English financial and commercial life that Morgan's people will find their power constantly decreasing on this side.[46]

J. P. Morgan's willingness to consider the obliteration of the firm which had provided much of his family's fortune suggests that he was inclined to agree with Revelstoke's assessment. There were certainly growing cultural tensions between the languor of the English house and the zest of its American cousin. Dawkins visited New York around this time and reported to Milner that

It is extremely interesting to find oneself in the very heart of the Wall Street excitement and combinations and to note the prodigious amount of nervous excitement and energy the Americans throw into their work. Part of the buoyancy and excitement is also due, I suppose, to the comparative youth of the majority of them. Few of them live through it to advanced years except physical and intellectual giants like Morgan who has something Titanic about him when he really gets to work. Most of them drop out suddenly. Total collapse very often.[47]

Yet Morgan feared he could not remove Dawkins without damaging the reputation of the house.

At the end of January 1905 Edward Grenfell cabled Jack Morgan in New York that Dawkins had suffered an attack of influenza and that one of his lungs was 'slightly touched'.[48] An earlier plan for Dawkins to return to India had come to naught, and perhaps more drastic solutions were in the offing when he obligingly fell ill. By December he was dead, apparently of a heart attack. Grenfell was already *de facto* senior partner when Dawkins fell ill, his status augmented by Dawkins's frequent absences on government business. In January 1904 he had been elevated to a full partnership, with a 4 per cent interest in the profits of the firm. His appointment as senior partner on Dawkins's death in December 1905 accelerated the already marked Anglicization of the house and during his tenure this process became complete. It began in September 1905 with the appointment to a junior partnership of his cousin, Vivian Hugh Smith, later the first Lord Bicester. Hugh Smith, a member of an old banking family (the 'banking Smiths') and a son of a former governor of the Bank of England, replaced his friend Jack Morgan, who returned to New York permanently at the end of 1905. It was an appointment with profound implications. The banking Smiths eventually took control of the London firm and gave it its distinctive aristocratic flavour until deep into the 1970s. In 1905 they were still overshadowed by the new senior partner, Edward Charles Grenfell.

Grenfell's early working life, like most successful careers in the City, was remarkably uninteresting. He was born in Pimlico on 29 May 1870, the son of Henry Riversdale Grenfell, a Member of Parliament and a director of the Bank of England. He was educated at Harrow and Trinity, Cambridge and took a second in history in 1892. He began by joining one of Morgan's rivals, Brown, Shipley & Co., the London branch of the Anglo-American merchant banking house Brown Brothers, but he cannot have enjoyed it, for in 1894 he moved to Smith Ellison's Bank at Lincoln. He was later manager of the Grimsby branch. In April 1900 family and social ties drew him back to London. He took up the position of salaried partner and manager at J. S. Morgan & Co., where J. P. Morgan hoped he would provide the technical support for Clinton Dawkins. In 1905, when he was thirty-five, he became, like his father before him, a director of the Bank of England, a post he held until 1940 and which became of enormous importance to the house of Morgan during the First World War.

In 1907–8 the battle with Baring's for supremacy in Argentina reached its climax. Undaunted by the disaster of 1890 and in accordance with the protocol of international merchant banking, it was only in Argentina that Baring's maintained its position tenaciously. It ceded Chile and Brazil to Rothschild's gracefully and Mexico to Morgan's apparently without demur.[49] With characteristic disdain for industry and commerce, Baring's dominated lending to the republic of Argentina and the city of Buenos Aires, handling thirteen bond issues worth some £27 million.[50] Morgan's shared Baring's distaste for manufacturing – it rejected both the Goodyear Tyre & Rubber Co. and the Edison Car Battery Co. as clients on the grounds they were 'too speculative' when horse traction was so cheap[51] – but happily lent to Argentinian Railways. They funded the construction of the transandine railway from Argentina to Chile (though difficulties with completion of the project eventually obliged the firm to acquire control of the Transandine Railway Company in 1901). In a particularly large and difficult loan to the republic in 1907 this amicable division of the spoils proved impossible to sustain. Three-quarters of the loan were unsold and, against Lord Revelstoke's will, Jack Morgan insisted to Grenfell that J. S. Morgan & Co. appear of equal rank with Baring's on all the sale documents:

The whole matter most trying and very sorry it has come up now, but see no reason why we should submit to being squeezed out without saying anything or why all friction should be on our side.[52]

In the end Argentina resolved the struggle, by attempting to take advantage of it. The Argentinian Government had for some time wanted direct access to the New York market and the house of Morgan was better equipped to provide this than Baring's. In September 1908 they opened negotiations with J. P. Morgan & Co. in New York for a new 50 million peso (£10 million) gold loan. In breach of a gentleman's agreement with Baring's, under which J. P. Morgan & Co. in New York was permitted to negotiate directly with Argentina, but J. S. Morgan & Co. was not, J. P. Morgan & Co. insisted that J. S. Morgan & Co. should syndicate part of the loan in London, offering Baring's a participation only. The Argentinians, scenting an auction which might rebound to their advantage, proposed to ask Baring's to bid separately for the London end of the loan. Morgan's attempt to bypass the gentleman's agreement caused apoplexy at Baring's, which refused to regard an issue in New York as outside its scope. Morgan's favoured forcing the issue. Grenfell and Hugh Smith cabled Jack Morgan:

If we can only secure this business even with a small profit [Baring's] would fear our competition and would probably approach us as to working jointly in the future.[53]

Jack, for his part, was game:

I don't care how we fight him [Lord Revelstoke] but am quite ready to fight him when we need to.[54]

For a time, it seemed that the two houses would bid against each other for the loan, but in January 1909 Grenfell and Revelstoke met to resolve the issue. The result was a complete victory for Morgan's, with Revelstoke conceding parity on any Argentinian business.[55] Though Baring's was disgruntled at the time, and showed it by snubbing Morgan's at a dinner for the Argentinian Ambassador the following year, the Baring's–Morgan's partnership in Argentina survived successfully into the 1920s.

The fact that Argentina had turned first to New York rather than London as early as 1908 was a melancholy reminder to the partners of the London house of their dwindling importance to the house of Morgan. The shift of emphasis across the

Atlantic was made actual in January 1910, with the admission
for the first time of a formal American interest in the profits of
the London house. Until 1910, J. P. Morgan and Jack had
remained partners in J. S. Morgan & Co. only as individuals
sharing a common ancestor, not as American business partners.
This was a powerful and a risky position. J. P. Morgan's
personal interest in the profits of the London house never
dipped below at least twice that of any other partner, but in
the 1907 panic he paid for nearly three-quarters of the losses of
the London firm.[56] His principal earnings, though, were
derived from New York, where he only twice collected less
than $1 million a year throughout the pre-war years. This
arrangement was dissolved in 1910. The partnership of J. S.
Morgan & Co. was replaced by a private unlimited company
called Morgan, Grenfell & Co. John and Jack Morgan reinvested immediately the £1 million due to them on the dissolution
of the old partnership, but for the first time it was a corporate,
rather than a family investment by the New York banking
house of J. P. Morgan & Co. New York, rather than London,
now guided the house of Morgan. This initially invisible re-
versal of fortunes, mirrored throughout British industrial and
commercial life, was laid bare by the enormous costs of financing the First World War.

John Pierpont Morgan died in the Grand Hotel, Rome on
31 March 1913, surrounded by art dealers anxious to sell him
another 'extraordinary bargain'. His last words were, 'I've got
to go up the hill.' Morgan had returned to Rome after weaken-
ing in Egypt, fearing that he might die in a country that was
not Christian. In the end his spirit had been broken by public
suggestions of greed and corruption. The sweeping consolida-
tions of American industry, of which J. P. Morgan and United
States Steel were the most potent symbols, had aroused considerable public and political disquiet, resulting in legislation
to curb the deleterious effects of these 'trusts' on competition.
In October 1911 J. P. Morgan himself was served with a writ
to dissolve United States Steel. 'Well, it has come to this!' he
thundered.[57] Many in Congress went further, contending that

a far more insidious influence was at work than that of the sprawling industrial monopolies: the conspiratorial 'money trust'. According to supporters of this theory, a handful of men, all known and bound to each other by a web of mutual shareholdings and directorships, controlled the vast resources of the American economy in their own, rather than the public's, interest. 'The public be damned,' as the railway magnate, Cornelius Vanderbilt, had put it. In 1901 Morgan himself had said 'I owe the public nothing', a remark which now delighted his enemies. In December 1912 J. P. Morgan was called to Washington to testify before a sub-committee of the Committee on Banking and Currency of the House of Representatives; though the prospect mortified him, unlike some others, notably William Rockefeller, he agreed to go. 'To think that after all these years I have been branded by my own government a criminal, fit only to be thrown into jail,' he wept.[58] Called the 'Pujo Committee', after its chairman, the Louisiana Congressman Arsene P. Pujo, it conducted hearings as part of a 'Money Trust Investigation'. The Pujo Committee showed that J. P. Morgan & Co., the First National City Bank of New York City, the National City Bank, the Bankers Trust Company and the Guaranty Trust Company held 341 directorships in various financial, industrial and commercial corporations. J. P. Morgan & Co. held 72 directorships in 47 financial and industrial corporations worth over $10 billion and controlled both Bankers and Guaranty Trusts. J. P. Morgan's testimony stupefied the members of the Pujo Committee by its transparent honesty. He conceded that he preferred combination to competition and that he controlled the boards, the voting shares and the financing of numerous corporations but persuaded the committee that because he and his associates were honourable men they would always behave honourably. It was during an exchange with the counsel to the committee, Samuel Untermyer, that he made his famous remark that 'the first thing is character'.[59] He would lend to any man, provided he trusted him. 'I have known a man come into my office, and I have given him a cheque for a million dollars when I knew he had not a cent in the world,' he said, recalling the sum he passed to Colgate Hoyt in 1893.[60] Pujo failed to prove the existence of a 'money trust'. In the end even Untermyer conceded that Morgan was 'animated by high purpose and that he never knowingly abused his almost incredible power'.[61]

Pierpont Morgan's fortune was modest by the standards of Vanderbilt or Carnegie, showing how little he had profited from the countless speculative opportunities that came his way. It totalled $68 million and his art collection another $50 million.[62] 'And to think that he wasn't even a rich man,' said Rockefeller. The will was generous. He left Jack $3 million and each of his three daughters $1 million each and every employee at 23 Wall Street was given a year's salary. The American Secretary of State, William Jennings Bryan, ordered his ambassador in Rome to send Morgan's body home in honour. A memorial service was conducted in Westminster Abbey. On the day of his funeral the New York and Chicago Stock Exchanges remained closed in silent tribute. The Kaiser, and the kings of England, Belgium and Italy, sent tributes and he was buried in Hartford, beside his father. The memory of the way in which he did business proved more durable than any of his legacies. He took personal responsibility for everything undertaken in his name and expected others to do the same. His claim to have written a cheque for a million dollars to a penniless man became the power of signature coveted by all Morgan bankers. Until their numbers were too much increased by the growth of the 1980s, all directors of Morgan Grenfell were given the power to bind the bank to a loan with a stroke of their pen. Once these links between personal and corporate responsibility were severed, as the processes of growth demanded, they were not replaced. Pierpont Morgan stood, said his friend Bishop Lawrence, for 'personal responsibility, personal control under personal supervision, personal enterprise and personal confidence'.[63]

Little came of the special relationship between the Morgan houses before the First World War, but during the conflict itself it was put to vigorous use. On the outbreak of war in August 1914, President Woodrow Wilson had immediately declared American neutrality, urging his countrymen to be 'neutral in fact as well as in name'.[64] For the house of Morgan, its business tied inextricably to Europe, this was scarcely realistic advice. Quite apart from its obvious ties to Britain, during the pre-war years Morgan's had done business in all of the Allied countries. The London house had participated in nearly a dozen Canadian loans between 1900 and 1913 and in January 1911 had joined forces with Lazard's in forming a company to encourage European investment in Canada.[65] Both the British and French arms of the house of Morgan had raised money for Imperial Russia and its nascent oil, cotton and mining industries before the war and though J. P. Morgan & Co. provided no capital to Russia until the outbreak of hostilities, the partners knew the country and its leaders well. Jack Morgan was in St Petersburg at the time of the 1905 revolution. The New York house maintained the Paris house, Morgan Harjes, that it had inherited from Pierpont Morgan's association with Anthony Drexel. As early as August 1914, the French Government – perhaps recalling 1870 – had approached J. P. Morgan & Co. not just for loans but for 10,000 horses too.[66]

The ties of affection with Britain were stronger still. J. P. Morgan had shared mistresses with Edward VII, and attended his funeral. He had paid for the electrification of St Paul's cathedral.[67] On the outbreak of war, Jack Morgan gave his grandfather's country house, Dover House, to the British Government for use as a hospital. One New York partner, Robert Bacon, was one of the earliest and most vociferous advocates of US intervention in the European war and another, Thomas Lamont, said, 'Our firm had never for one moment been neutral. We didn't know how to be.' This was not mere sentiment: ten years after the war was over, Lamont and Jack Morgan saved Stonehenge from destruction with anonymous donations. Senior members of the British Government certainly seem to have felt they could rely upon the support of the house of Morgan from the early days of the war. In November 1914 David Lloyd George, then Chancellor of the Exchequer, asked Edward Grenfell, whom he knew as a director of the Bank of England, to ask New York whether or not American rifle production could be increased.[68] When the firm asked Secretary of State William Jennings Bryan for advice on whether or not the firm could lend money as well, he replied that while loans were not unlawful, they certainly breached the spirit of neutrality. Bryan, who had invoked the Crucifixion against financiers during his presidential campaign in 1896, distrusted moneyed interests deeply.[69] He believed that 'money is the worst of contrabands – it commands all other things'.[70] Bryan's rectitude was soon supplanted by the ties of sentiment and those of greed. In October 1914 the State Department offered a distinction between United States Government loans, which would still be forbidden, and those made by private bankers acting in an individual capacity. This opened the floodgates. By April 1917 Great Britain had borrowed over $1 billion, France $300 million, Canada $400 million and Russia $50 million. The Central Powers had borrowed only $20 million. This disparity testified in large part to the refusal of the house of Morgan, among others, to cooperate with German efforts to secure American credits.[71] Bryan resigned in June 1915, disgusted by acts of flagrant American unneutrality, to be replaced by the explicitly pro-Allied Robert Lansing.

The loans were used as credit to purchase food and war *matériel*. Initially, British purchasing in the United States was chaotic. Different departments bid against each other and against private agents on commission for the same supplies, pushing up prices. Some private brokers bought options on *matériel* which they then sold to British agents, taking a percentage for themselves. Following Grenfell's request in November 1914, Jack Morgan had been barred from approaching Remington and Winchester, the two largest rifle firms in the United States, on the grounds that it would undermine the War Office purchasing agent.[72] It was against this background that the British Ambassador to Washington, Sir Cecil Spring-Rice, recommended Britain channel all its purchases through a single agent. He recommended J. S. Morgan & Co., not least because he had been best man at Jack Morgan's wedding. Though it is unclear who took the eventual decision to appoint Morgan's, a New York partner, Henry Davison, lunched with both the Prime Minister, Asquith, and the Chancellor, Lloyd George, in London in December 1914 and Asquith 'approved every word' of his proposal that Morgan's should become sole purchasing agent.[73] J. P. Morgan & Co. was appointed His Majesty's Government's sole purchasing agent in the United States in January 1915, with a brief to

> use their best endeavours to secure for His Majesty's Government the most favourable terms as to quality, price, delivery, discounts and rebates and also to aid and stimulate by all the means at their disposal sources of supply for the articles required.[74]

In return for this Morgan's were paid a commission of 2 per cent on purchases up to £10 million and 1 per cent thereafter. These were handsome fees but E. R. Stettinius, the former president of the Diamond Match company who ran the purchasing operations for Morgan's, recalled that the bank had wanted not so much the business as to aid the Allied cause and control the impact of the war on the American economy. Morgan's, with outlets in London, Paris and New York, was also ideally suited to link the major Allies with American suppliers. When Jack Morgan asked Woodrow Wilson if the appointment was a breach of neutrality he was told no action 'in furtherance of trade' could be construed as such. Though the 'Export Department', as it was called, was given space at 23 Wall Street, Stettinius was paid commission rather than a salary. Disgruntled middlemen and haughty civil servants still bypassed Morgan's in the early years, but Stettinius eventually made so much money that Jack was embarrassed into making him a partner in January 1916. In the two years in which the arrangement operated, $20 billion of orders were placed by Morgan's with over 500 firms in the United States, earning commissions of $30 million. At its peak in the spring of 1917, just before the United States entered the war, the Export Department employed 175 people.[75] Though they were scrupulous in selling stocks in those companies with which they placed orders, memories of the Money Trust Investigation were still fresh and there was criticism later that the partners of Morgan's had drawn the United States into the war to safeguard their own financial position. The immediate dangers were not inconsiderable. In July 1915 Jack Morgan and Sir Cecil Spring-Rice narrowly escaped assassination by a German nationalist who infiltrated the Morgan estate on East Island. Jack was shot twice, in the groin and the thigh, but overpowered his assailant. A second plot against his life was uncovered in April 1916 and he passed the war under constant police guard.[76]

Rather than use Foreign Office channels, British buyers transmitted their orders to New York through Morgan, Grenfell & Co. in London, an arrangement suggested by Morgan's. The Munitions Supply Department at the War Office even purchased the building next door to 22 Old Broad Street and knocked down the wall between them. Charles Whigham, a former senior clerk elevated to a partnership by Grenfell and Hugh Smith in January 1912, became Stettinius's counterpart in London, spending his mornings decoding cables from New York, his afternoons visiting government departments to collect orders and his evenings encoding and transmitting them to the United States.[77] Details of orders were recorded in ink on vast sheets of paper before transcription into an 'amazing elaborate code' for transmission to New York.[78] The use of a private code was an extraordinary privilege denied even to the War Office and the Admiralty, all of whose cables had to pass the censors at the Foreign Office. It was granted to the bank by Lloyd George in what Grenfell called 'a fit of broadmindedness'.[79] The lack of any German connections counted for something in this regard and, at times, the War Office found recourse to Morgan Grenfell's less circuitous network a useful alternative. The bank's role as purchasing agent expired once the United States entered the war in April 1917. The partners of J. P. Morgan & Co. were scattered. Stettinius went to Washington to organize American war purchasing; Henry Davison served as head of the Red Cross; and Thomas Lamont assisted General Pershing at his headquarters in Paris. Only Jack, because of the association of his name with bloated capitalism, stayed at home.

Before America entered the war, there was also the question of how Britain would pay for its war supplies. In assisting it to do this Morgan's was less successful. In 1915 imports from the United States were up by over two-thirds on their pre-war level. Though the rate of exchange of dollars for pounds was fixed at $4.86:1, the selling of pounds by Morgan's to buy dollars to pay for imports had put the pound under downward pressure. Grenfell had suggested to the Treasury in early 1915 that they issue a dollar bond in New York and apply the proceeds to the purchase of imports, but they had been unreceptive. He cabled New York:

This may appear to you very foolish procedure but from your own experience dealing with Government officials you will understand it is often impossible to make them appreciate a difficult situation, especially on such a complicated matter as Exchange.[80]

Jack Morgan lunched with Lloyd George in April and Davison implored Lord Cunliffe, the Governor of the Bank of England, in June, but nothing was done. It seems that the notion of a weak pound was as absurd to Asquith's Cabinet as a strong one is to a modern Cabinet. In July 1915 the new Chancellor, Reginald McKenna, told the Cabinet that Morgan's could not buy any more dollars at the prevailing rate and a $50 million loan, secured on American bonds supplied by the Prudential, was arranged. By August it was spent and Grenfell told Lloyd George that he had $17 million to pay and only $4 million in hand. The Cabinet agreed to a desperate expedient: buying dollar bonds held by British citizens and offering them for resale in New York. An Anglo-French Government mission was despatched to New York, led by Lord Reading.

Morgan's advised the Reading mission on the terms of a $500 million issue of Anglo-French bonds, which were offered for sale in September 1915. Subsequent generations of Morgan bankers were taught that the issue was a great patriotic act. In reality, it was a disaster. Scarcely a single investor bought the bonds; after three months $187 million were still unsold, and only heavy buying by Dupont, Westinghouse and Bethlehem Steel, all of whom had contracts outstanding with the British Government, saved the balance from being left almost entirely with the 1,570 banks Morgan had conscripted as underwriters. It was a dreadful embarrassment to the British Government, making subsequent borrowings in 1916 increasingly expensive. A plan by Davison in November that year to issue $1 billion of treasury bills only added to the humiliation when it was overruled by the Federal Reserve Board, despite being secured on British-owned dollar bonds and shares. Davison suspected the influence of the pro-German member of the Board, the New York banker Paul Warburg, but a British Government official blamed Morgan's 'overbearing and ill-advised' approach and castigated its 'want of organization and slipshod methods'. The *Times* correspondent accused the bank of being concerned solely with 'making as much for itself as possible' and even the favourably disposed Sir Cecil Spring-Rice accused Davison of 'aggressiveness'.[81] In fact, the Federal Reserve had been prompted by the President, who wished to pressurize the Allies into accepting a peace proposal, but the bank's role as financial agent was downgraded anyway. In January 1917 a Treasury official, Samuel Lever, was sent to New York instead.[82] In a memorandum to the Chancellor Lever disparaged almost all of Morgan's judgements about Britain's ability to raise funds in New York. He said the Anglo-French loan had been so widely syndicated that there was no one left to buy it; that the offer of security could and should have been avoided; and that Morgan's had reduced British credit to a state from which it would be hard to recover. This was slightly unfair. Settlers of German origin, who were especially numerous in mid-western America, refused to buy Allied bonds. One

Chicago banker who participated had his house burned down. The Morgans were also Republicans, and members of the widely distrusted eastern financial establishment, which did not endear them to middle America. Whatever the cause of the failure, after Lever's appointment Grenfell noticed a 'distinct indication of a desire on the part of the Authorities to work less closely with us'.[83] And though Morgan's own commitment to the Allied cause was undoubted – it ran an overdraft for the British Government which peaked in April 1917 at $437 million – its incompetence had jeopardized the entire war effort. When the United States resolved the dollar shortage by entering the war on the Allied side, Britain had enough dollars to fund its purchases for just three weeks.

For Morgan Grenfell the war turned the financial world upside down. Before the war Britain was the world's principal creditor nation. Its surplus of capital was reinvested around the world and the strength of the pound was assured. Morgan Grenfell's business of selling in London the bonds of foreign governments and companies and financing in pounds the trade of the world had reflected the nation's financial pre-eminence. The war had reversed the roles of Britain and America. After it, the victorious Allies collectively owed the United States about $10 billion. For Morgan Grenfell, Othello's occupation was gone. Throughout the firm's history the United States had been a debtor nation, borrowing from Britain to build its railways, canals, factories and waterworks. Morgan's had made its reputation and its livelihood channelling British capital to the United States for just these purposes. Between 1865 and 1914 the United States was the single most important area of British overseas investment. One-fifth of all the bonds sold in London during these years were of American origin and by the outbreak of war British citizens had invested £835 million in the United States.[84] British investors held millions in American securities but, as the war dragged on, Morgan's had to help the Bank of England commandeer and sell them to pay for it. They were joined in this work by Baring's, prompting one partner to joke that he would embargo the partners of

Morgan's and offer them as collateral for the next loan.[85] This gradually reversed American indebtedness in Europe until, by 1917, the United States had become a net creditor for the first time. At the end of the war, Britain owed the United States $5 billion.[86] From the end of the First World War until the emergence of the Eurobond market in London in the 1960s New York was the premier capital market of the world. The transformation of America from debtor to creditor was so rapid and so complete that during the 1930s it was used by isolationist American politicians to support the theory that loans to the Allies and Allied purchases of American goods had tied the health of the American economy so closely to the Allied war effort, that US involvement had become inevitable. Certainly a German victory would have jeopardized payments for goods sold and the repayment of the loans that were made, but it is hard to sustain the view that American involvement in the First World War was just a bankers' ramp.

Wartime spending had also drawn the American economy out of recession and revitalized its industries. As a result, American imports of goods from Europe decreased markedly at the very time when European debts could have been partially repaid by increasing their exports to America. America's high tariffs, introduced before the war to restrict imports, remained. The demands of the war with Germany had also prevented the Allies from exporting to other countries, which had formerly contributed to their favourable balance of trade. America had enjoyed a surplus of exports over imports with Europe for years before the war but, as a debtor nation, this was used to pay the interest on loans from Europe. Now that the United States was a creditor, payments of interest and principal were not deducted from the trade balance but added to it. Though the American surplus on trade was never especially large, exceeding $1 billion only once during the 1920s, European countries had somehow to cover their deficit on trade with the United States as well as repay their wartime debts. 'They hired the money, didn't they?' said one of Wilson's successors as President, Calvin Coolidge. During the 1920s the deficit was covered by payments of cash – gold, once most European countries had returned to the gold standard – extorted from the defeated Germany, whose war reparations were set at a staggering $33 billion, or borrowed from private bankers in the United States.[87] Paying through a mixture of gold, extortion and borrowing could not be sustained for long, since each of these was susceptible to exhaustion. This meant European countries had either to increase their exports to the United States, which was made impossible by an increase in the tariffs, or reduce their imports, or default on their wartime loans. In the 1930s both of these last two things occurred, precipitating the Depression. In Europe the question of international debt was further complicated by the fact that the Allies had also lent each other money. Britain alone had been a creditor for $10 billion, so Britain could honour its debts only if its former Allies honoured theirs.

The economic realignment of the world greatly strengthened the grip of the New York partnership on the house of Morgan. In London, Morgan Grenfell's substantial pre-war business in foreign bonds was forbidden by the governor of the Bank of England, Montagu Norman, who was an economic atavist, zealous for a return to the financial orthodoxy of the Edwardian era. Determined to protect sterling and to prepare for a return to the gold standard, he imposed from 1920 an embargo on all foreign loans maturing in less than twenty years. In April 1924 he restricted lending to reconstruction loans guaranteed by either the Treasury or the League of Nations. He had hoped, after the return to the gold standard in April 1925, to discourage foreign lending altogether but the Chancellor, Winston Churchill, sanctioned a resumption of lending in which Norman reluctantly acquiesced, though he issued private warnings to merchant banks not to lend to Russia or Germany. In 1930 Norman began to vet all foreign loans.[88] Though loans were not outlawed, neither Jack Morgan, who was close to Norman, nor Edward Grenfell, who was a director of the Bank of England, were minded to dispute the judgement of the governor. Others were less scrupulous. Morgan Grenfell had to refuse participations in loans for IT & T in December 1923, Belgium in September 1924, Tokyo in October 1925 and Italy in 1930.[89] To some extent, it could afford to indulge Norman, because the house of Morgan was insulated from the worst effects of the emergence of New York as the world's principal capital market. Morgan Grenfell was able to divert former clients to J. P. Morgan & Co. in New York and always secured the London tranche of any loan syndicated internationally.

Though dollar lending from New York meant that J. P. Morgan & Co. worked increasingly closely with the First National Bank and the National City Bank (the 'trio') rather than Morgan Grenfell, London retained its imprimatur of quality. Jack Morgan claimed that American investors were more willing to buy foreign bonds if they knew that Morgan Grenfell was involved. However, the demise of the pound meant that Morgan Grenfell drew closer to its peers in the London market like Baring's, Hambro's and Rothschild's. In 1923 Baring's and Morgan's, burying old differences, syndicated jointly a £2.5 million loan for the port of Buenos Aires.[90] Gaspard Farrer, a partner at Baring's, told Junius Morgan, Jack's eldest son, that 'if private firms are to survive amidst the constantly increasing competition of companies, the more friendly terms on which they are with each other the better it will be for their well-being'.[91] The feeling was mutual; Morgan Grenfell agreed, for example, to split all its Italian business with Baring's, Rothschild's and Hambro's. The London merchant banks even retained the club, the Accepting Houses Committee, which they had formed on the outbreak of war in 1914, principally to consider the implications of the fact that they were now unlikely to get their money back from the Central Powers. Its members, all close to the Bank of England, were an exclusive body of merchant banks whose bills qualified for the finest discount at the Bank of England. After the war it became a forum for discussion of matters of mutual interest with the Bank of England, which assured its members that they were, in the view of the governor, 'undoubted'. Foreigners were not permitted to join. By the 1980s it had become an institution principally of snob value, and faintly ludicrous in its exclusion of foreign banks. In 1980 one of the members, Antony Gibbs Limited, was expelled after being bought by a commercial bank from the colonies, the Hong Kong & Shanghai Bank. It was finally wound up in 1988.

'Financial conditions are overshadowed by political ones,' said Jack Morgan at the end of the war, but he spoke too soon.[92] The debt crisis of the 1920s provided a last platform on which merchant bankers could enact the drama of politics, diplomacy and private finance with which they had governed the fortunes of nations throughout the nineteenth century. Exchange rates had been much disrupted by the war and its legacy of vast international debts. Jack Morgan and Edward Grenfell shared the view of Montagu Norman and his American counterpart, Benjamin Strong, the governor of the New York Federal Reserve Bank, that stable exchange rates, as the prelude to a world-wide return to the gold standard, were central to a resumption of trade and economic growth. Morgan bankers often acted as intermediaries between the central bankers – especially in France, Belgium and Italy – but not always with good results. Their attempts in the winter of 1925–26 to encourage the stabilization of the French franc provoked waves of ill-feeling in France, postponing a return to the gold standard until 1928. In 1925 Belgium's desperation for a Morgan loan very nearly caused the Finance Minister to impose such Draconian cuts in public expenditure that they would have imperilled the survival of the Government. Italy's return to the gold standard was delayed by Montagu Norman's refusal to advance a central bank loan to the Banca d'Italia, on the grounds that Volpi, the Fascist Italian Finance Minister, had boasted to him that he controlled the central bank. It seems that Norman, speaking to Volpi in French, had misunderstood their conversation. After representations by Morgan's, Norman agreed grudgingly to the loan on the grounds that 'in Italy no one is independent'.[93]

The partners of Morgan Grenfell never questioned the wisdom of Britain's return to the gold standard, though it has been described as 'the most dramatically disastrous error by a government in modern economic history'.[94] Britain did not formally abandon the gold standard in 1914; instead, gold sovereigns were replaced by pound notes. Though the pound depreciated against the dollar during the war, in theory pound notes could still be exchanged into gold at the old fixed rate of $4.86. In reality, the number of pound notes in circulation vastly exceeded the supply of gold in the vaults of the Bank of England and, since wartime regulations required exports of gold to be licensed by the Bank of England, nobody availed themselves of the opportunity to exchange cash for gold. Once the wartime licensing rules were lifted in 1919, the Bank of England was relieved of its duty to sell gold at the old fixed price and, able at last to take account of the wartime inflation, the pound plunged to $3.50. It was against this background that Montagu Norman had sought to support the pound by banning foreign loans, which involved selling pounds for dollars. Norman, Benjamin Strong and the house of Morgan had then endeavoured to stabilize the currencies of Europe by lending central banks money with which to support them, until such time as a return to the gold standard could be effected. International adherence to the gold standard was in fact of relatively recent origin, dating from a European agreement in 1867 to settle international trade in gold. The United States had acquiesced in this arrangement at the turn of the century. Each currency was freely convertible into gold and this fixed the rate of exchange between currencies. For instance, in 1914 the same amount of gold could be bought in London for £1 and in New York for $4.86, and so the rate of exchange was £1 for $4.86. A balance of payments surplus caused an inflow of gold into the central bank's reserves, enabling it to increase the currency in circulation without fear of having insufficient gold to meet its international trade liabilities. The increase in the quantity of money raised domestic prices, diminishing demand for exports and so reducing the balance of payments surplus. The reverse happened in the event of a balance of payments deficit. In this manner, the economy adjusted itself naturally to the vicissitudes of trade without inflation. Norman hoped, by returning to the gold standard, to revert to this virtuous circle.

In April 1925 Montagu Norman persuaded the Chancellor of the Exchequer, Winston Churchill, a man not noted for his economic expertise, to return to the gold standard at the pre-war gold and dollar value of the pound of $4.86. Unfortunately, the decision took no account of the inflation that had occurred since the gold standard had been abandoned in 1919. Prices and wages had risen in Britain during and after the war much further than they had in other countries. This made British goods much more expensive than those of Britain's competitors, making a return to the gold standard at the pre-war rate a foolish decision, as Keynes pointed out at the time. Had Britain gone back to the gold standard at, say, $4.40 this would have compensated for the inflation, keeping the cost of British goods and services much more in line with those else-where, but at $4.86 British prices were a tenth or so higher than those of Britain's competitors. Trade went to the United States, Germany and France instead, leading to wage cuts and unemployment in Britain's export industries as companies lost markets. By 1930 2.5 million people were out of work. These consequences, predicted at the time by Keynes, were not considered by the house of Morgan to be its responsibility. Instead, it helped Norman impose his will on the Chancellor by topping up a loan of $200 million from the Federal Reserve to the Bank of England with a $100 million loan of its own, albeit at the behest of Benjamin Strong.[95] This was intended to convince speculators that parity would be maintained by the Bank of England selling dollars for pounds in the market. In the event neither loan was drawn upon during its two-year life (1925–27) and Morgan Grenfell simply collected £103,000 in commission, and a share of the $2 million commitment fee paid to J. P. Morgan & Co.

The dreadful problems of wartime indebtedness were also tackled largely by private bankers, in a manner which is unthinkable today, with our regular economic summits, the

International Monetary Fund and the World Bank. Their poor handling of the delicate structure of international debt and their failure to surmount Germany's manifest inability to pay the reparations imposed upon it arguably led directly to the Great Depression and the Second World War. After German defaults had led to the Franco-Belgian occupation of the Ruhr in 1923 it was left to a committee of private bankers headed by the Chicago financier, Charles Dawes, to investigate Germany's ability to pay. Jack Morgan, who accompanied Dawes in an unofficial capacity, demanded such a high price for the successful flotation of German reparations bonds that it could not possibly be paid. Kathleen Burk suggests that this was a diplomatic ruse concocted by the Bank of England and the British Government, designed to deny the French the right to occupy more of industrial Germany.[96] This scarcely squares with Morgan's well-known reluctance to do business with Germany, though his thinking was not entirely partisan:

As far as my own views are concerned I have considerable hesitation in undertaking a loan to an ex-enemy country, the very natural reason being the chief, with a secondary reason back of it, which is that our declining to do any ex-enemy business has in my opinion made it very much easier for us to do the Allies' business because our very active-minded competitors have been able to turn their attention to Germany and have I think competed not quite as intensely for our legitimate business as they otherwise would have done.[97]

The Dawes Committee nevertheless resulted in 1924 in a $200 million loan to Germany, most of it funded by American bankers and over half of it raised by the house of Morgan. This success encouraged the Allies to seek a permanent solution to the issue of German reparations and a second committee was formed in September 1928, chaired by the New York banker, Owen Young. The Young Committee, like the Dawes Committee, acted in a private capacity. It reduced German reparations by $9 billion and spread the payments over fifty-nine years, met largely by loans from American bankers. Jack Morgan was a member of its 'committee of experts' and played a leading role in the subsequent creation of the Bank for International Settlements, which was initially established solely to administer reparations payments. It grew in time into a central bank for central banks.[99] When Hitler seized power, Germany became the first and last borrower to default on one of Jack Morgan's loans.

It is hard now to recapture the loathing with which the house of Morgan was regarded in the inter-war years. Since the days of Pierpont Morgan and the 'money trust' the bank had been the most potent symbol of unbridled capitalism. Towards the end of the war a man was arrested trying to enter 23 Wall Street intending to kill Jack Morgan. In May Jack Morgan was sent a letter bomb, which was disarmed harmlessly.[100] A month later a man was convicted of trying to blackmail him. On 16 September 1920 a gang of anarchists detonated a bomb at the junction of Wall and Broad Streets in New York, killing thirty people outright and injuring hundreds more. It wrecked the interior of the Morgan offices and killed the chief clerk. Jack Morgan was abroad, but dozens of his staff were hurt and seventeen taken to hospital.[101] Much of this hostility was aroused by the refusal of United States Steel to recognize the trade unions as representatives of the workforce. As he moved on to the world stage in the 1920s, Jack Morgan became the architect of 'Morganization', by which a reliance on Morgan loans meant submission to economic policies approved by 23 Wall Street. Certainly Morgan's command of the American investment community gave it enormous influence. Both Cuba and Belgium modified their internal economic policies to suit the house of Morgan's criteria for a loan. In 1925 charges of 'Morganization' nearly unseated the French Prime Minister. As Russell Leffingwell, a New York partner, put it:

The American investment community believes in us and will take our word for it whenever we are in a position to give our word that France has turned the corner.[102]

In England, Ramsay MacDonald spent his last day as an independent socialist Prime Minister awaiting pathetically the terms of a dollar loan from Morgan's in New York, the terms of which were unacceptable to more than half the members of his Cabinet.[103] By then, of course, the house of Morgan had been overtaken by the catastrophe of the Great Crash, which split it asunder for ever.

The Great Crash changed everything. After the return to the gold standard in 1925 British prices remained high, handicapping exports and cheapening imports. Though Britain's surplus on current account did not plunge into chronic deficit until 1931, when shipping income and overseas investment earnings collapsed in the wake of the Depression, the size of the surplus shrank by a factor of ten between 1920 and 1930. In one year – 1926, the year of the General Strike – there was even a deficit of £26 million. By 1927 the balance of payments had deteriorated sufficiently for Montagu Norman to be alarmed by the loss of gold to the United States to pay for imports. That spring he travelled with Hjalmar Schacht, the governor of the Reichsbank, and Charles Rist, deputy governor of the Bank of France, to New York to persuade the Federal Reserve to cut interest rates. In theory, easier money would galvanize the American economy and raise prices, making it easier for British goods to make headway in American markets. In fact, the money went largely into playing the stock market instead. The expansion of credit that followed Norman's visit is held to have triggered the stock-market speculation of 1927–29, which ended amid unprecedented scenes of panic in October 1929. When the first crash came on 'Black Thursday', 24 October 1929, New York bankers gathered at Morgan's next door to the Stock Exchange, looking for a lead just as they had in the panic of 1907. Then J. P. Morgan had presided over an all-night meeting of bankers, arranging with James Stillman of Citibank a committee of the stronger banks to prop up the threatened trust companies. In 1929 Thomas Lamont of Morgan's presided over a similar meeting, which decided, as had been done twenty-two years earlier, to form a pool of $40 million to stabilize the market by buying shares. Richard Whitney, vice-president of the Exchange and a man known to all as the Morgan broker, was told to go into the market and buy. 'This, with great ostentation, he did,' as J. K. Galbraith put it.[104] The market rallied, and it seemed that Morgan's had saved the country once again. The market plunged again the following Tuesday, amid rumours that the bankers were offloading the stock they had bought the previous Thursday. A second meeting was held in the library at Morgan's, chaired this time by Jack Morgan, who had returned from Europe. George Harrison of the Federal Reserve was deputed to supply the market with liquidity by buying huge amounts of government bonds from the banks but, with occasional interruptions, the market carried on down for the next three years.[105]

The disaster was followed by unseemly revelations. Morgan's had been deeply involved in the most shocking of all the speculative acts that had preceded the Crash: investment trusts. These were companies formed solely to invest in other companies which, in turn, invested in still more companies. The layers were often five or ten deep. Through these delicate pyramids it was possible to control $100 million companies with an investment of a quarter of that amount. At the bottom of one of J. P. Morgan & Co.'s pyramids investigators found the fraudulent and now bankrupt railway speculators, the Van Schwerigen brothers. The partners had also maintained a preferred list of influential clients, even allotting stock in at least one flotation, that of the United Corporation, to themselves. The stock, bought at $75, was sold ten days later for $99. Richard Whitney, brother of a Morgan's partner and broker to the house of Morgan, was suspended from the New York Stock Exchange for theft of securities from the gratuity fund. He was later arrested and jailed. Worst of all, Jack Morgan had failed, unlike his father in 1907, to halt the Crash. The arrogance and power of the house of Morgan had been tolerated as long as it worked; once it failed it became, said J. K. Galbraith, 'fair game for congressional committees, courts, the press and comedians'. Galbraith added that

A banker need not be popular; indeed, a good banker in a healthy capitalist society should probably be much disliked. People do not wish to trust their money to a hail-fellow-well-met but to a misanthrope who can say no. However, a banker must not seem futile, ineffective or vaguely foolish. In contrast with the stern power of Morgan in 1907, that was precisely how his successors seemed, or were made to seem, in 1929.[106]

Samuel Untermyer, the scourge of Pierpont in 1912, emerged to declare that J. P. Morgan & Co. were responsible for all of America's problems. In 1932 the Banking and Currency Committee of the United States Senate began to explore the nature and origins of the Crash, reviving memories of the Pujo Committee. Unlike Pujo, when Morgan's protested that many of the questions submitted by the committee were of a private nature, Jack Morgan and ten of his partners were subpoenaed to appear before it in the spring of 1933. The public was outraged when it was revealed that Jack had paid no American taxes in 1931 or 1932. He made a spirited defence, submitting the famous statement that the house of Morgan had at all times sought 'only first-class business and that in a first-class way' and that their errors had been 'errors of judgment and not of principle'.[107] The spirit of the times was against him. The Glass-Steagall Act of 1933 and the legislation which followed it made it impossible for a banker ever again to exercise the power that Pierpont and Jack Morgan did and brought about the end of the house of Morgan as it had been constituted hitherto.

This was not immediately obvious in London, where financial paralysis crept over the City stealthily rather than vividly. In 1928 the partners of Morgan Grenfell felt confident enough to move offices, having found 22 Old Broad Street too small and old-fashioned. A new home was found at 23 Great Winchester Street, in a building designed in 1892 for the British India Steam Navigation Company and its associated concern, the great Indian merchant firm of Gray, Dawes & Co.[108] The occupants of the new building had changed considerably.

Edward Grenfell had been elected Member of Parliament for the City of London at a by-election in May 1922. In the House of Commons he spoke rarely and usually on matters of international and national finance, invariably counselling caution. He denounced the Labour Government's attempt in August 1924 to reach an accommodation with the Soviet Union over Britain's pre-revolutionary debts and the terms of the French war-debt agreement of July 1926. His transition to Parliament was in a family tradition: both his father and his grandfather had been MPs. In 1935 he was elevated to the peerage as the first Lord St Just of St Just-in-Penwith in the county of Cornwall and by the time he died on 26 November 1941 he was remembered more for a distinguished City career than any political heroics. A lieutenant of the City of London, a governor of Harrow School and a director of Sun Assurance, Shaw, Saville and the White Star Line, he left a fortune of £880,332.

Grenfell was not replaced for two years after he entered Parliament, but in 1924 the first new partners since Charles Whigham's elevation in 1912 were appointed. One, Michael George Herbert, was of little import and died almost unnoticed by posterity in 1932. The other, a recently created (1921) baronet called Sir Thomas Sivewright Catto, began a family association with the bank that persists today. Catto was chairman and managing director of Yule & Co., a wealthy mercantile house with which Morgan Grenfell had been connected since before the war. In 1908, Morgan's had lost £10,000 in the collapse of an old-established firm, India Development, and this led to the appointment of George Yule & Co., the London agency of Andrew Yule & Co., a large Calcutta merchant bank, as its agent in India.[109] In 1916, Morgan's agreed to acquire in Yule & Co. and Catto was invited in 1918 by Grenfell's cousin and fellow partner, Vivian Hugh Smith, to run it. He was sufficiently well known and respected in 1922-23 to be invited to serve on the Indian Government Retrenchment Commission, better known by its chairman's name as the Inchcape Commission. By the time he came back to London in 1924 to take up a partnership at Morgan Grenfell, Catto was a middle-aged man of recognized experience in both business and public affairs. He was born at Peterhead in Aberdeenshire on 15 March 1879 and began work at the age of sixteen in a Newcastle shipping office. Rising to be vice-president in charge of the New York operations of Macandrews & Forbes, a shipping company, he had acquired extensive knowledge of commerce in the Near and Far East. During the war he had been a Ministry of Shipping representative in the United States, helping to despatch to Britain, France and Russia the food and weapons bought by J. P. Morgan & Co. on behalf of the British Government.[110] In recognition of these services he was made baronet in 1921, and in 1936, for services to India, created the first Baron Catto of Cairncatto in Aberdeenshire, where one of his grandsons still manages the family estate, Schivas.

The house of Morgan in London was not exempt from the tendency of all forms of British commercial life to yield eventually to the aristocratic embrace. From an early age Jack Morgan had been friendly with the British nobility. In the late Victorian and Edwardian era many British families had married American money. The Duke of Marlborough had married Consuelo Vanderbilt for an initial payment of $2.5 million. The overlords of the East Coast business establishment like William Vanderbilt were happy to trade their daughters for the esteem that went with landed wealth and a title. Jack Morgan merely aped their manners, shooting grouse with the King at Balmoral and like his father becoming passionate about yachting. As Prince of Wales, Edward VIII would stay with the Morgans on Long Island. During the inter-war years Morgan Grenfell developed the nepotism and over-representation in the House of Lords that Anthony Sampson gently mocked in the first edition of his *Anatomy of Britain* in 1962. Edward Grenfell was created a peer in 1935. Vivian Hugh Smith, who had joined Morgan's from Hay's Wharf, a family firm, in 1905, became in 1938 the first Lord Bicester of Tusmoor. His son and heir, Randall Hugh Vivian Smith, joined Morgan Grenfell in 1930. In 1933 Francis James Rennell Rodd, a former diplomat, joined the bank, succeeding his father as

Lord Rennell of Rodd in 1941. Rodd had married Smith's daughter, Mary, in 1928. His brother, Peter, married Nancy Mitford, who lampooned Francis as a character who was rich and handsome, but a 'bore' and a 'cold fish.'[111] Michael Herbert's uncle was the Earl of Pembroke, and his brother was Captain Sidney Herbert, a Conservative MP. His mother's family was related to the Astors and the Vanderbilts. When Charles Whigham died hunting with the Bicester in 1938 he was replaced as partner by William Edward, Viscount Harcourt, who had joined the bank in 1931. Harcourt was the grandson of Walter Burns, the son-in-law asked by Junius Morgan to negotiate the French government loan of 1870. As such, he was a great-grandson of Junius Morgan himself, George Peabody's second partner and the co-founder of the bank.

In Britain the Great Crash on Wall Street completed the gruesome economic demolition begun by the ill-advised return to the gold standard in 1925. Since the war the countries of Europe had paid for their trade deficits with America and with each other by borrowing from the United States. In America the Crash blighted employment, consumer spending, business investment and the solvency of the banks. This brought the instant cessation of new American loans to Europe and the withdrawal of money already lent, as American lenders called in their debts to meet the demands of panic-stricken investors and depositors at home. This uncovered the wartime deficits which lending had hidden. As consumers lost their jobs, businessmen curtailed investment and politicians raised the duties on imported goods. World trade shrank, making it impossible for European countries to support themselves by an increase in exports. Most followed the dictates of financial orthodoxy, which prescribed a period of austerity while the deficits were erased. In Britain, two committees appointed to consider the crisis reported in July 1931. The committee on Finance and Industry was chaired by Lord Macmillan. It revealed to the public for the first time that Britain's trade account had been in deficit *since 1822* and that only invisible exports – banking, insurance, shipping and the interest on overseas investments – had put the balance right. These were the activities worst hit by the recession. It also revealed the City's exposure to German loans, which were repudiated in June 1931. The second committee, chaired by Sir George May, secretary of the Prudential Insurance Co., reported that the national budget was also in deficit, by £170 million. It recommended increases in taxes and cuts in public spending to eradicate it. When the socialist Prime Minister, Ramsay MacDonald, put the proposed economies to his Cabinet on the night of Sunday, 23 August 1931, nine of its twenty members offered their resignations rather than support them. The events that followed toppled MacDonald's Government and passed into the mythology of the Labour Party as a 'bankers' ramp' which had overturned a democratically elected government. The house of Morgan was at the centre of them.

American banks were hit especially hard by the Crash. Bankrupt businesses defaulted on their loans. As some collapsed, depositors grew nervous and withdrew their money from banks which had lent most of their cash to others on different terms. Between 1929 and 1933, 7,000 American banks failed, principally because borrowers defaulted on loans and they were unable to repay their depositors. The loss of confidence spread eventually to Europe, where in May 1931 the Rothschild bank in Vienna, the Kreditanstalt, failed to meet its obligations. German banks trying to rescue it were knocked down in the rush of withdrawals and repudiated the loans that had been made to them. One, the Darmstadter, failed. In Britain, the revelation by the Macmillan and May committees that the country's budget and balance of payments were both in deficit accelerated the withdrawal of banking deposits from the City of London, precipitating a run on the pound. London bankers were doubly threatened by the German repudiation in June. In a bid to attract capital, the bank rate was raised twice, to the then astronomical level of $4\frac{1}{2}$ per cent. The City pressed the government for some dramatic action to restore confidence in the pound, preferably a balanced budget. Prompted by the

Treasury, the Bank of England, itself directed by leading bankers like Edward Grenfell and Sir Thomas Catto, asked George Harrison, the governor of the New York Federal Reserve, whether or not it would be possible to support the pound with the proceeds of a dollar borrowing in New York. Harrison suggested that they contact J. P. Morgan & Co., who advised that a public loan was impossible until the economies proposed by Ramsay MacDonald and his Chancellor, Philip Snowden, had been implemented. The bank's initial response, cabled to the Cabinet in London on 21 August, read as follows:

Are we right in assuming that the programme under consideration will have the sincere support of the Bank of England and the City generally and thus go a long way towards resolving internal confidence in Great Britain? Of course our ability to do anything depends on the response of public opinion, particularly in Great Britain, to the Government's announcement of the programme.[112]

A second message the following day reiterated this point, warning that New York 'banks and banking houses have for a long time looked with great apprehension upon the continued neglect of the present Government to establish sound fiscal policies'.[113] This accorded with orthodox financial thinking. Cuts in public spending, coupled with wage cuts and higher taxes, would suppress demand for imports, restore the balance of trade and stabilize the pound.

Morgan's demands reduced Ramsay MacDonald to negotiating the sufficiency of the cuts in public expenditure (£68 million) not with his Cabinet alone, but also with American bankers. After accepting the resignations of nine Cabinet ministers on the night of 23 August, he remained in the Cabinet room to await the terms of the loan from J. P. Morgan & Co. in New York, relayed through the Bank of England. The news eventually came that Morgan's had agreed to raise £80 million in New York and Paris. With his government on the verge of collapse, Ramsay MacDonald agreed with the King the following morning to form a coalition government with the Liberal and the Conservative parties. MacDonald and those members of his Cabinet who joined him were expelled from the Labour Party but in the subsequent General Election his former comrades won only 52 of the 516 seats they contested against the National Government. For a few days the run on the pound was stayed but by late September the pressure was so intense that the gold standard was abandoned and the pound fell from $4.86 to $3.23. Sidney Webb, who as Lord Passfield was one of the eleven Labour Cabinet ministers to stick with MacDonald, said: 'Nobody told us we could do this.' Thereafter, the devaluation of the currency as a cure for economic ills became a commonplace. The era of economic management had begun. The events of August 1931 were the last occasion when the influence of the house of Morgan, or private bankers like them, proved decisive in the economic affairs of Great Britain. When the next financial crisis arose, in 1976, the Labour Government negotiated not with the house of Morgan but with the International Monetary Fund, an invention of the US Treasury economist John Maynard Keynes, who had described the May Committee report as 'the most foolish document I ever had the misfortune to read'. The myth that 'brutal foreign bankers had laid down terms, as regards the dole', as Grenfell put it, took root. It was significant that when the Labour Party assumed power in 1945 the very first institution it nationalized was the Bank of England.

The Crash had more immediate consequences for the house of Morgan than the curtailment of the power of private bankers. In the United States, President Franklin Roosevelt's New Deal after 1932 was only incidentally a reflationary corrective to the deflationary measures of the Hoover presidency. It was principally an attack on big business and the Eastern (and Republican) financial establishment that many Democratic politicians held responsible for the Crash and the Depression. In the Securities Act of 1933 and the Securities Exchange Act of 1934 the more egregious extravagances of 1928 and 1929, like inadequate disclosure, insider dealing, short selling and margin trading, were outlawed. The New York Stock Exchange was subjected to public regulation and the Securities and Exchange Commission was established to apply and enforce it. The legislation obliged American banks to choose between taking deposits and lending them (commercial banking), and the issue and underwriting of bonds and shares (investment banking). This was intended to make it harder for banks like J. P. Morgan & Co., which combined both activities, to mount inside operations or create the investment trusts which had led to the ruination of the stock market in 1929.

In 1934 J. P. Morgan & Co. chose incorporation as a bank, joining the Federal Reserve system in 1940. Jack Morgan's younger son, Henry Morgan, formed a new securities partnership, Morgan, Stanley & Co., in 1934. Because the legislation forbade an American bank to own or affiliate with a brokerage house, J. P. Morgan & Co. also cut its long-standing links with the investment house of Drexel & Co. in Philadelphia. The Paris partnership, Morgan & Cie, was absorbed as an independent banking subsidiary of the New York parent. The historic association with the London house, which would continue to be active in the securities business, was also curtailed. From June 1934, Morgan Grenfell & Co. ceased to be a private, unlimited company and became instead a private limited company, Morgan Grenfell & Co. Limited, with a paid-up share capital of £5 million. The partners – Grenfell, Hugh Smith, Whigham, Catto, Vivian Smith and Rodd – became directors, though the historic appellation of 'partner' lingered until the 1970s. This transformation into a limited company allowed J. P. Morgan & Co. to retain a one-third stake in the firm but, although Jack Morgan remained as a director, the former New York partners were precluded from any involvement in the management of the bank.

For the first time in the history of the London firm, its destiny was controlled exclusively by British men. Among these, the most important was Sir Thomas Catto. Because most of his experience had been in industry rather than merchant banking, he had kept most of his assets in cash rather than investments. This prudence allowed him to escape the Crash almost completely unscathed and in 1934 he emerged as the largest shareholder in the new London firm. The bank was also introduced to the perilous art of corporate advice by its acquisitive American clients and by the Bank of England, which sponsored a measure of industrial rationalisation between the wars. Morgan Grenfell encouraged merger talks between General Motors and the troubled Austin Motors in 1925; once these collapsed, the bank helped General Motors take an interest in Vauxhall Motors instead. In the 1930s, Catto became a director of the Union Castle Mail Company, formed from the merger of the Royal Mail Steamship Company and Union Castle. Until the war effaced the State's last inhibitions, industry faced no direct threats to its independence. The Bank of England's industrial reorganisation company, Barkers' Industrial Development Company Limited, achieved little and quickly became known as 'Brought in Dead'. Similarly, hostile bids were still unthinkable. In 1935 Morgan Grenfell advised United Steel Companies to abandon a bid for Lancashire Steel Corporation once the corporation made plain it was not welcome. In 1927 the bank helped the former Liberal Prime Minister, David Lloyd George, realise for £2.9 million his investment in the *Daily Chronicle*, a radical newspaper he bought in 1918 with the proceeds of the sale of political honours to, among others, war profiteers. Though Catto later sat on the Liberal benches in the House of Lords, even the official historians of the bank judged this a shameful transaction, but the shift of business from the almost limitless dangers of buying and selling securities to the sound and almost riskless business of earning fees testified to the sharp psychological shock delivered by the Crash.[113] It made a virtue of necessity too. Many former clients had lapsed into Communism or Fascism. After the war the dollar replaced sterling as the principal medium of international exchange and America became the capital market of the world. Sterling lapsed into chronic vacillation. Latin America was lost to American banks like Citibank and Chase, the house of Rockefeller. The financing of governments and the manipulation of currencies, when it resumed after the Second World War, passed into the cold hands of national governments and the new international organizations, the World Bank and the International Monetary Fund. The heroic age of merchant banking was over. The Crash, the Depression and the Second World War led in London to thirty years of decay and introspection.

The singular importance of the house in the First World War was not repeated in the Second. With the new-issue market shut and the lending business prostrate, merchant banking became impossible to practise. Three of the six directors and many of the staff were engaged on war duties and the bank went into hibernation.[114] Staff were evacuated to Haresfoot, a Smith family home near Berkhampsted. Of the 132 staff at the outbreak of war, 53 served in the armed forces. Six were killed. The panelling of the Partners' Room was damaged by a bomb which destroyed the nearby Dutch Church in Austin Friars on 16 October 1940, but there was little other excitement or activity until 1944, when the bank made its first acquisition, buying a private banking operation named after its founder, A. E. K. Cull. He had made a fortune backing the oil exploration company which became Ultramar, still clients of the bank today. The story goes that Morgan's only bought the firm to acquire its premises, which happened to be next door to 23 Great Winchester Street. Kathleen Burk, in her history of Morgan Grenfell, suggests that Cull approached Morgan's in 1943, on the grounds that his partners were too elderly to continue to do business. Cull added £241,000 to profits in 1944. At Cull's insistence all his staff were retained and one received an offer of employment from Morgan Grenfell by post while still a prisoner of war in Germany. There is a Cull's Room at 23 Great Winchester Street, reputed once to have been occupied by A. E. K. himself. A grandson of Cull's, Nicholas Gold, worked at the bank until 1987.

Summoned on account of his experience in the earlier conflict, Lord Catto served briefly between March and June 1940 as Director-General of Equipment and Stores and as a member of the Supply Council at the Ministry of Supply. When Churchill replaced Neville Chamberlain as Prime Minister in May 1940, Catto accepted the request of the new Chancellor of the Exchequer, Kingsley Wood, to serve in the specially created (and unpaid) position of financial adviser to the Treasury. He resigned all directorships, including that at Morgan Grenfell, on his appointment and though Kingsley Wood died in September 1943, Catto was rewarded for his sacrifices in the following year with the governorship of the Bank of England. As if to underline the alliance between the house of Morgan and the Bank of England, he succeeded Montagu (now Lord) Norman and though the temptation to dispose of a former partner in the firm most closely associated with the 'bankers' ramp' that undid the Labour Government in 1931 must have been extremely strong, he did not fall victim to the incoming Labour Government's nationalization of the Bank of England in 1945. The Chancellor, Hugh Dalton, decided that a massive upheaval of personnel would have undermined confidence in the City and abroad and Catto, his deputy governor and the court were all left untouched.[115] Catto served only one term as governor. He retired in 1949 and died in August 1959, having never rejoined Morgan Grenfell, though his son, Stephen, joined the bank in 1948 and his grandson, Alex, joined in 1984, the family shareholding passing down the generations. J. E. H. ('Tim') Collins joined at the same time as Stephen Catto. He too was 'family', having married Gillian, the elder daughter of the second Lord Bicester, Randall Smith, who became a director of Morgan Grenfell in 1938, and remained with the bank until only a year before his death in January 1968, aged 70. Of the directors who were prominent in the first fifteen years after the war only George Erskine (knighted in 1948) was an outsider. He joined the bank in 1929 from the National Bank of Scotland and became a director immediately after the war, in which he had served as deputy chairman of NAAFI.

Catto's governorship coincided with Britain's final relegation to the status of international beggar. Between 1939 and 1945

Britain had sacrificed its export trade to the prosecution of the war. By 1945 it was quite unable to pay its way in the world, and was absolutely dependent on American aid to cover its shortage of dollars, known as the 'dollar gap'. Initially some $5 billion was borrowed – at interest – in July 1946. All of it was spent by September 1947 and there was a run on the pound. In 1948 Britain received $1,263 million out of the total of $4,875 million offered in Marshall Aid, ranking it second only to France as a recipient of American charity. It was still not enough to cover Britain's balance of payments deficit, and in the second quarter of 1949 the Bank of England lost £160 million in gold reserves. Later that year the pound was drastically devalued, from $4.03 to $2.80, a near third reduction in its dollar value.[116] All this had profound implications for Morgan Grenfell's future. With sterling under perpetual pressure, the bank's traditional business of issuing and underwriting sterling bond issues for overseas borrowers was impossible to resume.

New activities had to be developed and these were found largely in the area pioneered in the 1920s and 1930s, that of offering advice for fees to industrial companies seeking finance. In 1945 Morgan Grenfell underwrote and managed its first offer for sale of shares – 4½ per cent preference shares of John Summons & Sons – since the outbreak of war.[117] By the early 1950s the devalued pound had improved the terms of trade sufficiently to eradicate the balance of payments problems of the 1940s. Between 1952 and 1955 there was even something of a stock-market boom. This breathed new life into the still moribund new-issue market, which was given added impetus by the denationalization programme. In 1953 the new Conservative Government redeemed its pledge to denationalize the road-haulage and iron and steel industries nationalized by the previous Labour Government. Long-distance road haulage was denationalized first, but shares in the companies were not offered for sale to the public through the Stock Exchange. The problems involved in denationalizing the steel industry were formidable. Much of the Conservative Party and many industrialists had grown used to regulation of the steel industry, which had undergone a measure of government-sponsored rationalization before the war and been subjugated completely to the demands of the war effort during the course of the conflict. One member of the Conservative Cabinet, Lord Salisbury, the Secretary of State for Commonwealth Relations, came close to resignation over the government's abdication of responsibility for the industry. The Labour Party's pledge to renationalize the industry immediately after resuming power (without full compensation) alarmed the investment institutions, many of which felt that they had escaped nationalization themselves only through the crowding of the legislative timetable and were not anxious to alienate the Labour Party by buying shares in a denationalized steel industry. Attempts to guarantee compensation for investors in the event of renationalization were fruitless and the Prudential and Pearl Assurance initially refused to consider underwriting the sale of shares at all. Once prevailed upon by the governor of the Bank of England, they insisted that a number of steel companies should be sold privately before they would invest, making it easier to judge a fair price for the public sales. There were no precedents on how to disentangle an industry from state control and no means of measuring the performance of nationalized companies by the orthodox criteria of the stock market. The newly nationalized Bank of England was anxious not to associate too closely with an issue so partisan in nature and threatening to the stability of a vital industry. The Government, itself disunited on the issue, needed to recoup at least the cost of purchasing the steel companies and any subsequent investment in the industry, when the sale price was likely to be severely depressed by the political threats emanating from the Labour Party. The involvement of Whitehall in the sale of shares was a new phenomenon. There were also fears that the trade unions would object forcibly and that the Iron and Steel Trades Confederation in particular would paralyse the industry by striking.

Morgan Grenfell, as merchant bankers to five of the six

largest steel companies since before the war, was the premier steel house in the City. Lord Bicester, the head of the house and a director of the Bank of England, and Sir George Erskine, the head of the bank's Corporate Finance Department, had worked on steel mergers and share issues during the 1930s. Bicester was also a Conservative, chairing the City of London Conservative Association for many years, and Erskine was regarded as the most innovative and inventive corporate financier of the day. It was therefore not surprising that in December 1950 Bicester and Erskine were invited by Sir Edward Peacock of Baring's to join the working party he had formed, at the behest of a number of steel industrialists, to ponder the feasibility of denationalization. This working party, meeting in conditions of great secrecy, had prepared a tentative scheme of denationalization even before the Conservative Party was restored to office in October 1951.[118] After the election, the working party was placed under the auspices of the Bank of England, though the governor of the Bank insisted that the sales be effected by the merchant banks involved without any special support, lest any abnormality alert investors to the risks involved. A committee of merchant banks was formed, which met for the first time at 23 Great Winchester Street on 13 April 1953. This formed a consortium to effect the sales. Its members were Morgan Grenfell, Baring's, Rothschild's, Lazard's, Hambro's, Schroder's, Helbert Wagg and Robert Benson, Lonsdale. Morgan Grenfell, which had numbered among its clients the largest of the steel companies, was the obvious candidate for leadership of it. George Erskine chaired its executive subcommittee and two colleagues, Kenneth Barrington and K. F. Chadwick, were joint secretaries to it.[119] 'Morgan's are getting an almost embarrassing lot of this business,' said Bicester to the governor.[120]

The subcommittee's first decision was to involve private investors as well as the insurance companies, pension funds and investment trusts, whose support was still lukewarm. The size of the operation, rather than any ideological desire to broaden the ownership of shares, dictated that they should.

The total value of the steel companies being offered for sale –
£300 million, or around £3 billion in today's money – was
unprecedented. It was roughly equivalent to the value of all
the ordinary shares held by the insurance companies at the
time (£320 million) and four times the value of all the ordinary
shares held by the pension funds (£75 million). A shortfall of
£30 or £40 million was anticipated if the merchant banks
relied on the institutions alone. It was eventually concluded
that the institutions would buy no more than half of the
companies and rather less if they were all sold at once. Erskine's
initial plan to sell the six largest companies simultaneously was
abandoned. As he put it to the governor:

The Pru [were] against both a powerful syndicate to take over the
bulk of the issues, and any attempt to do [i.e. float] the major companies simultaneously.[121]

Shares in the six largest steel companies were sold consecutively
between October 1953 and January 1955. United Steel Companies was sold first, for 25s a share with a handsome dividend.
Morgan Grenfell received just £6,369 for its part in the consortium and a fee of £10,000 for its advice to United Steel
Companies.[122] To ensure popular support, the advertisement
inviting applications for shares appeared in thirty-eight newspapers and four periodicals. When Morgan's analysed the
returns afterwards, it found more than a third of newspaper
applications came from readers of the *Daily Telegraph*. It attracted speculators. The issue was subscribed threefold and on
the first day of dealings the shares closed at a premium of 3d.
Thereafter they fell quickly for want of institutional buyers.
The sale of Lancashire Steel, which followed in January 1954,
was a flop. It took the balance of the decade to sell the rest of
the industry. Though nine-tenths of the shares in the steel
industry were in private ownership again by 1957, the debts of
the denationalized steel companies were not sold by Morgan
Grenfell until February 1961. Erskine reflected after the first
sale, apparently without cynicism:

The state of the 'after market' in United Steel shares ... indicated that although the public generally might come in for a quick turn, they did not appear at the present time to be permanent investors in any large volume in steel equities.[123]

The fears of investors were well founded. The steel industry was renationalized promptly by the incoming Labour Government in 1967. The merchant banks, of course, transacted this business too.

The denationalization of steel, and the economic growth of the 1950s and 1960s, allowed Morgan Grenfell to resume its traditional business of selling bond issues for industrial companies, but without being able to lend in dollars it was bound to be limited to Britain. Efforts were made to replace the severed connections with the United States within the sterling area. In 1949 Morgan Grenfell set up, jointly with Lazard Brothers and Consolidated Zinc, the Anglo-Australian Corporation Pty Limited in Melbourne to solicit business in Australia. Consolidated Zinc sold its share to the American cousins of Morgan Grenfell and Lazard Brothers in 1961; Stephen Catto, who had joined the bank a year earlier, was sent out to work for it. It joined in 1959 with the Australian United Corporation, the corporate finance arm of the stockbroker, Ian Potter & Co., to participate in the money markets. A full merger followed in 1963. This was the core of Morgan Grenfell's operations in Australia until 1977. It marked the beginnings of an especially close relationship in the London market with Lazard's, which to some extent supplanted J. P. Morgan in the bank's affections, at least in London. The two houses even shared a box at Covent Garden, and if one felt unable to transact a particular piece of business, the other was the first port of call. As the chairman of Lazard's, Lord Kindersley, told the Bank Rate tribunal – the proceedings of which remain a remarkable guide to the antediluvian life of the City – in a famous exchange in December 1957:

Morgans and ourselves are probably closer than any other two issuing houses in the City of London: we discuss intimate details of every kind and description. I do not think Lord Bicester would find it in the least surprising that I should come to him and say to him: 'Look here, Rufie, is it too late to stop this business or not?'[124]

There were obvious attractions. Both were heavily over-represented in the House of Lords and had developed a haughty manner to match. Lazard's, though descended from French-Jewish traders in New Orleans, was by the 1950s thoroughly Gentile and English. It was owned by Lord Cowdray and run by Lords Kindersley, Brand and Hampden. Though the family shareholdings of Lords Catto, Bicester, Harcourt and Rennell were not as dominant, because all the partners had stakes, the cultural effects were much the same. Harcourt was the brother-in-law of Lord Ashburton of Baring's, which had long been ensconced within the British aristocracy, boasting five peers in the 1950s. One, Lord Cromer, became governor of the Bank of England. Sir Edward Peacock, who led Baring's throughout the 1950s, was a Canadian and it was with Baring's that Morgan Grenfell expanded into Canada in 1952, buying the firm of Harris & Partners in Toronto. Tim Collins, Bicester's son-in-law and contemporary of Stephen Catto, was despatched to work with Harris & Partners. The association lasted into the 1960s and 1970s but little came of it, though a Canadian client took Morgan Grenfell into the field of fund management for the first time in 1953, when the bank agreed to manage the United Kingdom pension fund of the Canadian minerals company, Inco. Morgan Grenfell's interest in the firm was progressively diluted from 1961 and in 1967 Harris & Partners was merged with the local firm of Dominion Securities Corporation Limited.

Despite these new relationships in London and abroad, the actual and sentimental ties to J. P. Morgan & Co. in New York remained exceptionally strong. No separate office was established in New York and it was simply unthinkable that Morgan Grenfell would establish with Lazard Freres in New York a relationship similar to that obtaining with Lazard's in London. Bank officials visiting New York would always call at 23 Wall Street and, likely as not, reveal the nature of their business. Joint presentations to American clients were the norm. Both Stephen Catto and Tim Collins worked at J. P. Morgan & Co. in New York before returning to London as assistant managers in 1955, which was a common experience for trainees until the 1970s. J. P. Morgan & Co. – called Morgan Guaranty Trust Company after its merger with the Guaranty Trust in 1959 – and Morgan Stanley were regarded as 'associated' companies until deep into that decade. After the merger with the Guaranty Trust, J. P. Morgan & Co.'s business expanded and it opened a separate London office, but the historic ethos of the house of Morgan ensured that relations with Morgan Grenfell remained close.

The immediate post-war years witnessed profound changes in the nature of Morgan Grenfell's business, but not of its *modus operandi*. The bank remained small in numbers. The number of staff employed increased from about 150 in 1948 to no more than 250 in the early 1960s. There was a clear hierarchical division between directors, who wore suits, and managers, who wore black coats and striped trousers. The managers were the technicians; the directors merely supplied the contacts through which they could make money for the bank. Tea and smoking were banned at the staff's desk, in case a client passed. An anecdote is still told of Lord Harcourt addressing a clerk called Cockersell in the mid-1960s: 'Cockersell, I'm going to have my lunch now. You may go and have your dinner.'[125] Clerks sat on high stools writing up ledgers by hand, in the manner of P. G. Wodehouse's *Psmith in the City*. If a director was in the office before 10 a.m. it was assumed that the bank was going bust, and normal directional hours in the 1950s were from 11 a.m. to 4 p.m. Most messages travelled within the Square Mile by hand; only the most urgent were sent by telegraph, using Bentley's Code. The directors, who in the 1950s could still park their motor cars with ease under London Wall, took dry sherry before lunch in the Partners' Room, where they all sat together. The atmosphere was akin to that of a country-house library. A private history of Morgan Grenfell published in 1958 described the Partners' Room as follows:

As is still customary among the older Merchant Banking Houses of the City, all the partners sit together in one room and conduct the business of the firm from there. They can retire to other smaller rooms for private and uninterrupted conversation, but the convenience of all partners being in a position always to know what is going on and, tacitly or otherwise, to agree or disagree with each other, can only be met by their sitting together and hearing everything, including each other's telephone conversations.[126]

In the afternoon they were served with tea and biscuits from a silver service. There is still a Tea Room upstairs at 23 Great Winchester Street, where this ritual is reputed to have been enacted, often in the company of the editor of *The Times*. The practice of employing male secretaries had only recently been abandoned due to the exigencies of war, but most female staff still tended to work as stenographers, cleaners and switchboard operators rather than in intimate contact with the directors. Most were dressed in uniforms of 'Morgan Grenfell green', as if to distinguish it from the Lincoln Green of Robin Hood. Women who were taken ill would be driven home by Daimler-hire, a chauffeur-driven service with which Morgan's had a contract. They travelled always in pairs, in case the driver interfered with them. The paternalism ran deep. During one issue of shares underwritten by the bank, Lord Rennell came in to the office on a Sunday to sign the cheques payable to the other underwriters, knowing it would save time for the clerical staff on Monday. It was quaint, but it encapsulated a singular wisdom: each director knew what the others were doing and all were responsible for the welfare of the business and the staff. On his first day, a new recruit would be introduced to everybody who worked at the bank. There were no cabals or factions or struggles for self-aggrandizement. The integrity of the partners was unquestioned. These gems were swept away, along with all the detritus of the past, in the period of permanent revolution that overtook the bank in the 1960s.

NOTES

[1] Vincent P. Carosso, *The Morgans: Private International Bankers, 1854–1913*, Harvard University Press, 1987.
[2] Andrew Sinclair, *Corsair: The Life of J. Pierpont Morgan*, Weidenfeld & Nicolson, 1981.
[3] Sinclair, *op. cit.*
[4] *ibid.*
[5] As reported to C. W. Barron, in *ibid.*
[6] *ibid.*
[7] *ibid.*
[8] J. K. Galbraith, *The Age of Uncertainty*, André Deutsch, 1977.
[9] Sinclair, *op. cit.*
[10] *ibid.*
[11] Senator Aldrich, cited in Edwin Hoyt, *House of Morgan*, Muller, 1968.
[12] Sinclair, *op. cit.*
[13] *ibid.*
[14] Revelstoke to Gaspard Farrer, 19 April 1904, cited in Philip Ziegler, *The Sixth Great Power. Barings, 1722–1929*, Collins, 1988.
[15] Paul Ferris, *Gentlemen of Fortune*, Weidenfeld & Nicolson, 1984.
[16] Carosso, *op. cit.*
[17] Sinclair, *op. cit.*
[18] *ibid.*
[19] *ibid.*
[20] *ibid.*
[21] *ibid.*; also cited in Kathleen Burk, *Morgan Grenfell, op. cit.*
[22] *ibid.* A full verse ran as follows:
    It's Morgan's, it's Morgan's,
    The great financial gorgon!
    Get off that spot
    We're keeping it hot
    That seat is reserved for Morgan.
[23] H. G. Nicholas, *The American Union*, Pelican, 1950.
[24] Kathleen Burk in *Morgan Grenfell 1838–1988: The Biography of a Merchant Bank*, Oxford University Press, 1989, estimates J. S. Morgan & Co.'s losses on the IMM merger at more than £90,000. Carosso, *op. cit.*
[25] Letter to Bertram Currie of Glyn's, 3 May 1895, cited in *ibid.*
[26] *ibid.*
[27] Ziegler, *op. cit.*
[28] *ibid.*
[29] Carosso, *op. cit.*

[30] Goschen to Lord Salisbury, 9 May 1891, cited in Ziegler, *op. cit.*

[31] Carosso, *op. cit.*

[32] Robert Gordon to J. P. Morgan, 27 October 1899, cited in *ibid.*

[33] Cecil Baring to Lord Revelstoke, 28 December 1900, cited in Ziegler, *op. cit.*

[34] Lord Revelstoke to Cecil Baring, 23 November 1900, cited in *ibid.*

[35] Carosso, *op. cit.*

[36] *ibid.*

[37] *George Peabody & Co., J. S. Morgan & Co., Morgan Grenfell & Co., Morgan Grenfell & Co. Ltd, 1838–1958*, printed for private circulation by Oxford University Press, 1958, hereafter cited as *George Peabody & Co.*; Carosso, *op cit.*

[38] *ibid.*

[39] Letters to Lord Milner, 22 March 1901 and 2 November 1900, cited in Stanley Chapman, *The Rise of Merchant Banking*, Unwin Hyman, 1984.

[40] Ziegler, *op. cit.*

[41] Letter to Milner, dated 22 March 1901 and cited in *ibid.*

[42] Carosso, *op. cit.*

[43] *ibid.*

[44] It is unclear from which side the initiative came. In his history of Morgan's Vincent Carosso suggests that it was Lord Revelstoke's idea. Philip Ziegler, in his history of Baring's, suggests both that it came from J. P. Morgan and that 'the concept emerged in conversation between the two principals, each being convinced that the other was more eager.' Certainly Baring's had more to gain. (Carosso, *op. cit.*; Ziegler, *op. cit.*)

[45] Robert Winsor (of Kidder Peabody) to Gaspard Farrer, 10 September 1904, cited in Ziegler, *op. cit.*

[46] Lord Revelstoke to Hugo Baring, 8 August 1905, cited in *ibid.*

[47] Letter to Milner, 13 July 1901, cited in Chapman, *op. cit.*

[48] Carosso, *op. cit.*

[49] Ziegler, *op. cit.*

[50] *ibid.*

[51] Carosso, *op. cit.*

[52] Jack Morgan to Edward Grenfell, cited in Ziegler, *op. cit.*

[53] Grenfell and Hugh Smith to Jack Morgan, 12 December 1908, cited in Carosso, *op. cit.*

[54] Ziegler, *op. cit.*

[55] Carosso, *op. cit.*; Ziegler, *op. cit.*

[56] Carosso, *op. cit.*

[57] Hoyt, *op. cit.*
[58] Sinclair, *op. cit.*
[59] J. P. Morgan to Samuel Untermyer, *Money Trust Investigation Report*, 1913, cited in *ibid.*
[60] *ibid.*
[61] Carosso, *op. cit.*
[62] *ibid.*
[63] *ibid.*
[64] Ronald J. Caridi, *20th Century American Foreign Policy*, Prentice-Hall, 1974.
[65] Carosso, *op. cit.*
[66] Caridi, *op. cit.*
[67] Sinclair, *op. cit.*
[68] Cable from Edward Grenfell to Jack Morgan, 5 November 1914, cited in Kathleen Burk, *Britain, America and the Sinews of War 1914–18*, Allen & Unwin, 1985.
[69] Bryan was opposed to putting the dollar on the gold standard. His words at the Democratic National Convention in 1896 were: 'You shall not press down upon the brow of labour this crown of thorns . . . You shall not crucify mankind upon a cross of gold.' Cited in Caridi, *op. cit.*
[70] Arthur S. Link, *Wilson: The Struggle for Neutrality*, Princeton University Press, 1960.
[71] Caridi, *op. cit.*
[72] Burk, *op. cit.*
[73] *ibid.*
[74] Commercial Agreement between the Army Council, the Admiralty and J. P. Morgan & Co., signed on 15 January 1915. Cited in *ibid.*
[75] *ibid.*
[76] Hoyt, *op. cit.*
[77] Burk, *op. cit.*
[78] The phrase was George Booth's. He was Deputy Director of Munitions Supply at the War Office. Cited in *ibid.*
[79] Burk, *op. cit.*
[80] Edward Grenfell to H. P. Davison and Jack Morgan, 19 February 1915, cited in *ibid.*
[81] *ibid.*
[82] *ibid.*
[83] Grenfell to Morgan's in New York, 12 March 1917, cited in *ibid.*
[84] A. R. Hall, *The Export of Capital from Britain 1870–1914*, Methuen, 1968, cited in *ibid.*

[85] Gaspard Farrer to Edward Tuck, 19 October 1916, cited in Ziegler, *op. cit.*

[86] Burk, *op. cit.*

[87] Caridi, *op. cit.*

[88] Kathleen Burk, 'Diplomacy and the Private Banker: the Case of the House of Morgan', in Gustav Schmidt (ed.), *Konstellationen Internationaler Politik, 1924–1932. Politische und wirtschaftliche Faktoren in den Beziehungen zwischen West Europa und den Vereinigten Staaten 1924–1932*, Bochum: Studienverlag, Dr N. Brockmeyer, 1983, pp. 25–40.

[89] *ibid.*

[90] Ziegler, *op. cit.*

[91] Gaspard Farrer to Junius Morgan, 18 November 1923, cited in *ibid.*

[92] Hoyt *op. cit.*

[93] Burk, 'Diplomacy and the Private Banker', *op. cit.*

[94] J. K. Galbraith, *op. cit.*

[95] *George Peabody & Co., op. cit.*; Burk, *Morgan Grenfell, op. cit.*

[96] Burk, 'Diplomacy and the Private Banker', *op. cit.*

[97] Jack Morgan, 27 September 1927, cited in *ibid.*

[98] Hoyt, *op. cit.*

[99] Frank Costigliola, *The Other Side of Isolationism: the Establishment of the First World Bank, 1929–31*, Journal of American History, December 1972. Costigliola argues that Jack Morgan was instrumental in extending the power of the Bank for International Settlements against the wishes of the British Treasury. Burk, in *Morgan Grenfell, op. cit.*, explains that the Treasury wanted its functions limited to reports on payment, to be controlled by national governments, and to be located in London. Morgan insisted on political neutrality.

[100] Hoyt, *op. cit.*

[101] F. L. Allen, *Only Yesterday*, Pelican, 1938.

[102] Burk, 'Diplomacy and the Private Banker', *op. cit.*

[103] Roy Jenkins, *Baldwin*, Collins, 1987.

[104] Galbraith, *op. cit.*

[105] J. K. Galbraith, *The Great Crash 1929*, Penguin, 1975.

[106] *ibid.*

[107] Opening Statement submitted by J. P. Morgan to the Senate Banking and Currency Committee, 23 May 1933.

[108] *George Peabody & Co., op. cit.*

[109] Carosso, *op. cit.*

[110] Hugh Smith had first met Catto in the Caucasus in 1899. Smith became, according to Catto, his 'closest and most intimate

friend'. Burk, *Britain, America and the Sinews of War*, and *Morgan Grenfell, op. cit.*

[111] Burk, *Morgan Grenfell, op. cit.*

[112] Robert Skidelsky, *Politicians and the Slump: the Labour Government of 1929–31*, Macmillan, 1967; also cited in Burk, *Morgan Grenfell, op. cit.*

[113] Kathleen Burk, *The First Privatisation: The Politicians, the City and the Denationalisation of Steel*, Historians' Press, 1988; Burk, *Morgan Grenfell, op. cit.*

[114] *George Peabody & Co., op. cit.*

[115] Roger Eatwell, *The 1945–1951 Labour Governments*, Batsford, 1979.

[116] Alan Sked and Christopher Cook, *Post-War Britain*, Penguin, 1979.

[117] *The Services of Morgan Grenfell*, a publicity brochure published in 1986.

[118] Burk, *The First Privatisation, op. cit.*

[119] *ibid.*

[120] Bicester to Cobbold, 1 May 1953, cited in *ibid.*

[121] *ibid.*

[122] *ibid.*

[123] *ibid.*

[124] *Proceedings of the Tribunal appointed to inquire into allegations that information about the raising of Bank Rate was improperly disclosed*, Her Majesty's Stationery Office, 1958. Morgan's was at the time committed to an issue for Vickers, the success of which would have been imperilled by the raising of the bank rate. The suggestion was made that Bicester had advance warning of the rise in interest rates.

[125] The anecdote is probably apocryphal, because continuously updated versions of this story have circulated within the bank for decades. Nicholas Shakespeare reproduces it in *Londoners*, Sidgwick & Jackson, 1986, using the name Perkins. One account ascribes it to a conversation between Lord Rennell and the chief cashier, Bates, in the early 1950s. The Cockersell version is used here, because Cockersell – a colourful character known popularly as 'Jelly and Chips', on account of his unhealthy diet – is reported to have told the story about himself as recently as the early 1980s.

[126] *George Peabody & Co., op. cit.*

THREE

The Pendulum Years

The agent of the destruction of the old order in the City of London in the late 1950s and early 1960s was a Jewish refugee from Hamburg called Siegmund George Warburg. Though a scion of a famous German banking family, he and his tactics were received with horror. As Warburg himself put it:

I was not an English newcomer, but a German newcomer, a fellow who has not been educated in British schools, who speaks with a foreign accent . . . I remember some people in very good houses talked very nastily behind my back: 'Do you know this fellow Siegmund Warburg? He starts in the office at *eight o'clock* in the morning!' That was considered contemptible. Most of them came to the office at ten o'clock in the morning. I was awful. They looked down on me with utmost snobbism.[1]

He came as an outsider to a City in genteel decline. 'The traditional banks,' Jack Hambro told Anthony Sampson in 1960, 'are like the British Empire. There's nothing more to gain and quite a lot to lose.'[2] The cast of country house and military characters, many of them peers, reminded Sampson of a Victorian play, but their haughty manner was less aristocratic disdain than genuine bewilderment at modernity. For Lords Bicester, Harcourt, Catto and Rennell the selling of steel companies and the investment of the assets of the Inco pension fund were a far cry from the influence their forebears had wielded in the making and breaking of nations. There were real reasons for this. The burden of two world wars had left Britain unable to export its own capital in the form of the sterling bond issues on which George Peabody and J. S. Morgan had grown rich. Between J. P. Morgan's death in

97

1913 and the Festival of Britain in 1951, the country's real wealth remained static, as increasing domestic assets were offset by the sale of assets abroad to pay for war and economic recovery from war. For forty years, from the outbreak of Hitler's war in 1939 to the accession of Mrs Thatcher in 1979, a strict regime of exchange controls was in force to conserve scarce national reserves of foreign currency. Despite it, there was another run on the pound in 1956 in the wake of the Suez débâcle which could only be stopped by American support for a loan from the International Monetary Fund. By the late 1950s, the City of London was, in common with its political leaders, an also-ran. At the start of the 1960s nobody could think of any very good reason why it should ever again matter in world finance. Siegmund Warburg and the Euromarkets changed all that.

First, Warburg invented the contested takeover bid, in what became known as the Aluminium War. During the 1950s the aluminium market had become highly competitive. The principal British producer, the British Aluminium company, was already small and outdated when a disastrous investment in Quebec reduced it to virtual penury. By February 1958 its share price had slumped from a peak of 80s to only 37s, a performance which today would have put the company at the mercy of all manner of predators. At that time corporate warfare was still conducted in the eighteenth-century manner and hostile bids were virtually unknown. (When Charles Clore bid for Watney Mann, the pillar of the brewing establishment, its chairman, S. H. Combe, was astonished most of all by its impertinence. 'Preposterous. Utterly absurd. Who is this Mr Clore?' he bellowed.)[3] A bid from abroad was simply unthinkable; but Hans Vogelstein, the president of American Metal Climax Inc. – the American progeny of the German mining and metals house, Metallgesellschaft, with which Warburg bankers had been long associated – asked his friend Siegmund Warburg if he was prepared to try. The management of British Aluminium could scarcely have been in more traditional hands. The chairman was Marshal of the Royal Air Force, the Viscount

Portal of Hungerford, Chief of the Air Staff in the Second World War and now president of the Marylebone Cricket Club. The managing director was Geoffrey Cunliffe, the son of a former governor of the Bank of England. Warburg, anticipating a hostile response to Vogelstein, took the precaution of buying 10 per cent of British Aluminium before approaching Lord Portal's board with an offer to buy the rest in April 1958. He was treated with predictable disdain; Lazard's, Vogelstein's other advisers, told him the company was not for sale to foreigners. Vogelstein gave up but Warburg did not. In June he bought American Metal's 10 per cent stake, flew to New York and met the Reynolds brothers, who ran a large American aluminium producer. He told them British Aluminium was vulnerable provided they brought in a British majority partner, Tube Investments, whose chairman, the self-made Midlands industrialist, Sir Ivan Stedeford, was attracted by a large smelter British Aluminium was building in Quebec. By September Reynolds and Stedeford had formed a joint takeover vehicle 51 per cent owned by Tube Investments (TI–Reynolds). They stockpiled cash, bought another 5 per cent of British Aluminium and at the end of the month offered Lord Portal 78s a share.

Portal was disdainful and refused to pass the offer on to his shareholders. Even before receiving the offer from TI–Reynolds Portal had, without consulting his board, asked Olaf Hambro and Lord Kindersley, the chairman of Lazard's, to open negotiations with the giant Aluminum Company of America (Alcoa) on creating some unspecified form of partnership. These talks had not progressed very far by the time of the TI–Reynolds offer, mainly because Alcoa had no clear international strategy, but the irruption of Stedeford's bid enabled Portal to rush Alcoa into buying one-third of the shares in British Aluminium for 60s a share, considerably less than TI–Reynolds was offering.[4] Without telling the press of the deal with Alcoa, Portal then offered to buy back the stake his opponents had acquired. To his astonishment, they simply reiterated their offer to buy his stake for 78s. On 28 November

Portal, flanked by Kindersley and Hambro, announced to the press that a third of British Aluminium would be sold to Alcoa at 60s a share. He did not mention the offer of 78s a share by TI–Reynolds which, in an era when pressmen and shareholders tended to defer to the judgement of the board, he now deemed irrelevant.[5] Stedeford angrily called a press conference of his own and revealed the terms of the TI–Reynolds bid. William Davis, who was there, recalled that 'most of us readily agreed that they sounded a good deal more attractive than the deal which Portal and Cunliffe had made with Alcoa. One-third share stake, after all, amounted to effective control and it seemed somewhat high-handed for the directors to push ahead with the arrangement without seeking the prior approval of shareholders.'[6]

Warburg, Stedeford and Davis had grasped what Portal, Hambro and Kindersley had not: shareholders had the right to be asked whether or not they wished to forego the 18s. The next day the press was almost universal in its condemnation of Portal's deceit and the City establishment was unanimous in its loathing of Siegmund Warburg. The atmosphere in the Partners' Room at Morgan Grenfell, in common with most merchant banking parlours during those days, was thick with anti-Semitism. 'We must save British Aluminium for civilization,' Lord Portal was heard to say. There appeared in the press the first ever defensive advertisement, boasting that 'British Aluminium is not selling out to the Americans. It is going into partnership with them.'[7] The City's most blueblooded brokers, Cazenove and Rowe & Pitman, who had been brokers to both Tube Investments and British Aluminium, were persuaded to support British Aluminium. The members of the Accepting Houses Committee, led by Lazard's and Hambro's but including Morgan Grenfell, Baring's, Samuel Montagu, Hill Samuel, Brown Shipley and the rest, clubbed together in a 14-strong buying consortium to resist the upstart, muttering hypocritically about 'the national interest'. In fact no vital national interest was at stake; either bid would have left British Aluminium largely in British hands. The 'national interest' was only banking code for economic xenophobia. Unlike his opponents, Warburg had grasped that the nineteenth-century traffic in British capital was now flowing the other way. American industrial investment in Europe – the Continent's celebrated 'Coca-colaization' – was unstoppable. With the entire City establishment united against him, Warburg's decision to proceed with the bid was astonishingly bold, but he had several advantages. His champions, unlike Alcoa, were willing to pay a fair price. With money he could appeal directly to the shareholders of British Aluminium over the heads of their board of directors and win control of the company through the market rather than the old-boy network. This was where he eventually won the battle, without ever encountering serious counter-buying by the consortium. The intervention of the governor of the Bank of England in an increasingly acrimonious battle early in 1959 was sufficient for the consortium to stay its hand in the market, but Warburg continued to buy British Aluminium shares despite this august intercession.

By the end of December Warburg had reduced his opponents to the clumsy ploy of offering 82s for half of any shareholder's stock on condition that he agreed not to sell the other half to anybody else for three months. As the bitterness intensified, Olaf Hambro refused a proffered meeting with Warburg. On New Year's Day 1959, the governor of the Bank of England, Lord Cromer, and the Chancellor of the Exchequer, Derick Heathcoat Amory, asked Warburg to drop his bid and told him that the Prime Minister, Harold Macmillan, was of the same opinion.[8] They failed to persuade him. Lord Portal told his shareholders that TI–Reynolds were trying to 'acquire a powerful empire for the price of a small kingdom',[9] They disagreed and as Warburg raised his offer beyond £4 a share, they sold to TI–Reynolds in droves and he won control on 9 January 1959 with yards to spare, amid absurd accusations that British Aluminium shareholders were acting unpatriotically. Warburg had made fools of the establishment by the simple expedient of taking the battle to the shareholders rather than the management and offering them more money, and the City loathed him for it. As Lord Kindersley's bitter comment that 'there is still honour among thieves but one bank did not respect it',[10] suggested, the Old School resented deeply their defeat and Kindersley vowed that he would never speak to Warburg again. In an extraordinary letter to *The Times*, Olaf Hambro blamed the press for allowing Warburg to violate the wishes of the City.[11] In the wake of this tussle – and Charles Clore's unsuccessful £20 million bid for Watney Mann – the City formulated its first rules on the conduct of takeover bids. Before, it had simply relied on the players not to cut up rough. Warburg's buccaneering tactics had landed them with the threat of the thing they feared most: statutory regulation by a US-style Securities and Exchange Commission. The first Takeover Code was published in 1959. It lagged behind events then, as it does now. The threat of government intervention to clean things up became a perennial one.

Next, Warburg invented the Eurodollar bond issue, or Euro-bond. On 1 July 1963 S. G. Warburg & Co. Limited under-wrote, in conjunction with three European banks, an issue of $15 million of fixed-interest bonds for Autostrade, the Italian state motorway builder.[12] The bonds were then sold to European investors. Until then it had been unthinkable for a dollar bond issue not to be managed and underwritten by American banks and sold to American investors. The United States was the biggest capital market in the world; it had long since supplanted London as the principal source of capital for companies and countries looking to grow. Even Siegmund Warburg, who conceived and planned the idea of a foreign dollar bond issue, sold by Europeans to other Europeans, cannot have imagined the immense consequences of what he had done. It was among the most significant developments in the City of London in the twentieth century, because it allowed the City to resume its traditional role of channelling capital to companies and projects around the globe. By 1987 the Euro-bond market was worth $650 billion and had an annual turnover of $4.7 trillion.[13] Again, Warburg had grasped what his more traditional rivals had failed to spot: sterling, shunned and fickle, did not matter any more. London, with its long history of international banking, was the natural home for a new kind of stateless refugee, the Eurodollar.

Views differ on the origin of the prefix 'Euro'. The most popular explanation is that the first Eurodollars were placed by the Red Chinese in 1949 with a Soviet-owned bank in Paris called Banque Commerciale pour l'Europe du Nord, whose telex address happened to be 'Eurobank'. There is no disagreement on the ultimate source of the dollars. Eurodollars are just US dollars held outside the United States. They came to Europe for a variety of reasons. One was communist regimes keeping dollars outside American control in case the Cold War hotted up. Another was American investment in Europe, both by industrial corporations and by private investors seeking higher interest rates than they could get back home. But the Eurodollar markets did not really take off until the early 1960s, when the United States began to run persistent balance of payments deficits with Europe. The Eurodollar market tripled in 1959 and doubled again in 1960 as European exports boomed and American companies invested in Europe. By selling more to the United States than it bought, western Europe accumulated dollars. Initially they were just left on deposit and used to fund trade coming the other way. A Eurodollar deposit market developed, which is now synonymous with the term LIBOR (London Interbank Offered Rate). LIBOR is the rate of interest banks offer on Eurodollar deposits. Later Eurodollars were lent to companies and countries in exactly the same way sterling had once been lent to foreign borrowers. In 1958 most European countries – but not Britain – allowed their currencies to be converted into dollars for the first time since the war and banks began to swap dollars for other currencies too, so the prefix was extended to them as well. The Eurocurrency market was born. Then in 1963 President Kennedy, anxious about the increasing flow of dollars abroad, imposed the Interest Equalization Tax. By raising the cost of foreign borrowing of dollars in the United States by 1 per cent, it aimed to cauterize at least one haemorrhage: the export of capital. It was this that gave Siegmund Warburg the idea of a Eurodollar bond issue.

The City of London was the accidental beneficiary of all this. On the face of it, there was no reason for the Eurodollar business to gravitate to London, but the ties of history and sentiment proved stronger than any anxieties about the City's somnolent leadership. Indeed, its sleepy air was something of an advantage. Banks were governed not by state *apparatchiks* but by their own kind. The governor of the Bank of England and his court of sixteen directors were almost all merchant bankers. Regulation was light; the governor raised his eyebrow, not his hand, and there was no tax or exchange control on non-resident business. Besides, a banker could have fun in London, which was more cosmopolitan than Zurich or Frankfurt. Its market-making and stock-broking communities were established but sharp, its lawyers were inventive and it had the priceless advantage of being where it is. A Eurocurrency dealer could talk to Tokyo in the morning, New York in the afternoon and Los Angeles in the evening. Foreign banks flocked to London to ride the Eurocurrency boom, bringing with them new methods and mores. The first computers were bought and lunch succumbed to the American sandwich session. The merchant banks clung tenaciously to their historic addresses, arguing that they were required to maintain a banking hall at street level, but new skyscrapers shot up along London Wall to accommodate their American rivals. Rothschild's even knocked down its Victorian palazzo at New Court in St Swithin's Lane and embraced the future in the form of a colourless (but dwarfish) office block. For Morgan Grenfell the Euromarkets meant change, much of it rapid and not all of it welcome. Above all, it meant recruiting new types of people, with technical skills rather than a blue-blooded pedigree.

Change was felt first in the area of advice to companies, where the battle for British Aluminium had altered permanently the ethics of corporate warfare. In the 1960s the London stockmarket was subsumed in a welter of hostile takeover bids. Most takeovers are based on the supposition that the assets of the target are undervalued or badly managed or on the certainty that in business, if not in mathematics, two and two can make five. Bidders have to calculate the value of what they are buying by some conventional criteria, or else they will pay too much. Similarly, sellers have to calculate the value of what they own or they will sell their assets too cheaply. Both must demonstrate why the share price does not reflect the true value of the assets. Few of the peers in the Partners' Room, bar Rennell, were adept at reading a balance sheet, though Sir George Erskine had one of the sharpest financial brains in the City. Promising members of staff, like Kenneth Barrington, were paid while they took accountancy examinations. Barrington, who joined Morgan Grenfell as an eighteen-year-old bank clerk fourteen days before the Wall Street Crash in 1929, spent the whole of his working life at Morgan Grenfell, apart from war service with the Royal Navy. He qualified as an accountant in 1952 and he and Sir George Erskine, the only other outsider to ascend to the Partners' Room before the modern era, masterminded the denationalization of steel in the 1950s, which had called for a level of numeracy far beyond that possessed by Bicester or Harcourt.

Barrington finally became a director in 1961, and was charged with setting up a Corporate Finance Department. The technical demands of the merger boom necessarily involved some democratization. Guy Weston, one of the most buccaneering corporate financiers of his day, joined the Corporate Finance Department at this time. Technically brilliant, he devised a sale and leaseback of rolling stock for British Rail that is still remembered with awe. By syndicating British Rail's capital tax allowances amongst companies making taxable profits he saved them money and gave the bank a handsome income for years. To members of the old school, he remained cocky and vulgar. Until he came the word 'cunt' had never been uttered in the Partners' Room. The bank paid for his accountancy training but told him that he could never hope to become a director. In 1962 Peat, Marwick & Mitchell, the accountancy partnership, were asked to recommend a young accountant to join the Corporate Finance Department. They put forward the twenty-eight-year-old Charles Rawlinson, who had been educated at public school and Cambridge before qualifying as an accountant with a firm in Rugby, A. E. Limehouse. He had joined Peat, Marwick & Mitchell in 1958. Jonathan Perry, a twenty-seven-year-old grammar-school boy who had qualified as an accountant with Butler, Vines, Childs and Cooper Brothers, joined in 1966. Some younger, non-family men were also promoted from within. Philip Chappell, a gifted Oxford graduate of thirty-four who had joined the bank in 1954, became the bank's youngest ever director in 1964. Sir Dallas Bernard, a thirty-eight-year-old born into the City and who succeeded to his father's baronetcy in the 1970s, was a more conventional appointment as a director the same year. A nephew of his, Richard Strang, is currently a director at Morgan Grenfell. In 1965, the bank commissioned a report from Associated Industrial Consultants, as a result of which departments – Banking, Investments, Issues and Administration – were formed for the first time.[14]

The new skills were first tested in the ICI bid for Courtauld's in 1961, when Morgan's acted for ICI. In January 1962, having failed to secure an agreed merger, ICI bid £200 million for Courtauld's, making it by far the largest bid ever made in Britain. It was a generous bid, pitched 12s above the prevailing price of Courtauld's shares, which had been depressed by the company's dowdy image and a recent dividend cut. The bid became a battle of wills between Sir Paul Chambers, the chairman of ICI, and Frank Kearton, the dynamic deputy chairman of Courtauld's, who took over from the chairman, Sir John Hanbury-Williams, and the chairman-designate, Sir Alan Wilson, in the middle of the bid. Kearton pressed his merchant bankers Baring's for the financial ammunition – profit forecasts, asset revaluations and the like – which are now a routine aspect of takeover battles, but which were then greeted with astonishment. Morgan's was invited by Chambers to pour scorn on the figures produced by Baring's. The financial press became visibly involved. Though ICI raised its offer twice, for almost the first time in a takeover bid the share price of the target rose above the value of the offer. The Courtauld's board celebrated their eventual escape by going to church, but Kearton had introduced all the recognizable elements of a modern bid, bar a government concerned about competition (together ICI and Courtauld's controlled 90 per cent of Britain's manufacture of nylon).[15] He later complained that his merchant bankers, Baring's, were 'the most reticent bank of the day'. He was shocked by their poor stomach for the fight and, when Courtauld's embarked on the takeover trail themselves, their reticence. Later, as chairman of the Industrial Reorganization Corporation set up by the second Labour Government in 1966 – principally in response to the corporate bloodletting of the early 1960s – he dispensed with their services altogether and put the deals together himself.[16]

In 1964, the new team at Morgan Grenfell floated the shares of the General Motors Corporation on the London Stock Exchange. It was a prestigious transaction, showing how the bank could still draw upon its connections in the United States, but at the time strategic takeovers, conducted with the approval of Labour's Industrial Reorganization Corporation, were all the rage in Westminster, Whitehall and the City. In this ungentlemanly business, Morgan Grenfell found its seigneurial status placed it at a disadvantage. In the two biggest mergers of the 1960s, the bank had to withdraw because directors were on the boards of two of the companies involved. The two bids – GEC's hostile takeover of AEI in September 1967 and its agreed merger with English Electric in September 1968 – were both masterminded by the young Arnold Weinstock, who had reversed his father-in-law's television and radio manufacturing business into the ailing GEC in the early 1960s and emerged, within two years, as managing director. Weinstock used Kenneth Keith, the bruising head of corporate finance at Hill Samuel, in the takeover of AEI. Morgan Grenfell had until then been advisers to AEI, but Lord Catto had been a member of the board of GEC since 1959, which precluded involvement on either side. When Weinstock disrupted Plessey's hostile bid for the much larger English Electric, Morgan Grenfell was stymied again because Lord Harcourt was a director of Plessey. AEI's defence was conducted instead by Baring's who, stung by Kearton's critique, waged a brilliant campaign which forced Weinstock to raise his original offer by £1 a share. It incorporated many modern techniques. A £200,000 advertising campaign, the appointment of the scourge of British Rail, Lord Beeching, as a new and ruthless chairman and a series of timely asset disposals made it the longest and bloodiest takeover battle in memory.[16] It was galling for Morgan Grenfell that both Hill Samuel and Baring's gained much prestige and plenty of new business from the mutual destruction of one of its clients. Christopher Fildes recalled that at the time his City editor 'kept a headline in standing type: First Win for Morgan Grenfell. The time would come, he said, when he might have to use it.'[18] This folk memory was not unimportant in the shape of things to come.

As the Euromarkets developed during the 1960s, the Eurobond market proved a natural adjunct to Morgan Grenfell's business in underwriting fixed-interest loans for sale in the domestic market. After nationalization deprived a number of the bank's biggest clients – especially the renationalized iron and steel companies – of access to the sterling bond market, the newfangled Eurodollar bond market was explored as a possible substitute. Barrington understood immediately the implications of Kennedy's Interest Equalization Tax and of Warburg's Autostrade issue. The bank had already demonstrated a precocious grasp of offshore lending, in an issue of Swiss franc bonds for the City of Copenhagen, most of which had been sold to the major Swiss banks. This issue, which pre-dated even Warburg's Autostrade triumph, was the first attempt to bypass the opposition of the Swiss authorities to the use of the Swiss franc as a reserve currency, and complaints were received at the Bank of England. It was the first and last time it was done. The bank followed this cheeky issue with the first dollar-denominated issue for a Japanese company, Takeda

Chemicals'.[19] Though the issues were small, and invariably managed by other banks, Morgan Grenfell found its participations highly profitable. By 1966, the bank was helping to underwrite at least one $25 million bond issue a fortnight, each netting maybe $5,000 in commissions, then an unimaginably large sum. Eurobonds paid a fixed rate of interest but because Eurobond buyers tended to be rich individuals, like the legendary 'Belgian dentist' who took his bond to a Luxemburg bank to collect tax-free interest payments, the market catered for only the best company borrowers. Individuals were wary of governmental or municipal borrowers of the type that merchant banks had historically preferred, because they always taxed their populations and were liable in some cases to subside into revolution. Iran, Brazil and Mexico still had to borrow Eurodollars directly from the banks at rates of interest subject to periodic readjustment in line with market rates generally. At first, Morgan Grenfell would re-lend its own Eurodollar deposits; later, as the loans got bigger, it began to syndicate them among a group of banks, each of whom agreed to lend a proportion of the whole amount. Predictably, these loans became known as 'syndicated Eurocredits'.

Some borrowers did not actually want dollars but had to borrow them to buy the currency they actually needed, say Swiss francs or Deutschmarks. Until the early 1960s, Morgan Grenfell's foreign-currency team had been profitable but unspectacular. Consisting of the valetudinarian Bertie Hayes and an arbitrageur, Bill Braithwaite, they were adequate for the bank's own needs and those of its clients, but they did not generally exchange currencies or take deposits for profit. This paltry operation reflected the demise of sterling as a major trading currency. Peabody and Morgan had been able to finance most of the world's trade in sterling, because British exporters usually invoiced in sterling, leaving importers to sort out the currency problem on the spot. With sterling convertible into gold, even the buyers preferred the solidity of the pound. Where currency did need to be exchanged, a market of sorts operated in the Royal Exchange until the First World War.

The first dealing-rooms were opened by the clearing banks after the war as British imports were increasingly invoiced in the currency of the seller and British exporters began to invoice in foreign currencies too. Its development, though, was retarded by sterling's decline into vacillation and weakness. The events that marked its dismal progress – the return to the gold standard, the intervention of the 1930s, the exchange controls applied from 1939 – all inhibited its growth. Though the return of free convertibility for sterling in 1958 was a boost, it could not disguise the inexorable rise of the dollar as the world's principal reserve currency. Only the arrival in London of the Eurocurrency markets, dominated by the dollar, turned a sideshow into a thriving business. By 1966 Morgan Grenfell had a sizeable foreign-currency dealing-room, with foreign-exchange dealers dealing over the telephone with buyers and sellers of all the major currencies from all over the world. Geoff Munn, a man quite unfamiliar with public schools and Oxbridge, was hired to run the dealing-room. It proved remarkably successful and Munn became a popular chairman of the newly formed Foreign Exchange Dealers Association. The bank moved effortlessly into trading other money-market instruments, becoming one of the first authorized dealers when the Sterling Certificate of Deposit market opened in London in October 1968.[20] With very large sums of money crossing the exchanges every day as world trade expanded, foreign-currency dealing rapidly acquired a reputation as London's most stressful occupation.

During the early 1960s Morgan Grenfell, like other merchant banks, followed the reluctant lead of the clearing banks, who had bought the main hire-purchase companies and turned them into major finance houses with leasing arms, which bought major items of capital equipment like computers or aircraft and rented them to the user. For the finance houses, leasing was a form of secured lending, with the additional advantage of the generous capital allowances then accorded by the government to industrial investment. The bank was one of a number of London financial institutions approached by

Leaseway Inc., an American organization interested in tackling the British market. Tim Collins of Morgan Grenfell, who was also chairman of Royal Exchange Assurance, persuaded his insurance company to join Morgan Grenfell, United Dominions Trust (the secondary bank which became the biggest borrower from the Bank of England's 'lifeboat' in the secondary banking crisis of 1973–75) and Leaseway in the formation of the United Leasing Corporation in 1963. Morgan Grenfell was wary of acting alone and welcomed the involvement of those with experience of leasing. United Dominions Trust recruited David Berriman and John Sparrow (ironically from a client of Morgan Grenfell, AEI as general and assistant general manager) of the new company. Berriman and Sparrow had worked together in the financial planning department at the Ford Motor Company under John Barber, who became finance director at AEI in 1966, just before the company was taken over by GEC.[21] They were suitably technocratic. Berriman, a thirty-six-year-old Wykehamist and graduate of New College, Oxford, had been sent by AEI on a three-month management development course at the Harvard Business School in 1961. A product of a grammar school and the London School of Economics, the thirty-one-year-old Sparrow was an even more authentic representative of the new, technically minded order. He had qualified as a chartered accountant with Rawlinson & Hunter in 1959. These appointments were less revolutionary than they seem, for United Leasing ranked at first as a subsidiary of Leaseway Inc, in which Morgan Grenfell merely owned a stake, and the company was run not from Great Winchester Street, but from a separate office in London Wall. Nevertheless, the two appointments signified a new willingness to compete in unfamiliar areas.

The initial efforts of Berriman and Sparrow to lease low-value items like typewriters, duplicators and milk floats reflected the uneasy nature of the bank's shareholding in United Leasing. The company's wholly-owned competitors were able to lease larger pieces of capital equipment at much cheaper rates of interest because they could offset the capital tax allowances on their purchases against their profits, an advantage denied to United Leasing by its multiple shareholdings. The appearance in the banking hall at 23 Great Winchester Street of a debt collector, accompanied by two tatty Alsatians, causing considerable consternation among the cashiers, was an apt measure of just how *infra dignitatem* some of the new businesses were for an historic merchant bank. Within a year, Morgan Grenfell decided to buy out its partners and renamed the company Morgan Grenfell Finance Limited. The approach was changed to limit leasing to high-value capital goods leased to 'companies of good standing', as the bank's promotional literature put it.[22] Computers, which were then an extraordinarily novel and expensive investment, and quickly became obsolete, were an early success. Under one trading name, City Leasing, Morgan Grenfell Finance continued to offer facilities of up to only £100,000 in size, but it was joined by a second company, London Industrial Leasing Limited, in September 1967. This was jointly owned by Morgan Grenfell, Williams & Glyn's (where Tim Collins had trained as one of the bank's famous 'cadets') and Willis Faber, which became a shareholder in the bank at this time. London Industrial Leasing offered sums up to several million pounds for 'first-class companies'. Air Leasing, which leased aeroplanes, followed. Berriman became managing director of Morgan Grenfell in October 1967.

The exact nature and implications of what was happening were not well understood in the Partners' Room, where the managing directors sat. Despite all the changes, most managers could still not aspire to a directorship. The second Lord Bicester, whose tenure of the senior partnership until 1967 was more in the manner of *primus inter pares*, would not let his own nephew, then a trainee with the bank, draw cash without his consent. His anachronisms were legendary, if improbable. Once, spotting Philip Chappell looking tired after an overnight transatlantic flight, he expressed bewilderment: 'Can't understand that. Five days at sea with nothing to do.' He retired in 1967 and died, aged 70, in a car accident in January 1968.

He was succeeded as chairman by Viscount Harcourt, who had been a managing director since 1931. Bicester's forty-four-year-old son-in-law, Tim Collins, became vice-chairman. Harcourt, who personified the old City establishment – the great grandson of J. S. Morgan, Eton, Christ Church, Vice-Lord Lieutenant of Oxfordshire and a wartime staff officer – understood virtually nothing of leasing, Eurobonds or foreign-currency exchange. He did not know what a '60:40 commission split' was but would remember for years the wearer of a pair of dirty shoes. He cared little for the much-vaunted dynamism of the new men the bank had hired and regarded Guy Weston as its least acceptable face. After an acrimonious lunchtime argument with Weston – who had taunted him over Einstein's theory of relativity – he had simply walked out. Later he asked Barrington to sack Weston for his impertinence and would not be placated until he had received a formal apology. To the ordinary staff, he was a patrician figure, assuring one cowed employee who had lost over $17,000 in the Eurobond market that he could not understand why but that the young man should consider himself lucky it had happened early in his career. He was not a fool. He knew his talents were limited to 'gladhanding' the bank's impressionable clients and that he knew too little to be an effective executive chairman. His diplomatic talents were well deployed during his spell as head of the United Kingdom Treasury Delegation to the United States and Economic Minister at the British Embassy in Washington (1954–7), where he doubled as the United Kingdom Executive Director of the World Bank and the International Monetary Fund. In this capacity he had been greatly impressed by John Melior Stevens, a Bank of England official who was director of the European Department at the International Monetary Fund. In October 1967 he invited Stevens to join the board of Morgan Grenfell as a managing director. It was the most significant appointment of the post-war years at Morgan Grenfell.

John Stevens was born on 7 November 1913, the son of a solicitor. He was educated at Winchester and articled as a clerk to a small family firm of solicitors, Petch & Co., where he qualified in 1937. The war brought out a brilliant talent for languages, and great bravery, which were put to good use in the Special Operations Executive in Belgium, Occupied France, the Middle East and Greece before he was parachuted into Italy to join the Piedmont Liberation Committee of partisans fighting the retreating Nazis. He organized their financing and victualling. He ended the war with a Distinguished Service Order and the rank of colonel and joined the Bank of England as an adviser in 1946, travelling Europe and the Americas as a roving troubleshooter before his appointment to the IMF in 1954.[23] He returned from Washington in 1957 as an executive director of the Bank of England, where he remained until he followed in Harcourt's own footsteps by becoming Economic Minister and Treasury Delegate to the IMF and World Bank in Washington in 1965, for which he was knighted in 1967. His predecessor in these posts, Lord Cromer, had returned to become governor of the Bank and he was openly touted as a candidate for the governorship himself if an official, rather than a banker, was to be chosen. His contacts were legendary; in 1972 he was, like Peabody before him, received by the Pope.[24] Stevens's fluency in French, Spanish, Russian, German, Swedish and modern Greek made him an outstanding linguist. As the first Bank of England official to visit the Soviet State Bank in Moscow in 1958, he startled local officials by speaking to them in their own language. It was a useful gift, and Stevens's first brief from Harcourt was to sharpen up Morgan Grenfell's international impact. However, this belated drive overseas was initially overshadowed by more exciting events rather closer to home.

The takeovers boom of the 1960s peaked in 1968. The amount spent on them leapt from £502 million in 1964 to £1,653 million in 1968, much of it sponsored by the Industrial Reorganization Corporation.[25] Amid the confusion of this activity, in May 1968, Imperial Tobacco decided to sell a $36\frac{1}{2}$ per cent stake it held in Gallaher, Britain's second-biggest tobacco company and the maker of Senior Service and Benson

& Hedges cigarettes. Morgan Grenfell, in conjunction with another merchant bank to whom it was close, Robert Fleming, arranged a public offer for sale of Imperial's 26 million shares in Gallaher at £1 apiece, underwritten by themselves.[26] In keeping with the usual practice of laying off the risk, the banks deputed the stockbroker, Cazenove, to arrange for the shares to be sub-underwritten by a group of major institutional investors. These investors undertook, for a fee, to buy the shares if nobody else would, guaranteeing Imperial Tobacco its money even if the issue was not a success in the market. This was just as well, for the size of the sale – £26 million – made it the biggest public offering since the denationalization of steel in the 1950s, and £1 was widely regarded as a very ambitious price. Morgan Grenfell, smarting at its exclusion from the takeover of AEI in 1967, was hungry for a spectacular success. Unhappily, the sale of Gallaher did not provide it. Over a third of the issue – 10 million shares – was left with the underwriters and sub-underwriters, who watched helplessly as the price of Gallaher shares drifted down to 7s 6d, giving them a notional loss of 12s 6d a share.

There matters rested until 2 July, when Joseph Cullman III, president of the American tobacco giant, Philip Morris, slapped in a £46 million bid for half of every shareholder's stake. At an effective price of 25s a share, which was several shillings above the depressed Gallaher share price, it looked like a knock-out blow. 'I wish we could have been more genteel – but we had no choice,' Cullman said, as he organized a Eurodollar bond issue to pay for his prize.[27] The Gallaher board, chaired by the Old Etonian Mark Norman, responded initially with a questionnaire, before rejecting the bid, in the time-honoured phrase, as 'quite inadequate'. After a fortnight of frantic activity, American Tobacco, a 13 per cent shareholder in Gallaher, entered the fray on Gallaher's side. American Tobacco's move was purely defensive. It had discovered that if Philip Morris gained control of Gallaher, Philip Morris and American Tobacco would be partners in an overseas venture, which was in breach of American anti-trust legislation. American Tobacco would, as chairman Robert Heimann said, be forced 'to dump [its] holdings into Philip Morris's lap at bargain prices'. Like Philip Morris, American Tobacco did not want 100 per cent, just control. They capped Philip Morris's offer with a bid for half of each shareholder's stake at 35s a share. The Gallaher board welcomed American Tobacco's £20 million intervention, pointing out that the 35s a share it was offering valued the company at £130 million, as against Philip Morris's offer of £92 million.[28] This presented Morgan Grenfell and Cazenove, who were acting for American Tobacco, with an unusual opportunity. Since they had arranged the sub-underwriting of the Gallaher offer for sale, they knew exactly which institutions were holding large numbers of unwanted Gallaher shares. They had not only the support of the Gallaher board but instant access to a shareholding of sufficient size to defeat Philip Morris. On 16 July 1968 Cazenove, equipped with a list of the sub-underwriters, mounted a secret dawn raid on Gallaher shares on behalf of American Tobacco, and, by offering them the astonishingly high price of 35s a share, netted 28 per cent of the company in a single hour almost entirely from the large institutions that had underwritten the offer for sale in May. This arrangement suited both sides. Buying shares piecemeal in the market would have pushed the Gallaher share price far beyond 35s, but if the institutions had sold their substantial holdings *en masse*, the share price would have plummeted. Speculators who had acquired shares at £1 were angry that the old-boy network had been given privileged access to American Tobacco's largesse. It was widely believed in the City that Morgan Grenfell and Cazenove had mispriced the sale of Imperial's stake in Gallaher which had the effect of facilitating the entry to the fray of American Tobacco. It was bold and inventive stuff, but it infringed the spirit of the City's Takeover Code and Morgan Grenfell and Cazenove were plunged into a political crisis of unprecedented magnitude.

Earlier in 1968, the accelerating pace and scale of takeover activity had revived the Labour Government's interest in government control of corporate battles along the lines of the Securities and Exchange Commission in the United States, which even in 1968 had a staff of 1,400 people and an annual budget of $17 million.[29] To head off possible legislation, the City's first milk-and-water Takeover Code, devised in the late 1950s after Clore's surreptitious acquisition of a large stake in Watney Mann, coupled with an unrealized threat of a takeover, was replaced by a more incisive version, backed by the Bank of England, the Confederation of British Industry (CBI) and the leading City institutions. A panel of City worthies chaired by Sir Humphrey Mynors, a former deputy governor of the Bank of England, was set up to enforce it. The panel had cleared an application by Morgan Grenfell and Cazenove to make on behalf of American Tobacco a *pro rata* bid for half of the shares in Gallaher that it did not already own. This suited American Tobacco, which did not wish to bid for the whole of Gallaher but merely to 'protect' its investment. It also fitted with Section 7 of the new code, which obliged bidders to make the same offer to all shareholders in a company and not offer preferential prices to a chosen few, but it was not what Morgan Grenfell and Cazenove chose to do. The institutional shareholders approached by Cazenove were privately offered 35s a share to sell *all* the shares they owned, whilst the public were offered 35s a share for only up to *half* their shareholdings. In other words, different shareholders were, in effect, being offered different prices. Of course, Morgan Grenfell argued that only the amount had varied; the price had been the same. This was pure banter. It was a clear and deliberate violation of the spirit, if not the letter, of the rules of the City's new Takeover Code, but Morgan's and Cazenove were unrepentant and an apology had to be dragged out of them. The row that resulted was deafening.

Suspicions about Morgan's and Cazenove were all over the financial press the day after the raid. *The Times*, which rang round investment trusts, pension funds and rival merchant banks, reported virtually unanimous condemnation of Morgan's tactics.[30] Within a few days the paper was considering the issue in a leading article, which condemned Morgan

Grenfell. Reports circulated that representatives of Cazenove had been called to the Bank of England. The matter was even raised in Parliament.[31] At Morgan Grenfell Lord Harcourt confined himself to a single observation:

I am totally confident that the purchases are in full conformity with the code.[32]

He was relying on a loophole in the code. Clearly any buying in the market during a partial bid would lead to different prices being offered to different shareholders, and the code did not forbid it. Two days after the raid, on 18 July, the panel announced that it had concluded that 'certain dealings in Gallaher shares' had been in breach of Article 7 of the code, which stated unambiguously that 'all shareholders of a class of an offeree company shall be treated similarly by an offeror company'. It added that no shareholders in the offeree company should be made an offer 'which is more favourable than a general offer to be made thereafter to the other shareholders'. Morgan's disagreed. After a meeting with representatives of the panel, chaired by Martin Wilkinson, the chairman of the Stock Exchange Council, Morgan Grenfell and Cazenove told the panel that they would be dissociating themselves from its findings.[33] A hastily convened board meeting at Morgan Grenfell agreed a statement to the press. Within an hour of the panel's public announcement, Harcourt and Sir Antony Hornby, the senior partner of Cazenove, had issued a flat rejection of the panel's censure. The terse statement read as follows:

Morgan Grenfell and Cazenove cannot agree with the conclusions of the panel since both are firmly of the view that, so far as they are concerned, they have complied with the code in every respect.

This was unrealistic enough, but the statement's blunt conclusion was positively insolent:

No press enquiries will be answered by either Morgan Grenfell or Cazenove.[34]

The bank's aristocratic leadership was incredulous at the impertinence and tenacity of press questioning of what they had done. A reporter from the *Daily Express*, who had been particularly inquisitive, was physically ejected from the bank by the commissionaires. Lord Harcourt was disdainful:

If a man decides to invest a few pounds and can't do it, I don't see the point of having a Stock Exchange.

Morgan's hauteur was heightened by the knowledge that the panel had no teeth: it could explain itself and censure others, but only a revision of the rules could undo a trespass of them. The fact that the detestable S. G. Warburg was advising Philip Morris added a *frisson* of delight to their obstinate tactics. Yet Morgan Grenfell was being politically naive. The code had the moral backing of the governor of the Bank of England, Sir Leslie O'Brien, who had argued at the very highest levels of government for self-regulation rather than state interference. Morgan's must have known this, since Sir John Stevens was a member of the Court of the Bank of England. The panel could scarcely duck the first challenge to its authority, and the rest of the City, fearful that if Morgan's got away with it the case for statutory regulation would become unanswerable, was bound to support it.

The panel retired to consider what to do next. Meetings were held with Cazenove and Morgan Grenfell to find a face-saving solution. Meanwhile, Cazenove carried on buying Gallaher shares and Morgan's, as if to stress its intentions, busied itself with plans for a $50 million Eurobond issue for American Tobacco to pay for its recent purchases, though in the event it did not take place. A compromise was finally reached on 26 July, when the panel issued a statement to the press:

1. Morgan Grenfell and Cazenove have informed the Panel that they wish to refute any implication that the statement issued by Viscount Harcourt and Sir Antony Hornby on July 18, in which they expressed their disagreement with the conclusions of the Panel, indicated in any way that Morgan Grenfell and Cazenove contemplated flouting the authority of the Panel. Morgan Grenfell and

Cazenove have already given an undertaking that they would always comply with a definite ruling of the Panel and would never knowingly put themselves in breach of the Code.

2. The Panel accepts that, in their dealings in Gallaher shares on Tuesday July 16, American Tobacco, Morgan Grenfell and Cazenove acted in good faith in their belief that such dealings were in the letter and spirit of the Code.

3. Morgan Grenfell and Cazenove have represented to the Panel that the provisions of the Code concerning market purchases have not previously been tested in a partial bid situation and that, in such circumstances, those provisions could create difficulties to the point where they would seem to result in a total inability to make purchases. This would seem, in its turn, in Morgan Grenfell's and Cazenove's view, to conflict with Rule 29, which expresses that it is undesirable to fetter the market.

4. The Panel nevertheless reaffirms its conclusion that the dealings referred to in the Panel's statement of July 18 resulted in a breach of paragraph 7 of the general principles of the Code and has so informed the Stock Exchange and the Issuing Houses Association.

5. The Panel already has arrangements to keep the provisions of the Code under constant review. The points mentioned by Morgan Grenfell and Cazenove in paragraph 3 above will be examined under this procedure.[35]

The Stock Exchange Council probed the matter in relation to Cazenove, reporting on 13 August that it could find no evidence of wrongdoing, prompting Hornby's arrogant remark that 'we may have breached it the way they wish they had written it'.[36] Morgan Grenfell was not let off so lightly by either the Bank of England or the Issuing Houses Association (IHA). On 15 August Sir Leslie O'Brien wrote to the chairmen of the Stock Exchange, the Takeover Panel and the IHA, warning them that the City might face statutory control if it was unable to police itself effectively. Without naming Morgan Grenfell, he castigated 'wilful infringement' of the Code and the 'less than satisfactory' response to panel rulings.[37] His words were remarkably prescient:

I realise that a takeover battle will from time to time be only too well described as such. In these circumstances the urge to take quick and successful action is great. But action in breach of the Code is not justifiable in any circumstances. It harms the reputation of those who are guilty of it and is prejudicial to the good name of the City in general.[38]

After this, the IHA was left with no option but to issue a formal censure of Morgan Grenfell. In late August it stressed its 'great concern [at] the attitude towards the Panel which appears to have been adopted by Morgan Grenfell'.[39] It was the first time that the IHA had publicly censured a member and it contrasted bleakly with the Stock Exchange's exoneration of Cazenove. Lord Harcourt was even forced to pen a grovelling apology to the IHA (italics added):

We at Morgan Grenfell, as founder members of the IHA, have always endeavoured to be loyal supporters of the association. We have valued the work of the Committee highly, and have welcomed the opportunity of participating in it. I should, therefore, be grateful if you would convey to your Committee my firm's sincerest regret that anything said or done in recent weeks should have resulted in the Committee coming to the view which you have expressed to us.

I should like to assure the Committee that it was never my firm's intention to show any lack of respect for the authority of the Panel and that, in accordance with its original undertakings, *Morgan Grenfell & Co. will always observe the Code and will never knowingly put itself in breach of it.*[40]

At the end of October the Takeover Panel was re-equipped with a full-time staff, a freshly drafted code and sanctions for use against transgressors. It was prompted only by the fear of government interference and it remained a flawed body, run by merchant bankers for merchant bankers. The changes were sold to Tony Crosland, then president of the Board of

Trade, by Sir Leslie O'Brien at a meeting on 31 October and Crosland's dark mutterings about 'possible reinforcement' came to nothing.[41] Almost incredibly, Kenneth Barrington, the Morgan Grenfell director who had handled the American Tobacco bid for half of Gallaher, became chairman of both the IHA and the City's working party to counter pressure for a statutory code, introducing in 1972 the famous Rule 35, which obliged any bidder controlling over 40 per cent of a company's voting shares to bid for the rest of the company. This ruled out partial bids like that mounted by American Tobacco. Barrington was knighted in 1973.[42] Pharisaically, in view of his strictures, O'Brien, once clear of Threadneedle Street and elevated to the peerage, joined the Advisory Council of Morgan Grenfell in 1974. Barrington also served on it, after he retired in 1976.

Despite the extravagance of its apologies, Morgan Grenfell had still won. American Tobacco was not forced to bid for the whole company on the terms it had offered to the favoured few; it was not even suggested that the transaction should be undone. Its broker, Cazenove, was exonerated altogether. And the main objective – securing Gallaher's independence – was triumphantly achieved. The few regrets that had been wrung out of Lord Harcourt owed more to a taste on the part of the members of the IHA for kicking rivals when they are down than to any real need for redemption. The bank had engaged in megaphone diplomacy with the Panel and the Bank of England and cannot have been entirely displeased with the results. When in August 1968 the Panel changed the rules to insist that bidders should openly offer all shareholders the same price, it only underlined the fact that the rules had not just been interpreted or even flouted, but effectively renegotiated. The City could not police itself in the conventional sense of applying absolute rules which, once broken, incurred penalties. Instead, the rules were always pushed to breaking point, allowing the villains, rather than the police, to dictate the course of events. The members of Morgan Grenfell's young Corporate Finance Department could be forgiven for drawing the obvious conclusion, and they did. Versions of this unseemly episode were replayed countless times over the next twenty years and not just in the history of Morgan Grenfell.

Within weeks of the Bank's governor's speech in October 1968, Morgan Grenfell was involved in another highly public takeover battle which exposed the Panel's inadequacies again: the battle for control of the *News of the World*, a newspaper which had long thrived on titillation. The battle began with the sale by a disgruntled family shareholder, Professor Derek Jackson, of his quarter share in the newspaper to Robert Maxwell, an exiled Czechoslovakian Jew and Labour MP who had made a fortune from his publishing company, Pergamon Press. With 25 per cent of the company secured, Maxwell then launched a £27 million bid for the rest of the company. The chairman of the *News of the World*, Jackson's cousin Sir William Carr, condemned the bid as 'cheeky' and authorized his merchant bankers, Hambro's, to move into the market and buy up the company's shares, in open defiance of the Takeover Code's stipulation that shares should not be bought solely to frustrate a genuine bid. Despite the protestations of Maxwell, the Hambro's director handling the defence, Jack Sporborg, insisted that the Code forbade purchases only by the *company's* board and not by their bankers. The Panel was still pondering this latest blow to its authority when Morgan Grenfell announced that Rupert Murdoch, then a thirty-seven-year-old Australian newspaperman virtually unknown to the British public, was also buying up shares in the *News of the World*.

On hearing of Maxwell's bid, Lord Catto had telephoned Rupert Murdoch, who was plucked from the Melbourne racecourse to take the call. Catto had enjoyed strong links with Australia since he had worked there for the bank in the early 1950s, and returned frequently. In 1966 he was divorced from his wife Josephine Innes, on grounds of his adultery with Margaret Forrest, the family nanny, whom he married in January 1966. The Forrests are Tasmanian, adding the ties of family to those of business for Lord Catto. When Murdoch affirmed his interest in the *News of the World*, Catto contacted

Sporborg, who told Carr of Murdoch's interest and Carr, who had squared the other family shareholders, agreed that the Australian's intervention had merit. Murdoch flew to London and met with Carr over breakfast, where they agreed to a deal which gave Murdoch control. Hambro's delivered their stake to Morgan Grenfell and a tough and dirty takeover battle commenced, with Maxwell constantly urging the Panel to intervene and at one point trying to take over Murdoch's own group, News Limited. The contenders finally met face-to-face at a dramatic meeting of shareholders specially convened to consider the bid. The Panel, at last acting firmly, forbade Morgan's and Hambro's to vote at the meeting with the 51 per cent stake they had amassed, since it would have presented the remaining minority shareholders with a *fait accompli*. The meeting was worthy of the *News of the World*, a newspaper described by its editor with perceptible racialism during the Maxwell bid as being 'as British as roast beef and Yorkshire pudding'. Sir William Carr had given employees the day off to attend, and the forty-five-second ovation they accorded him and Murdoch contrasted vividly with the hisses, boos and shouts of 'Go home' which greeted the speech by Robert Maxwell. When Carr took a vote on the merger with Murdoch he won easily, despite the loss of the Carr family shareholdings and the Hambro–Morgan Grenfell stake. Maxwell shook hands with Murdoch but told reporters that 'the law of the jungle has prevailed'.[43]

Maxwell's verdict on the battle for the *News of the World* was echoed by Kenneth Barrington, whose City working party on the Code began soon after the bid to clear what he called 'the very considerable jungle' that had developed in the takeover arena.[44] The Murdoch bid received colourful press coverage – all of it flattering to Catto (though much of the detailed work had been done by Philip Chappell). Morgan Grenfell was seen to have acted quickly and decisively to scotch the Maxwell bid and the bank's morale began to lift.[45]

In 1972 the bank intervened in a takeover bid where it was not representing either party, then a highly unusual tactic.

P & O planned an agreed merger with Bovis, a client of War-burg's. Morgan Grenfell, owners of 0.66 per cent of P & O, judged the merger terms too cheap. The bank orchestrated shareholder opposition, and eventually coaxed a higher offer for P & O from Inchcape. Catto explains:

What P & O were actually doing was bidding for one man, Frank Sanderson, the property expert who was on the Bovis board. They weren't really bidding for the company. We thought that was wrong. So we rang all the big institutional shareholders, got a group of them together and after a great proxy battle we won.[46]

This was the second obvious instance in which Morgan Grenfell had not waited to be approached by a client before entering the battle for the future of a company.

The young Turks of the Corporate Finance Department like Philip Chappell, Dallas Bernard and Guy Weston were given their head and bright young men began to join the bank, after shunning it for years in favour of Hill Samuel or S. G. Warburg. In 1968 a thirty-two-year-old personnel specialist, Christopher Reeves, was hired by Lord Catto from Hill Samuel with a brief to recruit people who knew their way around a balance sheet and the Companies Acts. In January 1970 he became a director of the bank. George Law, a thirty-eight-year-old partner at Slaughter & May, the City solicitors preferred by Morgan Grenfell, joined the Corporate Finance Department in 1968. Patrick (later Lord) Spens, a twenty-seven-year-old Cambridge law graduate who had qualified as an accountant with Fuller, Wise & Foster (now part of Touche Ross), joined in January 1969. In 1972 he became the youngest director of a merchant bank in the history of the City. Roger Seelig, a computer wizard with a master's degree in economics from the London School of Economics and a graduate of the London Business School, asked to join Morgan Grenfell after Philip Chappell had given a talk at the London Business School in 1971. He was then just 26, and an assistant to the treasurer at Esso. Reeves recruited around a dozen other business-school graduates as well, but all but Seelig turned out to be unprepared for the ponderous ritual of a merchant bank and did not stay long. Catto pinpointed these years as the turning point for morale:

Our general image in the late sixties and early seventies was a stuffy one. We've always been called blue-blooded, largely because there were lots of Lords on the board. We didn't look after our corporate customers very well, expecting them to come and see us when they had problems, rather than the other way round.[47]

In fact these were years of crisis for the bank, but Lord Catto can be forgiven a little selective amnesia. In 1967 he had embarked upon a course that, far from boosting the morale of the bank, very nearly bankrupted it altogether.

NOTES

[1] The Confessions of Siegmund Warburg, *Institutional Investor*, March 1980.
[2] Anthony Sampson, *The Moneylenders*, Hodder & Stoughton, 1981.
[3] William Davis, *Merger Mania*, Constable, 1970.
[4] *Financial Times*, 7/8 January 1989. In this article David Kynaston cites a history of Alcoa (*From Monopoly to Competition*, by George David Smith, Cambridge University Press) which suggests that Alcoa was hustled into the deal by Portal.
[5] Jacques Attali, *A Man of Influence, Sir Siegmund Warburg, 1902–1982*, Weidenfeld & Nicolson, 1986.
[6] Davis, *op. cit.*
[7] *Financial Times*, 7/8 January 1989.
[8] Attali, *op. cit.*
[9] *The Times*, 6 December 1958.
[10] Sampson, *op. cit.*
[11] *The Times*, 12 January 1959.
[12] Ian Kerr, *A History of the Eurobond Market*, Euromoney Publications, 1984.
[13] Margaret Reid, *All-Change in the City*, Macmillan, 1988.
[14] Kathleen Burk, *Morgan Grenfell 1838–1988: The Biography of a Merchant Bank*, Oxford University Press, 1989.
[15] Davis, *op. cit.*

[16] Brian Widlake, *In the City*, Faber & Faber, 1986.

[17] Ivan Fallon and James Srodes, *Takeovers*, Hamish Hamilton, 1987.

[18] *Daily Telegraph*, 26 June 1986.

[19] Kerr, *op. cit.*, Burk, *Morgan Grenfell*, *op. cit.*

[20] *The Times*, 28 October 1968.

[21] Davis, *op. cit.*

[22] Morgan Grenfell & Co. Limited, *The Services of a Merchant Bank*, promotional brochure, *circa* 1969.

[23] Obituary, *The Times*, 30 October 1973.

[24] *The Times*, 16 October 1972.

[25] Board of Trade figures compiled for the Monopolies Commission report on Mergers, 1964–8.

[26] The partners of Morgan Grenfell were at least as close to their counterparts at Robert Fleming as they were to the directors of Lazard's. In the early 1970s a merger of Morgan Grenfell and Robert Fleming was seriously contemplated by both parties.

[27] Davis, *op. cit.*

[28] *The Times*, 17 July 1968.

[29] Davis, *op. cit.*

[30] *The Times*, 18 July 1968.

[31] *Hansard*, 17 July 1968.

[32] *The Times*, 17 July 1968.

[33] The chairman of the panel, Sir Humphrey Mynors, was debarred from attending because he was chairman of Imperial Tobacco, an interested party.

[34] *The Times*, 19 July 1968.

[35] *The Times*, 26 July 1968.

[36] *The Times*, 14 August 1968.

[37] *The Times*, 16 August 1968.

[38] *ibid.*

[39] *The Times*, 24 August 1968.

[40] *ibid.*

[41] *The Times*, 30 October 1968.

[42] Obituary, *The Times*, 14 September 1987.

[43] Davis, *op. cit.*

[44] Obituary, *The Times*, 14 September 1987.

[45] *The Times*, 25 October 1968.

[46] Widlake, *op. cit.*; Burk, *Morgan Grenfell*, *op. cit.*

[47] *ibid.*

FOUR

Making Movies

In the middle of the summer of 1967 Lord Catto invited to lunch at 23 Great Winchester Street a Russian-born film magnate called Dimitri de Grunwald.[1] It was, by all accounts, a formidable prandial occasion of the kind Old School merchant bankers still deploy to intimidate their social inferiors. It took place in Morgan Grenfell's elaborately decorated board room, where the ambience alone was enough to stifle any awkward questions. Lord Catto and Lord Harcourt were there and so was David Berriman, the boffin from the leasing department who became a director of the bank in the autumn of that year. De Grunwald was accompanied by his finance adviser, Anthony Zenaldy Landy, an Austrian-American film-finance expert who was mainly responsible for the lunch taking place at all. He had approached Lord Catto with a new method of financing feature films, which they had planned to discuss over the lunch. Despite this obvious purpose the proposal de Grunwald and Landy had brought with them was scarcely touched upon at all. Instead, the discussion ranged widely. The nervous film-makers assumed the circuitous nature of the conversation was part of an elaborate moral assessment, mistaking the technical ignorance of the peerage for a test of their commercial manhood. As they left they were assured by Lord Catto that Morgan Grenfell would like to take their proposal further. The following day Tony Landy received a letter saying much the same thing. Dimitri de Grunwald was the younger brother of one of the great names of cinema in the post-war years, Anatole de Grunwald, the producer of *Way to the Stars*, *Queen of Spades* and *The Winslow Boy*. They were White Russians, whose father had fled the Soviet Union while they were still children;

128

he became the leading historian of his native country from exile in Paris, producing seventeen volumes of Russian history. Dimitri had enjoyed a successful business career, becoming a managing director of the American pharmaceutical company, Vick's, at the age of twenty-seven. Anatole, though highly creative, was a poor businessman and he had brought Dimitri into his film business in the 1950s to help fulfil his dream of creating an independent production company capable of holding its own against the major American producers and withstanding the innate volatility of the British film industry. The partnership worked well until Anatole died very suddenly in 1965. Dimitri, after much deliberation, opted to carry on alone. He engaged Tony Landy, who boasted of widespread international connections, as his financial director. De Grunwald devised a completely new scheme for escaping the stranglehold the major American studios – MGM and Twentieth Century-Fox – exerted on global film distribution. It was this idea that de Grunwald and Landy put to Morgan Grenfell in 1967.

It was a sound scheme and is now the commonplace method of financing films, but in 1967 it was revolutionary. At that time most films were financed entirely by the major studios. Either they made their own films or they bought all the rights to show films made by independent producers, covering the costs of production by pre-selling films to their long-established network of distributors around the world. What the two film-makers proposed was to bypass this and develop a rival distribution network of their own to which de Grunwald films could be pre-sold. Morgan Grenfell would then lend de Grunwald's company, London Screenplays, further funds against the security of the proceeds of pre-selling the films. The loans would be repaid in a lump sum on delivery of the film to the distributors, so all the bank had to do was discount the value of the pre-sales back to a present value against which it felt able to lend. This involved two substantial risks: first, that the distributors might not pay and, second, that the films might not be made. The first problem was covered by guarantees of payment or a letter of credit – an order from a bank authorizing payment to a named person or company – from banks or private financiers whose credit Morgan Grenfell felt it could rely on. The second problem was trickier. Since the guarantees or letters of credit were contingent on the films actually being delivered, Morgan Grenfell was being asked to assume a production, rather than a banking, risk. The solution was provided by a guarantor of completion, Film Finances Limited, a specialist company which monitored the film's progress and guaranteed that it would be made and delivered on time. With these assurances Catto and Berriman undertook to discount – purchase for cash at a suitably discounted price – the letters of credit and the guarantees from the distributors. The discounted price enabled them to lend money to de Grunwald with adequate security and at a reasonable margin of 1 or 2 per cent over their own cost of borrowing in the money markets.

De Grunwald and Landy had approached Morgan Grenfell at an opportune moment. By the late 1960s, the Euromarkets were sufficiently well established for Morgan Grenfell to plan a massive expansion of its banking capability – the lending of money – to add to its traditional fee-earning corporate finance work and the commission-based, fixed-rate Eurobond and domestic bond issues sold and traded on its behalf by stockbrokers. Film financing offered good margins over the bank's own cost of funds and the potential for substantial export earnings, which fitted neatly with the bank's putative export and project financing businesses. These were a logical sequel to Berriman's leasing business, which had introduced the bank to difficult concepts like discounting future cash flows to a present value against which funds could be advanced. The same technique could be applied to export and project finance, whereby securities – bills of exchange or promissory notes – guaranteeing payment for the goods or the project at some future date could be discounted by the bank, and Berriman had already begun to take the bank into this area. This type of lending also matched the advice of Sir John Stevens, who argued strongly to the board that Morgan Grenfell should make a contribution to Britain's export drive by helping British companies finance exports and construction projects in foreign countries. Part of the rationale for backing de Grunwald was to ensure that the proceeds of distribution went to London rather than Los Angeles. In the case of both exports and projects, however, subsidized loans and guarantees were available from the Government's Export Credits Guarantee Department, which rendered the margins on lending rather thin. De Grunwald films appeared to offer much the same thing with the added bonus of a wider margin.

Morgan Grenfell regarded the arrangement of financing for de Grunwald as a normal banking risk. Though Lord Catto and David Berriman were nominally responsible, the newly recruited accountant, Jonathan Perry, was charged with monitoring payments and receipts. This was logical enough, since Perry had assumed the management of the leasing businesses after Berriman's elevation to the Partners' Room. At first all went well. De Grunwald acted as executive producer for all the films the company made and Albert Caraco, a Paris-based agent for the sale of foreign films, was engaged to collect distributors around the globe. By mid-July 1968, distributors had been collected in thirty-three countries and the International Film Consortium was launched with much ado in London. Eight films were planned, costing $33 million, which the distributors guaranteed to show in their cinemas in return for exclusive distribution rights. In fact, the banking syndicate formed in April 1969 supplied $11 million for six films. Between 1968 and 1970 Morgan's alone advanced £3 million to finance ten films in this way. In all $23 million (£9.6 million) was advanced.[2] The first film, a Western called *Shalako*, produced by Euan Lloyd and starring Sean Connery and Brigitte Bardot, was hugely successful in Britain and on the Continent, though it made little headway in the United States, where audiences were unable to decide whether it was a comedy or not (it was not). It was after Caraco had successfully pre-sold the distribution rights to this film that de Grunwald was persuaded to take him on. Independent distribution also suited Euan Lloyd, who did not wish to be tied to an American distributor. Rank's bought the British rights, paying cash before the film was shot. Flushed with this success in breaking what had been an American monopoly, Morgan's threw caution to the wind. Instead of carefully adding up actual pre-sales country by country and ensuring that distributors were contractually bound, the bank began to rely on estimates of pre-sales supplied by the lynchpin of the International Film Consortium, the sales agent Albert Caraco. He is remembered by most of those involved as a wishful thinker who failed to ensure that distributors were committed and whose projected sales rarely corresponded to the eventual outcome. Yet Morgan Grenfell took him at his word, rather than physically checking that he had performed the feats to which he laid claim.[3] The busy schedule of the film stars made it impossible to delay production while Caraco completed the contracts, and once a film was in production distributors were unwilling to commit themselves until they had seen the first 'runs' of the film. Things began to go wrong very early on – the second film was started without 100 per cent pre-distribution – but this was not immediately obvious.

Things began to go obviously wrong where they could least afford to do so – in the United States, where at least half of all pre-sales were made. In November 1969 Tony Landy tied up a North American distribution deal with the Winthrop Lawrence Corporation, a leisure-industry conglomerate with interests in bowling alleys, hotels and basketball stadia. Its head was the egregiously named Lammot du Pont Copeland Jnr, the son of the then chairman of the du Pont chemicals company, who introduced to London Screenplays his partner Thomas A. 'Al' Shaheen, a former US money broker based in London. Shaheen was made responsible for distribution of the films in the United States.[4] Morgan's, who had been bankers to the du Ponts since their nineteenth-century beginnings, thought the name was credit enough. De Grunwald and Catto, then in Paris, hailed him jubilantly as 'a vigorous American partner' who would help them break the stranglehold of MGM and Twentieth Century Fox on the film distribution business.[5] In

reality, they were lumbered with du Pont Copeland because
de Grunwald had failed to turn up any other distributors. Du
Pont Copeland had recently bought a firm of television film
distributors and was anxious to supply them with material. He
undertook to take up distribution rights on all the films not
otherwise pre-sold in the United States. With this generous
backstop, de Grunwald was pushed into producing films faster
than he would have liked and the quality of some was poor.
Shaheen pressed always for stars, irrespective of the quality of
the film. Although *Perfect Friday*, directed by Peter Hall and
starring Ursula Andress, was a good film, others – notably
Connecting Room, a pure vehicle for its stars, Bette Davis and
Michael Redgrave, *Grigsby*, *The MacMasters* and *A Soldier's
Tale* – were not. Without the muscle of MGM or Twentieth
Century Fox, they proved hard to distribute. Things began to
go wrong with others. *Murphy's War*, starring Peter O'Toole,
ran hideously over budget when the ship chartered to navigate
the Orinoco, the Greek-registered *Odysseus*, got stuck in the silt
and the actors and crew had to be flown by helicopter to the
location every day. Excess costs of $1.2 million were incurred.[6]
The film of D. H. Lawrence's *The Virgin and the Gypsy*, which
was made by Christopher Miles in 1969–70 and starred Franco
Nero and Joanna Shimkus, opened to rave reviews in New
York but its distribution was cut short by the sudden financial
collapse of Lammot du Pont Copeland, Jnr and the Winthrop
Lawrence Corporation, whose promissory notes at that time
were responsible for over $3 million of advance sales.[7] Though
Copeland later alleged fraud on the part of Shaheen and
others, the proximate cause of the collapse seems to have been
unwise property speculation.

In London, Morgan Grenfell found itself in ownership of
worthless Winthrop Lawrence promissory notes. With the American film market in the doldrums, Morgan Grenfell could not
find a new distributor, though de Grunwald's advisers claimed
that *The Virgin and the Gypsy* would gross $20 million in pre-
sales across the United States if they could. The bank chose to
cut its losses immediately, suggesting to the other members of

the bank syndicate that the loans be deemed interest-free, with any proceeds advanced first to them. It was rejected and one bank, First Wisconsin, threatened to sue Morgan for negligence. Morgan's repaid the other banks, and took the loan on to its own book.[8] After the inevitable litigation, Morgan Grenfell was left with eight films to administer. Michael Flint, then head of Paramount Pictures in London, was appointed by the bank as managing director of the ruined London Screenplays. He brought with him from Paramount an accountant called John Smith, who was despatched to Morgan Grenfell to administer the remaining films and recoup what he could of the money that had been lost. De Grunwald, who had warned Morgan Grenfell repeatedly of his serious doubts about the credentials of Al Shaheen and Du Pont Copeland, Jnr, handed his resignation to Flint, by coincidence once a partner at de Grunwald's former London solicitors, Denton, Hall & Burgin. Smith stayed on at Morgan Grenfell, eventually becoming a director in 1987. It took him so long to sort out the mess that even in the 1980s the legend persisted that he maintained a separate telephone line solely for dealing with it. Estimates of the sum the bank lost range between £6 million and £14 million but several of those close to the crisis remember a figure of £12 million, once interest forgone was added to the loss of principal of perhaps £6 million.[9] Provision for bad debts was £3 million in 1970 and £5 million in 1971. It was a ruinous sum for a bank whose disclosed capital and reserves in 1970 were only £6.9 million, and the bank was saved from collapse only by a revaluation of its freehold at 23 Great Winchester Street. Though the Bank of England was informed, it had not yet developed the inquisitorial role that it assumed during the secondary banking crisis of 1973–75, though it had expressed misgivings about the scale of the bank's lending during the expansion of banking assets in the 1960s. The shock was absorbed almost unnoticed by the City at large, though abortive merger talks were held with Baring's, Hill Samuel and Robert Fleming.[10] Tim Collins, the vice-chairman, told one member of staff that it was the biggest single loss the bank had

ever sustained, obliterating 120 years of hidden reserves. A
Holdings Company was formed, at least in part to conceal the
magnitude of the losses. Of course, it was not all written off at
once. The films came into the ownership of the bank and
continued to generate revenue, with Smith acting as distributor. One was sold to Home Box Office, the American
cable television network, for a handsome return, but provisions
had to be made in each of the immediately subsequent years
according to Smith's estimates of the likely recoverability on
each film.

Lord Catto somehow escaped his obvious culpability, eventually succeeding Tim Collins as chairman of the bank in
1979. Though Sir John Stevens asked him to stay, David
Berriman accepted the offer of the managing directorship at
Guinness Mahon in 1973. At Guinness Mahon he turned this
misfortune to good account by paving the way with Malcolm
Wilde for their emergence as one of the major forces in film
finance in London in the 1980s, using exactly the same techniques. In retrospect, it is hard enough to imagine why a group
of stuffy merchant bankers should have entered the perilous
waters of film finance at all, let alone treated with respect such
colourful and unreliable personalities of the cinema in the
1960s as Albert Caraco, Al Shaheen and Lammot du Pont
Copeland. Caraco was an outlandish figure, a consummate
salesman (especially of himself). Shaheen was scarcely the sort
of client with whom Morgan Grenfell ordinarily dealt. Yet
even dull merchant bankers are not immune to the lure of
glamour. Catto was on location at Almeria in Spain during the
filming of *Shalako* and dined with the stars at night. At its
première in Brussels he was introduced to the Queen of the
Belgians by the effervescent Tony Landy, an extraordinary
product of the ferment in Mittel-Europa during the first half of
the twentieth century. An Austrian who had taken American
citizenship after the Second World War, Landy claimed to
know most of Europe's royalty and probably did. He knew the
cinema business inside out, having worked before with Ciner-
ama, the wide screens pioneered by Nick Rossini in the 1950s

which never took off. Poached from Rossini by Dimitri de Grunwald, who relied on him absolutely for financial advice, he thought nothing impossible and comprehensively bamboozled Morgan Grenfell's slow aristocrats with his social connections and apparently easy grasp of numbers. In the company of Landy, it was easy to forget that they were merchant bankers, not merchant adventurers.

In one sense, the episode demonstrated how far the technology of banking had run ahead of the attitudes of its practitioners. Catto considered his decision to finance films an inventive one, of exactly the type the bank had to make if it was to shed its pedestrian image. It was around this time that the bank commissioned a survey of its standing in the business community from John Addey Associates. The research confirmed the high esteem in which the bank was held, but suggested also a reputation for fuddy-duddiness. So there was considerable internal pressure to look dynamic. Fittingly, Catto's mistake – to trust the word of those he dealt with – was one entirely in keeping with the historic ethos of Morgan bankers. He was not alone in making it. During the winter of 1969–70 a dynamic young director of the bank, Henry Gorell-Barnes, was similarly duped by two brazen con men, J. K. Howarth and Wayne Chambers. Howarth was the chairman of E. J. Austin International Limited, a company which claimed ownership of mineral and refining interests in Cyprus and possession of an extremely valuable ore body in California which Howarth claimed would yield £10 million a year by the end of 1970, thanks to a revolutionary new refining process perfected by Chambers.[11] Austin shares duly soared from 18s 6d to 45s, before they were suspended by the Stock Exchange pending substantiation of the claims.[12] Gorell-Barnes was flown by private plane to visit a mine ostensibly owned by Austin, and legend has it that Howarth plucked an ore sample from the wall of the lift shaft as they descended. Austin was an early client of Keyser Ullmann, the secondary bank rescued by the Bank of England in the mid-1970s, and it was assumed at one stage that Morgan Grenfell would succeed Keyser as bankers to the company.[13] Eventually two *Times* journalists visited Cyprus and California and found nothing of value, but not before Howarth and Chambers had borrowed £347,000, of which, according to a government report, 'substantial sums went into their own pockets'.[14] The same report described the Californian mine, the Cyprus mining venture and the Chambers process as 'worthless'[15] and E. J. Austin International was wound up in the High Court in December 1972 as a 'vehicle of fraud'.[16]

Some good came of the near-disaster in films. In September 1969 the Bank of England, informed of the mounting crisis, despatched one of its own men, David Keys, an executive in the discount office and a former assistant to the Chief Cashier, to ensure that the bank returned to more conventional methods of credit assessment. He became the much-feared and skinflint chairman of Morgan Grenfell's Credit Committee, formed, ironically, by David Berriman to assess all the lending risks assumed by the bank. It was a timely appointment. Morgan Grenfell lost virtually nothing in the property crash and consequent secondary banking crisis of 1973–5 which followed the Heath Government's foolhardy expansion of the money supply and the Bank of England's efforts, from 1971, to ginger up the lending markets by relaxing credit control and encouraging interest-rate competition between the banks. As in 1929, easy money, intended to encourage investment in productive industry, in fact flowed largely to property developers, stock-market speculators and the new 'secondary' banks which mushroomed around the City, mainly on the back of lending on property. A new generation of City financiers made quick fortunes lending on property, talking up share prices and stripping the assets of the companies they bought and sold with their inflated shares. The most famous of them, Jim Slater, almost succeeded in merging his rickety financial empire, Slater Walker, with a merchant bank, attracting, in turn, Lazard's, Warburg's and Hill Samuel. By November 1973 the near-collapse of London & County, the most vulnerable of the fringe banks, had forced the Bank of England to launch a financial lifeboat to rescue twenty-six secondary banking houses, which peaked in March 1975 at £1,285 million. Slater Walker was taken over by the Bank of England. Burmah Oil, Britain's oldest oil company, collapsed. Over a hundred Stock Exchange firms disappeared. The *Financial Times* index sank from a peak of 543 in May 1972 to 146 in January 1975.[17] From all this the film-financing crisis had immunized Morgan Grenfell.

The bank was not immune to the wider effects of the secondary banking crisis. The collapse of several property companies and the waning of the takeover boom of the 1960s all reduced the scope for lending money and selling advice. The domestic crisis was bad enough, but the outbreak of war in the Middle East on 6 October 1973, followed swiftly by an OPEC-inspired quadrupling of world oil prices, fundamentally altered the balance of world financial power. Suddenly, industrial countries were no longer spending money on each other's goods, but on oil. The OPEC countries would earn an extra $80 billion a year from their oil exports, of which they could spend only a few billion dollars on imports from the industrialized world. World trade shrank, with catastrophic effects on Morgan Grenfell's British industrial clients. They no longer took each other over or borrowed money in the banking or bond markets; they just sacked workers. Merchant bankers were rather luckier. Dealing only in money, they realized that the flood of petrodollars could actually be turned to their advantage. For one thing, the oil-rich Arabs and Africans could not possibly spend all their lavish gains on building pipelines and palaces at home but would need to reinvest some of them in foreign shares and bonds. They needed Western banking expertise to do so. In Arabia Islamic law forbade the practice of *riba* (usury), so they deposited their dollars with European banks instead, many of them in London. Just like Eurodollars, from which these 'petrodollars' have now become indistinguishable, they were re-lent by the Euromarket banks to those who needed them. At first re-lending was confined to developed countries. The British nationalized industries were early beneficiaries of dollar lending by Arabs, with the risk of borrowing dollars against sterling assets covered by the Bank of England.[18] The sheer magnitude of the sums available soon encouraged the London banks to lend to ever more exotic borrowers. Mexico, Brazil, South Korea, the Philippines, Peru, Argentina, Turkey and even Zaire were re-lent petrodollars. This business boomed until August 1982, when Mexico nearly defaulted and the exuberant lending of the 1970s was transformed into the biggest and most intractable debt the world has ever seen. At the end of 1988 fifteen developing countries in Latin America, Africa and the Pacific Basin owed Western banks and governments just under $500 billion.[19]

In the wake of the film-financing débâcle Sir John Stevens became executive vice-chairman of the bank. It was intended that he should eventually succeed Viscount Harcourt as chairman of Morgan Grenfell Holdings, the holding company formed in November 1971 as a vehicle for the bank's increasingly diversified businesses, uniting the offices of chairman and chief executive for the first time. Stevens believed passionately that if Morgan Grenfell was to survive and prosper it could not afford to depend upon the domestic market alone, or upon those incidental interests abroad which history had dictated that it should have. He wished to make Morgan Grenfell an international bank based in London rather than a London bank with international bases. He devised a *grand dessin*, code-named 'Project Triangle', in which the international businesses of Morgan Guaranty, Morgan Stanley and Morgan Grenfell would be reunited, bombarding directors with interminable memoranda on its advantages. Though the separate cultural and business development of each was propelling them inexorably towards mutual antagonism, he felt that there was still time to capture their strengths for their mutual benefit. The two American houses would give Morgan Grenfell powerful allies in the United States. Co-operation in the Eurobond market was already evident, because all the Morgan houses used Morgan & Cie International, the successor to Morgan Harjes, in Paris – though not for new issues. Morgan Grenfell

139

retained a 13 per cent stake in Morgan & Cie from its formation in 1963 until the early 1970s.[20] The other shareholders were Morgan Guaranty (70 per cent) and the Dutch merchant bank, Mees & Hope. Morgan & Cie consequently ranked among the top three Eurobond houses, ahead even of S. G. Warburg, creator of the market. Morgan Guaranty retained a one-third shareholding in Morgan Grenfell and informal links were strong. Project Triangle also matched the *Zeitgeist*. Britain had just joined the European Economic Community (EEC). Joint ventures and consortium banks were becoming commonplace in the Euromarkets. By the summer of 1973 even Siegmund Warburg had embarked on joint ventures in Europe and the United States with the French bank, Paribas.[21]

In January 1972, Stevens and three other directors met with partners of Morgan Stanley to discuss 'Project Triangle.' Morgan Guaranty was later drawn into the discussions too. Unfortunately, the plan aroused sufficient opposition from influential members of the board to occasion Stevens's defeat on a matter to which he had become dangerously overcommitted. Almost alone, he had taken negotiations with Morgan Guaranty and Morgan Stanley to the verge of a deal. A meeting of the board of directors was convened in the summer of 1973 to approve the concept. Stevens had his supporters among the directors. They included Kenneth Barrington and the head of Corporate Finance, George Law, and some of the young lions, like Philip Chappell and Roger Seelig. Among his opponents, the suspicion of surrender to more powerful cousins was strong, especially from David Bendall, a diplomat who joined the bank in 1971. The deal which Stevens was recommending gave Morgan Grenfell a shareholding of only 10 per cent in an international venture from which they judged that the bank would gain little. They felt that Triangle was a ploy by the more powerful American houses to trade their easily imitable skills in the Eurobond market for Morgan Grenfell's irreplaceable corporate contacts in Britain and future business within the European Community. They submitted a memorandum to this effect. Some privately despised Stevens's jet-setting, feeling it typified the international civil servant in him, or at best the clubbishness of central, as opposed to merchant, bankers. Project Triangle was resoundingly rejected by the board and the talk, collapsed, amid some acrimony, in June 1973.[22] Afterwards, Guy Weston submitted a letter suggesting that Stevens should resign. He chose not to, and instead took Morgan Grenfell back to its roots: the mobilization of capital on behalf of foreign borrowers. This time the capital was raised not from British savers but in the Euromarkets.

Morgan Grenfell was very active in the Eurodollar syndicated loan market throughout the 1970s, but took only small participations in the loans it arranged and for the most part resisted the temptation to lend to Latin America, where the New York banks were very active.[23] Instead, piloted initially by David Berriman, it used the Eurodollar markets to fund British firms exporting capital goods or building major projects abroad. Unlike takeovers, this was dour, unglamorous work, but the government subsidized it as a contribution to the balance of payments. Fixed exchange rates, which were not abandoned in Britain until 1972, made the country's balance of payments – the credit and debit account with the rest of the world – the ultimate arbiter of economic policy. As in the days of Montagu Norman and the gold standard (a measure of value replaced in the post-war world by the American dollar) a trade surplus strengthened the pound by increasing demand for it as foreigners bought sterling to pay for their British goods and a deficit weakened it as British importers bought foreign currencies to pay for foreign goods. Britain's anaemic economic performance had meant that from 1958 the trade balance, in deficit in real goods since the end of the Industrial Revolution, was no longer covered even by invisible exports. In November 1967 the pound had to be devalued from $2.80 to $2.40, a national economic humiliation which cost the Chancellor of the Exchequer, James Callaghan, his job.[24] Another record deficit of £700 million in 1972 forced Britain to abandon fixed exchange rates altogether and allow the pound to 'float' freely against other currencies. Amidst this, the promotion and subsidization of exports was a *sine qua non*.

Export finance of this kind was Morgan Grenfell's biggest single success of the 1970s. It won the bank Queen's Awards to Industry for export achievement in 1975, 1982 and 1986, and Morgan Grenfell remains the only merchant bank ever to have won such an award. David Berriman searched aggressively for business, pioneering the jet-setting approach that is *de rigueur* for modern merchant bankers but which was considered pushy and undignified as recently as the 1960s. He accompanied clients of the bank like GKN and Costain on journeys to Kinshasa and Dubai, where contracts to build railways, harbours and hospitals were agreed and financed simultaneously. Among the people Berriman used to secure lucrative construction contracts from Sheikh Rashid of Dubai was Mahdi Al-Tajir, sometime ambassador for the United Arab Emirates in London but then the Sheikh's *chef du cabinet*. Other directors of the bank, like Philip Chappell and David Douglas-Home (the son of the former Prime Minister and then Foreign Secretary, Alec Douglas-Home) dealt with Mohamed Al-Fayed, then factotum to Tajir but the eventual purchaser of the House of Fraser department-store chain which owns Harrod's in a bid which is now subject to investigation by the police. The use of 'fixers' of this kind was not unusual when doing business in the Middle East in the 1970s and Morgan Grenfell do not seem to have been perturbed by their presence. David Douglas-Home has admitted that Tajir and Fayed helped win contracts in a country where the wealth of the Sheikh and the wealth of the nation could not be easily disentangled, but believes Sheikh Rashid's knowledge of British contractors and trust in their business methods was probably the principal factor in the bank's success. Douglas-Home maintains that 'people like Mahdi and Mohamed' just 'happened to be in the right place at the right time'.[25]

Whatever the trials of negotiation in the Middle East, the lending techniques used by the bank were relatively straightforward. Foreign buyers of British products or expertise could arrange, in effect, to borrow the money to pay for them in London at a fixed rate of interest subsidized by the government. Export finance works in one of two ways. Most commonly, a British exporter is paid in a series of IOUs, either bills of exchange or promissory notes, which a merchant bank then sells to a syndicate of banks to enable the exporter to receive cash. These are called 'supplier credits'. However, in bigger contracts – say, the construction of a refinery, which takes longer to build, and to produce a return – the syndicate of banks lends the money required to the foreign buyer, usually by advancing it piecemeal as the project progresses. Because the buyer remains responsible for the payment of interest and the repayment of the principal, these are called 'buyer credits'. Project finance, as export finance for major capital projects is usually called, is essentially the same thing as a buyer credit. Most of the money lent by the banks at this time was raised by them in the Euromarkets.

Where export finance differs from ordinary lending is in the involvement of a government department, the Export Credits Guarantee Department (ECGD), which was set up in 1930 to insure British exporters against losses incurred abroad. It still guarantees to repay the banks if foreign buyers fail to pay, but it also subsidizes the financing by paying to the banks the difference between the rate offered to the buyers and normal commercial rates of interest. Similar government support for new oil and gas developments in the North Sea created a business of sufficient size for Morgan Grenfell to form a separate energy department in the early 1970s, Morgan Grenfell Energy Services Limited. As successive governments subsidized the cost of lending to North Sea oil companies, Morgan Grenfell helped finance the smaller independents like Charterhall, GOAL, Lasmo, Tricentrol and its oldest oil client, J. E. K. Cull's creation, Ultramar. Goal Petroleum, set up in 1973, was managed by Morgan Grenfell until 1981, when the Buchan Field came on stream.[26] For merchant banks like Morgan Grenfell it was not quite like a return to their traditional nineteenth-century function of channelling surplus capital to overseas borrowers. The involvement of the ECGD and the syndication of loans among a variety of banks blurred the age-old linkage between risk and reward. And it was hard to feel heroic about arranging a government-guaranteed syndicated credit facility at LIBOR plus a quarter to build a catalytic cracker in Colombia.

There were two major export markets where Morgan Grenfell had an edge over the competition. One was the Middle East, where it was the only London merchant bank sufficiently free of Zionist taint for Arabs to consider doing business with it. Certainly neither Morgan nor Grenfell, unlike Hambro, Rothschild, Samuel, or Warburg, had been Jewish, but this was more than happenstance. J. P. Morgan's vehement anti-Semitism had filtered down the generations. The bank's impact on the Eurobond market in the 1960s was severely hampered at the outset by its refusal to deal with the main market maker, Julius Strauss of Strauss, Turnbull & Co., though the bank eventually relented. Though the bank did employ Jews in small numbers, always below board level, only the greed of the 1980s overcame the prejudice against acting for Jewish firms like Ladbroke's and Dixon's or Jewish entrepreneurs like Robert Maxwell. A story is told – probably apocryphal – of an encounter in the lift as late as 1982 between Robert Shrager, an executive in the Corporate Finance Department, and Paul Gold, a Eurobond salesman, which relates Shrager saying: 'So you're the other Jew at Morgan Grenfell?'

In the charged atmosphere of the Middle East after the Yom Kippur War this pedigree paid rich dividends. Between 1969 and 1973 Morgan Grenfell raised $64 million in the Euromarkets for the Sultan of Dubai, culminating in a $10 million syndicated loan for the construction of a dry dock in July 1973.[27] In November 1973, shortly after the ceasefire in the Sinai desert, the bank arranged the syndication of an $180 million loan to Abu Dhabi. The participating banks were too timid to reveal their identities, fearing that their governments would disapprove of funding an Arab supporter of Egypt in the war, especially when an Arab oil embargo against the

United States was in force.[28] Morgan Grenfell did not allow the war to disrupt good business, whatever their sentiments about Israel. In 1973 it formed a joint banking company with the Jordan-based Arab Bank called the Arab and Morgan Grenfell Finance Company. The Morgan Grenfell and Egyptian Finance Company was also formed with several Egyptian and other Arab interests.[29] But, as Lord Catto admitted, the Middle Eastern lending business grew less out of Morgan eugenics than the efforts of the bank's industrial clients to export to the Middle East, where they were unhampered by American competition:

Our interest here [the Middle East] was part of our general attitude to overseas expansion. And to a large extent our Middle East business has grown out of business done by UK contractors for whom we were arranging finance.[30]

As the director in charge of the Middle East, David Douglas-Home rose to a position of some prominence, becoming a familiar figure to British businessmen on flights to the Gulf. There was much boasting about the first British export credit to be arranged in a foreign currency, which financed the building of a $600 million aluminium smelter and a $300 million gas-gathering complex in Dubai in May 1977. It involved export credits from four countries and Eurodollar loans of $460 million. Pre-revolutionary Iran proved very fruitful and a representative office was opened in Tehran. Morgan Grenfell executives were still there when the ayatollahs took over.

The other market where Morgan Grenfell outpaced the competition was behind the Iron Curtain. Morgan bankers had been active in Russia since Tsarist days, but in the early 1970s a concerted effort was made to break into Eastern European markets, led by the Russian-speaking Sir John Stevens. A team of Russian linguists was recruited, including Robert Owen from the Foreign Office and Frank Bicknell, from the Bank of London and South America.[31] The initial results, which included the co-management of two Hungarian

Eurobond issues and a participation in a $60 million syndicated loan to Comecon, were encouraging. The signing in 1972 of a £25 million line of credit to the Soviet Union, which was first used to help GKN build a factory in Russia, was an undeniable triumph.[32] It was the first loan to follow the announcement in July 1971 that the ECGD would finance £200 million of capital goods exports to the Soviet Union at a fixed cost of 6 per cent over two years and the deal was signed amid great ceremony in London by Sir John Stevens and S. A. Shevchenko, Chairman of the Moscow Narodny Bank.[33] It marked the beginning of a relationship with Russia that has secured for Morgan Grenfell fully four-fifths of all Anglo-Russian trade financing since 1972. Great drama surrounded the clinching of a contract by the Davy Corporation to build two methanol plants in the Soviet Union in 1976. The financial pyrotechnics involved a subsidized dollar loan from the ECGD and the forward selling of Davy's returns from the project and, when exchange rates threatened to allow a German company to undercut Davy's bid by £25 million, the contract was retrieved at the last minute by quoting Davy's price simultaneously in Deutschmarks, dollars and sterling. In November 1977 the bank opened a joint office in Moscow with Moscow Narodny and the Bank of Scotland, one of the signatories to the 1972 loan. Morgan's is still the only merchant bank represented in Moscow. Stevens himself became chairman of the East European Trade Council. It is said by those suspicious of the bank's long and fruitful relationship with the British Government, dating from the First World War, that Morgan Grenfell acts as paymaster for British spies in the Soviet Union.

Morgan Grenfell also began to sell abroad its ability to manage from London the international investments of overseas investors. Apart from a brief penchant for investment trusts between the wars, Morgan Grenfell, in common with the other London merchant banks, did not manage significant amounts of institutional investments at the start of the 1970s. This was mainly because savings in Britain did not really shift from bank deposit accounts and building societies to life assurance companies and pension funds until after the Second World War, when successive governments provided tax incentives to do so. During the 1950s private pension funds, once the prerogative of civil servants, spread rapidly through all sectors of the British economy. It was only natural that merchant bankers, who had long excelled in reinvesting the vast fortunes of themselves and others, should have commandeered this vast new source of organized capital just as private fortunes were shrinking under punitive levels of personal taxation. Though a private client department was run by W. W. H. ('Willy') Hill-Wood, a Cambridge cricketing blue who joined the bank in 1939, Morgan's had first entered the institutional market in 1953, with the contract to manage the pension fund of Inco, the Canadian minerals company. Part of the rationale for the merger discussions with Robert Fleming after the film financing débâcle was the Scottish bank's strength in investment management. A separate Investment Department was not established until Associated Industrial Consultant report was delivered in 1966.[34] It was run by Sidney Eburne, who stayed with the bank for over thirty years before becoming the senior Crown Agent in 1978, for which he was knighted. The department was not much expanded until 1974, when the thirty-five-year-old Henry Gorell-Barnes, the architect of the E. J. Austin débâcle and a director only since 1972, took charge. He worked under John Sparrow, who had been given a brief to make the department profitable, or close it. At the time it had just one major client and a paltry £195 million under management. It was also synonymous with the bank's bond-issuing business, which strained its independence of judgement. Gorell-Barnes split it from the securities operation and under his tutelage it grew rapidly. By 1979 it had 106 clients and £1.7 billion under management. Initially, the department tended to attract the pension funds of existing clients like Plessey, RHM and BICC, but from 1977 it began to market its services to American pension funds (called ERISA funds, after the US Employee Retirement Income Security Act of 1974) who were beginning for the first time to invest outside the North American markets. Morgan Grenfell Investment Services Limited was registered that year under the US Investment Advisors Act of 1940 to manage the international equity portfolios of American pension funds, foundations and endowment funds. Early clients included Alcan, Dupont and 3M.

Export and project finance and international portfolio management added substance to Stevens's messianic drive to internationalize the bank. Since not only Britain but most advanced industrialized countries operated export finance departments, Morgan Grenfell needed a presence in foreign countries to be sure of securing the cheapest finance for its clients. And the export financiers found the skills acquired in advising British exporters travelled well. The bank financed, for example, the first Italian export credit to be financed in the Eurodollar market. It was for a Colombian hydroelectric project, prompting the opening of a representative office in Bogota.[34] This was eclipsed by the co-ordination of £3 billion of loans between 1975 and 1978 to finance the construction by Davy McKee of a giant integrated steel mill for Aco Minas in Brazil, the largest overseas project ever handled by the bank. It involved export credits from Britain, France and Germany and a Euromarkets loan package of $500 million.[35] Though the mill itself was a disastrous white elephant, straying $2.5 billion over budget, the inauguration delayed until 1985 and the first phase not completed until 1986, Aco Minas became an internal symbol of the bank's re-emergence as a heavyweight force in world lending.[36] Export finance loans arranged by Morgan Grenfell grew from £91.9 million in 1972 to £820.5 million in 1976.

Eventually outposts were established abroad to root out potential business for referral to London. In 1969 Morgan Grenfell boasted only 'associations' with banking houses in Africa, Australia, the Bahamas, Canada, France, Holland, India, Ireland, Italy and the United States of varying degrees of significance. Many, like the ties with Morgan & Cie in Paris and Morgan Guaranty Trust Company in New York, were sentimental but substantive; others, like the tie with Andrew Yule & Co. Limited in Calcutta, reflected family involvements. For a long time, Yule shared a London office with Morgan Grenfell. The bank had only one overseas office of its own, in Munich. One legend has it that it received more enquiries for Morgan sports cars than anything else; another holds that it was borrowed by MI5 during the Czech crisis in 1968. In fact, Kenneth Grandville, the ex-diplomat chosen by Stevens to man the office, insisted on Munich. It was closed in 1978.[37] Under Stevens, representative offices were added in Rome and Sydney and banking companies were established in Guernsey and Jersey to attract deposits from non-residents. Within six years the bank had over twenty overseas offices and more than a hundred staff dotted around the globe. Stevens seemed to live life on the run, sprinting down the stairs at 23 Great Winchester Street locked in conversation with a fellow director before being sped to the airport in a Daimler driven by his faithful chauffeur, Stan Rozzi. He even added Japanese to his repertoire of eight foreign languages. To Stevens's detractors within the bank the representative offices were whimsical, an outcome of his preference for movement over action and his insatiable appetite for jet-setting, international junketing and foreign tongues. The representatives he appointed seemed to them to correspond to those he had shared his last cocktail with. They argued that representative offices in every European capital were an expensive luxury with no very obvious role that could not be performed in London and that some of the representatives he had found in European capitals were joyriding on the bank's naivety. This argument, among others, was still unresolved when death overtook Sir John Stevens on the last weekend in October 1973. He was not quite 60 years old.

For Morgan Grenfell, perched uneasily between the past and the future, the death of Stevens was a hammer blow. The proposed union in him of the offices of chairman and chief executive would have given the bank strong leadership at a time of rapid change. As it was, the momentum faltered temporarily as a caretaker regime took office in the Partners' Room. On Harcourt's retirement at Christmas 1973, Tim

Collins was appointed chairman of the Holdings Board and Lord Catto took charge at the operational level as chairman and chief executive of the bank.[38] An outsider, Gerard ('Bill') Mackworth-Young was interposed between them as vice-chairman of Morgan Grenfell Holdings. Mackworth-Young was a curious choice for a merchant bank. Though he had been to Eton, served in the Welsh Guards, started his City career with Baring's and was universally agreed to be absolutely charming, he was a stockbroker, not a merchant banker. However, Mackworth-Young was also an insider at Morgan's. He had since 1953 been a partner at the Queen's stockbrokers, Rowe & Pitman, where he had handled the broker's dealings with Morgan Grenfell, becoming close to Sir John Stevens. He had for many years visited the Partners' Room at Morgan Grenfell every morning to review with the bank's directors prospects and developments in the stock market. Publicly, he explained that, at forty-seven, he found Morgan Grenfell, with whom Rowe & Pitman had worked closely for years, an 'irresistible' challenge.[39] In reality he had recently narrowly lost the battle for succession to the senior partnership at Rowe & Pitman to Peter Wilmot-Sitwell and he felt that he could not stay. While Morgan's argued blithely that his flotation and takeover experience – he had floated Pilkington Brothers and Sainsbury's, advised on Harold Wilson's Chunnel and handled the GEC acquisition of AEI in 1967 – would be invaluable, it really only saw him as a useful buffer, if not an elderly one. Ostensibly, the strategic thinking at which Stevens had excelled was thrown to a new three-man Advisory Board made up of the great and the good. Its membership read like the beneficiaries of Morgan Grenfell's executive pension scheme. Chaired by Lord Harcourt, its membership included the outgoing governor of the Bank of England, Lord O'Brien of Lothbury, the scourge of Harcourt in 1968. The plan was to expand it with more superannuated staff and clients in the years to come.

It looked like a compromise and it was. Each of the partners had been unwilling to concede ultimate power to the others, so the incumbents had simply divided among themselves the baubles of office. This left the bank in safe but arthritic hands; from 1973 Morgan Grenfell was strategically rudderless. Ultimate responsibility was uncertain;, executive responsibility was split; and technical comprehension was limited. Control still rested with the families who owned the bank, dispiriting those who had hoped Stevens would make the bank more meritocratic. Apart from Willis Faber & Dumas, the Lloyd's insurance broker, whose shareholding had risen to 22 per cent by 1974, the Catto family were the largest shareholders in Morgan Grenfell. Throughout the 1970s Lord Catto, his mother, his first wife, the family firm of Yule Catto and various interests associated with them always controlled at least a tenth of the share capital. Though directors and long-serving staff were gradually admitted to the equity of the company, this only sharpened their appetite for personal aggrandizement. A group of younger directors like Christopher Reeves, John Sparrow, Charles Rawlinson, Christopher Whittington and Blaise Hardman felt that they made most of the profit and enjoyed little of the rewards. They wanted power not just to enrich themselves but because they were sure that they could make a better fist of running the bank than Tim Collins, Bill Mackworth-Young and Lord Catto. The younger directors also spoke for the layers of talent – men like Graham Walsh, George Magan, Roger Seelig, Henry Gorell-Barnes and others – who had not yet ascended to the board. It was an atmosphere in which political intrigue was almost certain to thrive, and did.

As if to underline its lack of imagination, the new regime that took office in late 1973 did not contest the need for joint ventures or overseas expansion. Indeed, with the domestic market depressed by the oil crisis, inflation and, after the election of a Labour Government in 1974, what Tim Collins called 'the sharpest switch towards socialist and collectivist economic policies ever seen in this country' the bank made a virtue of dullness.[40] In July 1974 a deal was concluded with two Japanese city banks, Tokai and Kyowa, on a joint venture to underwrite and sell Eurobonds, exchange corporate clients and swap research on companies.[41] It was the first example of the 'me-too' syndrome that gripped the bank throughout the vicissitudes of the 1970s and 1980s, and gave it a reputation for following timidly where others had led boldly. Similar deals had already been concluded between Kleinwort Benson and Fuji Bank, White Weld and Sumitomo, Hambro's and Mitsui, and Baring's and Sanwa Bank.[42] The move at least corresponded to the encroaching reality of Japan as the world's premier capitalist power. Once it shook off the effects of the high price of oil and other commodities in the 1980s Japan replaced the United States as the world's largest creditor, with profound implications for a bank rooted in transatlantic trade. In short, the Japanese and the Arabs – significantly, the Arab and Egyptian finance companies were formed at this time – had all the dollars, and Morgan Grenfell had to follow them wherever they went. Once Britain's membership of the European Economic Community was secured in the 1975 referendum, in which Morgan Grenfell gave £7,500 to the Britain in Europe campaign, the bank made moves, albeit desultory ones, in Europe.[43] Europe is not a natural market for a Morgan bank. Unlike Rothschild's or Hambro's, whose origins lay in Europe, the bank had allowed the American Morgans, through Morgan & Cie, to make the running on the Continent, as Lord Catto admitted:

The tie with Morgan Guaranty has meant that our interest in Europe has developed more slowly than that of other banks.[44]

In fact throughout the 1970s Morgan Grenfell made far too comfortable a living from financing exports to eastern Europe and recycling Arab petrodollars to attack European markets with conviction. Representative offices were opened in Paris, Milan and Madrid in 1974 and Morgan Grenfell Finance SA was opened in September of the same year in Switzerland, primarily to trade and sell bonds. In July 1974, in a pale imitation of Warburg's deal with Paribas, a joint venture was formed with the French bank, Compagnie Financière de Suez. Bold plans to swap directors and shareholdings and approach clients in tandem were announced and David Bendall, a

Morgan Grenfell director, swapped seats with Guy de la Presle. But Suez was the wrong choice; it was a wholesale commercial bank, lacking the entrepreneurial flair of Paribas. The pair established joint merchant banking subsidiaries in Singapore and Hong Kong but both sides found the relationship an uneasy one and it was concluded unhappily in 1976, leaving Morgan Grenfell in sole ownership of the Singapore operation and Suez of the Hong Kong bank.

The Young Turks on the board of Morgan Grenfell began to lose patience with the uninspiring nature of the leadership emanating from the Partners' Room. Everything that was done seemed to lack conviction. What finally stiffened their resolve to take charge was the splitting among the chosen few of the gains from the flotation of the insurance brokers Willis Faber & Dumas in 1976. Morgan Grenfell and Willis Faber had long enjoyed a close relationship, first exchanging shareholdings in 1967.[45] Morgan Grenfell bought 20 per cent of Willis Faber, who in turn bought 14 per cent of Morgan Grenfell, a holding which had risen to 22 per cent by 1974.[46] It is unclear what proportion of the Morgan Grenfell stake in Willis Faber was acquired by the bank on a corporate basis and what proportion was acquired by the directors of the bank in a personal capacity. However, at the time of the flotation of Willis Faber in November 1976, some directors of Morgan Grenfell certainly held shares in Willis Faber for their own account. These were worth about £100,000 each, and there was no evidence among the public records held at Companies House of a separate corporate shareholding. If there had been one, it must have been sold by 1976. The directors' holdings were congregated anonymously in a 'Morgan Nominees' account. It is most likely that they acquired their shares in the second half of 1971, perhaps by buying them from the bank.

Links between banks and insurance companies were not unusual in the 1960s. In 1967 Siegmund Warburg bought and merged two insurance brokers, Matthews Wrightson and Stewart Smith.[47] Hambro's backed Mark Weinberg, creator of Abbey Life and a pioneer of life assurance policies linked to unit trusts.[48] By the early 1970s virtually all merchant banks had formed insurance links of some kind, judging it a non-cyclical business which could see them through the troughs of the banking markets and grow without needing a lot of additional capital. Insurance brokers also generate large amounts of surplus cash, which the banks mobilized for their lending and Eurobond businesses. Banks would sell the brokers the securities they underwrote on the pretext of managing their surplus cash, a crafty ploy outlawed by the Insurance Companies Amendment Act 1973.[49] Together Morgan Grenfell and Willis Faber had formed a leasing company, London Industrial Leasing, and a company offering advice on 'staff motivation, participation and remuneration', MWP Incentives, in which PA Management Consultants also had a stake. They also set up two unit trusts for members of Lloyd's.[50] Willis still runs the Morgan Grenfell Pension Scheme and staff are offered cut-rate house and car insurance. It was also intended that Willis would insure or broke the insurance of certain of the bank's loans, especially in the area of export and project finance, which it has continued to do ever since. Willis Faber broked, for example, the political risk insurance of loans taken out by the South Pacific island of Palau for the purchase of a power station in 1983, arranged by Morgan Grenfell.[51]

The relationship never functioned as smoothly as intended, partly for reasons of personality but mainly because Morgan Grenfell's appetite for capital exceeded that of Willis Faber. This meant that Willis Faber continued to add to its shareholding in Morgan Grenfell while the directors of the bank steadily reduced the size of their stake in Willis Faber. The Morgan Nominees holding had shrunk to only 7 per cent of Willis Faber ordinary shares by 1975, and this figure was probably inflated by shares owned by clients of the bank.[52] By 1976 Willis Faber & Dumas was subject to similar strains and was finding it hard to sustain both growth and privacy. It was one of the four biggest insurance brokers in London and manifestly the most blue-blooded of them all, with a distinguished history stretching back to the merger of Henry Willis & Co. and

Faber Brothers in 1897. For most of its existence it had remained an utterly private company, only gradually ceding an interest to outsiders. In 1963 a quarter of its equity was sold to a group of institutional investors and by 1971 outsiders, including Morgan Grenfell, controlled only two-fifths of the company.[53] By 1976 there was pressure from the external shareholders like Morgan Grenfell to improve the marketability of their holdings by seeking a public quotation and the company itself was anxious to use listed shares to make acquisitions. The directors turned to Morgan Grenfell for advice on how to list their shares on the London Stock Exchange. At Morgan Grenfell, Guy Weston was put in charge of the flotation. His initial advice was to offer shares for sale to the public, but the spectacular failure of another issue underwritten by the bank – the offer for sale of Borthwick's, in which a record 98.4 per cent of the shares were left with the underwriters – discouraged Weston from pursuing the same course. The Hambro Life flotation had also flopped badly, making it hard to find buyers for insurance company shares. Just days before the Willis Faber sale was due to be announced, Weston switched to an Introduction, which did not require the issue of any new shares. At this point the question arose of what to do with the shares in Willis Faber held by the directors of the bank.

For the directors of Morgan Grenfell the flotation of Willis Faber was a tempting opportunity to increase dramatically the value of their shares. They had been chafing for some time at the gradual diminution in their spending power under the successive incomes policies of the Wilson and Callaghan governments in the 1970s. In April 1976 Tim Collins had contrasted the hard work of Morgan Grenfell's staff with 'their declining living standards brought about, particularly for the more senior and more responsible, by the combined effects of inflation, higher taxation and a stringent and egalitarian incomes policy'.[54] The value of the Willis Faber shares had multiplied many times since the directors acquired them in 1971 and a public flotation would increase it still further. The directors decided that they would not dispose of their shares ahead of the flotation but take advantage of it. Even in 1976, their decision to retain personal interests in a company being floated by the bank without disclosing the fact in the documentation of the offer for sale was faintly shocking. Knowledge of the directors' shareholdings was not widespread within Morgan Grenfell and when news of the decision filtered out, there was considerable resentment among the staff of the gains their superiors appeared to have made. This knowledge further sharpened the growing resentment of the Young Turks. Even some of the beneficiaries felt slightly embarrassed. For some, like Philip Chappell, it was probably the largest sum of money they had ever received. The Introduction took place on 10 November 1976. Ahead of it the directors' shareholdings were exchanged for 2,806,280 new ordinary shares in Willis Faber.[55] It is difficult to assess accurately the nominal gains which accrued to the directors on the flotation of Willis Faber, because their shareholdings in the Morgan Nominees account, along with those of clients of the bank, are indistinguishable. However, after the Introduction at £1.20 a share, capitalizing Willis Faber at £48 million, the share price rose to £2.05, and to a high of £3.10 in 1977, taking the value of the company to £124 million. An exact measure of the profit which accrued to directors of Morgan Grenfell is impossible to establish, but their immediate profit must have been of the order of £500,000, and rather more by the end of 1977. This was a very considerable sum of money in 1976, when the highest paid director on the Holdings Board earned only £33,700 and thirteen of his fellow directors earned less than £25,000.[56] After the flotation, a substantial number of shares held by Willis Faber directors, which were to have been sold in the Offer for Sale, were carefully marketed to outside investors, along with some of the shares held by Morgan Grenfell directors.

The arrangement was not a fraudulent one, its details being cleared with the Inland Revenue, but it was unethical. Though the directors of the Holdings Board had not, as some assumed at the time, benefited personally from the sale of a corporate shareholding, they had advised on the flotation of a company in which they had an interest which they had not disclosed. Their obvious material interest in the Introduction was not declared in the documentation of the issue prepared by Slaughter & May. Nor was Guy Weston's responsibility for the terms of the Introduction, though he was one of the benefici- aries of it. The documents admitted only the minimum required by law: that Willis Faber was a shareholder in Morgan Gren- fell, that the bank would receive a fee for its work and that Bill Mackworth-Young, the chief executive of Morgan Grenfell, was a non-executive director of Willis Faber.[57] Ironically, there was some disquiet in the press, and especially the specialist accountancy press, over the revelation in the documentation that two partners in Willis Faber's auditors, Baker Sutton (now part of Ernst & Whinney), had direct and indirect interests in over 3 million ordinary shares, or 7.5 per cent of the company.[58] Doubtless, this included shares held as trustees, but it was still highly unusual for a partner in an accounting firm to retain an interest in a client for whom he was re- sponsible. The Lex column in the *Financial Times* commented:

However, it should be noted that this disclosure was made volun- tarily, and is not part of the Stock Exchange's formal listing require- ments. It ought to be.[59]

It is tempting to portray the management coup of December 1979 as the dénouement of the power struggle between the Young Turks and the Old Guard at Morgan Grenfell, and in a sense it was. Its origins certainly lay in the unsatisfactory dispensation of power in October 1973, when no single figure proved big enough to replace Sir John Stevens. Though Catto quickly abandoned the executive role to Bill Mackworth- Young, who in December 1974 replaced him as chief executive, Mackworth-Young was a compromiser, not a leader. He repre- sented the enlightened amateurs of old, who were rapidly being replaced by professional men, lawyers and accountants. They despised the ignorance and venality of the Old Guard. They also feared for their future under it. In the Euromarkets the increasing involvement of the massive American money-centre banks – who lent money as well as arranged for others to lend it – was turning sentiment against banks like Morgan Grenfell, who could earn fees for arranging loans but lacked lending muscle of their own. To some extent this truth had been obscured by Morgan Grenfell's success in export finance, where the London clearing banks lent happily on the back of a government guarantee and the bank did not have to participate in the loans it arranged at all; now clients expected it to. It was this realization that had driven the bank towards Tokai, Kyowa and Suez. The bank's international presence was insubstantial and hopelessly compromised by the historic links with Morgan Guaranty and Morgan Stanley. These offered only the capricious safety of numbers and a permanent inhibition on open competition with them. Stevens's attempt to resolve this dilemma – Project Triangle – had foundered on an alliance of Young Turks anxious to retain control of the business and Old Guard anxious to protect their shareholdings. Somebody needed to take decisions on the future.

One man in particular thought he could: Christopher Reeves. He was in every way but one ill-equipped for the role he coveted. At thirty-nine, he had never done an ordinary banking job and was, in the words of one contemporary, 'not even qualified to drive a cab'. He was the son of a branch manager with the old National Provincial Bank. He went from Malvern College to the Rifle Brigade, serving in Kenya and Malaya, and later attributed his personal initiative and preference for working in small groups to this military experience. Declining a career in the army, he joined the Bank of England as a trainee, staying six years. Then, aged twenty-seven, he joined the merchant bank Philip Hill, to become personal assistant to Sir Derek Palmer. He also worked with Kenneth (now Lord) Keith, the archetypal City bruiser of the 1960s, on the merger of Philip Hill and Marcus Samuel.[60] He was hired by Lord Catto as personnel director in 1968, with a brief to recruit lawyers, accountants and others who knew what to do in the changing City of the late 1960s. He had no particular expertise of his own, but he was deeply ambitious and adept at corporate politics, gathering about him a group of like-minded supporters. One was Blaise Hardman, an Old Etonian who had joined Morgan Grenfell in 1961 after a three-year commission in the Guards. Graham Walsh, a bespectacled, fussy and valetudinarian accountant Reeves had met at Hill Samuel, and a neighbour of his in Dulwich, was less flamboyant but equally dependable. Christopher Whittington, a tall and self-effacing international banker, keen on squash and drily humorous, was the sort of clubbable functionary who survives every revolution. By the time of Morgan Grenfell's Queen's Award in April 1975, Christopher Reeves had emerged as head of banking, adroitly associating himself with the bank's signal success of the early 1970s. Since 1972 he had presided over a tenfold increase in ECGD-backed lending and now claimed a quarter of the total market for Morgan Grenfell. In this business, Reeves had one prime advantage: he could take decisions. Nobody else would sanction lending and underwriting decisions of the magnitude he did, apparently without losing sleep.

Reeves had only one serious rival – Philip Chappell. It would be hard to find a greater contrast. Educated at Marlborough and Christ Church, Chappell was prone to discourse on philosophy and in particular on the work of the philosopher Karl Popper, a refugee from the Nazis whose passionate demolition of totalitarianism, *The Open Society and Its Enemies*, had first inspired him at Oxford. Popper's vigorous defence of the individual is evident in Chappell's public commitment to radical tax reforms and wider share ownership. Unlike Reeves, he detested institutions and despised the politics necessary for advancement within them. His interests and ambitions were highly diverse. In May 1971, still in his early forties, Chappell was invited by the Transport Minister, John Peyton, to serve as chairman of the National Ports Council, where his deputy was Jack Jones, and earned himself a CBE. His directorships include Equity & Law, Fisons, GKN, Viking Oil and ICL, where he became non-executive chairman in 1980. He also served as a BBC governor for five years from 1976. All this had ensured that he was far better known than Christopher Reeves, but had spent too much of his time outside the City banking parlours where careers and fortunes are made. In October 1975 he was looking forward to spending more time at Morgan Grenfell, a bank he had loved and served since 1954. The improving climate at the Ports Council had allowed him to resume a part-time role at Morgan Grenfell, where he was appointed vice-chairman of Morgan Grenfell Holdings and shared an office with Christopher Reeves, who was simultaneously appointed deputy chairman of the bank. Chappell's job was to bring in corporate finance business; Reeves's job was to run the bank. As Chappell put it:

Christopher is paid to be in the office and I am paid to be out of it.[61]

He was out of it rather too often for his own good. His frequent absences, culminating in his appointment to the chair at the troubled computer giant, ICL, from early 1980, meant that he was powerless to halt the seizure of power by Christopher Reeves in December 1979.

The old order at Morgan Grenfell was crumbling. Sir Kenneth Barrington, former doyen of the Corporate Finance Department, retired at the end of 1976. In April 1978 Guy Weston, enriched by the proceeds of the Willis Faber flotation, was posted to Australia as managing director, though he was by then a broken man. Shortly before going he had succumbed to a dreadful personal tragedy. While crossing the Atlantic in his yacht, *Baltica*, his best friend was washed overboard and drowned. Weston searched for him for three days, but he was lost. Though he and Patrick McAfee – another director of the bank sailing with him – were blameless, for their companion had failed to clip himself in, Weston never fully overcame his sense of personal responsibility for the death. One of his replacements as a director in Corporate Finance was the then little-known George Magan. In April 1979 Sir Dallas Bernard was retired, in the time-honoured euphemism, 'to pursue other business interests'.[62] Two months later another unknown, Roger Seelig, became a director.[63] There were secular changes too. The expansion of the banking book had generated an insatiable appetite for fresh capital, necessitating rights issues in 1974 (£6.25 million) and 1978 (£8.2 million). The extra shares began to affect the price of the bank's shares, which were traded on an active internal market. After three years of steadily rising earnings between 1975 and 1977, which saw earnings per share rise from 16.2p to 41.3p, profits dipped sharply in 1978 and earnings per share fell to only 25p.[64] In December Reeves got what he wanted, successfully displacing Mackworth-Young as chief executive. Mackworth-Young and Catto were kicked upstairs as chairmen of the bank and the Holdings Board respectively. Tim Collins, the former chairman of the Holdings Board, was retired altogether, explaining pathetically to the press that the changes would 'centralize decision-making and administration at the Group'.[65] They certainly did. Reeves reduced both the bank and Holdings Board to ciphers and ruled through a seven-man 'management committee' packed with his cronies: Charles Rawlinson, Blaise Hardman and Christopher Whittington. Reeves was just forty-two; the average age of his management committee was forty. None was titled and nobody was very rich, yet.

NOTES

[1] *The Times*, 17 July 1968.
[2] *ibid.* Kathleen Burk, *Morgan Grenfell 1838–1988: The Biography of a Merchant Bank*, Oxford University Press, 1989.
[3] A memorandum prepared for Morgan Grenfell's solicitors in 1971, reads: 'The organisation used to obtain such guarantees (outside the US and UK) was Cinexport S.A., a company based in Paris . . . [which] exaggerated the extent to which guarantees had been or were being obtained' (cited in Burk, *Morgan Grenfell, op. cit.*).
[4] *The Times*, 19 November 1969; *Wall Street Journal*, 11 November 1970.

[5] *ibid.*

[6] Burk, *Morgan Grenfell, op. cit.*

[7] *ibid*. Wall Street Journal, 11, 16 and 23 November 1970; 28 December 1970.

[8] *ibid.*

[9] *ibid*. Kathleen Burk says John Smith cites an eventual loss of £6 million. It is not stated whether or not this figure includes interest forgone.

[10] *ibid.*

[11] *The Times*, 24 January 1970 and 15 February 1972.

[12] *The Times*, 22 January 1970.

[13] *ibid.*

[14] *The Times*, 15 February 1972.

[15] *ibid.*

[16] *The Times*, 12 December 1972.

[17] Margaret Reid, *The Secondary Banking Crisis 1974–75, Its Causes and Course*, Macmillan, 1982.

[18] Leo Pliatzky, *Getting and Spending*, Basil Blackwell, 1982.

[19] World Bank estimate, cited in *Financial Times*, 2 February 1989.

[20] Morgan Grenfell Holdings Limited, Annual Report and Accounts, 1971.

[21] Jacques Attali, *A Man of Influence, Sir Siegmund Warburg, 1902–1982*, Weidenfeld & Nicolson, 1986.

[22] Burk, *Morgan Grenfell, op. cit.*

[23] Zaire and Dubai were major clients in the early 1970s. In 1973 Morgan Grenfell joined Tokai Bank in a $50 million loan to Zaire, which was used to build an airport (*Financial Times*, 28 March 1973). In 1987 the bank wrote off the last of its Third World debt for only £8.7 million (*Standard*, 17 March 1988).

[24] Alan Sked and Christopher Cook, *Post-War Britain*, Penguin, 1979.

[25] *Observer*, Special Report, 30 March 1989.

[26] *The Worldwide Services of Morgan Grenfell*, a bank publicity brochure, 1982.

[27] *Financial Times*, 4 July 1973.

[28] *Financial Times*, 8 November 1973. Morgan Grenfell Holdings Limited, Annual Report and Accounts, 1974.

[29] *Standard*, 13 June 1974.

[30] *Financial Times*, 26 January and 8 May 1973.

[31] *Financial Times*, 26 January 1973.

[32] The loan was negotiated by David Douglas-Home. Fourteen months earlier his father, as Foreign Secretary, had expelled over 100 Russian diplomats from London (in *ibid.*).

[33] *The Worldwide Services of Morgan Grenfell, op. cit.*

[34] Burk, *Morgan Grenfell, op. cit.*
[35] *Australian Financial Review*, 11 May 1978.
[36] *Financial Times*, 28 February 1985.
[37] Burk, *Morgan Grenfell, op. cit.*
[38] *Financial Times*, 1 November 1973.
[39] *ibid.*
[40] Morgan Grenfell Holdings Limited, Annual Report and Accounts, 1974.
[41] *Financial Times*, 5 July 1974.
[42] *Financial Times*, 26 June 1974.
[43] Morgan Grenfell Holdings Limited, Annual Report and Accounts, 1974.
[44] *Standard*, 13 June 1974.
[45] *Financial Times*, 9 July 1974. This article suggests only that Willis Faber bought shares in Morgan Grenfell in 1967. Jacques Attali (*op. cit.*) suggests Morgan Grenfell took a reciprocal shareholding at the same time. Burk, *Morgan Grenfell, op. cit.*
[46] *ibid.* The *Financial Times* suggests Willis Faber's stake in Morgan Grenfell rose from 14 per cent to 22 per cent in the Morgan Grenfell rights issue of that year.
[47] Attali, *op. cit.*
[48] William Kay, *Tycoons*, Piatkus, 1985.
[49] Charles Clay and Bernard Wheble, *Modern Merchant Banking*, Woodhead Faulkner, 1976.
[50] MWP advises on share option schemes and the like, which first became popular in the 1970s. MWP is still associated with Morgan Grenfell. (Morgan Grenfell Holdings Limited, Annual Report and Accounts, 1974.) Burk, *Morgan Grenfell, op. cit.*
[51] This was the subject of litigation. A syndicate of five banks – Morgan Grenfell, Morgan Guaranty Trust, Orion Royal Bank, Bank of Scotland and Bank of Tokyo guaranteed repayment of a $24.3 million Export Credit Guarantee Department supported loan from two National Westminster Bank subsidiaries to Palau, a South Pacific island administered by the United States under a United Nations trusteeship. The loan was used to buy a power station from IPSECO International Power Systems. The five banks had covered themselves by taking out contract-frustration indemnity insurance at Lloyd's, broked by Willis Faber. Palau defaulted on the loan from National Westminster and the banks were called upon, but the Lloyd's underwriters refused to pay up on the grounds that the banks had not disclosed material facts when the policy was agreed. These facts related to a referendum in Palau over the island's continued association with the United States. In

the referendum the islanders voted for a continued association with the United States only if the Americans undertook not to test or store nuclear weapons there, which resulted in a withdrawal of US financial aid, precipitating the default. The Lloyd's underwriters argued that Morgan Grenfell and Willis Faber failed to disclose the risks associated with the referendum at the time that the policy was agreed. The underwriters later settled (*Financial Times*, 26 April 1989).

[52] According to the Willis Faber share register for 25 June 1975, Morgan Nominees of 23 Great Winchester Street owned 26,484 'A' ordinary shares and 43,673 deferred ordinary shares in Willis Faber, making a total of 70,157 ordinary shares in all, or 7 per cent of the ordinary share capital. It is likely that the Morgan Nominees shareholding was inflated by shares owned by clients of the bank, suggesting that the directors' stake was rather less than 7 per cent.

[53] *Financial Times*, 10 November 1976.

[54] Morgan Grenfell Holdings Limited, Annual Report and Accounts, 1975.

[55] Prior to the Introduction, Willis Faber had two classes of ordinary share: 465,000 'A' Ordinary Shares of £1 each and 535,000 deferred ordinary shares of £1 each, making a total nominal ordinary share capital of £1 million. As part of the arrangements for the Introduction, the 'A' and deferred ordinary shares of £1 each were subdivided and converted into four ordinary shares of 25p each. In addition to this, 36 million new ordinary shares were allocated to ordinary shareholders by way of capitalization of share premium and reserves, the monies retained by Willis Faber from issuing shares at a premium to their nominal value of £1 and from profits in past years. Morgan Grenfell's holding of 70,157 ordinary shares (see Note 45) was subdivided by four into 280,628 new ordinary shares of 25p each. To each of these was added nine new ordinary shares by way of the capitalization of share premium and reserves, making 2,806,280 shares in all.

[56] Morgan Grenfell Holdings Limited, Annual Report and Accounts, 1976.

[57] The flotation of Willis Faber cost the then unusually large sum of £550,000. This reflected the fees charged by Peat, Marwick & Mitchell, the reporting accountants, but also compensation to Morgan Grenfell for the loss of its anticipated $\frac{1}{2}$ per cent underwriting fee when the issue was switched from an Offer for Sale to an Introduction (*The Times*, 10 November 1976).

[58] *Financial Times*, 10 November 1976.
[59] *ibid.*
[60] *Observer*, 22 June 1986.
[61] *Financial Times*, 2 October 1975.
[62] *Financial Times*, 5 April 1979.
[63] *Financial Times*, 5 June 1979.
[64] *Financial Times*, 5 December 1979.
[65] *ibid.*

FIVE

Public School Bully Boys

In 1984 Baron Keith of Castleacre, the former Kenneth Keith, creator of Hill Samuel and sometime chairman of Rolls-Royce, told Paul Ferris that he had gone to the City in 1946 to make money:

We were interested in making money, you see ... I'm not certain these fellows are today. They may say they are, but the fact is that damned few have done it. They're interested in bigger and better salaries, bigger and better pensions. They're not so entrepreneurial as they used to be. People are concerned about perks and company cars. I was much more concerned about what heavy metal one has got at the end of the day ... I'm blatantly entrepreneurial ... We were eager young men ... People weren't so worried about dealing with information to which, as Lord Keynes said, you wouldn't normally be entitled. The whole thing has changed ... You've got bigger, monolithic institutions which are less entrepreneurial ... if I was going into the City today, I'd look for something thoroughly entrepreneurial, that was interested in making money ... I suppose, one way and another, I accumulated a million pounds. Somehow, I made ... money.[1]

As head of corporate finance at Hill Samuel, Keith was the star of the aggressive corporate restructuring of the 1950s and 1960s, working for Charles Clore, Jack Cotton and Arnold Weinstock. Christopher Reeves learned his trade under Keith at Hill Samuel during the 1960s and from December 1979 he began to apply the experience at Morgan Grenfell, rewarding what he called 'entrepreneurial ability' and running the bank through the tightly knit Management Committee he and his supporters controlled.[2] It did not include his principal rival, Philip Chappell, who, though cleverer than Reeves, was less tactful. In 1978–9 Chappell had also been much absorbed with the chairmanship and restructuring of the bank's loss-making Australian operations, which kept him out of the London office for longish spells. In 1980 Chappell became the non-executive chairman of ICL, a client of the bank. 'When I took on that job, I was unaware of how near the crisis was . . . I was only there for three months before the flak began to fly,' he recalled.[3] As the company plunged into financial crisis, he was summarily dismissed, returning to Morgan Grenfell with his confidence and his reputation badly shaken. At the bank, colleagues were astonished that he had thought it improper to inform Stephen Badger, the executive handling the ICL account, of the proximity of the crisis. This testified admirably to the rigour of Chappell's code of business ethics, but Christopher Reeves and Bill Mackworth-Young were formally carpeted for their ignorance by the governor of the Bank of England, Gordon Richardson. Legend has it that they were made to stand in his capacious office. Chappell resumed his responsibility for Morgan Grenfell Australia, with a brief to turn it from loss to profit, removing an influential dissident at a crucial time. Reeves's two-tier management structure matched his self-confessed preference for managing via a small group of trusted cronies; he had learned it with the Rifle Brigade, which also taught him to value personal initiative. Thus he made a virtue of his ignorance and neglect. 'We don't want to spend too much time mismanaging ourselves,' he quipped.[4] But the business ethics of the landed class had to be replaced with something. Without proper management controls, at some stage somebody was bound to go native.

Reeves started in January 1980 with one priceless advantage over his former mentor. In 1946 the principal obstacle between Kenneth Keith and a fortune was the fact that he was neither of nor married into a merchant banking family. At Morgan Grenfell the rights issues of 1974 and 1978 had already diluted the family shareholdings and brought in institutional investors more interested in share-price performance than the number of peers and cousins of peers on the Holdings Board. The first had increased Willis Faber's stake in the bank from 14 per cent to 22 per cent, allowing Willis to consolidate Morgan's results into their own for the first time, and Bill Mackworth-Young and Julian Faber swapped seats on each other's boards.[5] The second increased the stake of another long-standing shareholder, the Prudential, to $3\frac{1}{4}$ per cent.[6] Shareholders' funds grew from £6.9 million in 1970 to £45.4 million in 1979.[7] The first share option scheme for directors was introduced in 1974, bringing Reeves, Hardman, Walsh, Whittington and Rawlinson into the fold. None had been to university, let alone Oxbridge, and three – Rawlinson, Whittington and Walsh – were accountants. Hardman, who had replaced Reeves as head of banking, had been a Guards officer; Reeves himself had been factotum to Kenneth Keith. The old partnership was finally dissolved; the meritocrats had arrived. Lacking money of their own, their salaries and share options gave them, in the manner sensed by Lord Keith, a vested interest in increasing the bank's profitability and hence raising the share price. The methods they chose were threefold.

The first was aggressive recruitment of clients for the Corporate Finance Department. Reeves's first choice to handle the brief was Graham Walsh, his Dulwich neighbour. Walsh was very much a self-made man; he left school at seventeen and went straight to the accountancy firm of Harmood, Banner & Co., later absorbed by Deloitte's, where he was articled, enduring a five-year correspondence course in accountancy. He also owed much to Christopher Reeves, who had hired him first when Reeves was still at Hill Samuel, in 1964. They met, he claims, through a mutual love of opera. When Walsh resigned from Hill Samuel in September 1973 in protest at the proposed merger with Slater Walker[8] ('The fact that Hill Samuel would even consider it was enough,' he says), Reeves hired him again.[9] In May 1979 Reeves secured him a slot on the Holdings Board as head of the Corporate Finance Department. This was not a universally popular idea. Patrick Spens, then the driving force of the department, had little respect for Walsh whose hypochondria and fastidiousness had earned him the nickname of 'The Scorer'[10] and had to be persuaded by Reeves to stay on under him. Spens agreed to do so, but for only two years. In any event the matter was postponed, because in June 1979 Walsh was, at the astonishingly early age of thirty-nine, appointed director-general of the Takeover Panel. It was a two-year appointment, allowing Richard Webb a stint as caretaker head. Walsh returned in June 1981 with renewed vigour and a handy knowledge of how the rules of the City Code on Takeovers and Mergers could be warped or bypassed altogether in the interests of a client. 'It gives you a bird's eye view of the business,' as he put it.[11] Armed with this knowledge, Walsh embarked on an explicitly expansionist strategy, recruiting accountants and solicitors heavily and marketing ideas aggressively to clients. In four years he doubled the size of the Corporate Finance Department, forming six teams of eight to nine executives each headed by a director. One six-man team was formed solely to dream up potential deals.[12] This largely took the form of seeking out acquisitive companies that were not already clients of the bank and showering them with takeover propositions.[13] 'We've grown much more aggressive in seeking new clients,'[14] was Walsh's explanation:

At that time it was almost unheard of for one bank to approach another's client. And sometimes they would say, 'Thank you for the idea – we will discuss what you say with our advisers.' But more often than not, because we had taken the trouble to do our homework, they were very interested. And this led to a lot of new business of the kind we were looking for . . . It's very much a business where success breeds success. Your only real advertisement is the volume of business you can handle.[15]

This swashbuckling approach was a marked break with the past, where clients had been expected to approach the bank rather than vice versa, and what was in the interests of the client was assumed to be good for the profitability of the bank. Now what was good for the profitability of the bank took precedence over disinterested advice to the client. It won them eventually a reputation as 'public school bully boys'.[16] Patrick Spens left, bang on time, in July 1982.[17]

The second method was a renewed drive into the Eurobond market, which had been highly profitable during the 1960s and early 1970s. In 1972 Morgan & Cie had pioneered the sterling Eurobond market with a £10 million issue for the Standard Oil Company of Indiana[18] but sterling was too volatile for much to come of it. So the market had been rather neglected by Morgan Grenfell since the prime mover within the bank, John Hedges, had retired on health grounds in 1974. He was replaced immediately with Will Hopper, recruited, as usual, from Hill Samuel, but the first oil-price crisis and the consequent crash nearly destroyed the Eurodollar market as well.[19] It was shifted from the Investment Department, where clients of the bank's fund managers had been conscripted as buyers, to the Corporate Finance Department, where it became an adjunct to their activities, selling a few issues on behalf of the Corporate Finance Department's clients but totally inactive in the secondary markets. Though joint ventures, in the Euro-markets with both Morgan Stanley and Morgan Guaranty were discussed during the 1970s and with Morgan Guaranty as late as October 1978 – nothing came of them. Sir John Stevens had favoured a presence in the secondary markets, but his col-leagues cared little for the kind of person – market-making pioneers such as Julius Strauss and Stanley Ross – that you met there. Of the three salesmen, Barry Cook, Bob Riley and John Hobbs, Cook had been transferred to the foreign-exchange desk and Hobbs had left altogether. The decision to resurrect the operation came from Blaise Hardman, advised by John Forsyth, the egghead chief economist elevated to the board in February 1979.[20] In 1979 they submitted a paper to the board recommending the formation of a separate Eurobond Department which would hugely expand the bank's involve-ment in the market.

This was not foolish. The market was still almost wholly in dollars and the burgeoning Japanese trade surplus was rapidly replacing petrodollars as the biggest and most mobile pool of capital. Unlike Arabs, Japanese investors prefer buying bonds to making loans or leaving money on deposit and they were beginning to make their presence felt in the Euromarkets. Over 600 borrowers had raised over $30 billion in 1977 and 1978, suggesting that the market was in any event liquid enough to trade successfully and capable of renewing itself perennially on reinvestment of interest payments alone. Morgan Grenfell itself had sufficient funds under management by 1979 – £1.8 billion – to be sure of finding a friendly home for some dollar bonds at least.[21] From 1977, the Investment Division had been very successful in attracting management contracts from dollar-based United States pension funds and had also secured a contract to manage a proportion of the vast dollar fortune that was being withdrawn from the Crown Agents by the Sultan of Brunei. Sir Sidney Eburne, who chaired the Crown Agents until 1983, was a former director of the bank, and it was the bank which was invited by the Thatcher Government to advise on the future of the Crown Agents.[22]

Bonds also do not tie up a bank's capital in the same way as loans; ostensibly, they can always be sold to someone else. Most important of all, in October 1979 the incoming Thatcher Government had axed exchange controls, exposing Morgan's natural currency, sterling, to full participation in the Euro-markets for the first time. Trading bonds probably had a sub-liminal appeal for Hardman too; as a former head of foreign-exchange dealing, he regarded himself, and was regarded by his colleagues on the Management Committee, as a rather astute trader in his own right. Forsyth too, having advised the foreign-exchange dealers, in his capacity as chief economist, on the likely course of interest and exchange rates, considered himself a trader of sorts. Unhappily, they never completely grasped that the trading techniques of the foreign-exchange markets – taking positions and waiting for interest and ex-change rates to follow the pattern predicted – were ill-adapted to the Eurobond markets. Nor did they appreciate that it was the relatively unsophisticated nature of the Eurobond market in 1979 that allowed them to enter it, and that this would not persist indefinitely as more banks developed a presence. Whilst they were offered bonds by a variety of market-makers at widely different prices, fund managers were happy enough to shop around. As market-making improved, they tended to buy Eurodollar bonds consistently from those who offered the keenest prices. Without a natural constituency in dollars, Morgan Grenfell was at a disadvantage to the American investment banks. This was not perceived at the time of the formation of the Eurobond Department in June 1979. Instead, there was much optimism as Jonathan Perry, recently exiled to run the New York office, was recalled to London to run the new division. He was told that he need not make a profit for two years.[23]

The third method was headlong international expansion, not simply to sell the bank's traditional skills to new types of customer but to repeat under native conditions the services the bank offered in London. Reeves described it thus:

As I see it, the emphasis will be on expanding internationally in such a way that what we do elsewhere will be what we already do in London ... I don't think representative offices – other than New York – necessarily have an infinite life. We must look very closely at each office and decide whether there is a case for turning it into a trading operation as a sort of mirror image of London.[24]

This was a more exciting departure than it seemed. Until Reeves took charge, Morgan Grenfell's international efforts focused on selling abroad what the bank did best at home: fee-earning advice on how to borrow money or take companies over. Essentially, the logo followed trade and the local markets were largely ignored. Morgan Grenfell's Milan representative office, for example, had been established principally to tap the growing volume of Italian export credit business. This remained its principal function even after it was upgraded to a fully capitalized (200 million lire) subsidiary in June 1982. The first attempt to cut loose in a major way – through the faddish consortium ventures in Hong Kong and Singapore with Indo-suez and in the Eurobond market with Tokai in 1974 – had not worked out, though representatives of both banks lingered on pointlessly in the 'International Advisory Council' until 1987. It was an approach which even Siegmund Warburg, with the unparalleled international contacts derived from spending at least half of every year abroad, had found hard to manage. Yet through clever, if fluid, associations with Kuhn Loeb, Paribas, A. G. Becker and Effectenbank he had maintained an international profile on a slender amount of capital.[25]

There had been much debate at Morgan Grenfell on whether it was best to sell a single service worldwide, managed from London, or to own independent subsidiaries adapted to niches in local markets. Those like Philip Chappell, who were reared in a tradition which abhorred the possibility of a conflict of interest, favoured offering a single corporate finance service around the globe. But the rise to power of Christopher Reeves, with his messianic belief in the virtues of delegation, resolved the debate decisively in favour of the establishment of self-standing subsidiaries. Reeves favoured active trading operations in every major financial centre, complete with local corporate financiers, bankers, bond specialists and fund managers. It was an ambitious but flawed strategy. The old approach, necessarily biased towards former imperial possessions within the sterling area like Australia and Canada, or areas short on financial sophistication, like Eastern Europe or Arabia, had the cardinal virtues of cheapness and familiarity. Its principal defect, especially as the financial power of the United States and Arabia waned and that of Japan waxed, was that it bore little relation to the sources and destinations of world capital. Any bank with serious pretensions in the global market for capital had to have a presence in New York and Tokyo. Yet in both of these markets, each of sufficient size to warrant a presence in bear markets as well as bull, Morgan Grenfell was a puny Johnny-come-lately. The representative office opened in New York in 1974 was hamstrung for seven years while Morgan Grenfell reviewed the inhibitions of its relationship with Morgan Guaranty. Not even a representative appeared in Tokyo until 1981 apparently because the estimated cost – £250,000 a year – was regarded as too high.[26] This was by no means entirely the fault of the management; in both Tokyo and New York the bank faced regulatory impediments, behind which muscle-bound local banks had stockpiled prodigious amounts of capital. The question was whether it was worth trying to catch up.

Reeves thought it was, but the pace at which the strategy was enacted was not really under his control. The speed and manner of entry to almost every overseas market was dictated largely by the attitude of the local regulatory authorities. Though the early success in Singapore – where the joint venture with Indosuez was turned into an independent merchant bank in 1976 – must have encouraged Reeves, the experience was misleading. Morgan Grenfell (Asia) prospered mightily, precisely because there was no regulatory interference and minimal local competition in the foreign exchange, Eurodollar and Asian dollar loan and corporate, project and export finance markets it had tackled. By 1980 it was generating pre-tax profits of SF2.5 million on total assets of SF153 million. Switzerland and France, for example, offered the opposite experience. Though Banque Morgan Grenfell en Suisse S.A.[27] was allowed in 1982 by the Swiss authorities to maintain numbered bank accounts, and has prospered well enough, the Swiss franc bond trading arm, Morgan Grenfell Switzerland S.A. failed to pierce the armour of the major Swiss banking syndicates. Morgan Grenfell France S.A., the Paris subsidiary established in 1980 to provide advice on mergers and acquisitions, succumbed to more insidious forms of protection. Despite some newsworthy successes – like the acquisition in 1983 of Château Lagrange by the Japanese drinks company, Suntory – it has not prospered in a naturally xenophobic country where much of industry is enmeshed with either the state or jealous families.

Australia, though encouraging after a false start, showed

how hard it would be to make an impact in New York or Tokyo. The Anglo-Australian Pty merchant bank in Melbourne, set up by Morgan Grenfell in 1949 as a joint venture with Lazard's and Consolidated Zinc, was thrown together in 1962 with the stockbroker Ian Potter's corporate finance arm, Australian United Corporation (AUC), in which Morgan Grenfell retained a 10 per cent interest until 1977. This inhibited an independent presence, though the bank began to develop one from 1973, opening a representative office in Sydney that year.[28] A proper merchant-banking outlet was not established until 1977 when, following the lead of Schroder Wagg and Hill Samuel, the bank announced that it would sell corporate finance advice in Australia on its own account.[29] In early October 1977, the stake in AUC was sold to Morgan Guaranty for around A$800,000[30] and, following an invitation from the Australian Mutual Provident Society, the proceeds were reinvested a week later in a 25 per cent stake in the insurance company's money-market operations.[31] Lord Catto joined the board of the new company, AMP-Morgan Grenfell, and Guy Weston was installed as managing director of a new, wholly-owned merchant bank, Morgan Grenfell Australia Limited.[32] At first all went well. In May 1978 the London office's experience in the North Sea landed the Australian operation the job of advising Woodside Petroleum Limited, a new company 43 per cent owned by Shell and BP, on raising the finance for an oil and gas exploration project in the North-West Shelf.[33] In 1981 the bank advised on a $1,400 million loan to finance the first phase, then the largest project financing ever raised.[34] It was a major, and highly lucrative, coup, culminating in the flotation of the company in 1985.[35] But Weston was unable to stop the operation losing money. It was this mess that Philip Chappell, freshly sacked from the chair at ICL, was asked by Reeves to clear up in 1982.

Chappell, who visited Australia frequently, and Jamie Dundas, the thirty-year-old managing director sent out from London, were fairly ruthless. They quintupled staff numbers, but of the twenty staff they found on arrival, only three survived. Their first major move came in December 1982. That month they recruited as joint managing director Geoffrey Hill, a burly Australian then running his own entrepreneurial merchant bank, Bancorp Holdings. He brought with him his closest associate, Pat Elliott, and two regional staff, Bill O'Neill in Melbourne and Steve Chapman in Adelaide. His impressive client list included two of Australia's most imaginative entrepreneurs, John Spalvins of Adelaide Steamship and Alan Bond, creator of the ubiquitous Bond Corporation.[36] Merger and acquisition work picked up accordingly. In 1983 Morgan Grenfell Australia helped Griffin Group acquire W. R. Carpenter in one of the largest takeovers in Australian corporate history; another, the A$1.2 billion takeover of Myer Corporation by G. J. Coles in 1985, was the largest ever.[37] A drive into fund management followed. In March 1984 the bank poached four of BT Australia's fund managers, adding A$300,000 to the wage bill overnight, but they succeeded in more than doubling funds under management, from only A$200 million in 1984 to A$450 million in 1986.[38] Neither this quartet nor Bancorp were especially expensive acquisitions, the price of Bancorp in particular being linked to future performance, but in June 1983 the interest in AMP-Morgan Grenfell was sold back to AMP. Links were maintained; Lord Catto, his Australian connections as strong as ever, kept a seat on the AMP board and the bank was still acting for AMP in its controversial takeover of London Life in 1988, but the split reflected the need for additional capital ahead of the deregulation of Australian financial markets initiated by the incoming Hawke Government in 1984. This local Big Bang offered Reeves an ideal testing ground for his concept of global expansion. In August 1984, even before a broker had been bought in London, Morgan Grenfell Australia took a 14.9 per cent stake in a Sydney stockbroker, Hordern, Utz and Bode.[39] Despite his own misgivings about the strategy Reeves had evolved, by early 1985 Philip Chappell was justly proud of what he had built in Australia, and his confidence revived. But in London things were changing. As it turned out, the resurrection of Morgan Grenfell Australia was the last major task he undertook for the bank to which he had devoted his working life.

The Corporate Finance Department became the flagship of Morgan Grenfell's businesses in the 1980s. This was part chance; the early 1980s saw a merger wave which exceeded even the officially sanctioned ructions of the 1960s. The 1970s were blighted by the inflation and industrial stagnation which followed the oil shock and, with takeover activity quiescent, Morgan Grenfell's Corporate Finance Department had earned an unexceptional living underwriting loan stocks and arranging rights issues. In the five years between 1972 and 1976, the bank acted in only 101 takeovers worth just £1 billion; yet in a single year in the 1980s (1986) it acted in 111 takeovers worth £15.2 billion.[40] In the year before Reeves took over in 1980, the bank had advised just fifteen clients in bids worth the paltry total of £341 million. So in one sense the aggressive stance adopted thereafter was a necessary one; all Walsh did was rediscover the boldness Harcourt and Barrington had summoned up in the battle for Gallaher in 1968. But signs of impatient aggression were evident long before the discovery of the two companies – BTR and Guinness – whose ambitions matched exactly those of the new regime at the bank. The prolonged but ultimately successful acquisition between 1976 and 1978 of Beyer Peacock by the oil-rich Arab, Sheikh Mohamed Y. al Bedrawi, managed by Patrick Spens, attracted criticism.[41] Here, the interests of the client prevailed above other considerations and this was to become a familiar theme in the years ahead. When, in January 1979, Stenhouse floated its industrial operations on the stock market as Caledonian Holdings, Morgan Grenfell advised its client, London & Midland Industrials, to apply heavily for shares. The strategic stake thus acquired was then used as a springboard to mount a full takeover bid.[42] In this case the lure of invention proved stronger than the pull of tradition. This, too, became characteristic. Later the same year the bank abetted Ladbroke's in a reconstruction of its shareholdings in subsidiary companies designed to distance the parent company from its casino interests, which were being probed by the Gaming Board, while retaining the profits from them for shareholders.[43] It was a clear attempt to 'negotiate' with the authorities, including the police. This time it ended ignominiously and unsuccessfully, with Philip Chappell giving evidence in court on behalf of Ladbroke's; in some of the bids to come it worked rather better.[44] In May 1980 the bank literally *bought* Asprey & Co., the silversmiths, for £7 million to save it from a hostile bid by Dunhill, sponsored by a dissident Asprey family faction.[45] It was George Magan's first major triumph and it won him a place on the Asprey board. His next major success, BTR's victory over Thomas Tilling in 1983, made Morgan Grenfell undisputed takeover champions of the City of London for the next five years.

BTR is an abbreviation of the British Tyre & Rubber Company, a dowdy conglomerate run by the skinflint Owen Green, who created it out of odds and ends in the engineering and rubber industries that he had picked up from Jim Slater.[46] BTR is a company fit for accountants to work in, a predatory conglomerate acquiring businesses, imposing cost controls, cutting out the dead wood and selling the bits it does not want but, like Hanson, definitely post-Slater. Green was not an asset-stripper like Slater and was genuinely more interested in running businesses than in acquiring them. Morgan Grenfell could not have invented a client better suited to its new approach. Graham Walsh had also acted for BTR for over twenty years.[47] The relationship was resumed modestly enough. In 1981 Morgan Grenfell helped BTR buy Serck Limited, for £25 million. Walsh secured for BTR an option on 29 per cent of Serck and bought 15 per cent of the company in the open market at the same time. 'BTR controlled 44 per cent of the stock before anyone knew it,' Walsh boasted.[48] It was after that that George Magan took to Owen Green the idea of taking over Thomas Tilling, the former omnibus company, now an ailing industrial conglomerate with interests spanning Pilkington Tiles, Heinemann publishing, Cornhill Insurance and Pretty Polly tights. The timing was impeccable. British industry had been put through the wringer in the early years of the Thatcher Government by a combination of high interest rates and a strong pound. The first signs of an industrial recovery could be glimpsed, and even Tilling was on the mend, but the long recession had stretched the old loyalties of institutional shareholders to incumbent managements to break-ing point. They were looking for more vigorous management. Magan knew this, Green liked his idea and together Green, Magan, Walsh and Guy Dawson, a young but rising executive in the Corporate Finance Department, began preparing a bid. The offer document, when it came, played the management card for all it was worth.

In April 1983 George Magan was still only thirty-eight. Though avaricious and deeply ambitious, he was markedly less relaxed with the press than his co-star Roger Seelig, preferring to coin a clever or literate phrase rather than drop an indiscretion. Some attribute his reticence to his family. His father, Bill Magan, was a brave and distinguished soldier who had served on the Northwest Frontier and in Persia, where he had lived rough with the natives, speaking their languages. He subse-quently joined MI5, working with Peter Wright in Cyprus in the late 1950s.[49] George was the only member of the family to go into the City. Of his two brothers, one committed suicide and the other became a monk. His mother, though, is an entrepreneurial sort, creating the highly successful Cuckoo Designs company in Tunbridge Wells after Bill's retirement from MI5. Schooled at Winchester, George skipped university and trained as an accountant at Peat, Marwick & Mitchell instead. After a spell at Kleinwort Benson under Charles Ball and John Gillum, he joined Morgan Grenfell.[50] Magan felt uncomfortable at first in the snobbish atmosphere of Morgan Grenfell and, after two glum and ineffectual years, he came close to leaving the bank. He was only revitalized by an intervention by Patrick Spens.[51] Perhaps as a result of this narrow escape, he became almost a caricature of a merchant banker. A diminutive and bespectacled figure, Magan sported suits with the stripes placed suitably far apart, a gold watch-chain and Brylcreem (or some similar concoction supplied by his Bond Street barber, Truefitt & Hill) in his hair, an affectation that earned him the nickname 'Teddy'.[52] He revelled in the freebooting atmosphere Reeves had allowed to develop:

We are not the sort of bank employing two or three hundred people with nice lunches, mahogany furniture, comfortably watching the world go by.[53]

Tilling, he must have thought, was like that. The campaign to take it over was plotted with great secrecy, lest bid speculation drove the price out of BTR's reach. Despite the mounting excitement inside the Corporate Finance Department, which was sustained throughout the bid, Tilling suspected nothing at all when the battle for its future began on Tuesday 5 April 1983 with a dawn raid on its shares.

At 11.30 a.m. the same morning Owen Green and his chairman, Sir David Nicholson, went round to Tilling's head-quarters to tell the chairman, Sir Patrick Meaney, what they had done.[54] Cazenove had been instructed by Morgan Grenfell to buy up to 14.99 per cent of Tilling in the market, the maximum then permitted without triggering a compulsory bid for the whole company. In the event, they netted only 6 per cent, but it still cost BTR £30 million. Meaney, meanwhile, had been deserted by his usual bankers, Schroder Wagg; they were acting for Hanson Trust, who had defeated Tilling in a three-cornered fight for the battery maker, Berec.[55] They were replaced with S. G. Warburg, rekindling a rivalry that had smouldered since the aluminium war of 1959 and which, for Morgan Grenfell at least, seemed at times to make BTR and Tilling almost incidental to the battle. Though Cazenove stayed in the market for a few days, it picked up few shares in a market anticipating a full bid. This duly came on Tuesday 12 April; it was worth £576 million. In money terms, it was the largest bid ever attempted on the London Stock Exchange, dwarfing even Grand Metropolitan's £378 million (£1.38 billion in 1983 prices) takeover of Watney Mann in 1972. The merger boom had started, the battle for Tilling fixing a mood which was to engulf the City for the next five years.

Bids had long been fierce but this was the first to become publicly acrimonious. Meaney, and much of the financial press, thought Tilling would brush off the bid. 'Even if Owen Green went to 240p, that wouldn't get us,' claimed Meaney.[56] Tilling's slogan – 'Don't Sell Tilling Short – Don't Sell Tilling At All' – was trumpeted in full-page advertisements in the quality press, whilst the Morgan Grenfell camp assiduously courted sympathetic financial journalists. At one stage, Morgan's let it be known that the Takeover Code would not allow BTR to carry on buying unless it acquired at least 30 per cent of Tilling, forcing Tilling to contend that they were trying to panic shareholders into accepting the bid. This ploy was coupled with heavy buying of Tilling stock in the market, which gave the predator nearly a quarter of the company by the time the bid was increased to £655 million on 17 May. The Morgan approach, though dangerous, was indubitably more effective. One Tilling slogan – 'The Sum Of Our Parts Makes Us Strong' – seemed to miss BTR's point entirely; it was discreetly dropped altogether when in late May the Tilling management announced plans to sell for £175 million all or part of its two most marketable subsidiaries, the healthcare group Inter Med and Cornhill Insurance, the Test Match sponsors. It was a dreadful error, validating instantly everything that BTR had said and giving it a platform to repeat the message, since the sales needed approval from three-quarters of Tilling's shareholders at a time when BTR controlled over a quarter of the company.[57] In keeping with the austere image of its creator, and in stark contrast to the lavish and imperious defence of Sir Patrick Meaney, BTR stuck thereafter to its own more prosaic message in press advertisements: 'The increased BTR offer gives an immediate and massive 95 per cent increase in Tilling's capital value. The offer is final. Accept the BTR bid now.'[58] Despite the verve and brass of the BTR campaign the result was in doubt to the end. The increased offer was timed to expire on the eve of the General Election of 9 June, adding to the uncertainty of wavering shareholders. The lobbying of the thirty or so undecided institutional shareholders was intense. On 6 June the Prudential, a major shareholder in Morgan Grenfell which also held 2.5 per cent of Tilling, faltered and announced it would support 'incumbent management . . . of good standing'.[59] After this, most commentators predicted a late swing of sentiment to Tilling, but they were mistaken. On 8 June Morgan Grenfell announced that BTR had won 61 per cent support in a bid even George Magan conceded 'could have gone either way'.[60] The same could not be said of the General Election. The next day Mrs Thatcher won a parliamentary majority of 144 seats.

The twin victories of Owen Green and Mrs Thatcher were more than coincidence. The City, like the country, had endorsed the revolution in attitudes the Prime Minister had brought about. No company, however large and established, was safe any more. The total value of takeovers in the City of London climbed from £2.34 billion in 1983 to £5.24 billion in 1984[61] and to £9.8 billion in 1985.[62] In the first half of 1986 alone this figure was doubled, with £19.2 billion of bids either completed or still outstanding[63] and by the end of the year bidders had spent £25.13 billion on 1,323 public and private companies.[64] For Morgan Grenfell, which had positioned itself for an outcome of exactly this kind, it was a bonanza. In 1983, the bank advised on only 17 takeovers worth £1.3 billion; in 1984 on 32 worth £2.4 billion; in 1985 on 92 worth £8.8 billion; in 1986 on 111 worth £15.2 billion. In the market the vanquished Tilling was the best possible advertisement for ambitious businessmen. In November 1983 Jeffrey Sterling, newly installed as chief executive at P & O, then under bid threat from Trafalgar House, sacked the company's traditional bankers, Schroder Wagg, and switched to Morgan Grenfell. He explained why:

Having taken over, I decided I wanted to work with people more in tune with my style.[65]

He was doubtless partly persuaded by Blaise Hardman, then a

non-executive director of P & O. The account was given to the man of the hour, George Magan. Sterling was the first of many to switch. The 1981–2 edition of *Crawford's Directory of City Connections* recorded Morgan Grenfell as having 98 corporate clients; the 1986 edition counted 143. Morgan Grenfell's own estimates were higher, at 100 and 163 respectively.[66] Among the most spectacular defections were Jaguar,[67] newly privatized by Hill Samuel in the summer of 1984 and Boot's the chemist, which appointed Morgan Grenfell as its advisers in July 1985.[68]

The battle for Tilling had generated tremendous excitement within the bank as well as outside it. It had been the first major contested bid for an old and revered name; for the first time institutions had deserted an established Board; and the nose of Warburg had been bloodied. In its aftermath, an insolent pride took root, leading to aggressive tactics and the adoption of aquisitive clients. Even during the Tilling bid, an Illinois circuit court stopped BTR acquiring Tilling shares in the United States on the grounds that disclosure to the authorities was incomplete.[69] In a bid launched on the same day as the BTR bid for Tilling, Roger Seelig had agreed to act for Marshall Cogan and Steven Swid, two unusual Americans who wanted to acquire Sotheby's. Though their vehicle, General Felt/Knoll International (GFI), did acquire a 29.9 per cent stake, the bid was eventually referred to the Monopolies and Mergers Commission after intensive lobbying of the Trade Secretary, Lord Cockfield, by Sotheby's advisers, S. G. Warburg. The referral caused considerable surprise at the time, since the Office of Fair Trading had cleared it. Warburg, using the political lobbyists GJW, had cleverly lobbied the Trade Secretary, Lord Cockfield, while Morgan Grenfell concentrated on the Office of Fair Trading.[70] Sotheby's eventually fell to an American shopping-centre millionaire, Alfred Taubman, who was widely understood to have bought it as a birthday present for his wife. In September 1983 there were furious exchanges with Kleinwort Benson when Morgan Grenfell declared victory for its client, Pritchard Services, in the bid for the laundry group, Spring Grove. Kleinwort claimed to the Takeover Panel that unexercised share options reduced Pritchard's support below the crucial 50 per cent mark, a claim irreverently dismissed by Morgan's as 'absolute rubbish'.[71]

It was in the long battle for control of the insurer, Eagle Star, that Morgan Grenfell first established its reputation for testing the takeover rules to the limit. Throughout this prolonged bid, which lasted on and off for two and a half years, the intentions of Morgan Grenfell's client, Allianz Versicherungs, Germany's biggest insurance group, remained resolutely inscrutable. To some extent, this reflected the sensitivity of the target. Hitherto British insurance companies, like banks, had been regarded as untouchable, not least by foreigners. Allianz recognized this and had talked patiently about an equity stake and joint ventures abroad with the Eagle Star board, chaired by Sir Denis Mountain, since the autumn of 1980 without overt aggression. This was an unusual strategy in Britain, though less so in Europe, where cross-holdings of equity are often used to cement business relationships. The talks led nowhere and Morgan's instructed Rowe & Pitman to barge into Eagle Star in a dawn raid in June 1981, netting 14.9 per cent of the company. The raid was accompanied by a tender offer aimed at raising this to 29.9 per cent, the maximum allowable without a formal offer for the whole company. This was almost completely successful and secured for Allianz 28.1 per cent of the company. Sir Denis was asked again if he would co-operate with Allianz abroad, a suggestion coupled this time with a demand for another 10 per cent of the equity and two seats on the board. The result was still stalemate. With nothing to show for the £100 million or so that they had spent, the Allianz board became understandably exasperated. They did not want to buy the whole company, yet they could not buy any more than 30 per cent without the agreement of the Eagle Star shareholders and board, which was not forthcoming. After briefly considering pulling out and buying Cornhill instead – now in the gift of Owen Green at BTR – they agreed with George Magan to an offensive tactic not seen in a major hostile bid since the battle for Gallaher's in 1968: a partial bid.[72]

Since Gallaher's, the customs, practices and rules of the hostile takeover business in London had dictated that one company bidding for another must bid for it all. Yet on 19 October 1983 Allianz offered to buy Eagle Star in a manner clearly designed to appeal to Eagle Star shareholders over the heads of their board, but not with total success in mind. The size of the bid – £692 million – narrowly eclipsed the four-month-old bid for Tilling as the largest takeover ever made in London, but the price per share (£5) was 22p short of the prevailing share price. Morgan's clearly did not expect the bid to succeed; it admitted as much in the accompanying press blurb, which stipulated that the bid would lapse unless Allianz secured the consent of 90 per cent of Eagle Star shareholders. In this way Morgan's hoped to gradually pick up another 10 per cent or so of the company without the consent of the board. It was an ingenious way round the 30 per cent rule, but in early November it was rudely overturned. Unknown to George Magan, two days after the Allianz partial bid Sir Denis Mountain was approached by Patrick Sheehy, the chairman of BAT Industries, then looking for a 'fourth leg' to add to its tobacco, retailing and paper businesses.[73] The Eagle Star chairman was receptive to Sheehy's entreaties and when BAT, advised by Lazard's, bid £792 million for his company, he recommended it to shareholders, who later approved it. Surprised, Magan played for time, announcing on 8 November that Allianz was considering raising its offer, pending the release of further financial information by Eagle Star and clearance for a full bid from the Trade Secretary, Norman Tebbit. This prevented BAT acquiring any further stock in the market, but it broke Rule 8 of the Takeover Code, which stipulates that 'when a firm intention to make an offer is announced, the terms of the offer must be disclosed'. Despite this, Magan repeated the treatment when, on 28 November, Allianz finally made a full offer of £900 million which was capped within thirteen minutes by a £913 million revised offer from BAT.[74] Again, the market dried up, but this time Magan had given a hostage to fortune: Allianz had said it would not advance on £900 million.

Lazard's, led by vice-chairman Tom Manners and rising star Marcus Agius, complained to the Takeover Panel about Magan's tactics. The Panel concurred, telling Morgan Grenfell to clarify Allianz's intentions by 9.30 a.m. the following Monday. As the deadline passed, Morgan Grenfell announced that Allianz would increase its offer, but not until it had met the board of Eagle Star and received assurances about the future. This was obviously playing for time and Lazard's, joined this time by Eagle Star's advisers, Hill Samuel, complained to the Panel again. Surprisingly, the Panel was unmoved. Sir Denis Mountain wrote to the Allianz chairman, Dr Wolfgang Schieren, to complain that his tactics had resulted in a 'loss of business and staff morale'.[75] The meeting was held on Thursday 8 December when George Magan and Philip Evans took two Allianz directors, Dr Bierich and Herr Van den Burg, to see Sir Denis Mountain and three members of his board. Sir Robert Clark of Hill Samuel was also there.[76] There took place, in the words of George Magan, a 'very full, frank and confidential discussion'. After it Sir Denis told the press that the ball was back in Allianz's court; Magan, in one of the witticisms for which he was fast becoming famous, riposted that 'nobody knows where the ball is'.[77] Relations grew strained and Mountain, backed by the Panel, told Allianz and Morgan Grenfell to put up or shut up:

I feel the time has come where they have got to do something. A takeover of this size dragging on for this long is not right. No further meetings with Allianz are planned. It is now up to them to decide what they are going to do.[78]

On Friday 9 December Magan pleaded with the Panel for more time.[79] That day a series of crisis meetings was held between Hill Samuel and Morgan Grenfell. Over the weekend of 10–11 December Magan flew to Munich to tell Allianz that the Panel's patience was running out. They considered a technical swerve, increasing their bid by 1p, but rejected the idea as too controversial. On the Monday the Panel met Morgan Grenfell, Lazard's and Hill Samuel separately.[80] It warned Morgan Grenfell that it had thus far reacted too slowly to its strictures and that Allianz must up its offer by 9.30 a.m., Wednesday 14 December. Allianz duly raised its offer by £20 million, to £920 million. It was capped within an hour by BAT, who offered £990 million. Choosing his words carefully, Magan said 'the battle must be seen to be continuing'[81] and urged Eagle Star shareholders not to sell to BAT. This was too much, even for the Panel, and on 21 December it finally imposed its will. The three banks were called in and told they had until 4.30 p.m. on 30 December to work out their final offers.[82] It involved a minor alteration to the rule requiring offers to be posted by the 46th day of a bid. Absurdly, Magan protested at the 'major alteration' to rules which he had himself apparently regarded with contempt:

We are very surprised that the Panel is taking a route which involves sealed tenders being made on a final closing date in a major bid of this sort . . . It has become a sort of Russian roulette.[83]

The following day Allianz matched BAT's latest offer of £934 million. Magan conceded that this was a surrender to 'certain pressures' from the Panel, who insisted that Allianz should 'up their offer or withdraw'.[84] In the event, neither Allianz nor BAT had the stomach for Russian roulette. Allianz made the first move on the Wednesday before Christmas, despatching a 'well known personality in the German political and economic world' to see Patrick Sheehy, who flew to Munich immediately for talks with the Allianz board. These were resumed on the Wednesday after Christmas, 28 December, and over the next two days they hammered out in Munich and London the rudiments of a deal, which they made public on 30 December. Allianz withdrew, advised by Magan that BAT was paying too much, and BAT upped its offer to £968 million, allowing Allianz to sell its 30 per cent shareholding to them for £7 a share. So while the promised shoot-out never took place,

Morgan Grenfell was able to exact satisfaction even from this apparent defeat. Its delaying tactics had not won it the prize, but they had forced BAT to pay £172 million more than it had originally intended, most of which went straight to Allianz, who collected a profit of £163 million on its stake.[85] Allianz had successfully doubled the stock-market value of Eagle Star in just two years, driving the bidding up to twenty-eight times its 1982 earnings. Magan hinted cheekily that in the end Allianz were not serious bidders at all:

We were all along alert not to let valour get the better of discretion.[86]

The *Financial Times* noted the darker side of this quip. Morgan Grenfell had advised Eagle Star shareholders not to sell in the market, though the price had reached £7.16 at one point in December, as a fresh bid from Allianz was expected. Now Allianz itself had settled for only £7 a share. The panel, it thought, should ponder deeply 'the desirability of vague coat-trailing announcements from a bidder determined to keep the share price of the target company out of the reach of a rival.'[87]

All this excitement completely overshadowed the humdrum work of the Corporate Finance Department, which in 1983 overtook S. G. Warburg as the biggest underwriter of rights issues, handling 19 worth £485 million.[88] But even in its routine business, the bank was acting for a type of client not readily associated with the ponderous ritual of a merchant bank like Morgan Grenfell. Between 1983 and 1985 it floated on the London Stock Exchange the advertising agencies Boase Massimi Pollitt and Lowe Howard Spink Campbell Ewald, the record retailer Our Price, the Surrey estate agents Mann & Co and the discotheque and party organizers, Juliana's Holdings. The offering circular for Lowe Howard Spink Campbell Ewald failed to disclose the conviction of the chairman, Frank Lowe, in a case in 1980, an omission labelled 'arrogance of the worst kind' by one newspaper'.[89] Adhering perhaps to the letter rather than the spirit of the law, Morgan's argued that the omission contravened no regulation. George Magan even joined the board of one advertising agency, Wight, Collins, Rutherford, Scott. In 1986 the bank floated Virgin Group, a disparate entertainments company involved in cheap air travel, rock records, book publishing and condoms etc, and run by the hirsute balloonist Richard Branson, a compulsive showman who was ill-advised to approach the stock market. After it became evident that the City preferred steadily rising earnings to his hunches about the next development in youth culture, in 1988 Branson took his company private again, arguing that the flotation had been an expensive mistake (this time using Samuel Montagu).

One activity – privatization – was notable only for its absence. After the Thatcher Government took office in June 1979, this rapidly became a major business for the City. By the end of 1988 the British taxpayer had paid out some £660 million in fees to City firms, mainly for underwriting shares in the former state firms.[90] Kleinwort Benson has been involved in nine sales, where fees have totalled £38 million, and Rothschild's has been involved in five worth £23 million.[91] Much of this income has been redistributed to the investment institutions which sub-underwrote the issues, but it was a potentially lucrative business. In fact, Morgan Grenfell arranged the first major privatization in February 1982, the offer for sale for £69 million of the government-owned radiochemicals company, Amersham International, which earned fees of £900,000.[92] After this, the bank was confined to the role of underwriter in the major privatizations of British Aerospace, Britoil, BP, Cable & Wireless, Enterprise Oil, British Telecom and British Gas. The most prestigious accounts – Telecom and Gas – went to Kleinwort Benson. The reasons for this are unclear, though certainly there was sharp criticism that Amersham had been badly underpriced. There was also the sale organized by Morgan Grenfell in 1983 of twenty-one British Rail hotels, selling some of them to a consortium of financial institutions that formed Gleneagles Hotels. This company was subsequently taken over by a long-standing Morgan Grenfell client, the Bell's whisky company, in February 1984, sparking suggestions that Morgan Grenfell had somehow 'delivered' the hotels to a favourite client.[93] Perhaps an eagle eye or elephantine memory in Downing Street noted that although the bank gave £95,000 to the Conservative Party between 1983 and 1985, Bill Mackworth-Young had in January 1981 appointed the new Social Democratic Party's leading light, Roy Jenkins, to a part-time board position after he returned from Brussels and in 1983 sent a personal cheque to the nascent SDP.[94] Worse, in September 1983 he invited the retiring Department of Industry mandarin, Sir Peter Carey, to join the board. As Permanent Secretary, Carey had handled the earliest privatizations of Jaguar, British Aerospace and Cable & Wireless without noticeable enthusiasm.

The real explanation was probably more prosaic. Competitors reported that the arrogant manner of Morgan Grenfell staff at presentations was not supported by a comparable amount of homework and they were simply outclassed. Once the arrogance spilt into insolent mockery of most forms of authority in the City, culminating in the Guinness scandal, it was simply unthinkable that the government could use Morgan Grenfell. The bank made a virtue of this, arguing that privatization work was unprofitable. Often it was, but both Kleinwort and Rothschild's have used their experience with conspicuous success to market themselves at home and abroad, particularly in the developing world. David Suratgar, the Persian Oxford-educated lawyer responsible for marketing Morgan Grenfell's services to the developing world, certainly regarded the bank's lack of privatization work as a weakness. The head of Morgan Grenfell's Paris office, Jean-Pierre Souviron, a former Directeur Général de l'Industrie under Giscard d'Estaing and Directeur Délégué at the state-owned electronics company, Matra, was well placed to secure privatization business in France after the right-wing election victory in 1986.[95] Though he secured work on the privatization of Compagnie Générale des Constructions Téléphoniques in December 1986, this was small beer compared with Kleinwort, which worked on two of the major privatizations in France. Kleinwort was also appointed financial adviser to British Gas and Associated British Ports after handling their stock-market flotations.

Morgan Grenfell's approach to the takeover boom was not a reflective one. Few questions were asked of anyone, provided they made money. This they certainly did, earning sums of unprecedented magnitude for the bank. Earnings from merger and acquisition work soared from 14 per cent of Morgan Grenfell's total revenues in 1981 to 32 per cent in 1985[96] and actual earnings increased tenfold from around £3 million a year in the 1970s to over £30 million a year by the mid-1980s.[97] The first £100,000 fee had been charged in the mid-1970s; in 1983 the BTR/Tilling bid alone had yielded fees and commissions worth £4 million. By the time of the Guinness bid for Distillers in 1986, these had risen to £60 million.[98] The remuneration of directors kept pace. In 1979 the highest-paid director earned just £44,000 and no other director of the Holdings Board earned over £40,000. The 36 directors of the bank shared £1.5 million, or an average of roughly £42,000 a head.[99] By 1986, the last year before the bank was overtaken by a great nemesis, the highest-paid director was earning £475,317 and thirty-five other directors earned over £100,000. Between them the forty-six directors collected £10.37 million, or £225,000 a head.[100] (That year, Christopher Reeves earned £310,000.[101] Of course, their responsibilities had increased, not least in terms of the numbers of people they had to manage, which soared from 639 in 1979 to nearly 2,700 in 1986, of whom 760 were based overseas, but there was no conspicuous change of management style, and preferment continued to depend on a mixture of patronage and success. As executives approached a directorship, they were showered with shares and share options. Gavin Lickley, a young director who made heavy profits in the leasing business, owned just 132 shares in Morgan Grenfell in 1981, but 10,532 by 1985. The number of share options he was granted rose from 13,000 to 60,333 in the same period. Giorgio Cefis, an expert in Italian export finance, increased his shareholding from 80,110 shares and 15,000 options in 1981 to 216,021 shares and 65,333 options in 1985. These represented not inconsiderable sums of money when the bank was offered for sale to the public at £5 a share in 1986. Reeves's approach to management, which blended Keith's 'heavy metal' with the wide discretion given to officers of the Rifle Brigade, had unintended consequences. It allowed takeover 'stars' to emerge, investing the business with a glamour foreign to its real nature of endless number-crunching and mindnumbing adherence to the intricate provisions of the Companies Acts and the Takeover Code. Roger Seelig began to generate his own business deals, using the department merely as a processing service. Clients felt that they were receiving second-class treatment if they were not allotted George Magan or Roger Seelig. The emergence of this pair as the 'stars' of the department undoubtedly made takeover battles more gladiatorial; it sharpened resentments between departments within the bank; it undermined the morale of their duller confrères; and it reduced luckless clients, as one observer put it, to 'a football field around which the players run'.[102] Reeves himself had a favourite, telling a colleague that 'if I had to choose between Roger and George, I'd pick Roger'.[103] More importantly, as senior management – and Christopher Reeves in particular – became increasingly caught up in the false glamour of takeovers, the bank was unbalanced at the very moment in its history when it was seeking to broaden its earning power in the securities markets. Corporate financiers, among whom the most vociferous were Roger Seelig and George Magan, argued that they could work for six months to earn the bank £1 million which could be lost in six minutes by a teenage bond- or share-dealer. It was a powerful argument which Reeves never comprehensively countered, and it does much to explain Morgan Grenfell's tentative approach to the momentous changes unleashed by Big Bang, the liberation of the London stock market that was set in motion in the late summer of 1983.

NOTES

[1] Paul Ferris, *Gentlemen of Fortune*, Weidenfeld & Nicolson, 1984.
[2] *Business*, July 1986.
[3] *Planned Savings*, July 1988.
[4] *Financial Times*, 29 December 1979.
[5] *Financial Times*, 9 July 1974.
[6] *Financial Times*, 18 April 1978.
[7] Morgan Grenfell Holdings Limited, Annual Report and Accounts, 1971 and 1979.
[8] *Sunday Telegraph*, 20 May 1979.
[9] *Acquisitions Monthly*, January 1986.
[10] *The Observer Magazine*, 30 July 1989
[11] *Wall Street Journal*, 12 April 1983.
[12] *Acquisitions Monthly*, January 1986.
[13] *Financial Weekly*, 27 September 1985.
[14] *Wall Street Journal* 12 April 1983.
[15] *Sunday Times*, 29 December 1985.
[16] Martin Green, banking analyst at Smith New Court, quoted in the *Wall Street Journal*, 24 October 1986.
[17] *Financial Times*, 9 July 1982.
[18] Ian M. Kerr, *A History of the Eurobond Market*, Euromoney Publications, 1984.
[19] *Financial Times*, 17 October 1974.
[20] *Financial Times*, 1 February 1979.
[21] *Financial Times*, 1 April 1980 and Morgan Grenfell Holdings Limited, Annual Report and Accounts, 1979.
[22] Brunei's General Reserve Fund was managed by a committee whose membership included Lord Catto. It amounted to $13.4 billion at the start of 1983. Morgan Grenfell shares its management with James Capel, Citibank, Morgan Guaranty, Daiwa, Nomura and Wardley. In January 1984 Morgan Grenfell was asked by the government to advise on the feasibility of privatizing the Crown Agents (*Sunday Telegraph*, 26 June 1983, *Guardian*, 19 January 1984, *Daily Mail*, 16 March 1984, *Far Eastern Economic Review*, 16 May 1985). The Sultan's investment advisers have included figures as diverse as Lord Shawcross and the Egyptian Al Fayed brothers, owners of Harrod's. 'Tiny' Rowland, chairman of Lonrho, alleges that the Sultan supplied the money with which the Al Fayeds bought Harrod's (*A Hero From Zero*, Lonrho, 1988), an allegation supported, if not substantiated, by a government report on the takeover (*Observer*, 30 March 1989).

23 *Financial Times*, 1 April 1980; Kathleen Burk *Morgan Grenfell 1838–1988: The Biography of a Merchant Bank*, Oxford University Press, 1989.
24 *Financial Times*, 29 December 1979.
25 Jacques Attali, *A Man of Influence: Sir Siegmund Warburg, 1902–1982*, Weidenfeld & Nicolson, 1986.
26 Burk, *Morgan Grenfell, op. cit.*
27 *Financial Times*, 11 February 1981.
28 *Financial Times*, 12 February 1973.
29 *Financial Times*, 26 October 1977.
30 *Financial Times*, 19 October 1977.
31 *Daily Telegraph*, 26 October 1977; Burk, *Morgan Grenfell, op. cit.*
32 *Australian Financial Review*, 26 October 1977.
33 *Australian Financial Review*, 11 May 1978.
34 *The Worldwide Services of Morgan Grenfell*, a bank publicity brochure, 1982.
35 *Australian Financial Review*, 10 May 1985.
36 *Australian Financial Review*, 14 December 1982.
37 Morgan Grenfell Holdings Limited, Annual Report and Accounts, 1983 and 1985; *The Services of Morgan Grenfell*, a bank publicity brochure, 1986.
38 *Australian Financial Review*, 13 March 1984; Morgan Grenfell Australia Limited, Annual Report, 1986.
39 *Australian Financial Review*, 16 August 1984.
40 Morgan Grenfell Group plc, Annual Report and Accounts, 1986.
41 *Sunday Times*, 2 July 1978.
42 *Daily Express*, 2 February 1979.
43 *Daily Telegraph*, 10 October 1979.
44 *Financial Times*, 15 November 1979.
45 *Birmingham Post*, 15 May 1980.
46 Ivan Fallon and James Srodes, *Takeovers*, Hamish Hamilton, 1987.
47 *Acquisitions Monthly*, January 1987.
48 *Wall Street Journal*, 12 April 1983.
49 Peter Wright, *Spycatcher*, Heinemann Australia, 1987.
50 *Sunday Times*, 27 January 1985.
51 *The Observer Magazine*, August 1989.
52 *Business*, July 1986; Fallon and Srodes, *op. cit.*
53 *Sunday Times*, 27 January 1985.
54 *Financial Times*, 6 April 1983.
55 Fallon and Srodes, *op. cit.*
56 *Daily Express*, 9 May 1983.

[57] *The Times*, 26 May 1983.
[58] *ibid.*
[59] *The Times*, 7 June 1983.
[60] *The Times*, 9 June 1983.
[61] *Acquisitions Monthly*, March 1985.
[62] Fallon and Srodes, *op. cit.*
[63] *Acquisitions Monthly*, July 1986.
[64] *Acquisitions Monthly*, December 1986.
[65] *Financial Times*, 8 November 1983.
[66] Morgan Grenfell Group plc, Offer of Ordinary Shares by Tender, Prospectus, June 1986.
[67] *Daily Mail*, 14 August 1984.
[68] *Sunday Times*, 28 July 1985.
[69] *Wall Street Journal*, 25 April 1983.
[70] *Financial Times*, 6 May 1983.
[71] *Daily Telegraph*, 29 September 1983.
[72] *Financial Times*, 20 October 1983.
[73] *Financial Times*, 3 November 1983.
[74] *Financial Times*, 3 January 1984.
[75] *Financial Times*, 9 December 1983.
[76] *Financial Times*, 9 December 1983.
[77] *ibid.*
[78] *Financial Times*, 10 December 1983.
[79] *ibid.*
[80] *Financial Times*, 12 December 1983.
[81] *Financial Times*, 15 December 1983.
[82] *Financial Times*, 22 December 1983.
[83] *ibid.*
[84] *Financial Times*, 23 December 1983.
[85] *Financial Times*, 29 December 1983.
[86] *Financial Times*, 4 January 1984.
[87] *Financial Times*, 30 December 1983.
[88] *Daily Telegraph*, 10 January 1984.
[89] *Sunday Express*, 10 June 1984.
[90] Price Waterhouse estimate, cited in *The Independent*, 5 December 1988.
[91] *Sunday Times*, 4 December 1988.
[92] *The Scotsman*, 23 February 1982.
[93] Nick Kochan and Hugh Pym, *The Guinness Affair*, Christopher Helm Publishers, 1987.
[94] *Sunday Times*, 27 May 1984.
[95] *Financial Times*, 7 March 1986.
[96] Morgan Grenfell Group plc, Offer for Sale Document, June 1986.

[97] Fallon and Srodes, *op. cit.*
[98] Peter Pugh, *Is Guinness Good for You?*, Financial Training Publications, 1987.
[99] Morgan Grenfell & Co. Limited, Annual Report and Accounts, 1980.
[100] Morgan Grenfell & Co. Limited, Annual Report and Accounts, 1986.
[101] *The Observer Magazine*, 30 July 1989.
[102] *Acquisitions Monthly*, January 1987.
[103] *The Observer Magazine*, 30 July 1989.

SIX

Big Bang

The sounds of Morgan Grenfell's elaborate war-dance over the prostrate form of Thomas Tilling had hardly subsided by 1 July 1983, when the chairman of the London Stock Exchange, Sir Nicholas Goodison, went to the drab, 1960s office block in Victoria Street that houses the Department of Trade and Industry. He had been invited to what he thought was a routine meeting some days previously by the new Secretary of State, Cecil Parkinson, but at it Goodison received some rather unexpected news. Parkinson told him that he would call off the court case that had been brought against the Stock Exchange by the Office of Fair Trading (OFT), which had spent the past six years uncovering evidence of price-fixing and other anti-competitive practices in the way the Stock Exchange went about its business. The Stock Exchange had spent over £1 million since February 1979 fighting a rearguard action against the OFT but looked by July 1983 to have lost; the case was due for a hearing in early 1984. The *quid pro quo* for Goodison was an assurance that the Stock Exchange would reform itself within four years, to which he acceded. After several days of discussion, they settled on a date: 27 October 1986. When Parkinson announced the deal to the House of Commons on 27 July it was roundly denounced by virtually all sides as a cosy deal between a Conservative Government and its cronies in the City, especially as it came so soon after a General Election campaign masterminded by Parkinson and in which the City had been conspicuously generous to the Party. For all the City knew, the carpers could have been right. Nobody really understood the magnitude of the forces Parkinson and Goodison had unleashed that summer afternoon.

In 1983 the London Stock Exchange was still characterized by job demarcations, closed shops and price-fixing arrangements which would not have disgraced a trade union. According to the Rule Book, stocks (in England, negotiable debt, or bonds) and shares (equity in a company) could be bought or sold on the London Stock Exchange only by a stockbroker through a stockjobber, both of whom had to be members.[1] The stockbroker acted as an agent only, dealing on behalf of his clients with a stockjobber, who would buy or sell stocks and shares on his own account, maintaining a 'book' of them for the purpose. For this service, the stockbroker charged his client a commission, fixed according to the size of the transaction. Generally speaking, the bigger the deal, the lower the commission, but there were still fixed minimum rates of commission. The stockjobbers, who occupied the once-familiar hexagonal booths on the floor of the Stock Exchange building, hoped to make money by selling stocks and shares for slightly more than they had paid for them or buying them for slightly less than they had sold them. The largest and most active market in bonds was the Government bond market, or the 'gilt-edged' market in which the Bank of England borrowed money on behalf of the Government. It did this by offering gilts for sale through one particular broker, Mullens & Co., whose senior partner was the Government Broker. He and all the other partners of Mullens wore top hats, as evidence of their seigneurial status, though the practice was imitated by a number of lesser brokers. A stockbroker was not allowed to be a stockjobber and vice versa, ostensibly because of the obvious conflict of interest between a broker needing to buy at the lowest price (or sell at the highest) and a jobber needing to sell at the highest price (or buy at the lowest). This system was known as 'single capacity'. Its opponents regarded it as the very worst kind of closed shop, defended unreflectingly by its beneficiaries, but its proponents maintained that single capacity was hallowed not just by the passage of time, but by bitter memories of the chaos caused by dual capacity during the Crash of 1929.

Theoretically, single capacity ensured that a broker always

went to the cheapest jobber. Competition between them for the broker's business was meant to ensure that the gap – or 'spread' – between the price which jobbers paid for a share and the price at which they sold it did not get too wide. In practice, there was not much of it. The number of jobbing firms had shrunk from 187 in 1950 to only 14 by 1978, of which a mere five accounted for nine-tenths of turnover.[2] In the gilt-edged market, which throughout the 1960s and 1970s had been kept far busier than the share market by a succession of spendthrift governments, two jobbers, Akroyd & Smithers and Wedd Durilacher Mordaunt, controlled at least three-quarters of turnover. Mutual agreements between the few that remained on the minimum spread they would charge were rife. Short of capital, few jobbers could guarantee a single price for a single trade and by 1983 brokers had resorted increasingly to matching big institutional buyers and sellers themselves. Because the rules of the Stock Exchange insisted that all business went through a jobber (except in one or two closely defined circumstances) these 'put-throughs' were sometimes purely cynical transactions, with the business going through the jobber as a formality only and the broker pocketing double commission. But brokers defended them as a valuable spur to competition since, once they were in possession of a large order, they were keen to complete the business before their rivals and they could dictate the terms of the exchange. The Wilson Committee estimated that 'put-throughs' accounted for a tenth of all equity turnover.[3] Worse, the fixed commissions paid to brokers directly linked their personal incomes to the number and size of their deals. Some brokers deliberately 'churned' the portfolios of their discretionary clients just to generate extra income for themselves. Innovation was a dirty word. The new derivative instruments developing in North America – traded options and financial futures – were simply ignored by a Stock Exchange with no incentive to change its ways. It took an entirely new market outside the ambit of the Stock Exchange, the London International Financial Futures Exchange (LIFFE), to bring financial futures to London. This prompted typical grumbling among the members of the broking community that it was poaching the Exchange's traditional gilt-edged business, though jobbers were more enthusiastic and both Akroyd and Wedd took seats. Less forgivably, the Stock Exchange (like most of the merchant banks) had almost completely ignored the Eurobond market. Of 120 London houses listed in 1983 as Eurobond dealers by the Association of International Bond Dealers, only four were members of the London Stock Exchange.[4] No outsiders could belong to the Exchange; there had been no new member firm since the end of the Second World War. Until 1973 outsiders included women. Even in the 1980s many women became familiar with the chanting and pointing which accompanied the appearance of a trousered female on the floor of the Exchange. In 1971 Graham Greenwell, then senior partner of the stockbroker, W. Greenwell & Co., had startled readers of *The Times* by claiming that the Exchange need not admit women because it was not 'an institution which exists to perform a public service' but a private gentlemen's club.[5]

Graham Greenwell was not an ironist. The system had given the members of the Stock Exchange like him a handsome living in recent years: commission income had climbed from only £190 million in 1976–7 to perhaps £580 million in 1982–3, implying a gross income of around £135,000 a head for the 4,269 members of the Exchange in 1983.[6] The future, already at hand in the Euromarkets and in the United States, was not therefore a pleasing prospect. In the Eurobond market banks acted as banker, broker and jobber rolled into one, with bonds syndicated among banks, each of whom had to buy or find buyers for the bonds it was allotted. Commissions were fixed by custom, not the Rule Book, and always deducted from the price of the bonds rather than charged separately. The bonds were traded not on the floor of the London Stock Exchange but in a vast and amorphous telephone market which traversed the globe, with prices displayed on electronic screens. Salesmen and traders, hunched over workstations groaning with telephones and VDUs, were a familiar sight in the Euromarkets long before Big Bang extended the phenomenon to the London equity market. Nor was the American precedent an encouraging one. The deregulation of commissions in the United States in May 1975 had precipitated a wholesale reconstruction of the New York stock market: some houses had gone out of business altogether while others, like Dean Witter and Bache, had had to seek capital and protection from wealthy patrons.

The OFT had studied American stock-market deregulation in detail. By 1983 it had narrowed down its critique of the Stock Exchange's 170-item Rule Book to three specific restrictions: fixed minimum commissions, single capacity and the fact that brokers could not trade on their own account. Even the members of the Stock Exchange knew that fixed commissions could not survive a rigorous examination. They were already under attack from institutional investors, who were no longer consoled by free research, air tickets, office furniture and VDUs, the 'soft commissions' which by 1983 had become commonplace props to an indefensible system. As early as 1972, the merchant banks had clubbed together to set up a separate computer-based dealing system for their fund managers and institutional clients, to provide a cheaper alternative. Called ARIEL (Automated Real Time Investments Exchange Limited) it never attracted more than one per cent of London equity turnover and was undone completely in the gilt-edged market by the Bank of England's refusal to participate. It did, however, prompt a cut in Stock Exchange commissions on major deals in 1973, and commissions on short-dated gilts were already negotiable. So fixed commissions were doomed from the outset; but the Stock Exchange did think that single capacity – because it worked against conflicts of interest – might be vindicated even by the OFT. So their defence cleverly centred on the so-called 'link' argument: that fixed commissions and single capacity were indissolubly linked. If brokers' income shrunk under the impact of squeezed commissions, they would be tempted to cut the jobbers out altogether and, where bargains could not be matched, to job the stocks themselves. Diehards maintained that fixed commissions had been introduced specifically to save single capacity, which broke down without them. Though linkage did not save the traditional Stock Exchange, it was a remarkably successful theory. By 1984 virtually everybody who mattered in the City of London believed that the abolition of fixed commissions made dual capacity inevitable. Thus from this Byzantine defence flowed everything that happened next.

Stockbrokers and stockjobbers concluded fairly rapidly after the deal between Parkinson and Goodison that their days as independents were numbered. Although the agreement, to the horror of Sir Gordon Borrie, included no formal understanding on the admission of outsiders to membership of the Stock Exchange, most brokers and jobbers took it for granted that dual capacity implied the involvement of outsiders because they did not have sufficient capital of their own to buy, sell and trade stocks and shares on their own account on the scale likely to be required. The entire capital of the member firms of the Stock Exchange at the start of 1983 amounted to only £150–200 million. Even the biggest jobber, Akroyd & Smithers, had only £37 million in capital.[7] Banks, be they British, American or Japanese, could supply capital and, while that was not reason enough for the banks to do so, by 1983 a number of developments had made it highly likely that they would. The boom business of the City in the 1970s – recycling the petrodollar surpluses of the Arab countries to the Third World – came to an abrupt halt in August 1982 when Mexico partially defaulted on its debts. A lethal combination of falling commodity prices, low inflation, high nominal interest rates and a strong dollar meant that thirty-five countries were unable to service their debts by the end of 1984. Only three years earlier bankers had been busily pumping another $133 billion into developing economies, taking total sovereign debt up to some $500 billion.[8] Now they needed other ways to spend it and in 1983 the securities business was all the rage. As the oil price fell, the most significant global imbalance of payments was no longer between the Arabs and the West but between Japan and the United States. By spending more and taxing less, the Reagan administration had turned the United States into the world's principal debtor nation, while Japan, by exporting more and saving more, had become the world's principal creditor nation. The Japanese banks, whose South American debtors owed them $90 billion, had been badly scalded by the debt crisis, and revised their lending criteria accordingly. Similarly, Japanese investors, who anyway preferred bonds to deposits, chose not to lend money to countries unlikely to pay it back; they bought securities from creditworthy countries instead. Thus it was largely Japanese savers who bought the Treasury bonds issued by the US Government to fund its massive budget and trade deficits. But Japan's enormous current-account surplus could not be absorbed by the United States alone and Japanese investment in all manner of foreign securities during the 1980s sharply tilted the balance in the world's financial markets away from lending money and towards the buying and selling of securities. The debt crisis had also changed perceptions about the balance of risk and reward. The big central banks in London, New York and Frankfurt try to control the risks lending banks incur by restricting loans to fixed multiples of each bank's own capital, weighted according to the type of risk incurred. In the 1970s banks had lent a lot of money to bad risks in the Third World, using up a lot of their capital in the process. Though different ratios are applied to different risks, banks can currently lend £100 for every £8 of shareholders' capital.[9] Securities, because they can in principle always be sold to another bank or investor, are not subject to the same rules and so do not tie up the capital of the bank in the same way. By buying securities rather than lending money, banks reasoned that they could do more business with less risk. If 'country risk' was the catchphrase of the 1970s, 'securitization' was the buzzword of the 1980s.

Big Bang would not have happened the way it did without good reasons for brokers and jobbers to sell and for bankers to buy, but the process was discreetly nudged along by the Bank of England too. David Walker, then the Bank's executive director in charge of City organization and now chairman of the Securities and Investments Board, described the Bank's role as that of the 'midwife of change'.[10] By 1983 the Bank had become extremely worried by the City's failure to compete at the leading edge of financial technology. Smugness and inertia were spread far beyond the confines of the Stock Exchange and down the narrow streets and alleyways of the Square Mile until they infected almost every indigenous City institution. In the domestic capital market, companies, bankers, brokers, jobbers and investors existed in an almost marsupial relationship with each other. If a merchant bank underwrote a company's bonds or rights issue or offer for sale, the shares would be sub-underwritten by a broker with a group of institutional investors, with a proportion of the issue reserved for the jobbers at a concessionary price. Everyone who participated was paid large, fixed fees. Merger and acquisition work, by drumming up turnover and fees, relied on much the same network. Walker and his colleagues were concerned that failure was most obvious in the markets where all the forces unleashed by Big Bang on 27 October 1986 were already present: the Euromarkets. Some 550 foreign banks had congregated in London, virtually all of them active in Eurocurrency lending. Of the top twenty 'lead managers' – banks that initiate a loan, fix the terms, write the documentation and underwrite the largest part of it – of syndicated Eurocurrency loans in 1981, only three were British.[11] By 1982 one foreign securities house, Credit Suisse First Boston, controlled 14 per cent of the Eurobond market, substantially more than all the London merchant banks put together. New ideas – floating-rate bonds and interest-rate and currency swaps – abounded, but went unexploited by the merchant banks. To bypass the archaic settlement and clearing systems of the London Stock Exchange, the Euromarkets had even developed their own clearing and settlement operations – Euroclear in Brussels and CEDEL in Luxemburg. The abolition of exchange controls in October 1979, which exposed the London houses for the first time to the twin possibilities of unlimited overseas investment and full participation in the Euromarkets, provoked only a limp response. Of the £20 billion of British funds invested overseas in the first five years after the abolition of exchange controls, only a twentieth passed through the books of British intermediaries.[12] The Bank believed that by unifying banks, brokers and jobbers it might not only help the City to survive Big Bang but also catch up with the foreign competition. Between September and November 1983 David Walker spoke with the senior partners of forty Stock Exchange firms, gently encouraging them to consider links with banks.

The countdown to Big Bang had begun. For banks like Morgan Grenfell, the challenge was twofold. Once the 'link' argument prevailed it was clear that single-capacity brokers and jobbers in both the equity market and the gilt-edged market would be supplanted by a much larger number of dual-capacity market-makers competing with each other for business on price alone. The members of the Stock Exchange affirmed this by vote in October 1983; by April 1984 they had agreed on the shape of the new equity market. Instead of brokers checking prices with jobbers on the floor of the Stock Exchange, prices would be disseminated through a computerized system of electronic screens called Stock Exchange Automatic Quotations (SEAQ). Similarly, the Bank of England announced that it would no longer use Mullens & Co. as its broker to sell gilts on the floor of the Exchange, but would instead establish dealing relationships with authorized 'primary dealers'. The Bank would buy gilt-edged stock from the primary dealers or sell it to them according to the borrowing requirements of the Government or the influence it wished to exert over interest rates. Price was the principal factor for the first time. The primary dealers would also make markets in gilt-edged stocks. Morgan Grenfell had to decide, quite quickly, whether it wished to be a dual-capacity dealer in either or both of these markets and then to work out how to get there. The income of the Stock Exchange had shot up from £265 million in 1979 to £580 million in 1983 and many of the senior directors of Morgan Grenfell imagined that it might enrich them too, though their enthusiasm was tempered by a threatened dilution of the value of their shareholdings to pay for the expansion. They hesitated to apply for authorization as a dealer in the new gilt-edged market, although they believed that the bank understood fixed-rate bond issues and knew that it was already active in the dual-capacity Eurobond market. But there was no firm decision and by mid-March 1984 Lord Catto was having to explain to impatient staff and shareholders why nothing had been done:

Today, it is not only the international banking sector that is in a state of flux: securities markets, both international and domestic, are going through a period of rapid change. We have to study these developments carefully and survey the many options open to us. It is our belief that, over the coming years, more funds will tend to be raised through the international capital markets and relatively less through bank intermediation; the development and growth of our business in the securities markets, in which we are already active, has thus assumed considerable importance. Our involvement, through our merchant-banking operations, in the primary securities markets is of long standing; more recently, we have strengthened our presence in the secondary Eurobond markets. As the securities markets and our competitors change around us, we are likely to become more widely involved in secondary markets while continuing to enhance our position as a leading international issuing house.[13]

This statement came nearly five months after S. G. Warburg had boldly proclaimed its intentions by taking a one-third stake in the biggest and best stockjobber, Akroyd & Smithers, for £41 million. It would probably have bought it all, but Stock Exchange rules formulated in 1982 allowed outsiders to own only up to 29.9 per cent of any one member firm and only 5 per cent of any second member firm. A few weeks later Warburg acquired the maximum permissible stake (5 per cent) in the Queen's stockbrokers, Rowe & Pitman, with whom Akroyd had already been holding discussions.[14] They immediately formed an international equity dealership, as a dry run for the domestic deregulation of the equity market. Though informal discussions were held, Morgan Grenfell does not seem to have contemplated seriously an acquisition of Akroyd. Both Warburg and Akroyd were already public companies, so the ultimate price could be paid in shares. Morgan Grenfell was not then a publicly quoted company, a limitation which was of considerable import in deciding what could be afforded. An alliance between Morgan Grenfell and Rowe & Pitman was anticipated by the City before news of the arrangement with Warburg, and Rowe & Pitman was widely believed to have offered itself to Morgan Grenfell. The two firms had always worked closely together and Rowe probably did more merchant banking business with Morgan Grenfell than any other merchant bank. During the 1960s and 1970s Bill Mackworth-Young, as a partner at Rowe & Pitman, had come to the Partners' Room every morning to review developments in the stock market. After striking the deal with Warburg, Peter Wilmot-Sitwell, the partner of Rowe & Pitman to whom he had lost the succession to the senior partnership in 1973, rang Mackworth-Young to tell him the news, knowing that it would upset him terribly, and it did. In the end, Morgan Grenfell was finessed by a superior strategist. As a director of both Union Discount and the Bank of England, David Scholey, the chairman of S. G. Warburg, understood much better than Christopher Reeves the nature of the securities business. He had identified Akroyd very early on as the best firm on the London Stock Exchange. He had also had some luck. When Warburg approached Akroyd, Scholey found Ackroyd had already reached an understanding with Rowe & Pitman, which Warburg insisted was honoured. Thereafter Morgan Grenfell was romantically linked with several firms. In late January 1984 both John Robertson, senior partner of the other major jobber, Wedd Durlacher Mordaunt, and Christopher Reeves admitted to talks.[15] 'Morgan are talking to a whole variety of institutions,' conceded Reeves.[16]

The prevarication reflected major divisions of opinion on the board. Morgan Grenfell had been dithering for years over what to do in the event of a major deregulation of the London Stock Exchange. A committee chaired by Patrick Spens had vaguely recommended links with the stockbroker Strauss Turnbull, whose strength in the Eurobond market fitted neatly with the bank's strategy in the early 1980s, but nothing came of this. Blaise Hardman and John Forsyth, creators of the successful Treasury division and architects of the burgeoning Eurobond Department, were aggressively enthusiastic for full participation in the securities markets, where they judged that they could repeat their earlier successes. Philip Chappell, already an isolated figure, thought participation in the secondary securities markets had little or nothing to do with the art of merchant banking as he understood it. Influential figures in the Corporate Finance Department, among them Roger Seelig, were strongly opposed to an uncertain and expensive adventure in the gilt-edged market. Buying Wedd, they argued, would involve paying a lot of goodwill for a gilt-edged market-making business in a sector about to become ruinously competitive. In this they were quite right. The amount of capital committed to the gilt-edged market rose from £80 million to £600 million overnight in 1986, squeezing spreads severely.[17] They also argued, again quite plausibly, that buying a particular broker would lose them equity-underwriting business if a client wanted to use his usual broker. Most importantly, they argued from a position of strength, since they made most of the profits of the bank. Reeves, trapped in the glamour of bid-making, was sympathetic to this view, which was also supported by a group of diehards who felt the cost of any acquisitions would undermine the share price. But the stock of Hardman and Forsyth also stood high. The Treasury division, which lent at handsome margins, had supplied dependable income while the Corporate Finance Department was being built up, and the putative Eurobond operation was growing successfully. They could count on the support of some of the younger directors in Corporate Finance, like Richard Westcott, who suspected that the older generation was putting its future at risk by failing to endorse Big Bang wholeheartedly.[18] Their argument – for an 'integrated' investment bank which could issue, underwrite, sell and make markets in the stocks and shares of its clients under one roof – was in danger of going by default. Jon Perry, the head of the Eurobond Department and by 1983 a member of the select Management Committee, regarded a gilt-edged market-making capability and a strong broking distribution arm as essential to the business he was building, especially in the sterling Eurobond market, and entertained few doubts about the need to embrace the future, but he carried little weight with Reeves. Bill Mackworth-Young, the only senior figure with long experience of the securities business, regarded himself as a representative rather than a leader. Only one man – Henry Gorell-Barnes, the head of the Investment Division – would have had the strength and vision to persuade Reeves to think strategically, and he had died of a heart attack whilst shooting in November 1983, aged only forty-four.[19] His death deprived the Big Bang enthusiasts of their most powerful spokesman at a crucial moment.

The divisions were accentuated by the troubled question of capital. Even before Big Bang, the bank's capital was increasingly insufficient. During the boom years of Eurocurrency lending, the pressures to participate in loans, as well as arrange them, had intensified; the aggressive takeover strategies of the early 1980s, by requiring the bank to buy shares on behalf of clients, added to them; and the forays into the securities markets, starting with Eurobonds, caused the management to think periodically of a stock-market flotation. Talk of an impending flotation of the bank was current throughout the first half of the 1980s but, fearful of vulnerability to a predator once the shares were publicly available, the bank adopted a series of increasingly desperate stratagems to avoid this apparently ineluctable conclusion. The failure to establish a joint venture in the Eurobond market in 1978 had undermined much of the rationale behind Morgan Guaranty's one third shareholding. The rights issues of 1974 and 1978 had tried Morgan Guaranty's patience, and a third capital-raising exercise of £12.5 million in May 1981 finally exhausted it. Morgan

Guaranty did not take up its allocation of rights and, in a complex restructuring of Morgan Grenfell's capital, surrendered all but 4 per cent of its interest. This was a momentous change, finally severing the historic ties between the Morgan banks and freeing Morgan Grenfell to pursue its own destiny. The two banks had found each other encroaching more and more on one another's markets both at home and abroad. Breaking with Morgan Guaranty allowed Morgan Grenfell to compete openly for corporate advisory business with its larger cousin in the United States and to pursue its ambitions in the securities markets at home. The bank's New York representative office was transformed immediately into a $1 million trading subsidiary, Morgan Grenfell Inc.[20] A former managing director of First Boston, John Fraser, was installed as president.[21] Amid great ceremony, a great-great-grandson of J. S. Morgan, John A. Morgan, was installed as chairman.[22] Morgan Guaranty's unwanted rights were taken up mainly by Willis Faber, which increased its stake to 24 per cent, and the Prudential, which increased its stake to 9 per cent. Though no other single shareholder then owned more than 5 per cent of the bank, the balance was still held tightly by either employees and their families (13 per cent) or a group of twenty-one friendly institutional investors, some of whom, and Willis in particular, had deep misgivings about Morgan's decision to endorse Big Bang.

In December 1983 the bank issued a $50 million floating-rate bond issue, its first issue of publicly quoted securities. This was a pointer of enormous significance which went almost unnoticed at the time.[23] By the beginning of 1984 Morgan Grenfell was seriously short of money by comparison with its rivals for the hands of brokers and jobbers. These rivals were not confined to the publicly listed merchant banks, like Warburg, who could raise funds on the open market. They included the Big Four clearing banks and the 'Thundering Herd', the phrase originally applied to Merrill Lynch, but by 1984 a generic term encompassing the enormous American money-centre banks Citibank, Chase Manhattan and Security Pacific, the financial conglomerate Shearson Lehman-American Express, the big three Swiss banks and the Japanese securities houses, Nomura, Daiwa, Yamaichi and Nikko. One of them, Nomura, had over £1 billion in equity at the end of 1982, ten times the amount deployed by Morgan Grenfell, but, officially discouraged by the Bank of England, the Japanese bought nothing. It was a curious choice, in view of Morgan Grenfell's hesitancy and indecision, that Mackworth-Young was appointed in May 1984 to serve on the ten-man Big Bang committee set up by the governor of the Bank of England, Robin Leigh-Pemberton, to advise him on regulatory changes.[24] Two months earlier Mackworth-Young had announced that Morgan Grenfell was resolved to be in the new markets but was undecided about whom to buy:

We have made our decision to expand into the secondary securities market. We want to be in market making and distribution of all fixed interest securities we issue and are likely to issue and in British Government securities as well.[25]

By then the market had made up Morgan Grenfell's mind for it. In December 1983, Rothschild's had bought Smith Brothers, a quoted stockjobber. Another minor jobber, Bisgood Bishop, had gone to National Westminster Bank in February. Two major brokers, W. Greenwell and De Zoete & Bevan, had gone to Midland Bank and Barclay's Bank respectively. Even Wedd Durlacher, after lengthy discussions with Kleinwort Benson, was bought by Barclay's Bank, for a figure widely believed at the time to have been close to £100 million. Asked to comment on whether Morgan Grenfell would have liked to buy Wedd, Mackworth-Young said:

Not at that price. There's a large amount of goodwill in that figure.[26]

This missed the point. With few assets of substance changing hands, goodwill and staff skills, many of which might be irrelevant to the new markets, was all anyone was buying. All the buyers (and the sellers) knew that goodwill might count for nothing in the fiercely competitive markets that would follow

Big Bang and that staff, bought at high cost, might leave without warning. More importantly, Mackworth-Young had missed the bus. By the end of March 1984 there was only one jobber of any size left without a partner: Pinchin, Denny & Co. At the beginning of April Morgan Grenfell duly bought the maximum permissible stake (29.9 per cent.) in Pinchin and undertook to acquire the balance as soon as Stock Exchange rules permitted.[27] Though the overall cost was not disclosed at the time, it was subsequently revealed to be £21 million.[28] It had made £4.25 million in the year to April 1984, but the partners clearly did not expect this to continue, since they smartly withdrew their cash reserves of £2.99 million before the sale.[29] This was not an unusual move – for example, the partners of Rowe & Pitman withdrew £17.9 million ahead of the sale to Warburg – but it underlined just how little, even in terms of faith, Morgan Grenfell was acquiring. Indeed, the purchase agreement specified that the partners would withdraw their capital, leaving Morgan Grenfell nothing but the fixed assets – old desks and the like – and the goodwill. Morgan Grenfell understood the risk it was taking, since it knew that the partners would not have chosen to sell if they had been optimistic about an independent future. The initial purchase was nevertheless accompanied by many brave words. 'Pinchin was my first choice,' said Mackworth-Young, and Reeves called it 'rather aggressive'[30] but in reality it was a case of Hobson's Choice. 'We were beginning to feel a bit lonely, like a boulder in the middle of a stream,' said Pinchin's senior partner, V.A.L. ('Val') Powell, realistically. Pinchin Denny was still a private partnership. It was founded in 1926 and by 1984 had 37 partners and 220 staff. It considered itself the third-largest jobber in London behind Akroyd and Wedd, making markets in maybe 5,500 stocks and shares but specializing in electrical, chemical and financial companies and investment trusts.[31] It also had a small but unprofitable business making markets in London in European, and especially French, shares, but its presence in gilts was almost negligible, being only 6 or 7 per cent of the market. At the time of the sale Powell put its share at about a tenth, implying, since Smith had pulled out, that Akroyd and Wedd controlled the balance. The Bank of England certainly considered them of little consequence. Given Morgan Grenfell's plans to become a major force in the gilt-edged market, this was a crucial mistake, for if it bought a stockbroker with a large business in gilt-edged securities, Pinchin would simply not be able to handle the volume.

There was widespread astonishment in the City at Morgan Grenfell's failure to secure a sizeable broker. Cazenove, the obvious alternative to the betrothed Rowe & Pitman, was approached, but had decided, unlike most others, to go it alone. This attitude did not waver throughout the 18 months ahead of Big Bang, though Morgan's checked its stance regularly.[32] In any event, Morgan Grenfell could not have afforded Cazenove. Though the director in charge of negotiating the bank's purchases, Blaise Hardman, was singularly averse to spending money, the bank's real shortage of cash was a more serious impediment. For a house with a disclosed net worth at the end of 1983 of only £115 million, the sums reputed to be changing hands in the prelude to Big Bang were extremely alarming. Though the exact prices have never been revealed, Akroyd probably cost Warburg £96 million in the end. Wedd is understood to have cost Barclay's £90 million, not far short of the £100 million rumoured at the time, and De Zoete fetched another £50 million.[33] Yet in May 1984 Morgan Grenfell struggled to spend £10.4 million on a 20 per cent stake in the £52 million Target Group plc, a new life-assurance and unit-trust company created by Roger Seelig out of debris jettisoned by Jacob Rothschild and Saul Steinberg ahead of the ill-fated £1 billion merger of Rothschild's Charterhouse J. Rothschild with Mark Weinberg's Hambro Life. The Target deal also hardened the convictions of some in the Corporate Finance Department that the securities markets could and should be ignored. It was the kind of entrepreneurial deal at which Seelig excelled. The bank not only gained a £440,000 fee for placing the rest of the equity with institutional investors; it also secured an option on another 20 per cent of the equity if the company was floated *and* picked up a £30 million investment advisory contract worth another £500,000 a year.[34] Pinchin, they argued, would cost £21 million for tenuous access to a cut-throat market in government bonds.

Expansion abroad was adding to the cash shortage. A trading subsidiary was opened by Lord and Lady Catto in Hong Kong in mid-May, capitalized at $6 million and run by Rupert Carrington, son of the former Foreign Secretary, Lord Carrington.[35] Morgan's had not been active in Hong Kong since the break with Indosuez in 1976 and Carrington was vague on what it would do, but thought project finance in Communist China was the most likely reason he was there.[36] This was typical of the blunderbuss approach Morgan Grenfell could not afford with all the changes taking place in London. It would be expensive to carve a niche in the Hong Kong market, which was dominated by the great Oriental houses of Wardley, Jardine and Schroder, who controlled three-quarters of the Hong Kong new-issue market and managed funds locally worth $3.5 billion already.[37] In July 1984 Carrington bought Euro Management Limited, an offshore private-client business along the lines of the bank's operations in the Channel Islands.[38] Further capital was also absorbed by the operations in New York and Australia. When in late May 1984 the bank tapped its shareholders for another £45 million in a one-for-four rights issue, Willis Faber, still the largest shareholder, made clear its lack of enthusiasm for further cash calls. It was, after all, the fourth rights issue since 1974. Significantly, the board announced publicly for the first time that it was 'giving consideration to the desirability of obtaining, possibly in 1985, a listing for the company on the Stock Exchange'.[39]

So it was money, as much as irresolution and lack of choice, that finally settled Morgan's selection of Pember & Boyle as its broker in October 1984. At the time of the rights issue in May, Mackworth-Young had conceded the need for a brokerage arm but hinted that 'it might be cheaper to build up our own broking capacity'.[40] In the circumstances, an additional attraction of Pember & Boyle seemed to be its stupendous cheapness.

It eventually cost just £10.35 million, and even this was offset by the acquisition of over £1 billion of local-authority pension funds managed by the partnership, which were shipped smartly into the bank's own fund-management arm.[41] Reeves described the terms at the time as 'extremely affordable'.[42] As with Pinchin, the partners ensured that Morgan Grenfell bought nothing but the fixed assets and goodwill. They withdrew £2.33 million of their own tax reserves and personal cash balances rather than risk them on an uncertain future, though many subsequently put the money on deposit with Morgan Grenfell.[43] Privately, they were delighted that a merchant bank, apparently so well versed in asset valuation, was prepared to pay anything for them at all. 'We've been kissed by the Holy Ghost', quipped one partner.[44] It was exactly the kind of firm which, in more rational surroundings than the City of London in 1984, would have meekly awaited its extinction beneath the feet of the Thundering Herd. It was exclusively a gilt-edged broker, with no presence in equities. It had once had a blue-chip client list – the Halifax Building Society, Barclay's Bank, Midland Bank, Royal Insurance, Phoenix and a large collection of local authorities. It still had the best settlement department in the City, but by 1984 it was manifestly living on borrowed time, and the partners knew it even if Morgan Grenfell did not. For all that, it courted, and was courted by, virtually every house seeking an *entrée* to the securities markets. After negotiations with no fewer than nineteen potential buyers, it was on the verge of concluding a deal with Orion Royal Bank, the investment-banking arm of the Royal Bank of Canada, when it approached Morgan Grenfell to see if they were interested. It was a timely intervention. At that moment Morgan Grenfell was breaking off a tumultuous courtship of Phillips & Drew, who had shocked them by courting wealthier suitors. 'They seem to have been talking to everybody in the City,' complained Blaise Hardman with naive incredulity. By the autumn of 1984, with Rowe & Pitman, De Zoete & Bevan, W. Greenwell, Grieveson Grant, Wood Mackenzie, Laing & Cruickshank, L. Messel, Savory

Milln, Fielding Newson Smith and a host of lesser brokers already gone, the internal pressure at Morgan Grenfell to do a deal with someone – anyone – was intense. An opportunity to buy Scott Goff Layton, a good equity broker, for £3 million had been passed up; they went to Rothschild's in December. Sadly, Bill Mackworth-Young, the one man in the hierarchy with real experience of the equity markets, was dying of cancer during these last critical weeks. His death came four days after the deal between Morgan Grenfell and Pember & Boyle was finally struck on 14 October. The acquisition followed the pre-Big Bang pattern laid down by the Stock Exchange. Because Morgan's already owned 29.9 per cent of Pinchin Denny, it could buy only 5 per cent of Pember & Boyle now, with a firm commitment to buy the balance once Stock Exchange rules permitted.[45] It was a necessity rather than a blunder, but none the less disastrous for that.

Pember & Boyle brought with it little that was relevant to the problem at hand. Its ambience was donnish but more fraternal than that of most Oxbridge colleges. It had been clannish, but by 1984 virtually nobody could recall either a Pember or a Boyle. George Ross Pember had died within the memory of some of the older partners, but for much of the twentieth century the firm had been dominated by two families, the Althauses (whom legend said were illegitimate offspring of the Rothschilds) and the Hanson-Lawsons. The last of the Althauses, Nigel, left in 1982 to become the Government Broker, taking much prestige and personal expertise with him. The last of the Hanson-Lawsons, Johnny, though a brave wartime tank officer, would often pass the afternoon alone with a client and a decanter of port. It was said that the habit of holding two lunches, one at 12.30 p.m. and one at 1.30 p.m., was designed to accommodate the separate guests of each family and the two sittings continued, in a shadowy way, to represent different factions within the firm. The lunches persisted in the 1980s but had become altogether more sober affairs; men of learning or state would be invited to discourse over the school puddings. The partners prided themselves on their connections. Professor

Brian Griffiths, now head of Mrs Thatcher's Policy Unit, was retained by Pember & Boyle as economics adviser from 1973 until his elevation to the Court of the Bank of England, and remained a frequent visitor at lunch until the firm was sold.

Few of the partners looked forward to the new gilt-edged market, which it was already obvious would be murderous. The number of market-makers was set to increase tenfold, the capital committed to the market over sevenfold. The economy was recovering, boosting the tax receipts of a Government already committed to a tight fiscal and monetary policy. Heavy sales of state assets and further cuts in public expenditure suggested that the supply of new gilts would dry up just as capacity multiplied. The equity market, by contrast, was daily clearing new highs. Yet Pember & Boyle was primarily a gilt-edged broker, with virtually no equity salesmen or research analysts. Its gilt-edged business, like that of any business relying on fixed commissions, was derived largely from the turnover it could generate, and Pember & Boyle was more than usually dependent on the generation of turnover by artificial means which by 1984 were becoming increasingly ineffective. Speculative trading, which was popular in the volatile markets of the 1970s, was implausible in the calmer atmosphere of the 1980s. The technique invented by John Hanson-Lawson in the 1920s – switching to take advantage of anomalies in the market, by buying cheap stocks and exchanging them for expensive ones, and vice versa – had become increasingly unprofitable, as the use of computers erased the remaining anomalies. Switching stocks to take advantage of the different rates of tax applicable to capital gains, as opposed to income, which some estimates suggested was responsible for up to a quarter of turnover in the gilt-edged market, was outlawed by the Government in the budget of 1985.[46] Tax-loss switching, in which insurance companies would sell gilts on which they had a tax-allowable loss within the year, but sell those on which they had a gain after a year and a day – because gains were tax-free provided they had held the gilt for a year – was hit hard. The gilt-edged activities of the Halifax Building Society, which used Pember & Boyle to transact all of its business, were also curtailed.

Morgan Grenfell had not only bought into a cyclical business at the top of the cycle; they had also probably bought the firm most likely to fall off the cycle altogether. The 14 partners and 100 staff of Pember & Boyle could hardly believe their luck. Reeves, who had now added the chairmanship of the bank to his role as group chief executive after Mackworth-Young's death, did not even seem to know what he had bought:

We could not get involved in equity distribution without a broker – and Pember comes a lot cheaper than others.[47]

He had asked Blaise Hardman, a man with a legendary appetite for detailed committee work, to handle the purchase of the two firms. His duties were now extended to their integration. Though accepted at first by the partners of Pinchin Denny and Pember & Boyle as a logical choice for this task, they found that Hardman, with his inexperience of their business and obsession with paperwork and committees, became an irksome reminder of the independence they had lost. The appointment of a negotiator more sensitive to their anguish would have been a wiser choice, but by now Reeves was too thoroughly absorbed with the triumphs of George Magan and Roger Seelig to care very much about that.

NOTES

[1] In the United States, 'common stock' refers to ordinary shares. Strictly speaking, in England 'stock' refers to bonds available in registered form, whereas 'bonds' refers to those available in bearer form.
[2] Margaret Reid, *All-Change in the City*, Macmillan, 1988.
[3] Committee to Review the Functioning of Financial Institutions, Cmnd 7937, 1980.
[4] Hamish McRae and Frances Cairncross, *Capital City*, Methuen, 1985.
[5] Brian Widlake, *In The City*, Faber and Faber, 1986.
[6] Reid, *op. cit.*
[7] *ibid.*

[8] Estimates made by Euromoney Publications.

[9] Guidelines published by the Cooke Committee of Central Bank Governors, published in July 1988.

[10] Reid, *op. cit.*

[11] McRae and Cairncross, *op. cit.*

[12] Widlake, *op. cit.*

[13] Morgan Grenfell Holdings Limited, Annual Report and Accounts, 1983.

[14] Jacques Attali, *A Man of Influence, Siegmund Warburg 1902–82*, Weidenfeld & Nicolson, 1986.

[15] *Evening Standard*, 27 January 1984.

[16] *Observer*, 29 January 1984.

[17] *Financial Times*, 13 December 1988.

[18] *The Economist*, 17 January 1987.

[19] *Evening Standard*, 15 November 1983.

[20] *Daily Telegraph*, 15 April 1981.

[21] *Financial Times*, 7 April 1981.

[22] *Financial Times*, 17 April 1981.

[23] *Financial Times*, 13 December 1983.

[24] *Financial Times*, 24 May 1984.

[25] *Guardian*, 20 March 1984.

[26] *ibid.*,

[27] *Financial Times*, 10 April 1984.

[28] Morgan Grenfell Group plc, Offer of Ordinary Shares by Tender, Prospectus, June 1986. Morgan Grenfell's initial offer was £10 million. Pinchin Denny hoped for £17 million. (*The Observer Magazine*, August 1989)

[29] *ibid.*

[30] *Financial Times*, 10 April 1984.

[31] *ibid.*

[32] *Standard*, 19 September 1984; *Observer*, 16 September 1984 and 7 October 1984.

[33] Reid, *op. cit.*

[34] *Financial Times*, 3 May 1984.

[35] *South China Morning Post*, 11 May 1984.

[36] *ibid.*

[37] *Asian Wall Street Journal*, 7 January 1985.

[38] Morgan Grenfell Holdings Limited, Annual Report and Accounts, 1984.

[39] *Financial Times*, 22 May 1984.

[40] *Daily Telegraph*, 22 May 1984.

[41] Morgan Grenfell Group plc, Offer of Ordinary Shares by Tender, Prospectus, June 1986.

[42] *Daily Telegraph*, 15 October 1984.
[43] Morgan Grenfell Group plc, Offer of Ordinary Shares by Tender, Prospectus, June 1986.
[44] *The Observer Magazine*, 30 July 1989.
[45] *Daily Telegraph*, 15 October 1984.
[46] *Financial Times*, 1 March 1985.
[47] *Sunday Times*, 21 October 1984.

SEVEN

Tough Smoothies

'Why doesn't George Magan pick on somebody his own size?'
exclaimed the diminutive Sir Michael Edwardes, the newly
appointed chairman of Dunlop after hearing that BTR, via
Morgan Grenfell, had captured twenty-eight per cent of
Dunlop's preference shares in a dawn raid in January 1985,
scattering with a single blow the fruits of months of tortuous
and patient negotiation with the creditors of the beleaguered
tyre company. His irritation was fuelled by the knowledge that
Magan had also led the earlier £425 million bid by STC
for ICL in late 1984, where Edwardes had replaced Philip
Chappell's successor, Christopher Laidlaw, as chairman. At
Brooke Bond, also corralled by Magan for £389 million in
1984, the first news of a raid by Unilever was one Friday
afternoon, when Magan and Unilever's chairmen, Sir Kenneth Durham and H. F. Van der Hoven, called on the company's chairman, Sir John Cuckney, with a 'take it or leave
it' offer. Cuckney demurred, only to learn of the bid that
followed from a journalist who rang him at home on a
Sunday. After failing to contact senior managers at Brooke
Bond, Magan simply delivered the offer document to the
company's offices.[1] Magan was a ruthless takeover tactician,
who identified closely with clients and insisted that they bid
with verve and conviction. Competitors accused him of warlike
attitudes and of railroading potential bidders. Graham Walsh
had to deny publicly that the bank dominated its clients.[2]
Magan was condescending:

We are not as aggressive personally as many of our competitors.
There is no point in being aggressive – it does more damage than

good. We tend to be decisive. When we've determined what to do, we push on with it.[3]

Distaste for the bank's tactics was spreading beyond its traditional rivals. 'Morgan Grenfell think they are God's gift to merchant banking. It makes them absolutely insufferable at times,' said one partner of a law firm.[4] 'The merchant-banking contestants may feel that, because they are treated like gladiators, they have to behave like gladiators,' noted one company chairman.[5] 'They are the team on song. Tough smoothies and smooth toughies,' observed a cynical fund manager, tautologically.[6] By the winter of 1984–5, resentment of Morgan Grenfell's cockiness was widespread in the City of London and this counted for much when the Guinness scandal erupted two years later. Then, as Bernard Donoughue put it, 'a great house stumbled, and not a hand went out to help'.

On Tuesday, 15 January 1985, Sir Michael Edwardes and his merchant bankers, Hill Samuel and S. G. Warburg, unveiled one of the most complicated rescue packages ever put together by the City of London: an impenetrable mixture of rights, new preference shares, convertible bonds and new bank borrowings designed to reduce Dunlop's £453 million debt burden to a more manageable £125 million by the end of the year.[7] The plan, and a self-congratulatory share-option scheme that netted Edwardes and two fellow directors a notional profit of £2.6 million on the re-listing of the company two days later, was subject to the approval of 75 per cent of Dunlop shareholders at a meeting scheduled for 8 February. Few doubted that the new Dunlop board would get it. Indeed, the applause at their ingenuity had scarcely died away when, at dawn on Thursday morning, George Magan authorized a raid on the new Dunlop preference shares, listed on the Stock Exchange for the first time that day. In the raid, the bank picked up 28 per cent of the stock, sufficient to block the Edwardes reconstruction plan. The client was Magan's favourite predator, BTR, the conqueror of Tilling. The following day George Magan and BTR chairman Owen Green solemnly offered to buy the rest of Dunlop for a paltry £33.4 million. 'The only way to make sure we could get a bid that would run was to command the restructuring situation,' said Green, impassively.[8] It was a brilliantly opportunistic intervention but, as usual, what followed was pungent with insolence. For a company which, despite all its problems, still turned over £1.25 billion and employed 30,000 people, the value of the bid was utterly specious. Only 0.26 per cent of Dunlop shareholders accepted BTR's offer at its first closing date, a figure which rose to only 0.34 per cent when the offer was extended.[9] With Dunlop shares trading at 38p in the market, the BTR offer document focused exclusively on a fatuous comparison between the 14p price at which shareholders and banks were offered new shares in the Edwardes reconstruction plan and the 20p they were offered by Green, ignoring the value of the other securities Edwardes was offering to shareholders. The Takeover Panel duly rapped Morgan Grenfell's knuckles for failing to present the figures 'in an appropriate or helpful manner'.[10]

Walsh thought this transgression just a 'matter of opinion'.[11] The bank still ran a misleading advertisement – 'BTR think your shares are worth more than Dunlop do' – in the regional press, and planned to run it in the *Daily Telegraph* too, when the Panel stepped in a second time to halt it.[12] Similarly, a Panel request to Morgan Grenfell to state which way BTR would vote its shares at the shareholders' meeting on 8 February was greeted with scarcely veiled insolence:

BTR has not yet decided whether, and in what manner, to vote its preference shares.[13]

At the meeting, where BTR voted against the Edwardes plan, George Magan maliciously drew attention to the extraordinarily favourable share options Edwardes had awarded himself. When Sir Michael pointed out that he had put his options into abeyance on 20 January, Magan remarked superciliously that 'the options, like Chernenko, were capable of being revived'.[14] Dunlop's request for a copy of the BTR shareholders' register – a perfectly legitimate request, sanctioned by company law – was countered with a letter to Dunlop's advisers, S. G. Warburg, threatening to make Dunlop liable for the costs of any letters sent to BTR shareholders, prompting Edwardes to accuse BTR of personal threats.[15] At one stage Morgan Grenfell suggested that the original Edwardes re-construction plan, which had been approved by the Stock Exchange, was in breach of the law and Edwardes threatened to sue for defamation.[16] All these moves were, as Dunlop correctly alleged, part of a 'campaign to intimidate Dunlop's shareholders into accepting BTR's absurdly low offer'.[17] Edwardes countered with a threat to sell Dunlop's much-prized American assets. This brought an almost instant climb-down from Green, who requested a meeting with Edwardes. After three hours of bargaining, Green raised his offer to nearly three times his sighting shot: £101 million. Dunlop accepted. A Morgan client had triumphed again, but the bank had forfeited much goodwill in the process.

Much goodwill had already been written off in earlier bids. In the summer of 1984 Roger Seelig had suggested to Stanley Kalms, chairman of the electrical retailer Dixon's, that he might bid for the family-controlled Curry's, precipitating a ferocious struggle which ended amid scenes of unprecedented acrimony in the High Court.[18] Kalms had until then used S. G. Warburg, turning to Morgan's only after Seelig promised him a less compromising approach to bid tactics. The final stages of the £233 million bid for Curry's in late November 1984 were a close-run thing, with both sides lobbying hard. At the last minute, one investor, the Scottish Amicable life-assurance company, tried to change its mind. An attempt to withdraw its acceptance of the bid was ignored by Morgan's, who declared Dixon's the winner at 12.15 p.m. on 30 November with just 50.6 per cent of the shares. The Scottish Amicable shareholding had amounted to 0.68 per cent of Curry's – just enough to frustrate Kalms. Late on Friday afternoon, Curry's and Scottish Amicable obtained an injunction blocking the bid. Although, after two days of hearings in the High Court, Mr Justice Vinelott dismissed the Curry's claim as 'fanciful' and 'flimsy', it was an apt conclusion to an intemperate bid.[19] More prescient observers noted for the first time that, although Dixon's was paying for the acquisition with its own shares, thereby vastly increasing the number in circulation, the Dixon's share price had still *doubled* during the course of the bid. This could not be accounted for solely by the unshakeable logic of the deal. Morgan Grenfell was anyway quite open about using its own financial muscle in support of its clients. During 1985 the bank underwrote over £2 billion of cash alternatives for its clients. 'It would be impossible for us to have achieved what we have without that sort of backing,' said George Magan.[20] The bank's own resources were also used to buy shares in both the bidder and the target, though the target's shares would also be 'shorted' – selling shares the seller does not own in the expectation of buying them at a cheaper price later on – to depress their value. In fact it was a late flurry of buying that finally tilted the Curry's battle Dixon's way.[21] Although Seelig claimed it was genuine institutional interest and a subsequent review by the Takeover Panel cleared both him and Kalms of any malfeasance, the Panel still changed the rules to forbid purchases of a target's stock within twenty-four hours of a purchase of a bidder's stock. Competitors sensed a whitewash. 'If you believe it's a coincidence that's up to you. They've got a fairly well-tuned system,' said one.[22] In 1984 another of the acquisitive clients recruited by the bank, Alec Monk, the chairman of the then 'glamour stock' supermarket chain, Dee Corporation, bid for Booker McConnell, a food-distribution business. Dee accumulated a 20 per cent stake in Booker before the Office of Fair Trading intervened in June and referred the bid to the Monopolies and Mergers Commission. After the usual six-month probe, Dee was allowed to renew its assault in February 1985. It did, with a £328 million bid at exactly the Booker share price of £2.60. Rather than offer a premium, Morgan Grenfell cunningly coupled the revised bid with an announcement that Dee was selling part of the 20 per cent stake it had built up at the first attempt and would probably sell more, on the grounds that the Booker share price, buoyed by months of takeover speculation, was unrealistic. Selling a target's shares was a common enough tactic in bids, but coupling a public sale with a public offer to buy was an especially inflammatory ruse. Yet again the Takeover Panel had to rewrite the code, banning bidders from increasing an offer whilst selling the target's stock.[23]

Elsewhere, the scale of Morgan Grenfell's purchases on behalf of clients was alarming and alienating some of the bank's more sedate competitors, especially as it was coupled increasingly with an elastic interpretation of the rules of the Takeover Code. Some began to fight back. Among the first was Schroder Wagg, Morgan's opponents in the long and bitter struggle for control of a small Cumberland brewer called Matthew Brown against repeated bids from a Morgan client, Scottish & Newcastle Breweries. This bruising encounter, spread over three bids and thirty months, was characterized by a formidable and tenacious defence by Schroder's. It frustrated two dawn raids by buying shares on its own account; persuaded a friendly investor, the Whitbread Investment Company, to increase its stake; primed two north-west Labour MPs, Dale Campbell-Savours and Jack Straw, to raise the bid at Prime Minister's Question Time; and staged demonstrations, rallies, petitions and a local advertising campaign, featuring the chat-show host, Russell Harty, which turned an otherwise dull bid into something of a media event. The initial bid was referred to the Monopolies and Mergers Commission on 29 April 1985, which stalled it for six months. Though it was cleared on 12 November, and Scottish & Newcastle immediately renewed the assault, it was denied victory for another two years. Morgan Grenfell, led in this instance not by one of the stars but by the tall and patrician Richard Webb, the caretaker chief of the Corporate Finance Department while Walsh was at the Take-over Panel, for once did not get its own way with the Panel.[24] After repeated public announcements that its second bid was final and would not be increased, Scottish & Newcastle's final letter to Matthew Brown shareholders, prepared by Morgan Grenfell, stipulated that any bid acceptances received after

3.30 p.m. on 11 December 1985 would not be counted. Schroder's itself stopped buying in the market at 3.30 p.m., assuming that Morgan's would follow suit.

Morgan's did not; indeed, it not only carried on buying, but extended the offer period to allow itself to do it for longer. At 4 p.m. the Takeover Panel Executive – the administrative arm of the full panel – rang Schroder's to say that, although Morgan Grenfell had counted acceptances from only 47 per cent of Matthew Brown shareholders, the bid was being extended to 5 p.m. The ruling was made under a rule designed solely to allow more time for counting acceptances, not for making further purchases in the market. It was not hard to discern why the limitation was necessary. Obviously, without counter-bidding from Schroder's, Morgan Grenfell was free to mop up any loose stock, so creating a false market in Matthew Brown shares. Schroder's was appalled at this flagrant breach not just of the rules, but of protocol. Nicholas Jones, the Schroder's director handling the defence, takes up the story:

We sought an immediate meeting with the Panel and during that meeting an announcement was made at 5 p.m. to the effect that Scottish & Newcastle were over 50 per cent and the offer was unconditional as to acceptances. We later discovered that the final market purchases by Scottish & Newcastle which had taken them over 50 per cent had been made at 4.55 p.m. We appealed against the Panel executive's decision and sought a full Panel hearing and also requested that the offer should not be allowed to become fully unconditional. To effect this it was agreed that the Stock Exchange listing of new Scottish & Newcastle shares would not be granted ahead of the hearing the following day.[25]

At the two-hour hearing the following day Jones was completely vindicated. The full Panel overturned the executive's decision to allow an extension of the bid. Though Matthew Brown eventually lost its independence to a third bid in October 1987, Schroder's defence against Morgan Grenfell was a turning-point for morale badly shaken by the Tilling and P & O defections. Scottish & Newcastle's winning bid in October 1987 was £194 million, over twice the original offer. By then Morgan's was immersed in the Guinness affair; and soon Schroder's was to replace Morgan Grenfell at the top of the takeover league table.

There had been other controversial incidents. During the £24 million bid by the construction group French Kier for Abbey, an Irish housebuilder, writs were served on Morgan Grenfell and French Kier for an unscrupulous advertising campaign.[26] Roger Seelig suggested to a client of the bank, Woolworth's, that it might like to be taken over by another client of the bank, Dixon's. When it demurred, in April 1986 Dixon's launched a hostile bid. Morgan Grenfell, associated with both parties, had to stand aside, but the Woolworth board was not impressed. 'Right at the beginning it was Morgan's who suggested that the two companies should talk together,' said Kalms.[27] By Christmas 1985 the City rumour mill was openly speculating on the possibility of a mole in the Corporate Finance Department at Morgan Grenfell, after suspicious price rises ahead of three Morgan bids: the Guinness bid for Bell's, the Scottish & Newcastle bid for Matthew Brown, and the merger of Habitat Mothercare with British Home Stores.[28] By January 1986 the head of surveillance at the Stock Exchange, Bob Wilkinson, had discussed 'possible breaches of security' during the three bids with George Law, the bank's newly appointed 'compliance officer', or director in charge of ensuring that price-sensitive information did not pass from one part of the bank to another. Law conceded as much:

Yes, I have had contact with the Stock Exchange . . . As far as we are concerned it is about which individuals knew what at what stage.[29]

By March 1986 Roger Seelig was being publicly criticized by a rival corporate financier, Hill Samuel's Trevor Swete, who described Seelig's view that Morgan's, Warburg's and Kleinwort Benson were the only worthwhile banks as 'fairly idiosyncratic'.[30] All the elements that erupted into crisis in 1986 – liberal interpretations of the rules, disregard for authority, intimations of insider dealing and an apparent lack of formal or informal constraints within the bank itself – were already present in the Corporate Finance Department by the end of 1985. Reeves was unrepentant about the tactics the bank had adopted in recent bids:

It is a tough business. By their nature, they are very contentious. I do not think we have behaved improperly.[31]

He had lost sight completely of how much external perceptions really mattered.

'Pinchin Denny and Pember & Boyle are no more than the building blocks for our new dealing subsidiary,' was Blaise Hardman's assessment of the £31.3 million the bank had spent on human capital for Big Bang.[32] Lumbered with what Christopher Reeves optimistically called a 'do-it-ourselves' approach to building a major securities business, Hardman's most difficult task was to recruit the salesmen, analysts and traders who would spearhead the bank's drive into the deregulated equity markets after Big Bang. But his first job was to fix the terms of the two purchases, which were finally completed in April 1986 when the Stock Exchange rules permitted outsiders to take full control of member firms. This Hardman tackled with his customary passion for detail, appointing endless committees who wrangled for over five months and produced enough paper to have satisfied the bureaucratic zeal of Philip II.[33] The triplicate of Whitehall was parodied by negotiations which required each side to field its own lawyers, bankers and accountants. (Pember & Boyle chose Lazard's, because it was the only major merchant bank to abjure Big Bang altogether.) The unindustrious brokers and jobbers with whom Hardman negotiated were genuinely astonished at the quantities of paper he could devour, even at weekends, and they all grumbled about the way in which he gradually abandoned the terms of the initial letter of intent, in which Morgan Grenfell listed its benign (but unbinding) intentions towards the captive jobbers and brokers. In the two years before Big Bang, endless planning meetings were held, usually at the end of the day's normal business. With days starting at 7.30 a.m., few brokers or jobbers were inclined to contest Hardman's decisions in a meeting held at 8.30 p.m. Most suspected that the timing was deliberate. Certainly the original plan – to form a semi-auton-omous gilt-edged broker-dealer controlled equally by Morgan Grenfell, Pinchin Denny and Pember & Boyle – bore little relation to the eventual outcome. The fourteen-strong board of directors of the gilt-edged company at the end of 1986 was chaired by Hardman and included six Morgan Grenfell direc-tors or outside appointees. Commitments to appoint Val Powell head of equity trading, and on salary scales, were similarly ditched.[34]

They had no complaints about the money or the conditions attached to it. A team from the Corporate Finance Depart-ment, led by Richard Webb and Guy Dawson, devised a takeover plan designed to tether the two companies' partners to the bank without losing their goodwill. Morgan Grenfell was not anxious, in a phrase of Ian Fraser's, then the chairman of Lazard's, to buy 'goodwill which is two-legged and walks out as quickly as it walks in'.[35] This fear was real enough; eight people from Wedd Durlacher left for Kleinwort Benson even after the deal with Barclay's was signed.[36] To engender loyalty, Christopher Reeves pledged verbally that there would be no redundancies in either Pinchin Denny or Pember & Boyle as a result of their integration. Luckily, the yearning for independence of the former partners of Pinchin Denny and Pember & Boyle was tempered by an unwillingness to lose most of their windfall gains from the purchase of their firms to the Inland Revenue. Both sides were satisfied by a formula that eschewed cash 'golden hallos' of the type then becoming increasingly familiar in the City in favour of partially deferred payment with pieces of paper. 'Golden hallos', unlike share pay-offs, then attracted tax at the higher rates of income tax rather than the lower rates of capital gains tax. Because of this, the partners of both firms were happy to accept part of the purchase price in Morgan Grenfell sold for cash and part in securities convertible into Morgan Grenfell shares, whose con-version rights were deferred for five years and so depended on continued employment at Morgan Grenfell. This formula was

applied to both purchases. Pember & Boyle was bought for
£10.3 million, of which £3.1 million was paid in shares placeable for cash and £7.2 million in 5 per cent convertible
preference shares. Pinchin Denny, bought for £21 million, was
paid for with £5.8 million in shares placeable for cash, £14.4
million in 5 per cent convertible loan stock and a cash payment
of £813,164. Any partner who resigned without the agreement
of Morgan Grenfell before five years were up would forgo his
conversion rights; anybody who was sacked (unless for dis-
honesty) would keep them.[37] Though the proceeds in each
case were split among the partners according to the size of
their stake in the partnership, and so the sums involved varied
considerably between individuals, most had incentive enough
to stay. It was a condition of the sale that Pember & Boyle
should create new partners, so Morgan Grenfell's largesse
filtered through to the 'marzipan layer', the long-serving
employees on the threshold of ascension to the 'icing layer' of a
partnership. One, Peter Mockford, was pleasantly surprised to
find himself aboard the gravy train.

Hardman then had to fuse the brokers of Pember & Boyle
with the jobbers of Pinchin Denny to form the new primary
dealership in the gilt-edged market. Morgan Grenfell was one
of thirty-one institutions which applied to the Bank of England
in June 1985 to trade gilts.[38] Like the others, the bank had
been examined searchingly by Eddie George, the Bank official
responsible for the new market. Morgan Grenfell entered the
market primarily for defensive reasons. It feared that once the
principal brokers and jobbers were in the hands of its rivals,
they would no longer sell or make markets in the new issues
the bank managed for its clients, which would deny it new-
issue business. But, given the evidence available even then, it is
hard to believe that the decision to apply for a licence was
entirely rational; the supposition lingers that Morgan Grenfell
entered the gilt-edged market partly for reasons of prestige.
Though the over-capitalized Japanese securities houses were
precluded pending the opening of the Tokyo markets to British
firms, the opposition included American giants like Shearson

Lehman, Citicorp, Chase Manhattan and Merrill Lynch. Five jobbers would be replaced by thirty-one, while the capital committed to the market was likely to rise from £80 million to £600 or £700 million as new firms were admitted to the market. Commission rates, always negotiable on short gilts and razor thin – 0.05 per cent – were likely to disappear altogether on longs. The supply of new stock was drying up and the projected market share of the thirty-one applicants added up to twice the prevailing size of the entire market. Within a fortnight of submitting their formal applications, Schroder Wagg and the American investment bank, Drexel Burnham Lambert, had withdrawn them, citing the probable lack of a reasonable return.[39] The only justification for staying, as Morgan Grenfell argued at the time, was that a sales and market-making presence was an indispensable corollary to the bank's new-issue business, especially in sterling Eurobonds, which were priced in relation to gilts and increasingly sold to the same investors. Unfortunately, by 1985 the Eurobond Department was a house of cards.

The Eurobond market had grown explosively during the 1980s as interest rates and inflation tumbled around the globe, encouraging investors to put more of their money into fixed-rate bonds. Companies flocked to the London-based international banks who – because Eurobond investors were prepared to trade lower interest rates for anonymity and tax-free income – could usually raise finance at cheaper rates than they could manage at home. The amount of paper issued rose tenfold from $18.8 billion in 1980[40] to $180 billion in 1986.[41] It was a market in which any merchant bank with pretensions to becoming an international investment house had to be active, and Morgan Grenfell accepted the challenge eagerly. Jon Perry, head of the Eurobond Department, had been busily recruiting bankers, salesmen and traders since the division's constitution as a separate department in 1980.[42] Needing to make an impression quickly, he had been forced to abandon the bank's traditional reliance on home-grown talent and to poach from houses already active in the market. This in itself posed the novel problem of integrating staff raised in different corporate cultures, and was answered partially by choosing from a narrow range of firms. A complete team was gradually assembled from members of the Eurobond department at Orion Royal Bank, then one of the leading houses in the market. Among the recruits was Keith Harris, a Eurobond specialist who marketed the United States for Orion.[43] He was by no means a typical recruit. Educated at Buckhurst Hill County High School, Essex, and at Bradford and Surrey Universities, he was a meritocrat impatient with the social gradations of a bank like Morgan Grenfell. He succeeded nonetheless, becoming a director in 1985.[44] David Whitehead, a bond trader, was recruited from Continental Illinois to run a trading book.[45] Paul Gold, then a salesman with Credit Suisse First Boston, the dominant force in the Eurobond market throughout the first half of the 1980s, was hired to head the sales drive.[46] It was hoped that the new division could capitalize on the impeccable corporate contacts of the Corporate Finance Department.

At first everything went well. The number of bond issues of which the bank underwrote at least a part increased from just 23 in 1980 to 256 worth $30.5 billion in 1984.[47] The number of 'lead managements' – where the bank fixed the terms of the borrowing, wrote the documentation and underwrote the largest amount – increased from six to twenty-five in the same period.[48] That year the bank finished twenty-second in the *Euromoney* league table of lead managers, well adrift of the major American, Swiss and Japanese banks but ahead of every other merchant bank except S. G. Warburg.[49] There were even some notable innovations. After an uncomfortable reception, a $20 million convertible bond issue for an unknown Danish pharmaceutical company, Novo Industri A/S, was a runaway success of exactly the kind at which merchant banks had always excelled.[50] It presaged a steady flow of business arranging convertible bond issues in London for smaller companies.[51] They included a macabre coffin manufacturer called Amedco[52] and two US Mid-Western cable-television companies called Comcast and Heritage.[53] The lead management for United

Biscuits of a sterling bond issue with 'equity warrants' – detachable options to buy United Biscuits shares – was genuinely pioneering, though the warrants sold at a pace sufficiently brisk to suggest that they had been badly underpriced.[54] After the abolition of exchange controls, the bank handled the first placing of foreign-currency bonds in London since the war – DM100 million of bonds for the European Investment Bank. The bank also managed the first sterling bond issue sold in London for a Japanese company, a £20 million convertible for the retailer, The Daiei Inc.,[55] and the first floating-rate sterling bonds, for Scandinavian Bank.[56] A $100 million deal of hideous complexity for ICI, which offered buyers warrants to buy shares in ICI and an option to convert their dollar bonds into sterling ones at a fixed exchange rate, was lead managed in conjunction with Goldman Sachs. Though the technology completely outstripped understanding and the bonds sold poorly, the innovation won plaudits.[57] So did a dual-currency bond for General Motors where interest on dollar bonds was paid in Swiss francs.[58] But good ideas were not enough; the initial success was illusory.

The bank had been prepared to run its Eurobond Department as a loss leader for at least two years, and was pleasantly surprised to find that it was marginally profitable at once. The Eurobond market between 1979 and 1984 was still generous to newcomers, and to some extent Morgan Grenfell could trade on its reputation alone as borrowers and investors were happy to see what it could do. One or two clients were referred to the division by the Corporate Finance Department, and the outsiders recruited from Orion brought with them established contacts and rudimentary expertise. As at other banks before the era of 'Chinese Walls', the bank's own Investment Department could be relied upon to buy some of the bonds the division underwrote. Even the increased number of banks involved in the market seemed to redound to Morgan Grenfell's advantage. There was immense competition to gain access to syndicates. Banks who accepted loss-making deals knew that the favour would be repaid in time with an underwriting slot in a profitable one. Many underwriters – and Morgan Grenfell was no exception – had no idea of where to sell some types of bond, but accepted anyway, confident that the lead manager would buy back their allotment at a profitable price. It could be argued that syndicate desks around the market existed for this express purpose. Lead managers would deliberately allot underwriting banks more bonds than they had said they could sell, in the expectation that they could pick them up later at a lower price. It meant that prices of new issues – the 'primary' market – often bore little relation to the prices of seasoned issues – the 'secondary' market. The bleak 'tombstone' advertisements – the dull lists of banks who underwrote a loan or a bond issue – which fattened the pages of the financial press, grew absurdly long and cosmopolitan, but gave few clues as to where bonds actually ended up. By 1984 the average underwriting group might contain 150 institutions, of which only a handful impinged in any way on the success or failure of a bond issue. It was not a system built to last.

It did not become fully apparent until 1984 that the Eurobond market was changing profoundly, but from then on it was clear that it was nothing more than a commodity business responsive to price alone, akin to selling sacks of potatoes. Historically, this was the point at which merchant banks usually abandoned the field to their better capitalized competitors, but to have done so in 1984 would have contradicted the entire rationale of Morgan Grenfell's approach to Big Bang. The bank had bought Pinchin Denny and Pember & Boyle and applied for a place in the new gilt-edged market specifically because it wanted to be in the new-issue business. This was unfortunate, because the terms of the debate were changing. The market had been growing steadily less friendly since the late 1970s, as aggressive techniques were imported by the American houses active in London. Among the first was the introduction of bond brokers, a familiar sight on Wall Street, but unknown in the Eurobond market until 1978. By advertising the prices at which they were prepared to buy and sell new issues, they offered incompetent banks a discreet exit from bond issues they could not sell, allowing underwriters to accept positions in the knowledge that they could sell them back to the lead manager without the embarrassment of doing it directly. In this way brokers' prices for new issues in the primary market – so called 'grey-market' prices – fell out of joint with real secondary-market prices. Yet banks like Morgan Grenfell, which were still feeling their way in the new market, tended to price new issues by reference to the grey market, where prices were unrepresentative of the real state of the Eurodollar bond market.

This led to a split on whether Morgan Grenfell should compete in the Eurodollar bond markets or not.[59] Keith Harris thought that if Morgan Grenfell was to become an international investment bank, it must be able to service its clients in all the key capital markets.[60] 'I felt that the ability to issue debt securities was an essential part of being an international investment bank,' said Harris.[61] A slavish devotion to league tables – journalistic assessments of a bank's impact on the market measured solely by the number and volume of issues a bank has managed in any particular year or half-year – was common among banks at the time. Most bankers affected to despise the rankings, but they all knew that a high placing in a *Euromoney* or *International Financing Review* league table was an unanswerable argument for doing business with one bank rather than another. Since the Eurodollar bond market constituted four-fifths of the entire market, it was impossible to secure promotion in the league tables without issuing Eurodollar bonds. This lumbered banks with new issues designed not to make money but to propel them up the league tables. To traders like David Whitehead, profitability, rather than volume, was the only appropriate measure of success. Profits were easier to generate in the more liquid American treasury-bond market, or the less crowded European government-bond markets, where the gradual removal of withholding taxes was internationalizing the markets. It was also hard to price Eurodollar bond issues correctly without active participation in the American treasury market. At Morgan Grenfell, as else-

Left: George Peabody (1795–1869), merchant, philanthropist, miser and bore. 'A regular old bachelor,' said J. P. Morgan, but he had a mistress in Brighton. *Right:* Junius Spencer Morgan (1813–1890), George Peabody's first partner and founder of the Morgan dynasty, photographed in London in 1890. 'Do not let the desire of success or of accumulating induce you ever to do a single action which will cause you regret,' he told his son. (Courtesy of the Pierpont Morgan Library, New York)

H.M.S. *Monarch*, having on board the remains of George Peabody, leaves Portsmouth Harbour for the United States on 11 December 1869, accompanied by U.S.S. *Plymouth*.

Right: John Pierpont Morgan (1837–1913), banker, art collector and priapist. 'The first thing is character,' he told his critics, though not about his nose, which he called 'part of the American business structure'.

Below: Jack Morgan (1867–1943), the last Morgan to run the family bank. He is pictured aboard *Corsair*, arriving in England in 1937 to shoot with the King.

Below right: Montagu Norman (1871–1950), governor of the Bank of England throughout the inter-war years.

Left: Thomas Sivewright Catto (1879–1959), posing as the laird of Schivas. Created the first Baron Catto of Cairncatto in 1936, he was Montagu Norman's successor as governor of the Bank of England in 1944.

Above: Sir Siegmund Warburg (1902–1982). Creator of the Eurobond market and inventor of hostile bids, he was despised for starting work at 8 a.m. 'They looked down on me with utmost snobbism,' he said of his City contemporaries.

Stephen Gordon, the second Baron Catto of Cairncatto (1923–), outside Caxton Hall Registry Office with Margaret Forrest, the family nanny he married in 1966.

Above: Dr. Ashraf Marwan, the Egyptian financier and client of Lord Spens, who made a dividend cheque homeless when he asked for his money back.

Above right: Ephraim Margulies, chairman and chief executive of S & W Berisford, who prudently dealt via the secretive Swiss. He is so far untouched.

Right: Alistair Buchanan, the money markets man who thought he had joined the premier merchant bank in London, but found instead a 'corporate *soixante-neuf*'.

Left: Sir Peter Carey, the Whitehall mandarin dumped in the chairman's seat by the Guinness affair, pictured upstairs at 23 Great Winchester Street. 'We are quite determined to clean ourselves,' he assured the press.

Below: John Craven, at 23 Great Winchester Street, watching 450 leave from 20 Finsbury Circus. 'To take a zero market share and build a meaningful business was frankly a hell of an uphill task which I don't think that anybody could have achieved,' he said after they had left.

John Craven, with Teddy Grenfell: a dealmaker joins the establishment.

where in the Eurobond market, the need of corporate financiers to service their clients was at odds with the need of traders to trade profitably.

The split was exacerbated by the diminishing realism of the Eurobond new-issue market, where fierce competition was a bonanza only for borrowers. Increasingly, bonds were being underwritten at prices which made them impossible to sell. The most obvious reason for this was the 'bought deal', invented in April 1980 by Credit Suisse First Boston who, rather than test the reaction of underwriters, simply bought $100 million of fixed-rate bonds issued by the General Motors Corporation. For borrowers this was a godsend, insulating them completely from a rise in interest rates after the terms were agreed, but for banks it raised the stakes significantly. If interest rates fell before the bonds were sold, banks made a fortune; if they rose, they lost a fortune. By 1984 most issues were 'bought' in this way, usually after a telephone auction. It put a premium on knowing where to sell an issue quickly, but as a small and hitherto introspective British merchant bank Morgan Grenfell naturally found investors in Eurodollar bond issues very hard to come by. In the earliest days of the market it had relied on Morgan & Cie in Paris to place bonds almost exclusively in Switzerland via the big three Swiss banks and their lesser private brethren, and so had developed no network of its own.[62] In the relatively generous market of the early 1980s, when in-house investment departments were ready buyers, the absence of an exclusive sales network did not matter very much. In the competitive markets after 1984, which were characterized by keen price competition and mounting concern about conflicts of interest, it did. Swiss investors, still important to the success of an issue, were inaccessible except via the Big Three, who were active in the Eurobond market on their own account. Alternative Eurodollar bond investors in the United States, Japan and the Middle East were heavily courted. Historic relationships broke down and borrowers began to shop around. They were encouraged by the large Eurobond houses, which thrived on the publicity which accompanied a borrower's decision to change lead managers. At Morgan Grenfell, the cautious counselled withdrawal but, at least initially, the bolder spirits like Harris prevailed.[63]

Competition was not the only factor. 'Hedging' – a technique which allows buyers and sellers to protect their business against a change in prices – encouraged banks to think that Eurobonds could be underwritten at the wrong price and still break even. A fixed-rate Eurodollar bond bought the day before a massive rise in dollar interest rates could still be virtually riskless provided that the buyer simultaneously 'shorted' – sold a bond he did not own – on the American treasury-bond market. If interest rates did rise, the price of the Eurobond fell, but so did the price of the treasury bond, so the treasury bond could be bought at the lower price and sold at the higher price, offsetting the loss on the Eurobond. The most significant development of all was the invention of the 'swap'. Though some have pinpointed the first swap in the exchange of American gold reserves for pounds sterling by the house of Morgan to assist Britain's return to the gold standard in 1925, swaps are generally agreed to have their origins in 'parallel' and 'back-to-back' loans, which became a popular way round British exchange controls in the 1960s and 1970s.[64] Unable to buy dollars at will, British companies would lend sterling to American companies in return for dollars. Their descendant, the modern swap, owes as much to the unpredictability of world-wide interest and exchange rates since the abandonment of fixed exchange rates in the early 1970s. The gyrating costs of money and currencies have allowed borrowers to 'arbitrage' – essentially, borrow cheaply in one market and lend dearly in another – the various domestic and Eurocurrency bond markets. This is what swaps do. In theory, currency markets are 'perfectly arbitraged'. Any gain from borrowing cheaply in one currency market should be lost when investing in another; it is for this reason that the calculation of exchange rates incorporates interest rates. If this theory – called 'interest-rate parity theory' – held true, all interest rates would, after covering for foreign exchange, be the same. Swaps prove that they are not.

They come in two forms, which can be combined. The first is the *interest-rate swap*. In its classic form, one borrower borrows at a fixed rate of interest and the other at a floating rate of interest; they then simply swap their obligations. This works only because an arbitrage exists: one party can borrow more cheaply in the fixed-rate market, whilst the other party can borrow more cheaply in the floating-rate market. The second is the *currency swap*, where the two parties do much the same thing, but exchange currencies as well. Any permutation of these two is possible. Swaps are arguably the single most important innovation since the advent of the Euro-markets. Swap opportunities are now actively traded, with borrowers using the market continuously to adjust their pattern of interest- and exchange-rate risk. It may be worth as much as $500 billion.[65] In the Eurobond market, borrowers no longer simply borrow the currency they need; they borrow another one and swap it instead if the end result is cheaper money. Often bankers deliberately misprice a bond issue to meet the demands of a swap, confident that their earnings from arranging the swap will outweigh their losses on the bond. Issues 'swap driven' in this way were reckoned to account for over a quarter of all Eurobond issues in 1987.[66] The number of mispriced Eurobond issues has increased commensurately, but to stay in the Eurobond business at all Morgan Grenfell had to be in swaps. At the beginning of 1984 a swaps team was formed within the Eurobond Department.[67] This brought to the Eurobond Department a highly ambitious director of the bank, a thirty-seven-year-old Whitgift and Cambridge man who joined the international banking operations of Morgan Grenfell in 1973, after five years in the Diplomatic Service. He was called John Rawlings.

The perils of unrestricted involvement in the Eurodollar bond market became starkly apparent at Morgan Grenfell in April 1984. It was agreed with Citicorp, the giant American money-centre bank, that Morgan Grenfell would underwrite $100 million of fifteen-year bonds for it at a fixed rate of interest of $11\frac{3}{4}$ per cent. A similar issue for ITT had sold well the previous day, and the following day Morgan Grenfell began to syndicate the bonds. That afternoon the Eurodollar bond market, following a lead from New York, tumbled on news of a fresh debt crisis in Mexico. The value of bonds issued by Citicorp, with its large exposure to Latin American debt, tumbled with it. It proved virtually impossible to syndicate the bonds that afternoon.[68] They were refused even by Citicorp's London office, which persuaded other banks to reject them too.[69] Morgan Grenfell, faced with the choice of losing money or losing face, chose money. Though a syndicate was eventually formed, the decision to support the bank's client in the expectation that the market would recover cost the bank over $1 million.[70]

It was a substantial loss, highlighting the value of the riskless fees and low appetite for capital of the Corporate Finance Department. The cautious were vindicated. The bank's annual reports for 1983 and 1984 record not an increased involvement in the Eurodollar bond market but deepening involvement in the sterling domestic ('Bulldog') and Eurobond markets instead. This, combined with cleverer products like convertibles and combined bond and equity warrant issues, were judged much safer ground. The bank began to make markets in sterling Eurobond issues.[71] In 1985 it arranged the first Eurobond issue by a British building society, raising £150 million for the country's biggest home-loans institution, the Halifax.[72] Successful Eurodollar convertible-bond issues were arranged for two French companies, Moët Hennessy and ACCOR.[73] The change of direction was absolute: in the five years to the end of 1985 Morgan Grenfell lead-managed nine fixed-rate dollar Eurobonds worth $650 million, but in the three years preceding the final closure of the division in 1987, it led just one, a swap-driven $75 million deal for Inco in July 1985.[74] Whereas from 1980 to 1984 the bank lead managed only nineteen sterling Bulldog and Eurobonds worth £818 million, in the following three it led thirty-three worth £2.2 billion.[75] In 1986 Morgan Grenfell led more sterling Eurobond issues than any other bank.[76]

There was a renewed emphasis on innovation in the hope that quality might compensate for quantity. In December 1984 Morgan Grenfell conceived a novel way of using the Eurobond markets to finance British exports to Brazil. Instead of borrowing the money to lend to Brazil from Euromarket banks in London, with an interest-rate subsidy from the ECGD, the scheme raised the money by an issue of $155 million of floating-rate bonds. Because the interest payments on the bonds were secured on ECGD-guaranteed loans to Brazil, the bonds proved very popular.[77] A similar $230 million deal followed a year later, with the formation of Italex, which raised money to lend to Brazil under the guarantee of SACE, the Italian export credit agency.[78] It was thought in the city at the time that these deals would revolutionize export financing but they proved to be one-offs. The same fate befell MINI, the first company formed to issue £50 million of bonds whose interest payments were secured on household mortgage payments. At the time the American market in bonds of this kind was worth $15 billion, and a number of firms had been working out how to bring the technology to London, but Morgan Grenfell was the first to clear the jungle of tax and legal obstacles.[79] Had the bank's technological lead been translated patiently into further business, it might not have had to close its bond operations in 1988; today S. G. Warburg and Salomon Brothers routinely issue mortgage-backed bonds in sizes of up to £500 million.[80] Other ideas were borrowed from abroad. In March 1985 the bank lead managed the first zero-coupon sterling Eurobond. These bonds, which roll up all the interest payments into a single payment at the end, were very popular in New York, but flopped badly in London, where few investors were interested in deferred income.[81] Another idea, the first sterling Eurobond to be issued at a long maturity, a £100 million issue for ICI, was a runaway success. The bond took advantage of the Bank of England's increasingly liberal attitude towards investment in Eurobonds by London institutions. It was fêted in the specialist press, but success was increasingly a matter of chance rather than judgement.[82]

The decision to concentrate on sterling was vindicated by a revival in the popularity of the currency among international investors, but the fixed-rate sterling Eurobond market was an insufficient foundation for continued prosperity. It was a marginal corner of the market, highly volatile and utterly dependent on changing international perceptions about the strength of the pound. The bank's rivals, many of whom had bought much better brokers than Pember & Boyle, had access to much larger groups of potential buyers. A potential niche in sterling convertible Eurobonds for British companies was lost to a foreign house, Credit Suisse First Boston, who boasted that it made £30 million from it in 1987. Unlike other merchant banks, who were similarly cornered in the sterling Eurobond market, Morgan Grenfell also failed to develop a complementary specialization which could be sold to the same clients as bought sterling Eurobonds. Hambro's became one of the City's leading underwriters of Australian dollar bond issues, while Baring's specialized in Japanese equity warrants, but Morgan's was hamstrung by a sterile debate over the economics of entry to the Eurodollar bond markets, which eventually spilled into the public domain.[83]

Entry to the Eurodollar bond market involved recruiting experienced Eurodollar bond traders. Unfortunately, they did not come cheap. In the first half of the 1980s the Eurobond market was a byword for excessive salaries, Porsches and a champagne lifestyle. Competition for experienced staff had sent salaries up to stratospheric levels. According to one survey, Eurobond professionals were the best paid in the City, with nearly two-thirds of departmental heads paid over £100,000 per annum and 93 per cent of sales and trading staff earning annual bonuses on top of sums often of similar magnitude.[84] Peregrine Moncrieff left Shearson Lehman to run the Eurobond operations of E. F. Hutton, an American brokerage house, for a reputed $1 million salary.[85] The spectacular 'team' defection, in which entire teams of experts change sides overnight, was routine. It was pioneered, to general astonishment, by Merrill Lynch, who poached ten senior professionals from the rival

Credit Suisse First Boston in a single day.[86] This made the costs and risks of hiring Eurodollar bond traders unjustifiably high. At Morgan's, Harris, frustrated and disillusioned, considered resigning, but accepted the managing directorship of Morgan Grenfell Inc. in New York.[87] On his return, he planned to assume leadership of the Eurobond Department.[88]

Harris's departure for New York removed from London the foremost advocate of full-blooded participation in the Eurodollar bond markets. He left behind John Rawlings, the manager of the newly formed swaps group, who opposed Harris's Eurodollar strategy.[89] Rawlings was a banker, not a securities man, and had little truck with a commodities business like Eurobonds. He was reluctant to use the swaps team as a lever for new-issue business and stuck to those swap opportunities where he felt the bank could add value. These tended to be complex cross-currency swaps, where the returns were higher, though the group also traded sterling interest rate swaps and was active in high swap technology like options and asset swaps.[90] There was no room for swapping Eurodollar bonds into other currencies. Rawlings's methods represented a return to the classical view of the business of merchant bankers, in which they lived, in the celebrated phrase of Sir Edward Reid, on their wits rather than their assets, pioneering new markets but abandoning mature ones to better capitalized competitors. He had applied them successfully in the bank's international banking division. Fortuitously for him, this approach matched the changing nature of the Euromarkets.

Rawlings's arrival in the Eurobond Department was symptomatic of the increasing 'securitization' of bank lending. All the factors which had encouraged the growth of the Eurobond market – Japan's recycled trade surplus, profitable companies looking to invest surplus cash, the Third World debt crisis and the looser central banking controls on buying securities as opposed to lending money – had a profound effect on the syndicated Eurocurrency loan market which had developed in London during the 1970s. In 1981 the Eurocurrency loan market was one and a half times the size of the Eurobond market; yet by 1986 the Eurobond market was nearly six times the size of the syndicated loan market.[91] Borrowers, mainly banks and governments, found that they could raise money more cheaply by issuing Floating Rate Notes – Eurobonds on which interest payments fluctuate in line with interest rates generally – than by borrowing from the bank. The number of Floating Rate Notes issued soared to $15.7 billion in 1987, stealing business from the syndicated-loan market.[92] Morgan Grenfell, anxious not to be squeezed out, began to make markets in Floating Rate Notes.[93] Unlike fixed-rate Eurodollar bonds, which were hard for Morgan Grenfell to find and trade after the initial flurry of interest, this seemed to make sense. It was a large market, dominated by very large issues from top credits like banks and governments, in which it was easy to buy and sell without losing money. Unfortunately, the bank did not become a major face in the market.

More traditional banking markets were also overrun by securitization. Until the 1980s, the Treasury operations of most merchant banks were a backwater untouched by the excitement elsewhere in the City, taking deposits, lending money for short periods and exchanging foreign currencies much as they had done since their formation in the 1960s. At Morgan Grenfell, the anachronistic nature of Treasury operations was typified by Julian Stanford, its Old School director, whose short working day and antiquated sartorial taste made him a figure of fun to the eager young men of the Eurobond Department.[94] One was delighted when he mistook the obscure Japanese bank, Norinchukin, for the Norwich Union assurance company. The invention of Euronotes and Eurocommercial paper, which enable companies to borrow by repeatedly selling quickly maturing (three- or six-month) securities, threatened the quiescent existence of Treasury departments. By selling the Euronotes or Eurocommercial paper directly to investors, companies cut banks out of the lending chain – 'disintermediated' them, in the jargon – and denied them the turn they usually took on syndicating a Euroloan or a Eurobond with other banks and investors. It also affected the deposit-taking business.

Rather than leave surplus funds on deposit with banks at a low rate of interest, companies invested directly in the Euronotes and Eurocommercial paper issued by other companies, most of which paid higher rates of interest. By 1985 Morgan Grenfell was sufficiently worried by the trend towards securitization to merge the domestic lending business of the bank with the Eurobond Department.[95] The Eurobond Department was immediately renamed the Banking and Capital Markets Division – in recognition, as Lord Catto put it, of 'the continuing trend towards the securitization of lending'.[96] Experts were recruited, some from outside the bank. One of them was Alex Catto, the thirty-two-year-old son of the second Lord Catto, who left a banking post at Morgan Guaranty to join the family bank as a senior assistant director.[97] The plan was to use the contacts of the Corporate Finance Department to win business. This worked quite well, and a new money-market division, incorporating foreign exchange, Eurocommercial paper, Euronotes and certificates of deposit, was set up in early 1987.[98]

These changes fundamentally altered the nature of the business of the Eurobond Department. They would not have done so had the Eurobond market not become unprofitable, but in mid-1986 the biggest buyers of Floating Rate Notes, the Japanese banks, started to withdraw from the market because the returns were too small. They turned, *inter alia*, to investment in Euronotes and Eurocommercial paper. Liquidity – the ability to buy and sell bonds in large quantities without moving the price – began to dry up. Investors shunned a market in which they could not sell, obliging borrowers to look elsewhere. With no new issues, salesmen and traders fell idle and banks started to lose money. Any commitment to further expansion in the Eurobond market became insupportable. The stock of John Rawlings, who had long opposed unrestricted participation in the Eurobond markets and whose own swaps team continued to make money, rose commensurately.[99] When in December that year the Corporate Finance Department finally ran into serious trouble, its reverberations were felt most keenly and most immediately in the Eurobond Department, where the

Guinness Affair administered the *coup de grâce* to an operation which had been struggling to find its way for over two years.

NOTES

[1] *Sunday Times*, 27 January 1985; *The Observer Magazine*, 30 July 1989.
[2] *Financial Times*, 11 March 1985.
[3] *ibid.*
[4] *Financial Weekly*, 27 September 1985.
[5] *Financial Times*, 11 March 1985.
[6] *Sunday Times*, 27 January 1985.
[7] *Financial Times*, 16 January 1985.
[8] *Financial Times*, 19 January 1985.
[9] *Financial Times*, 23 February 1985 and 19 March 1985.
[10] *Financial Times*, 1 February 1985.
[11] *Financial Times*, 3 March 1985.
[12] *Financial Times*, 6 February 1985.
[13] *Financial Times*, 11 March 1985.
[14] *Sunday Times*, 29 December 1985. Chernenko was one of Brezhnev's successors as Soviet leader. His death was concealed from the public.
[15] *Financial Times*, 12 February 1985.
[16] *Financial Times*, 23 February 1985.
[17] *Financial Times*, 27 February 1985.
[18] *Sunday Telegraph*, 25 November 1984.
[19] *Financial Times*, 5 December 1984.
[20] *Sunday Times*, 27 January 1985.
[21] *Institutional Investor*, December 1985.
[22] Ivan Fallon and James Srodes, *Takeovers*, Hamish Hamilton, 1987.
[23] *Financial Times*, 14 February 1985; *Daily Telgraph*, 16 February 1985.
[24] *The Economist*, 5 February 1987.
[25] *Acquisitions Monthly*, March 1986.
[26] *Guardian*, 7 December 1985; *Financial Times*, 7 December 1985; *Irish Times*, 6 December 1985.
[27] *Standard*, 10 April 1986; *Financial Weekly*, 10 April 1986.
[28] *Mail on Sunday*, 22 December 1985.
[29] *Mail on Sunday*, 5 January 1986.
[30] *Standard*, 14 March 1986. Seelig's original views appeared in *Financial Decisions*, March 1986.

[31] *Financial Times*, 19 March 1985.
[32] *Sunday Times*, 21 October 1984.
[33] *Daily Telegraph*, 15 October 1984.
[34] Morgan Grenfell Government Securities, Accounts, 1986; *The Observer Magazine*, 30 July 1989.
[35] *Financial Times*, 10 August 1985.
[36] Margaret Reid, *All-Change in the City*, Macmillan, 1988.
[37] Morgan Grenfell Group plc, Offer of Ordinary Shares by Tender, Prospectus, June 1986.
[38] *Financial Times*, 4 June 1985.
[39] *Financial Times*, 18 June 1985.
[40] Ian Kerr, *A History of the Eurobond Market*, Euromoney Publications, 1984.
[41] 'A Survey of the Euromarkets', *The Economist*, 16 May 1987.
[42] Morgan Grenfell Holdings Limited, Annual Report and Accounts, 1980.
[43] *Financial Times*, 2 April 1982.
[44] *The Observer Magazine*, 30 July 1989; Financial Times, 5 January 1985.
[45] *International Insider*, 17 November 1980.
[46] *Financial Times*, 7 November 1981.
[47] Morgan Grenfell Holdings Limited, Annual Report and Accounts, 1980 and 1984.
[48] Morgan Grenfell Holdings Limited, Annual Report and Accounts, 1984.
[49] Annual Financing Report, *Euromoney*, March 1986.
[50] Kerr, *op. cit.*
[51] Morgan Grenfell Holdings, Annual Report and Accounts, 1983.
[52] *Financial Times*, 16 May 1983.
[53] *Financial Times*, 17 November 1982 and 20 March 1984.
[54] *Financial Times*, 20 March 1984; *The Times*, 20 March 1984; *Daily Telegraph*, 20 March 1984.
[55] *Guardian*, 18 June 1980.
[56] Morgan Grenfell Holdings Limited, Annual Report and Accounts, 1983.
[57] *Financial Times*, 4 May 1983.
[58] *Financial Times*, 4 October 1983.
[59] *The Economist*, 17 January 1987.
[60] *ibid.*
[61] *Euromoney*, June 1988.
[62] Kerr, *op. cit.*
[63] *The Economist*, 17 January 1987.

[64] *Inside the Swap Market*, International Financing Review Publishing Limited, November 1985.

[65] Reid, *op. cit.*

[66] Bank for International Settlements, International Banking and Financial Market Developments, 30 October 1987.

[67] *Euromoney*, November 1985; Morgan Grenfell Holdings Limited, Annual Report and Accounts, 1984.

[68] *International Financing Review*, 7 April 1984.

[69] *Financial Times*, 5 April 1984.

[70] Losses are incurred when a bond is bought at a discount greater than its underwriting fees. The loss has been calculated by subtracting from Morgan Grenfell's underwriting fees of 1.375 per cent ($1.38 million on $100 million), the 2.5 per cent ($2.5 million) discount at which, according to *International Financing Review* (7 April 1984), investors were prepared to buy the bonds.

[71] Morgan Grenfell Holdings Limited, Annual Report and Accounts, 1984.

[72] Morgan Grenfell Holdings Limited, Annual Report and Accounts, 1985.

[73] *Financial Times*, 3 July 1984; *Daily Mail*, 3 July 1984; *Financial Times*, 25 September 1984.

[74] *Financial Times*, 10 July 1985.

[75] *International Financing Review, passim.*

[76] Morgan Grenfell Group plc, Annual Report and Accounts, 1986.

[77] *Financial Times*, 14 December 1985; *Daily Telegraph*, 14 December 1984; *Financial Times*, 20 December 1984.

[78] *Financial Times*, 5 December 1985; Morgan Grenfell Holdings Limited, Annual Report and Accounts, 1985.

[79] *International Insider*, 14 January 1985. In 1987 the bank was finally persuaded by an outside consultant, Nick Deutsch, to set up First Mortgage Securities in conjunction with GEC, the Bank of Scotland and Foreign and Colonial, a £20 million company designed to provide bond finance for lenders secured on mortgage repayments. By then it was hard to penetrate a sophisticated market (*Financial Times*, 6 June 1987).

[80] *Euromoney*, March 1985.

[81] *Financial Times*, 6 April 1985; *International Insider*, 1 April 1985.

[82] *Financial Times*, 20 March 1986; *Daily Telegraph*, 20 March 1986; *The Times*, 20 March 1986.

[83] *The Economist*, 17 January 1987 and 7 November 1987; *Euromoney*, June 1988.

[84] Coopers & Lybrand, 'The Big Bang, Earnings and Benefits of Key Specialists', cited in Reid, *op. cit.*

[85] *The Economist*, 19 July 1986.
[86] *Daily Mail*, 30 January 1984.
[87] *Euromoney*, June 1988.
[88] *The Economist*, 12 November 1987.
[89] *ibid.*
[90] Morgan Grenfell Holdings Limited, Annual Report and Accounts, 1985.
[91] Bank for International Settlements, International Banking and Financial Market Developments, 30 October 1987.
[92] *International Financing Review*, 2 January 1988.
[93] Morgan Grenfell Holdings Limited, Annual Report and Accounts, 1984.
[94] *Business*, July 1986.
[95] Morgan Grenfell Holdings Limited, Annual Report and Accounts, 1985.
[96] *ibid.*
[97] *Financial Times*, 20 December 1985.
[98] *Daily Telegraph*, 9 February 1987.
[99] *The Economist*, 12 November 1987.

EIGHT

Revolving Doors

In the spring of 1985 Geoffrey Collier, the thirty-five-year-old president of Vickers da Costa Securities Inc. in New York, received an invitation from Michael Dobson, the managing director of Morgan Grenfell Inc., to breakfast with him at Manhattan's exclusive Racquets Club.[1] Collier was surprised by the venue, since he assumed that it was well known that he had only recently been blackballed by the Racquets Club, a bastion of British expatriate snobbery which considered him far too brash, but there was no reason for him to suspect anything unusual. Though they did not know each other well, he and Dobson had often bumped into each other on New York's incestuous social circuit for Englishmen in exile. But when he arrived at the Racquets Club he found that they would not be eating alone; Christopher Reeves and the group director of Morgan's overseas companies, Christopher Whittington, were also present. The breakfast began stiffly. After eleven years of blunt exchanges in New York and Far Eastern dealing rooms Collier had forgotten the long and inconsequential ramblings that precede any discussion of money amongst Englishmen. It was not until they were preparing to leave that Reeves finally asked Collier if he would be interested in joining Morgan Grenfell as managing director of the equity-securities business the bank was piecing together in London ahead of Big Bang in October 1986. Collier was an unusual choice for a merchant bank to make but he was undoubtedly the right man for the job. Even his detractors acknowledged that he was a brilliant trader, able, in the words of one observer, 'to read the stock market like the bottom of his glass'.[2] He was also a proven builder of businesses, having steered Vickers da Costa's American operations from nothing to a staff of forty in New York and six in Los Angeles in just five years. Collier had started with the stockbrokers Grieveson Grant as a twenty-two-year-old research analyst in 1972. After three years he moved to Laurence Prust, working in Singapore and Malaysia and opening their Hong Kong office, before joining Vickers da Costa's prosperous Hong Kong operation in the summer of 1977, as a salesman. Vickers was something of a gamble. After resigning from Laurence Prust, Collier had taken a consultancy post under Alan Knapp, the senior partner of the Hong Kong stockbroker, Sandelson & Co., but the firm folded within four months of his appointment amid allegations of shady dealings. Vickers approached him in the wake of the confidential Stock Exchange probe into Sandelson that followed the firm's collapse.[3] Though he worked initially with Vickers in Hong Kong and Tokyo, his transfer to New York in 1979 was his first big break. At the time, Vickers da Costa had nothing in New York. Collier's brief, as a vice-president under the firm's senior partner in London, Jeremy Paulson-Ellis, was to start a full trading operation. He made the most of his opportunity, assuming full responsibility as president just a year later, at the age of only thirty. Morgan Grenfell could not have invented a man better suited to their purposes. He had already created one business from scratch and New York, which had deregulated its market in 1975, had given him experience of dual-capacity trading of exactly the kind that would pertain in London after Big Bang.

Reeves had also asked the question at an opportune moment. Collier had been thinking of returning to London anyway, enticed by the excitements and opportunities of the prelude to Big Bang. Furthermore, Vickers da Costa wanted to merge with the giant American money-centre bank, Citicorp, promising an end to his freedom of action. Like the partners of Pember & Boyle and Pinchin Denny, he believed that Morgan Grenfell was an inventive, unbureaucratic and entrepreneurial merchant bank bubbling with talent and ideas, and he was particularly attracted by the challenge of building up an international equity-dealing operation from scratch. He had only two misgivings. One was money. Reeves had made a generous offer but if he left Vickers before the full consummation of its merger with Citicorp he would forgo his share of the takeover price, because any partner who left within five years was automatically disinherited. This was easily solved. Reeves assured Collier that he would be amply compensated in cash for any financial sacrifice, and a cash payment was eventually made. The other was whether his experience qualified him for the job. Vickers had an unrivalled reputation among British stockbrokers in the New York and Far Eastern markets but little of substance in London. Collier, had been out of the City a long time and his knowledge of the London scene was extremely skimpy. As they left the Racquets Club, Reeves explained to Collier that he would initially rank as a partner in Pember & Boyle, and was shocked to discover that Collier had not heard of the firm. A deeper worry was the reaction of potential clients. There was no reason to suppose that London investors would be willing to deal with a new firm headed by a man who had worked abroad since 1975. Blaise Hardman later told him that the bank had also been talking to another English exile in New York, John Holmes. 'That's the best reason for joining I've heard yet,' said Collier.

In 1985 John Holmes was president and chief executive of Hoare Govett Inc. in New York.[4] Though he had been on Wall Street for only three years he had already developed a transatlantic accent. Just forty-one, he had come a long way. After leaving York University nearly twenty years earlier with a second in politics and economics, he had joined Hoare Govett as a chemical-sector analyst. Within five years he was running his own team. A switch in 1973 to institutional sales, where he showed unusual flair, had secured him a partnership by 1976. Hoare Govett had posted him to its New York operation in 1982 where, like Dobson, he had met Geoff Collier. The two men liked and respected each other and, even better, Holmes's personality and experience complemented Collier's perfectly. Hoare Govett Inc. was only an agency broker – merely selling shares in New York for settlement in London – whereas Vickers da Costa Securities Inc. was a fully fledged and well capitalized trading operation as well. Holmes had good sales contacts in London; Collier knew how to trade and settle shares in a dual-capacity market. Unpretentious and instantly likeable, Holmes's openness enticed and retained talented people, who shared his belief that profit would follow market share. Geoffrey Collier was the opposite: blunt, clever and obviously ambitious. He believed that profit was the sole measure of success. The differences extended to their physical appearances too, but Collier enjoyed the parody and would often start presentations by describing Holmes as the 'short, thin, nice one' and himself as the 'short, fat, nasty one'. They quickly became known round the City as 'Mr Nice' and 'Mr Nasty'. Given their respective skills, it was odd that Collier was put in charge of sales and research and Holmes in charge of market-making. It should have been the other way round but, being unfamiliar with titles, they simply ignored the error. For Val Powell, Senior Partner of Pinchin Denny, Collier's appointment was a major surprise. Hardman had assured him in the firm's letter of intent that he would be head of equity trading.[5] Together, Holmes and Collier set about recruiting equity analysts, salesmen and traders. They were both disappointed that Morgan Grenfell had failed to buy what they considered to be a decent equity broker, but warmed to the challenge of rolling their own. It proved much more difficult and expensive than they had imagined.

Meanwhile, Reeves and Hardman were still looking for someone to run the bond business. He had to come from outside, since nobody in the bank was up to the job and choosing as the great panjandrum a partner from either Pinchin Denny or Pember & Boyle would be fraught with fratricidal peril. After several candidates had rejected his entreaties, Reeves finally decided on Alistair Buchanan, the retiring chairman of the discount house, Cater Allen. Buchanan, a tall, ramrod-straight Etonian and ex-Guards officer, who had been born into the City – his grandfather was a Messel and his wife a Baring – was easily caricatured, but his intelligence and integrity were unquestioned. After taking a first in PPE at Oxford, he had qualified as an accountant, rising eventually to the chairmanship at Cater Allen. Morgan Grenfell was merchant banker to Cater Allen, and Buchanan had first met Reeves through George Magan. Reeves subsequently joined a shoot on Buchanan's estate in Wiltshire, and it was among the coverts that Reeves first broached with him his possible role in easing the frictions between Pinchin Denny and Pember & Boyle. For Reeves, Buchanan's greatest value lay in his experience as chairman of Cater Allen, one of the three small, intimate firms which buy and sell government and other securities worth many times the value of their own capital. Before Big Bang, they used to borrow spare cash from the banks and use it for buying Treasury bills and gilts from the Bank of England. There is much of the flavour of an older City in the description of their work by Hamish McRae:

Discount-house men remain a dignified breed, renowned, slightly unfairly, for the short hours they put in and their enjoyment of the daily rite of putting on a silk top hat to call on the major banks and the Bank of England. Despite this genteel atmosphere, the discount men are, like everyone else in the City's money markets, doing much the same job as a bookie.[6]

Buchanan emerged from this cultural milieu unprepared for the infighting of a merchant bank but, on the face of it, his experience and standing were well suited to developing Morgan Grenfell's plans for the gilt-edged market. He had served from 1981 to 1984 as a director of LIFFE, the financial futures market set up by the banks, stockbrokers and discount houses in 1982 and in which Morgan Grenfell intended to participate. The Bank of England, which lacked confidence in Morgan Grenfell's ability to integrate its new businesses, was also delighted with Buchanan's appointment. Finally, and most importantly, he was available. Then forty-nine years old, in July 1985 he was following a succession plan agreed in 1981 at the time of the merger of his firm, Allen, Harvey & Ross, with Cater Ryder and making way for a younger successor, James Barclay, in

the chair at the new firm of Cater Allen.[7] After three months'
holiday, he started work at Morgan Grenfell in October
1985 as managing director of the new primary dealership in the gilt-edged market, Morgan Grenfell Government
Securities.

By September 1985 the new corporate structure of the bank
had been finalized. It was probably the greatest upheaval in
the history of the bank. From November that year the bank
split banking, investment and securities into separate companies. Corporate finance and banking were left with Morgan
Grenfell & Co. Limited, whilst investment management was
transferred to a new subsidiary, Morgan Grenfell Asset Management Limited. The gilt-edged and equity securities operations
were invested in a wholly new subsidiary, Morgan Grenfell
Securities Limited. Each business was then transferred to a
separate building. Corporate finance and banking remained at
the ancestral home, 23 Great Winchester Street, whilst Morgan
Grenfell Asset Management moved to 46 New Broad Street
and Morgan Grenfell Securities to 20 Finsbury Circus. There
were no common operating directors. Reeves and Rawlinson
ran the bank; Sir John Sparrow the Asset Management company; and Hardman ran Securities.[8] The separation was
designed to erect physical and managerial barriers as well as
metaphorical 'Chinese Walls' between the corporate finance,
investment management and securities operations. Potential
conflicts of interest between them were a novel problem,
recognized by Reeves:

It is almost inevitable that conflicts of interest will be perceived in a
group that engages in both securities dealing and investment management and is one of the City's foremost issuing houses and advisers on
mergers and acquisitions. Separation of the day-today management
and physical location of those three distinct functions is therefore
implicit in the new Group structure.[9]

Insider dealing had been tackled already, but only because
it might have prejudiced the outcome of a profitable deal. The
Corporate Finance Department had always operated behind

255

locked doors and staff had long since been banned from buying or selling shares through an outside broker. To enforce the rules, the bank's own dealers were equipped with a daily 'stop list' of shares where the bank was working with the company involved. Other major conflicts of interest were of recent origin and had to some extent been institutionalized. Substantial conflicts of interest did not often arise within banks when labour in the City was divided between bankers, brokers and jobbers. With all three now under the same roof, the temptation, say, to park an unsold Eurobond issue with the unwitting clients of the Investment Department or to adjust the market-makers' bid and offer prices in a particular share just ahead of a rights issue underwritten by the bank might prove irresistible without formal safeguards. A whole new industry – dubbed 'compliance', a term borrowed from Wall Street – sprang up in the City to police actual and potential conflicts of interest. In common with other banks, Morgan Grenfell appointed a group compliance director, the former head of Corporate Finance and sometime partner of Slaughter & May, George Law. He defined his task as follows:

What we have to do before Big Bang is to formalize what we already do into a written-down code setting out the way in which people behave, according to the highest professional and ethical standards, to demonstrate to the outside world that there really are rules, and put in place various policing mechanisms.[10]

This gave rise to a fat booklet, the *Group Compliance Manual* and by 1987 Law had a staff of eight working for him to ensure that the bank no longer deemed the interests of its borrowing clients ever to coincide with those of its investing clients.

The dictates of compliance resulted in some startling oddities. Eurobond sales and trading, for example, were transferred to Morgan Grenfell Securities, whilst the Eurobond new-issue and underwriting team stayed with Morgan Grenfell & Co. Limited, but only a single flight of stairs at 20 Finsbury Circus actually separated them.[11] Hardman became a legend around the City for his tiresome explanations of the intricacies

of the new structure to the bored former partners of Pember
& Boyle and Pinchin Denny. Rival firms were much amused
by Alistair Buchanan's riposte to one particularly incomprehensible *tours d'horizon*, which, he suggested to Hardman,
was best understood as a 'sort of corporate *soixante-neuf*'.
The obsession with structure reflected a naive belief that a
viable business would somehow follow in its train. Buchanan
made no secret of his dismay that when he arrived in October
1985 he found that whilst reams of paper had been expended
on corporate organograms, nobody had composed, decided
and set out in writing the bank's strategy for the gilt-edged
market. Hardman, of course, could not have written it, since
he had no experience of the gilt-edged market. Nor could
Reeves, whose skimpy knowledge of the securities markets was
not enhanced by his formidable travelling schedule and growing fascination with takeovers. The rapid changes of personnel
at the top of Morgan Grenfell Securities bewildered rival firms
in the gilt-edged market. They were bemused that two Morgan
Grenfell bankers – John Forsyth and Jamie Dundas – were
given responsibility for gilt-edged sales and trading. In common
with other firms, joint responsibility for gilts and Eurobonds
made reasonable sense. By late 1985 the historic barriers to
global bond trading – exchange controls and discriminatory
taxation – were being dismantled virtually everywhere.
Though exchange-rate fluctuations made the job as hard as
ever, bond traders and investors were treating all the world's
bond markets as a single whole. David Whitehead, John
Stevens and the other Eurobond traders were buying and
selling not just gilts and sterling Eurobonds but US Treasury
bonds and all the major European government bonds as well.
They came in each morning to adjust their holdings in line
with the overnight news from Tokyo and left each evening
worried that events in New York would prove them wrong.
Tokyo, which turned over $21 trillion of bonds in 1986, and
New York, which turned over $24 trillion, were the world's
biggest bond markets. The Eurobond market – the third
biggest market in the world – turned over a relatively paltry

$3 trillion in 1986. Morgan Grenfell lacked a serious presence in any of these markets. The gilt-edged market, in which the bank nursed its greatest ambitions, had a turnover of only $630 billion in 1986.[12] Though its turnover was likely to rise sharply after 27 October 1986, its profitability was likely to do exactly the opposite. Survival would be possible only if Morgan Grenfell Government Securities could establish a large group of loyal investors, and improve its understanding of the market sufficiently to make sensible judgements about whether to be 'long' (agree to buy securities, in the expectation that their value will rise) or 'short' (sell securities, in the expectation their value will fall) of stock.

This was an almost insuperable challenge for the Pember & Boyle sales force, who had been reared on artificial tax-driven trades between 60 or so large institutions whose loyalty would clearly be strained by the competition which followed Big Bang. Nor were they prepared to try and persuade their clients to buy bonds underwritten by Morgan Grenfell if they felt themselves that the terms were inappropriate. This first became evident in a disastrous issue of £75 million of bonds for the Bank of Greece in September 1985. Pember & Boyle's sales force were not consulted about the terms of the issue, which they judged to be unreasonable, and refused to sell it to their clients. With single capacity still in place, they could argue quite plausibly that they were obliged to offer their clients disinterested advice. The experience strained relations between Morgan Grenfell, which contrasted Pember & Boyle's failure to place a single bond with Hoare Govett's relative success in placing £15 million, and Pember & Boyle, which was proud that none of its clients was in possession of an issue which fell quickly to a substantial discount.[13] It was an inauspicious start to Morgan Grenfell's 'integrated' securities operation, caused by a failure of communication between the Eurobond Department, which devised the terms for the Bank of Greece issue, and Pember & Boyle, which was simply deputed to sell it. Despite this, the disaster prompted no serious reassignation of responsibilities. Responsibility for sales passed eventually from

John Scrope and Bob Pearce to Jeremy Wormell, a junior partner of Pember & Boyle, but he was not invited to contribute regularly to the pricing of the bank's Eurobond issues and Eurobond sales and trading continued to be run separately by Jamie Dundas. Wormell, noting the reluctance of his colleagues to lumber their old and trusting clients with bonds from an unpredictable source, expanded Pember & Boyle's list of potential clients to over 200, without much confidence of success. Whether or not Wormell succeeded, the gilt-edged market was already a sideshow beside the salient economic fact of the bond markets in the 1980s: Japanese savings were funding the enormous American budget deficit by buying US Treasury bonds in huge and profitable volumes. As the American budget deficit climbed inexorably to $221 billion in 1986, foreign buying of Treasury bonds increased from $10 billion a year in 1980 to $80 billion a year.[14] This huge debt, its effect on the value of the dollar and the movement of the sums of money needed to finance it, became the key indicator of world interest rates. Unless Morgan Grenfell understood it and, preferably, somehow interposed itself between buyers in Tokyo and sellers in New York, it would be virtually impossible to make any money.

Christopher Whittington, appointed by Reeves as group director of overseas companies in 1985, professed to understand this:

You cannot have a successful securities business without significant subsidiaries in New York and Tokyo. It would be very sad to depend on the UK economy.[15]

In reality, Morgan Grenfell had been slow to recognize the changing balance of world financial power. Once the ties to Morgan Guaranty were undone in 1981, the bank had opened a subsidiary in New York, Morgan Grenfell Inc., but it was designed principally to capitalize on the bank's first major success in the Anglo-American takeover business: Imperial Group's hotly contested, and fateful, offer for the Howard Johnson motel chain in 1980.[16] 'If we can scratch 0.01 per cent of the fee income in New York we shall be doing nicely,' quipped Richard Webb, then acting head of Corporate Finance in London.[17] Roger Seelig was appointed to the board of Morgan Grenfell Inc. in February 1982,[18] and a resident corporate-finance team was established with a brief to drum up transatlantic acquisition activity.[19] In 1984 a risk-arbitrage department was set up. It aimed, like Ivan Boesky, to make a profit by acquiring shareholdings in companies just before they were taken over. Certainly it was a bold decision, and the arbitrageurs (traders in the shares of companies likely to be taken over), renowned for their indifference to the traditional mores of merchant bankers, were a novel kind of employee. Leasing and project finance teams followed. Michael Dobson, the young Eton and Cambridge pin-up who had headhunted Geoff Collier and John Holmes, was at the time on a three-year secondment from the Investment Division in London,[20] successfully persuading US pension funds to invest abroad via Morgan Grenfell. The bank was registered with the Securities and Exchange Commission as an investment adviser and a new operation, Morgan Grenfell Capital Management Inc., was established in 1985 to provide fund-management services in the United States to American clients. By 1985 some $2 billion of American pensioners' money had been invested abroad by Morgan Grenfell.[21] In the autumn of 1986 a team of four fund managers was poached from Chase Manhattan and though their first invention in May 1987 – a fund for investment in growth companies – was a flop, their decision to defect testified to the growing seriousness of Morgan Grenfell's reputation as a fund manager.[22] Although Morgan Grenfell Inc. joined NASDAQ, the over-the-counter stock exchange, in 1983 and was admitted to the New York Stock Exchange in April 1985, these moves were principally to facilitate the buying and selling of American shares on behalf of fund-management clients in London. Nobody had thought very seriously about the securities business until the arrival from the Eurobond Department of the disgruntled Keith Harris as managing director.

When Harris arrived in New York Morgan Grenfell Inc.

had made little substantial progress. His predecessor, John Franklin, was affectionately known as 'Lord Greenwich', for his idle boasting about the prowess of the bank and his posh Connecticut address. Harris was an appropriate choice. He had marketed the United States with both Orion and Morgan Grenfell for several years, and nursed a genuine affection for America and Americans (not least because, as a high-school boy, they were refreshingly free of snobbery), but his real ambitions still lay back home, where his failure to persuade the bank to make a resolute commitment to the Eurodollar bond market had been off-set by assurances that he was in line to become the next deputy chief executive.[23] Anxious to bolster his claims, and advance his vision of how the bank should tackle the Eurobond market, he acted boldly. Reared in the capital markets of London, where spectacular hirings were *de rigueur* by 1985, in May 1986 he poached an entire six-man team of currency and interest-rate swap experts from Chemical Bank in New York. 'Where else but New York could you hire a team made up of a Chinese, a Belgian, an Irishman, a Dutch-woman, a Greek and a regular American?' he crowed.[24] The New York swaps team, with access to dollar-based counterparties, plugged at a stroke the Eurobond division's most glaring weakness: its inability to win and execute mandates for swap-driven Eurodollar bond issues in London.[25] In June he added a bond-dealing team, but Harris still had to persuade the board in London to support him rather than Rawlings.[26] This Harris ultimately failed to do.

Similar Eurobond and swaps teams were assembled in Singapore, Tokyo and Australia. Booming Far Eastern stock markets easily paid their salaries. In Singapore the bank even bought a 49 per cent stake in Su F-Min, a Singapore stock-broker, thereby picking up a seat on the local Stock Exchange.[27] Bull-market euphoria went furthest in Australia, where an Antipodean version of the Big Bang, initiated by the Hawke Government, was in full swing. Morgan Grenfell Australia bought two stockbrokers, Hordern, Utz & Bode in Sydney and Barnes, Tolhurst & Milner in Adelaide,[28] and set up Morgan

Grenfell Australia Securities Limited. This was accompanied by the usual noises about using the securities firm to sell stock generated by the corporate financiers. In a booming market alive with takeovers, underwriting activity in 1986 soared to A$160 million.[29] An indigenous money-market operation, complete with a swaps team, was set up in late 1985 and within a year had attracted deposits of A$150 million.[30] In April 1986 Morgan Grenfell expanded across the Tasman Sea, setting up Morgan Grenfell New Zealand Limited, a two-man subsidiary in Auckland.[31] By the end of the year Morgan Grenfell Australia was making pre-tax profits of A$4.25 million on total assets of A$170 million and employed over a hundred staff at offices in Sydney, Melbourne, Adelaide and Perth, but the booming Australian stock market concealed just how fragile the operation really was. In the previous year (1985) *half* of pre-tax profits were derived from mergers and acquisitions, the bulk from a single takeover. Most of the rest came from the still massive Woodside project financing.[32] Worse, Pat Elliott and Geoff Hill, the principal architects of the corporate-finance miracle, were restless. In January 1986 Pat Elliott got fed up and left to start his own show, Nat Corp Holdings, the former Bancorp Holdings once 80 per cent owned by Geoff Hill and his family.[33] Significantly, Hill, who stayed on, took a 35 per cent stake in the new venture. That Christmas he accepted an invitation from London to move to New York as joint managing director with Harris, where changes had been set in train to repeat the apparent Australian success.

Japan was altogether more worrying. The workaholic Japanese, with their incomprehensible language, elaborate etiquette, unspeakable cuisine, *karioke* bars and almost impertinently large sums of money made almost everybody at Morgan Grenfell feel uncomfortable. Geoff Collier, who had worked in Tokyo and secured the first branch licence for a British stockbroker to deal in securities for Vickers da Costa in 1978, did not yet count as a Morgan Grenfell banker. This reluctance to engage with the Japanese, though common among British bankers, undoubtedly retarded the bank's relative progress in Japan. The bank's first representative in Tokyo was not appointed until 1981, and he did little beyond gladhand Japanese financiers, more in hope than expectation of the odd fund-management contract, project financing, or underwriting slot in a Eurodollar or Swiss franc bond issue for Mitsubishi or Sanyo. Siegmund Warburg had visited and invested in Japan as early as 1962, when it was virtually impossible to sell a single Japanese share or bond in London. Kleinwort Benson, Schroder Wagg and Baring Brothers had also been building up in Japan for years. Japanese markets, long made hostile to foreigners by the restrictions imposed by the Ministry of Finance, were not easy to penetrate in the 1980s. Prompted by those merchant banks that could see the potential in Tokyo, the British Government made the official protection of Japanese financial markets a major diplomatic issue, leading at one stage to the exclusion of Japanese banks from the new gilt-edged market in London. Progress was still tortuously slow. The Ministry of Finance did not license Morgan Grenfell to open a branch to trade securities until the end of 1986[34] and the actual branch, Morgan Grenfell Japan, was not opened until April 1987. It sold European and American shares to Japanese investors. An investment-management licence, when it came in May 1987, was strictly circumscribed to exclude the giant Japanese pension funds, which continued to be monopolized by the indigenous trust banks and insurance companies.[35] But Morgan Grenfell's Japanese investment-management business, Morgan Grenfell International Asset Management Co., set up in 1985 in anticipation of deregulation, worked well enough. It had attracted funds worth $900 million by the end of 1987[36] and linked up with the retailer, Daiei Inc., to provide an investment counselling service.[37]

Meanwhile Holmes, only partially restrained by the more cautious Collier, had embarked on an orgy of public hiring to plug the gaps left by buying two firms so weak in the equity markets. Pember & Boyle offered virtually nothing in terms of research analysts or salesmen. Pinchin was flush with market-makers, but they were demoralized, and Collier improved their performance with better pay. He also re-organized and re-named Pinchin Denny's small London dealership in European shares, turning it into an effective and profitable business for almost the first time. Morgan Grenfell Securities International (MGSI), as it became known, also provided valuable experience of dual-capacity trading in London ahead of Big Bang. But the rest of the staff had to be recruited from outside. Two senior appointments were made first. Alan Bartlett, a former client of John Holmes, and an East End grammar-school boy who had worked his way up the City hierarchy via London University and the National Coal Board Pension Fund and County Bank, was hired from the Shell pension fund to run the forty United Kingdom research analysts. Basil Postan, a forty-year-old analyst then working at Citibank, was appointed by Collier to run the sales and research side of MGSI. Postan, unlike Holmes, Collier or Bartlett, was more in the Morgan Grenfell social mode. Clever, hard-working and popular, after Westminster he had studied at Strasbourg and Corpus Christi, Oxford, where, like Buchanan, he took a first in PPE. His career had not been damaged by a noticeable but disarming stutter and he was immensely experienced. Since 1967 he had worked at Vickers da Costa, Hoare Govett and Cazenove as well as Citibank. Immensely intelligent, he felt that his unhappy spell at Cazenove reflected its contempt for intellect. He feared a repetition at Morgan Grenfell, but was persuaded by Collier to join in spite of these misgivings.

As in the gilt-edged market, the key to ultimate success lay in salesmen who knew (or could find) investors to sell shares to. This was the greatest shortcoming facing Morgan Grenfell Securities' equity operations and it was directly attributable to the decision not to buy an established stockbroker. Holmes thought that 'in future a powerful ability to distribute shares is going to prove critical to securing deals'.[38] Reeves, probed on why Morgan Grenfell had bought a broker so weak in equities, could only answer lamely that 'we're doing it in a unique way'.[39] Yet it was in this crucial area that Morgan Grenfell Securities was least successful in attracting talent. With Big

Bang only three months away, Holmes had secured only ten out of a projected twenty-five salesmen. He announced publicly that he was prepared to pay virtually anything for more:

The good people are underpaid . . . The best stockbrokers' salesmen should be earning half a million pounds a year.[40]

Analysts were easier and cheaper to come by. In May 1986 Holmes and Collier recruited three of the four-man property research team from Scrimgeour Kemp-Gee, then poised to merge with Citicorp and Vickers da Costa.[41] Three analysts defected from Smith New Court to Morgan Grenfell in August 1986[42] and others came from De Zoete and Grieveson Grant.[43] By March 1986 forty-eight people had been hired. Collier also hired Vickers da Costa's five-strong settlements team, headed by Ken Holcombe. This demonstrated a proper sense of priorities. Within a year of Big Bang, turnover in the London equity market had risen so fast that settlements systems at many firms had broken down completely. At one stage London securities houses had collectively borrowed £7.6 billion to pay clients before they were paid themselves.[44] Morgan Grenfell, thanks to Holcombe, was not among them.

Spiralling City salaries made a nonsense of Reeves's economical approach to Big Bang. Mounting wage inflation was the first and biggest cost attached to Reeves's 'unique' approach, with office space a close second. Each of the 86,000 square feet at 20 Finsbury Circus cost £27. Once rates and other services were added to this the cost per square foot rose to £65, lumbering the new operation with an annual overhead of £5.6 million before it had sold even a single share.[45] By the eve of Big Bang Collier was reflecting internal concern about costs publicly:

We're about survival. Let's keep the ship tight. Don't let's go and spend vast amounts of money.[46]

With so many firms scrambling for scarce skills, salaries were bid up to absurd levels in 1986. With entire firms changing hands few City people had any compunction about job-hopping. In February 1986 Morgan Grenfell poached two top-ranked pharmaceuticals analysts, Angela Buxton and Alastair Kilgour, from Quilter Goodison; within four months they had left to rejoin former colleagues at another firm, Ark Securities. Ironically, the salesman they brought with them, David Gray, stayed on to embarrass the bank in other ways two and a half years later.[47] The Prime Minister expressed 'great concern' that twenty-five-year-olds in the City were paid in six figures while the dole queue was measured in seven.[48] Morgan Grenfell took eight from Smith New Court in August 1986, including a five-man traded-options team.[49] Holmes and Collier soon found that they were paying most of the people who worked for them more than they earned themselves. The Wood Mackenzie retailing team was falsely rumoured to have rejected a £1 million transfer offer from Morgan Grenfell.[50]

In March Morgan Grenfell Securities did pick up Grieveson Grant's four-man financial-research team, including one analyst, the insurance expert Derek Elias, whom Grieveson had itself poached from Citibank only three months earlier. One report suggested that they and one other, the De Zoete banking analyst, Tom Bennett, were tempted by a £500,000 'golden hallo' and another £350,000 in salary.[51] Grieveson's head of research, Bernard (Lord) Donoughue, said he could not persuade them to stay after Morgan's had offered them 'golden hallos' of £150,000 each and annual salaries of £100,000 apiece.[52] Another report claimed that the whole package was costing Morgan Grenfell £1.5 million in the first year.[53] The reports underlined the havoc wage inflation was wreaking with pay differentials at Morgan Grenfell Securities, as elsewhere. Collier himself, though he collected options over 25,000 Morgan Grenfell shares, was paid a salary of only £70,000, albeit with a guaranteed bonus of £50,000.[54] His celebrated 'golden hallo' of £250,000 was in fact the one-off cash payment Reeves had promised him as compensation for the loss of his share of the takeover price paid by Citicorp for Vickers da Costa. Bennett explained implausibly that:

It's nothing to do with money. We shall be joining an aggressive operation with no bureaucracy and computers that work.[55]

In fact they were joining an operation riddled with cultural conflict between brokers, jobbers and bankers, bound together only by a common love of money and lacking in any distinctive *esprit de corps*. The hiring spree had only added an unsustainable cost base to these already formidable problems.

On 9 September 1985 Morgan Grenfell's preparations for Big Bang took a bizarre turn. The bank announced that day that it had agreed to merge its property arm, Morgan Grenfell Property Services, with Michael Laurie & Partners, a firm of chartered surveyors. It was not unusual for a merchant bank to be involved in property. Most of Morgan Grenfell's corporate clients owned property, which might from time to time be refinanced, revalued, or sold. Some property companies, like Wates and MEPC, were clients and the bank periodically led bond or share issues for them. The investment department also deployed other people's money in the property market; most balanced investment portfolios contain properties. In June 1973, amid both a domestic property boom and widespread enthusiasm for investing in Europe following Britain's entry into the European Community, Morgan Grenfell had joined with Knight, Frank & Rutley, MEPC and a group of European banks to create the European Property Investment Company N.V. (EUPIC). After raising £20 million on the Amsterdam Stock Exchange it bought a string of properties across the Continent. Like the Eurotrusts which were then taking the stock market by storm, shareholders appeared to be cutting the risks of investing in Continental property by buying EUPIC instead.[56] Though EUPIC proved somewhat ahead of its time – it was eventually sold off to the Dutch property company, Rodamco-Morgan Grenfell Property Services was formed in the same year.[57]

In February of 1974 Henry Gorell-Barnes appointed Patrick Dawnay, then a partner in Laing & Cruickshank, to set up property unit trusts for sale to investors who would not have to pay tax on the returns, like pension funds and charities.[58] The Industrial and Commercial Property Unit Trust (ICPUT) was started in 1976 and by the end of 1982 had accumulated properties worth around £70 million. A second unit trust, the British American Property Unit Trust (BAPUT), was started jointly with Citibank in 1982. By the end of that year it had bought properties in the United States worth around $30 million. Property unit trusts, popular as a hedge against inflation in the 1970s, were hard to sell in the booming equity markets of the 1980s. The property market had lagged behind the bull market in shares and pension funds were cashing in their units and reinvesting the proceeds in the stock market. In March 1983 Morgan Grenfell assumed the management of four unit trusts managed by the beleaguered Property Unit Trusts Group, a trust Morgan Grenfell had helped to set up in 1966, and the bank's unit trusts were subsumed in a larger organization. By 1983 it was buying more units than it was selling. Its biggest fund, the £247 million Pension Fund Property Unit Trust (PFPUT), had a net outflow of £21 million in 1982.[59] The takeover created a group of trusts which controlled properties worth over £450 million. Morgan Grenfell Property Services, hitherto run as an adjunct to the investment department, moved closer to the professional property market, taking over PFPUT's prestigious offices at 73 Brook Street, and Patrick Dawnay was despatched to the West End as chairman.[60] With property unit trusts still unpopular, the first problem facing him and his chief executive, Neil Borrett, was to protect the business from its over-dependence on property unit trusts at a time when fund managers were investing more in the equity markets and less in property. Their next problem was how to make it grow. Buying a property company was too risky. It was then that they thought of buying a firm of estate agents.

This was not unthinkable. Lloyd's Bank and Hambro's, neither of which had embraced Big Bang wholeheartedly, had substantial interests in retail estate agents. Baring's, similarly reticent, had absorbed the tiny surveying firm of Houston &

Saunders after they had been disgorged by Rowe & Pitman following the merger with Warburg's. Some residential agencies, like Bairstow Eves and Mann & Co., had gone public. Other banks thought fee-earning property services – like valuing the property of takeover candidates – could be grafted successfully on to a bank's corporate-finance operations. Other advantages were obvious – notably property investment and managing as well as funding major property developments – but Morgan's also had the singular advantage of having one of the longest client lists in the City.[61] There was considerable surprise in both the City and the property communities that Morgan Grenfell had chosen to tie up with a firm like Michael Laurie rather than a blue-blooded partnership like Jones Lang Wootton or Hillier Parker. Most noted that its chairman, Elliott Bernerd, was a close friend and business associate of Roger Seelig. They had formed the property-development company, Stockley, in late 1983 and served together on the board of the retail chemist, Underwood's, which Morgan Grenfell floated on the stock market in October 1985. Though Seelig himself did not handle the flotation, the fact that in the spring both he and Bernerd had been allotted shares in Underwood's that netted them a combined instant paper profit of over £600,000 at the flotation price raised eyebrows at the time.[62] It was a fellowship that persisted into the even murkier depths of the Guinness bid for Distillers. Seelig's profound influence over the decision to acquire Michael Laurie was obvious to all in the City.

Laurie & Partners was first approached by Seelig in November 1984. Elliott Bernerd was not the sort of man with whom Morgan Grenfell usually did business. For one thing, he was Jewish. For another, he was an exceptionally natty dresser, not averse to over-equipped Mercedes and BMWs or to personal adornment. He had left school at fifteen to work for an estate agent, joining Michael Laurie & Partners two years later and becoming a partner by the age of twenty-one. He not only built the partnership up – in conjunction with Stephen, one of Michael Laurie's sons – but began to buy and sell properties on his own account. In the property boom of the early 1970s he was associated with 'Black Jack' Dellal, deputy chairman of Keyser Ullman, the secondary bank which crashed after over-lending to property companies. One of the companies to which Keyser Ullmann lent was C.S.T. Investments, a private company controlled by Christopher Selmes, which in 1973 took over Grendon Trust, chaired by the Duke of St Albans.[63] Coincidentally, Grendon's defence, which was managed by Morgan Grenfell, was among the earliest deals Roger Seelig worked on after joining the bank.

By 1985 Bernerd was forty and a multimillionaire, seeking respectability in antiquarian books, patronage of modern painters and the chairmanship of the National Philharmonic Orchestra.[64] It was, however, his skill as the most brilliant property deal-maker of the day that Morgan Grenfell hoped to tap and, unlike some others, Bernerd was prepared to deal. Gossip in the property market indicated that talks were also held with a variety of other chartered surveyors, and serious discussions begun with at least two of them, but it was widely believed that Seelig's choice would prevail. None of the other possibilities was likely to agree to a takeover, because they feared a loss of business from other banks. Unlike most chartered surveyors, Laurie's was a private company rather than a partnership, making it easier to pay for it in shares. The shares were also tightly held by a small group of the directors, principally Bernerd and his chief executive, John Lockhart, which limited the need for discussion with outsiders. For a bank looking to increase its transatlantic business, Laurie's had the added attraction of an operation in New York, though it was barely profitable. Laurie's hoped the merger would dilute its colourful image and improve the willingness of the City to finance its activities. With major property developments costing £100 million or more, at the time there was considerable excitement about new methods of property finance, including 'non-recourse' lending – where the only security for the bank is the building, rather than the developer – and 'unitization' – where the capital appreciation and rental income on the completed properties would, in keeping with the prevailing *Zeitgeist*, be 'securitized'. Laurie's New York office had observed securitization in practice in the United States and, at the time, Elliott Bernerd cited this as one of the main reasons for the merger. Indeed, it was discussed at a special 'brainstorming' session at Brockett Hall, the Hertfordshire stately home, within weeks of the merger.[65]

The failure of a unitized property market to develop may explain why the deal between Morgan Grenfell and Michael Laurie remains a lonely one. In any event, the final shortlist of possible partners submitted to the board was strongly biased in Laurie's favour. The supporting evidence was heavily influenced by Seelig, especially in its bold claims about Laurie's expertise in the retail property sector, where Seelig had strong connections. At the time the deal with Laurie was concluded in September 1985, he had also just worked with them on the controversial Burton bid for Debenham's, concluded in August 1985 amid rancorous accusations of foul play. Seelig had advised his friend Terence Conran, who had agreed with the Burton chairman Ralph Halpern to redesign the Debenham stores in the event of Burton winning and Michael Laurie had valued the stores for the bank. Later, Seelig masterminded the £1.5 billion merger of Habitat Mothercare with British Home Stores, which was concluded in December 1985. The property advisers to Habitat Mothercare was Michael Laurie. Negotiations were duly opened with Laurie.

The deal they struck with the four principal shareholders in Michael Laurie – Elliott Bernerd, John Lockhart, the chief executive, Ron Lang and Richard Townley – was a clever one, at least for Laurie's. Morgan Grenfell paid £2.5 million for a 51 per cent stake, paid by issuing 500,000 shares at £5 each to the Laurie shareholders. Nearly three-quarters of these were then placed elsewhere immediately, giving the shareholders £1.78 million of the purchase price in cash. A complex formula then gave Laurie's the right to require Morgan Grenfell to buy the rest of the firm at any time between 1987 and 1995, provided it met profit performance targets. Morgan Grenfell would be given a countervailing right before 1995 only if it already controlled most of the firm.[66] Elliott Bernerd could be forgiven a wry smile as he described the deal to the press in October:

I think some other firms will sell out for more money than we have. But I think we will always have the best deal.[67]

Indeed he did. Dawnay and Borrett soon left the firm, giving Bernerd and Lockhart virtually unfettered control of the business. With an obvious incentive to generate income, they set about breaking up Morgan Grenfell's £450 million property unit-trust portfolio. Half of UNIPUT was sold to Taylor Woodrow and BAPUT was offered to John Ritblat of British Land, though the deal fell through.[68] The entire PFPUT property portfolio was sold to the buyers of Bernerd's Stockley development company – Tony Clegg's Mountleigh Group – with the new company, Morgan Grenfell Laurie, collecting a fee on any properties in the portfolio that it managed to re-sell. Bernerd subsequently reacquired PFPUT's old headquarters, 73 Brook Street, from Clegg as part of a special deal. With deals like this, matching Morgan Grenfell's performance criteria was easy. By the end of 1987 Morgan Grenfell had been forced to buy up over three-quarters of Michael Laurie, whose pre-tax profits climbed from £1.5 million in 1985 to £3.4 million in 1986.[69] By then Roger Seelig, the architect of the deal, and Elliott Bernerd, its principal *raison d'être*, had both resigned their posts, chased from office in the fallout from the Guinness affair.

NOTES

[1] *Financial Times*, 6 June 1985.
[2] *The Independent*, 2 July 1987.
[3] *The Times*, 25 March 1987.
[4] *The Times*, 5 June 1985.
[5] *The Observer Magazine*, 30 July 1989.

[6] Hamish McRae and Frances Cairncross, *Capital City*, Methuen, 1983.

[7] *Standard*, 8 July 1985.

[8] *Daily Telegraph*, 13 September 1985.

[9] *Financial Times*, 13 September 1985.

[10] *Sunday Telegraph*, 27 October 1985.

[11] Morgan Grenfell & Co. Limited, Annual Report, 1985.

[12] Margaret Reid, *All-Change in the City*, Macmillan, 1988.

[13] *Financial Times*, 4 September 1985.

[14] Reid, *op. cit.*

[15] *Business*, July 1986.

[16] *Daily Telegraph*, 15 April 1981.

[17] *Financial Times*, 15 April 1981.

[18] *Financial Times*, 9 February 1982.

[19] *The Worldwide Services of Morgan Grenfell*, a bank publicity brochure, 1982.

[20] Nicholas Shakespeare, *Londoners*, Sidgwick & Jackson, 1986.

[21] *Morgan Grenfell Incorporated* and *The Services of Morgan Grenfell*, bank publicity brochures.

[22] *Wall Street Journal*, 11 May 1987.

[23] *Euromoney*, June 1986.

[24] *Forbes Magazine*, 2 June 1986.

[25] *Wall Street Journal*, 7 May 1986; *Financial Times*, 8 May 1986.

[26] *Euromoney*, June 1986; *The Economist*, 12 November 1987.

[27] *Financial Times*, 9 December 1986.

[28] *Australian Financial Review*, 16 August 1984.

[29] Morgan Grenfell Holdings Limited, Annual Report and Accounts, 1986.

[30] Morgan Grenfell Australia Limited, Annual Report, 1986.

[31] *Australian Financial Review*, 17 April 1986.

[32] *Australian Financial Review*, 3 April 1986.

[33] *Australian Financial Review*, 31 January 1986.

[34] Morgan Grenfell Group plc, Annual Report and Accounts, 1986.

[35] *Daily Telegraph*, 26 May 1987.

[36] Morgan Grenfell Group plc, Annual Report and Accounts, 1987.

[37] *Financial Times*, 16 January 1986.

[38] *Business*, July 1986.

[39] *Financial Weekly*, 19 June 1986.

[40] *Investors Chronicle*, 20 June 1986.

[41] *Standard*, 16 May 1986.

[42] *The Times*, 12 August 1986.

[43] *Financial Weekly*, 19 June 1986.
[44] Reid, *op. cit.*
[45] *Estates Gazette*, 13 July 1985.
[46] *Wall Street Journal*, 24 October 1986.
[47] *Standard*, 12 February 1986.
[48] *Sunday Times*, 16 February 1986.
[49] *The Times*, 12 August 1986.
[50] *Daily Mail*, 9 July 1986.
[51] *Sunday Times*, 23 March 1986.
[52] *Financial Times*, 24 March 1986.
[53] *Observer*, 23 March 1986.
[54] *The Times*, 2 July 1987.
[55] *Sunday Times*, 23 March 1986.
[56] *Financial Times*, 5 and 8 June 1973; *Daily Telegraph*, 5 June 1973; *The Times*, 5 June 1973; *Investors Chronicle*, 8 June 1973.
[57] *The Worldwide Services of Morgan Grenfell, op. cit.*
[58] *Financial Times*, 12 December 1973.
[59] PFPUT was the first property unit trust.
[60] *Financial Times*, 23 February 1983; *Investors Chronicle*, 25 February 1983.
[61] Morgan Grenfell Group plc, Offer of Ordinary Shares by Tender, June 1986. This cites *Crawford's Directory of City Connections* recording Morgan Grenfell as having 143 clients in 1986.
[62] *Daily Mail*, 1 November 1985; *Standard*, 31 October 1985; *Private Eye*, 21 August 1987.
[63] Margaret Reid, *The Secondary Banking Crisis, Its Causes and Course*, Macmillan, 1982.
[64] *Daily Express*, 7 July 1986.
[65] *Estates Gazette*, 14 September 1985; *CSYR*, 7 November 1985.
[66] Morgan Grenfell Group plc, Offer of Ordinary Shares by Tender, June 1986.
[67] *Financial Times*, 10 September 1985.
[68] Subsequently, ICPUT and one of the Property Unit Trust Group's trusts, PUTPAGS, were merged to form UNIPUT.
[69] Morgan Grenfell Laurie Holdings Limited, Accounts, 1986.

NINE

Ten Grand Short

On 4 July 1985 the chairman of Morgan Grenfell, Lord Catto, called his deputy, Philip Chappell, into his office at Great Winchester Street. It was a perfunctory meeting, prefaced by a blunt explanation from Catto of its purpose: 'Reeves wants your job.' News of the encounter quickly achieved wide currency in the City. Though he shed many crocodile tears for the benefit of shareholders and staff when the news of Chappell's resignation 'to pursue other interests' was officially announced at Christmas, in the eyes of the City, Lord Catto had been reduced to doing the dirty work of his chief executive, Christopher Reeves. It was an apt measure of how far relations between Reeves and Chappell had deteriorated, and how weak the office of chairman had become. Though he was deputy chairman of the bank, Chappell had long since been cut out of its innermost counsels; Reeves had even taken to cutting him at official cocktail parties. His dismissal also removed the last influential dissident from the highest echelons of the bank, making possible much of what followed. For Chappell, the blow was shocking and hurtful but not unexpected. He had been active with other interests and out of the London office too long and too often to have prevailed against a regime from which he felt increasingly alienated. In contrast to the openness of the Partners' Room, where each knew what the others were doing, Reeves managed the bank in a different way. Surrounded by men of his own choice – Walsh, Hardman, Rawlinson, Whittington – he rarely heard unwelcome views. With this *modus operandi*, Chappell was profoundly out of sympathy. In a career spanning over thirty years with the bank he had clung tenaciously to the historic ethos of

Morgan bankers: 'Only first-class business and that in a first-class way.' The ethic was sufficiently deeply imbued for him to have added 'first-class people' to his personal version of it.[1] Yet under Reeves, clients, and with them the reputation of the bank, often ranked second to fees, which were increasingly agreed in advance of a transaction. In time, it tied the bank to the clients that paid the biggest fees, like Ernest Saunders of Guinness.[2]

In the decision to enter the securities markets, avarice was not tempered by modesty. Anxious to boost the value of their shares and share options, but unwilling to cede control, men who knew nothing of new markets took decisions to enter them. One younger director described it:

Decisions have to wait for the oligarchy to relearn the business so they can understand the decision, and then they have to arrive at a consensus after that.[3]

It was a perilous form of management for a bank not just tripling in size but embarking upon a wholly new business fraught with unfamiliar risks. Not least because it would stretch their expertise very thin, Chappell had thought the decision to enter the securities markets an unequivocally foolish one. Reeves later acknowledged publicly that he had failed to give operational directors a sufficient say in the overall policy and management of the bank.[4] Issues of which they understood increasingly little were habitually resolved out of earshot of those who might have disagreed. Those newcomers to the bank who were excluded from its innermost counsels complained to former colleagues that 'the car telephone had replaced the board meeting'. In this way, the effects of insensitive management spread far beyond the retired vice-chairman. For young and gifted directors like the newly promoted director of money-market activities, Martin Knight, it bred resentment at their exclusion from decisions which jeopardized their livelihood.[5] For the newcomers – Holmes, Collier, Buchanan – it was a danger to the businesses they were building and an insult to their ability. Unfortunately, there was no tribunal to which any of them could appeal, for the office of chairman was weak. Lord Catto's deal-making days were over, and he divided his time between the chairs at Yule Catto, the family company, and Morgan Grenfell, the family bank. The great and the good on the board of directors, like Sir Peter Carey, Sir Kenneth Durham and Ray (Lord) Pennock, were superannuated civil servants or industrialists unfamiliar with the day-to-day complexities of contested bids and unlikely to ask probing questions, such as why the Guinness share price was so strong. Those that did rebel, like Philip Chappell, were retired early. Others of unorthodox views, like Richard Westcott, grew tired of their exclusion and resigned. The rest of the staff, whose numbers quadrupled from 639 in 1979 to 2,675 in 1986, just crossed their fingers and cashed their pay cheques.[6]

Until they were ruthlessly exposed by the fierce competition that followed Big Bang, the bank's severe managerial shortcomings were obscured by an apparently effortless rise in profits. Net profits rose tenfold between 1979 and 1986, from £5 million to £54 million.[7] Though traditional banking assets – loans – were a declining proportion of the whole, the balance sheet had swollen commensurately in the same period, from footings of only £1.26 billion in 1979 to £6 billion in 1986. The nature of the bank's business was also changing. Fee-earning corporate-finance work had risen from around a tenth of total revenues to a third, but increasingly necessitated the use of the bank's own money to buy shares on behalf of clients.[8] In the two biggest bids of the winter of 1985–6 – the United Biscuits bid for Imperial Group and the Guinness bid for Distillers – the bank spent £430 million buying shares in the target companies.[9] David Ewart, the bank's finance director, explained the problem later:

We increasingly find ourselves in the position where a client has said if we can't handle [a large underwriting] it will find someone else with larger capital resources.[10]

In addition to these entanglements, involvement in the Euro-bond, gilt-edged and equity markets meant that money tied up in securities-trading balances – the gilts, Eurobonds and shares retained by the bank for market-making and sales purposes – rose from just £35 million in 1983 to £1.4 billion in 1986.[11] This spectacular growth put the bank's capital under enormous strain. Total disclosed shareholders' funds climbed from only £45 million in 1979 to £212 million at the end of 1985. Though, in common with other merchant banks, Morgan Grenfell retained undisclosed 'hidden reserves' – monies which were salted away to even out profits in the bad years – by the end of 1985 Morgan Grenfell was seriously stretched financially.[12] At Christmas, soup and liqueurs were cut from the menu at the annual office party at the Grosvenor House hotel. Tickled, Lazard's sent Reeves a tin of Campbell's soup and a bottle of three-star brandy to wish him 'not a very prosperous New Year'.[13] Within twelve months, their wish was fulfilled, though not in the manner that they had anticipated, since they could not have known that at that very moment Morgan Grenfell executives were finalizing details of the Guinness bid for Distillers, which was launched on Monday 20 January 1986.[14]

Capital was an increasingly vexed but persistent question for Morgan Grenfell. The last rights issue in May 1984 had raised £45 million. It had been accompanied by news that the bank was seriously considering going public in 1985, but this was withdrawn the following spring. Cynics noted that the quoted merchant banks – Warburg's, Kleinwort's, Schroder's and others – had conspicuously underperformed the all-share index over the previous year.[15] Reeves and Rawlinson, who handled the bank's relations with its biggest shareholder, had also failed to sell the idea to Willis Faber, which had expressed grave doubts about the bank's entire strategy for Big Bang. This mattered less than it might have done, because in November 1984 Reeves persuaded the giant Deutsche Bank to spend nearly £14 million on a 4.99 per cent stake in the bank. Rawlinson later claimed that Deutsche had approached Morgan Grenfell but, if it did, its reasoning was obscure.[16] Morgan Grenfell's need for capital from any source was obvious, but it is unclear why Deutsche Bank paid such a high price for its shareholding without securing any board representation. The price per share – £4.95 – was nearly a pound above the price of the rights issue in May and nearly 50p above the price at which shares were changing hands among staff at the time. Deutsche's explanations included access to Morgan Grenfell's takeover skills, pooling their knowledge of export and project finance and vicarious access to the gilt-edged market – but only vague talk of increased co-operation in the Eurobond market really rang true. Deutsche Bank was sensitive to criticism that it was lagging behind in the Eurobond market and had recently moved its Eurobond operations from Frankfurt to London.[17] Reeves was pushed to name a specific rationale:

We like to think of our shareholders as people we can work with. Both sides will get a lot out of this.[18]

It was easy to see what Morgan Grenfell got out of it – a £14 million capital injection at a premium price without any loss of authority. Flotation, with the earnings dilution and loss of control that it implied, could be postponed again. It was rather harder to see what Deutsche gained.

From Saturday 8 March 1986 members of the London Stock Exchange were permitted to cede full control of their businesses to the banks to which they were betrothed. In April 1986, Pinchin Denny and Pember & Boyle duly became wholly-owned subsidiaries of Morgan Grenfell Securities, which was allocated an initial capital of £40 million.[19] By then Morgan Grenfell had earmarked some £270 million for the securities markets, rather less than publicly quoted banks like Kleinwort Benson and Warburg, each of whom was committing over £450 million, but still a very substantial sum of money.[20] Capital was again an issue, but the evils of flotation – dilution, loss of control and shareholder scrutiny – were unchanged. It was in this context that Reeves was by February 1986 toying seriously with an idea which Roger Seelig had put to him the previous Christmas. If it worked, it would massively increase the capital of the bank without dilution, cession of control to outsiders or exposure to shareholders and their allies in the financial press. On the contrary, it promised the existing shareholders a handsome rise in the price of their shares, to perhaps £7 or even £9 a share. The idea was an agreed takeover of Morgan Grenfell by Exco, the international moneybroking, stockbroking and financial services group created by John Gunn, to create a financial services giant with a stock-market value of £1.2 billion and capital of £700 million.[21] In mid-February Reeves took the idea to the Exco chief executive, Bill Matthews. Exco was in a vulnerable position. The Stock Exchange had rebuffed its attempt in 1984 to set up a broking arm and its shareholders had tired of the ceaseless rights issues used to pay for acquisitions. Gunn had left the conglomerate in September 1985, leaving it rudderless. After a series of controversial stock-market transactions, the Malaysian financier, Tan Sri Khoo Teck Puat, had emerged as the holder of a 22 per cent stake in Exco previously owned by British and Commonwealth Shipping, whence John Gunn had decamped to plot the creation of a second financial empire. Tan Sri Khoo's plans were uncertain, and Reeves argued that a merger with Morgan Grenfell would satisfy him and resolve Exco's future. The attraction for Morgan Grenfell was the company's enormous pile of cash, derived from the sale in July 1985 of its half share in the screen information system, Telerate, for £360 million.[22] Tan Sri Khoo flew into London in late February to join the discussions. Unfortunately, they had not got very far when they were leaked to the press. Following a rumour in Hong Kong, where Exco controlled the stockbroker W. I. Carr, the *Sunday Telegraph* ran an obviously informed account of the story on 23 February. The story suggested, correctly, that the Bank of England, which then barred shareholding links between merchant banks and moneybrokers, had been asked for its blessing.

Although, as Reeves conceded later, both sides 'were a long way from agreement over details when our talks were leaked', not all the parties to the putative deal were steaming in exactly the same direction at the time.[23] Exco was bigger than Morgan Grenfell – it was a publicly listed company capitalized at £530 million, whereas Morgan Grenfell was valued at only £400 million even at £7 a share – but Reeves seems to have assumed that he would naturally be in charge. 'We needed the capital and Exco was simply an opportunity that came up,' was his assessment.[24] 'This is an opportunity of expanding our capital base and obtaining a listing. This merger will approximately double our size, which is necessary if we are to go on doing bigger and better things,' was Roger Seelig's.[25] '£1 billion would give us the resources we feel will be needed to compete. We'll have made a start on solving our capital problems before Big Bang,' was Hardman's.[26] 'Exco were under the misapprehension that they were going to take over Morgan Grenfell, whereas we were simply after Exco's surplus funds to finance our own expansion plans,' was the assessment of another director.[27] Once Reeves and Seelig had sold this version to the press, Matthews was forced into an embarrassing public defence:

We certainly see it in no way as a reverse takeover.[28]

Much hinged on the attitude of Tan Sri Khoo, whose stake, now raised to 27 per cent, would be severely diluted by the merger to only 10 or 12 per cent. Initially, he was annoyed not to have been consulted. On 24 February, the day after the story broke publicly, he met Christopher Reeves and asked for financial details of both Morgan Grenfell and the proposed terms of the merger, which he was given the following day.[29] An associate and fellow Exco director, Alan Ng, said he thought the idea was a 'very good one', but he wanted to see the figures first.[30] Tan's adviser, Nicholas Jones at Schroder Wagg, was not confident that the merger could be agreed quickly, but Tan seems not to have been actively hostile at any stage, specifically ruling out a bid of his own on 26 February. The other party to the transaction, the Bank of England, was much less happy to wait and see.

The Exco negotiations coincided exactly with Morgan Grenfell's most audacious flouting of the takeover rules yet. On 20 February Morgan Grenfell had successfully relaunched the Guinness bid for Distillers despite a reference by the Office of Fair Trading to the Monopolies and Mergers Commission. It had done so by offering to buy five whisky brands from Distillers.[31] On 21 February Morgan's opponents in the battles for both Imperial and Distillers, Rothschild's (acting for Hanson Trust) and Samuel Montagu (acting for Argyll), had complained to the Stock Exchange that the bank's aggressive buying of shares had breached rules debarring companies from overspending on takeovers.[32] The inability of the Stock Exchange to counter Morgan Grenfell's insouciant dismissal of the complaints eventually prompted an intervention by the Bank of England to curb the direct financial involvement of banks in support of their clients. Reeves had earlier chosen to ignore gentle warnings from Threadneedle Street. 'The Bank of England is saying "cool it",' opined the *Guardian*.[33] In the judgement of Neil Collins, writing in the *Sunday Times*, the Bank's move was

as hard a rap on the knuckles of a leading merchant bank as I can remember and it is a direct response to the swashbuckling tactics that Morgan is developing to avoid losing takeover tussles.[34]

It was not a propitious moment to be asking favours of the Bank of England, though Morgan Grenfell now had to do exactly that. The so-called 'O'Brien letters', outlined in the early 1970s by the then governor of the Bank of England, Sir Leslie O'Brien, limited the involvement of banks in money- and foreign-exchange broking houses. The original limit was 5 per cent, but this was raised to 10 per cent in 1984 so that it did not accidentally prevent some of the mergers in hand ahead of Big Bang. The Bank of England felt that, as intermediaries between banks, moneybrokers should not be owned by them because of the potential conflict of interest between a moneybroker and a bank which would be one of its clients. In any event, many moneybrokers believed that banks would not deal with a tied broker who might reveal their confidences to the market. The merger between Morgan Grenfell and Exco posed a direct challenge to this rule. Since a forced divestment of Exco's moneybroking operations would rob the deal of much of its logic – roughly two-thirds of Exco's profits derived from Astley & Pearce, its moneybroking arm – Morgan Grenfell had to ask the Bank either to abolish the rule or to make an exception to it. The precedents were not encouraging. The Bank had forced Barclay's to ditch Wedd Durlacher's stake in the moneybroker Charles Fulton, but deregulation was in the air and, given the puny capitalizations of the British securities houses about to confront the Americans and the Japanese, it was reasonable to hope that the Bank might look benignly on a merger which would have created the biggest merchant bank in Britain.

That the Bank did not at any point do so suggests that other considerations swayed it against the merger. Tightening the takeover and the O'Brien rules simultaneously only underlined the rebuke that had been delivered to Morgan Grenfell: the bank was being denied capital just when it needed it most. Arguably, the merger would have created conflicts of interest no more unwieldy than most of those taking shape around the Square Mile just ahead of Big Bang. In 1985 the Bank had approved Mercantile House's application to own both a gilt-edged market-maker and a gilt-edged inter-dealer broker, a new organization specifically designed to transmit information between market-makers.[35] Of course, rules are not bent lightly and with Big Bang only six months off, it cannot have been keen to appear slack. The Government, then piloting the flagship of self-regulation, the Financial Services Bill, through the House of Commons cannot have been encouraging it to be so. Nor could the Bank view with equanimity the holding of a sizeable stake in a merchant bank by a foreign financier. But the suspicion lingers that the Bank was simply not willing, unlike the Stock Exchange, the Takeover Panel and the Office of Fair Trading before it, to bargain with Morgan Grenfell. An anonymous spokesman for the Bank told *The Times*:

The rule was introduced primarily because the market wanted it. It is unlikely that the Bank can make an exception in particular cases . . . We would not contemplate changing the rules unilaterally without consulting the market.[36]

This was an authentic sighting of the raising of the gubernatorial eyebrow: Threadneedle Street was fed up with Morgan Grenfell renegotiating the rules of the City. Either Morgan's sold Astley & Pearce or it persuaded the rest of the market to persuade the Bank to scrap the rule.

The Bank's intransigence was enough to wreck the deal. Crisis talks between Exco and Morgan Grenfell on possible ways round the O'Brien letters were held late into the night of 24 February. The results were put to the Bank of England and the Exco board the following day, but were unacceptable to the Bank.[37] Tan Sri Khoo flew home and the talks were officially called off on 5 March, though Bill Matthews made an unheeded plea for the market to change the Bank's mind.[38] Other banks did not rush to the assistance of a bank that had gouged most of them in one way or another in recent years, though both the British Bankers Association and the Foreign Currency and Deposit Brokers Association subsequently said that they did not care very much about the O'Brien letters. As if to ram home its point, the Bank changed the rules in November 1986 to allow banks to own moneybrokers provided that they did not then deal with them, without consulting the market at all.[39] Three days after this change Exco was devoured inside two hours for £672 million by its creator John Gunn, prompted by Tan Sri Khoo Teck Puat. It was too quick for Morgan's. 'We would have been perfectly able to put together the finance,' said Reeves, looking rather leaden-footed.[40] Later, he argued that the merger would not have worked anyway:

The one major disservice I could have done our group would have been to get us into such a disunited situation that we started neglecting our clients, so that they went off to other merchant banks.[41]

Ironically, the architect of the letters, now Lord O'Brien of Lothbury, was a member of Morgan Grenfell's International Advisory Council. It is hard to underestimate the disappointment that was felt in the Morgan Grenfell board room at the final loss of Exco. The 1985 accounts show that there were some 3.7 million share options outstanding in early 1986 exercisable at prices between £1 and £4.45. Assuming the merger with Exco had valued Morgan Grenfell at somewhere between £7 and £9 a share, the holders – mainly directors and senior staff – might have clocked up profits of up to £20 million or so, irrespective of any further gains on ordinary shares they held. At £9 a share, Reeves himself, who held 118,000 shares and options over another 35,000, would have netted somewhere between £700,000 and £1.23 million. No wonder Reeves said 'I am obviously sorry'.[42] At bottom, it is hard to escape the conclusion that the putative Exco merger was primarily an attempt by the directors to extract short-term value, rather than a considered strategic move, but its failure finally obliged them to swallow their chronic reluctance to absorb the dilution of their shareholdings, and ponder a public flotation.

Talks about talks with Exco flickered on and off until the final denouement in November, but were revived seriously only in late April when John Gunn first registered his interest in his old firm by offering to buy out Exco's money-market operations.[43] There was a brief flirtation with another business friend of Seelig's, Jacob Rothschild, with whom he and Elliott Bernerd had created the property-development company which became Stockley plc.[44] The rumour of talks with Rothschild was confirmed in most people's minds by an official denial from Lord Catto.[45] There was even idle talk from Reeves of a £100 million rights issue, and a madcap scheme for some kind of triangular arrangement between Willis Faber, Exco and Morgan Grenfell seems to have been mooted briefly, but in reality the skinflint attitude of the Bank of England had left Morgan Grenfell with only one option.[46] At the shareholders' meeting on 14 May 1986, after a week of leaks, the bank announced that it was taking it. Lord Catto, after claiming in

March that a listing was 'not essential . . . most of our shareholders are content that the bank is unquoted'[47], effected the
volte face effortlessly:

We have always thought in the long term it was essential. If you
want to be in the big league you cannot do it without a listing.[48]

Rawlinson's assessment – 'Obviously, if we'd merged with
Exco this wouldn't have been necessary'[49] – was closer to the
mark. The major shareholders – Willis Faber, Deutsche Bank
and the Prudential – had all been sounded out about a rights
issue after the Exco deal collapsed.[50] Willis Faber had baulked
at another call on its resources and went along with the
flotation only reluctantly. To continue including Morgan Grenfell's contribution to its profits, which amounted to £12 million
in 1985, Willis Faber would have to buy sufficient shares to
keep its stake above 20 per cent. Otherwise, the timing was
propitious. Profits in 1985, made public in mid-March, were
up 40 per cent and had been accompanied by suitably encouraging noises about earnings per share and dividends, the
key stock-market valuation tools. The bank had just clocked
up huge fees in the Distillers and Imperial Group takeovers,
which allowed Reeves to forecast profits of £48 million for the
first half of 1986, only just short of earnings for the whole of
1985.[51] The flotation in March of the bank's American cousin,
Morgan Stanley, had been a runaway success, profiting the
partners handsomely. Reeves noted as much:

On balance now is a good time to go for a listing because we will be
able to raise a really sizeable sum of money and be able to position
ourselves for the Big Bang . . . We need to feel we have the firepower
to help our clients.[52]

The plan was to raise around £100 million by doubling the
number of shares, halving their value from an expensive £8–
£9 a share to a more manageable £4–£5 a share and selling
32 million new shares to outside investors, bringing the total
number in issue to around 150 million. In other words, the
bank would sell about a fifth of its enlarged self to outsiders.[53]

This would be coupled with the sale of $200 million of perpetual Floating Rate Notes, a new type of Eurobond popular with banks because the debt does not have to be repaid, enabling them to count the proceeds as part of their capital.[54] The 'perpetual' was sold successfully in August, after the share sale. Together, they increased the bank's capital to a total of £560 million.[55]

The sale of shares in the bank exposed Morgan Grenfell for the first time to public scrutiny. Shareholdings in takeover targets, hidden reserves, the profit contribution of each division and the manner and cost of buying Pinchin Denny, Pember & Boyle and Michael Laurie would all have to be disclosed to potential investors. The strong temptation to let the Corporate Finance Department write the documents and Morgan Grenfell Securities sell the shares was successfully resisted, on the grounds that nobody would believe the sales pitch, but only up to a point. The appointment of another merchant bank as advisers was unthinkable, so the unspecific role of 'sponsor' fell to Cazenove, one of the last independent stockbrokers, instead. Since Rowe & Pitman had sold itself to Warburg's, Cazenove had been the Corporate Finance Department's first choice as broker in contested takeovers, and it generated some useful hype ahead of the sale, but was incapable of handling the flotation alone. 'Due diligence' – the process whereby an independent financial adviser explores the probity of all the claims made in the sales documents – was inevitably done mainly by Morgan Grenfell itself. Guy Dawson, a corporate finance director, was the principal interrogator.[56] Morgan Grenfell Securities was appointed joint brokers with Cazenove.

A triumph at the time, the extraordinary success of the flotation seems with hindsight more, not less, remarkable. Somehow a small merchant bank, its current revenues dependent on the takeover boom and a few key investment-management accounts and its future revenues mortgaged to an expensive excursion into the unfamiliar and highly competitive securities markets, persuaded investors to stump up £160 million to buy just a fifth of the company. Merchant banking, in common with most City activities, is a highly cyclical business and June 1986 was very close to the top of the cycle. Less than half of 1985 revenues was earned from predictable activities like lending money. One-third came from corporate finance advice, and was highly inflated by just two takeovers. A fifth was earned in investment management, which could easily dive if the market crashed or a key account was lost. No one knew what Morgan Grenfell Securities earned, because the bank had owned it only since April and Big Bang was still five months off, but Pember & Boyle made only £1.9 million in the year to April 1986, in a protected market that would soon cease to exist. Pinchin Denny's domestic business made less than £300,000, but its former international trading arm, renamed Morgan Grenfell Securities International (MGSI), had made over £1 million by the time of Big Bang, having been allowed by the Stock Exchange to simulate Big Bang conditions for six months by practising since December 1985 as a dual-capacity broker dealer in European and Far Eastern shares.[57] Apart from MGSI, it was hardly an encouraging performance ahead of the main event, beginning on 27 October, when it was widely agreed that most firms would be counting losses rather than profits. Despite this frightening prognosis, Morgan Grenfell eschewed the guaranteed success of offering shares for sale at a fixed price and asked investors to bid for them at anywhere above a minimum price of £4.25, maximizing the proceeds of the sale for the bank but minimizing the possibility of speculative gains for early investors.

Paradoxically, the higher the price demanded, the less absurd it seemed. The shares of other merchant banks began to look cheap and investors bought them too, making the whole sector look much more exciting than it was. When the offer document was published on 20 June, the real profit for 1985 turned out to be a full fifth higher, sufficient to obscure the disappointing size (£16.5 million) of the much-vaunted 'hidden reserves'. The sale, which closed six days later, was an enormous success. On Thursday, 26 June, a large crowd gathered outside Lloyd's Bank in Moorgate, where applications for shares were accepted up to 10 a.m.[58] The following day Morgan Grenfell announced that enough applications had been received to buy 144 million shares, four and a half times the number on offer. Though it later emerged that the registrar, Lloyd's Bank, had left another 19 million applications un-counted it hardly seemed to matter. The shares were rationed, a price of £5 a share was confidently struck and when dealings began on 3 July a handsome premium of 16p developed in early trading. It was the apogee of the achievements of the bank under Christopher Reeves. With 163 accredited clients, the Corporate Finance Department topped the mergers and acquisitions league table for the first half of 1986, advising in 28 transactions worth £11.7 billion.[59] The recently completed Guinness bid for Distillers was the largest ever to succeed in Britain. Morgan Grenfell Asset Management was advising over 300 pension funds, charities, unit trusts, investment trusts and private clients in the deployment of £12.6 billion of savings.[60] At Morgan Grenfell Securities a staff of 350 had been assembled and equipped to analyse, trade, sell and settle British and foreign shares from 27 October. Of the £155 million raised by the flotation, £100 million was earmarked for them, bringing the total invested in the securities venture to £140 million.[61] Banking assets exceeded £1 billion and deposits totalled over £2 billion. The bank's reputation for service and innovation in the field of export and project finance was still unrivalled. Even the faltering Eurobond divis-ion, playing carefully to its strengths, controlled a quarter of all new-issue activity in the Eurosterling bond market.[62] The manpower employed at home and abroad had quintupled in seven years to nearly 3,000 people. Above all, it seemed to work. In the previous five years the balance sheet had doubled but net profits had quadrupled.

The staff were enthusiastic buyers of the shares. Ahead of the flotation 650 staff owned 9.5 per cent of the shares in Morgan Grenfell, or perhaps 11 million shares after their number was doubled. Ownership was concentrated among senior staff and directors. At the turn of the year the 49 directors of Morgan Grenfell & Co. Limited alone owned 1.9 million shares, or 3.8 million after the number was doubled. These were worth over £18 million at the sale price. They also had options to buy another 3.4 million at prices ranging between less than 19p and £3.75, rather less than the £5 flotation price.[63] Similar interests were scattered around the various subsidiaries of the bank. For instance, Elliott Bernerd, the chairman of Morgan Grenfell Laurie, owned over 100,000 shares in Morgan Grenfell at the beginning of 1986.[64] Up to a tenth of the shares offered for sale were withheld to allow staff to top up their shareholdings and 800, though warned dutifully by directors that shares can go down as well up, invested £5.5 million in 1.1 million shares in their employer, some taking out loans to do so.[65] Many directors sold their own shares at the time of the flotation, thinking £5 was a good price. Lord Catto, Reeves, Hardman, Law, Rawlinson, Walsh, Whittington and 'other shareholders' even agreed to pre-sell 4.4 million shares worth £22 million to Willis Faber and Deutsche Bank at £5, to enable both to maintain the size of their shareholdings in the enlarged company.[66] Though the profit they made cannot be calculated accurately, the first six netted £1.5 million as a result, Lord Catto alone pocketing £500,000. His son, Alex, also sold a portion of the family shareholding. It demonstrated a perspicacity in personal dealings belied by their management of the bank's affairs in subsequent months. The wave of selling by directors quickly erased the 16p premium. The shares ended the first day's trading at a discount of 15p, dismissed by Guy Dawson as a 'temporary situation'.[67] The price did not clear £5 again until serious bid speculation set in a year or so later. It was especially disappointing for the partners of Pember & Boyle and Pinchin Denny, much of whose wealth now depended upon a strong share price.

When Morgan Grenfell & Co. moved from 22 Old Broad Street to 23 Great Winchester Street in 1928 the partners were appalled by the grandiloquence of the new building's nineteenth-century façade. Its 'florid incrustations which included a Hindu and a Pathan with cornucopias and vegetation' were stripped off at once.[68] Visitors were greeted instead with an expanse of cold and empty marble space, abruptly terminated by the glass panels of the banking hall, that was calculated to make them feel uneasy. In Sir Edward Reid's famous phrase, merchant bankers had long had to live on their wits rather than their assets, and wit extended to giving their austere mystique this palpable form. Walter Bagehot's phrase about the British monarchy – 'We must not let daylight in upon magic' – is often misquoted by merchant bankers as an apt description of their method. Bagehot's real assessment, that bankers were 'imprudent in so carefully concealing the details of their government and in secluding those details from the risk of discussion' would have pleased them less.[69]

Today the opulence of the entrance at 23 Great Winchester Street is much less discreet. The intimidating glass panels have been removed from view completely. The sullen greetings of the commissionaires have been replaced by a bevy of pretty girls. Parts of the hall have been carpeted and copies of glossy brochures and magazines favourable to the bank are plentiful. Time was when no director of Morgan Grenfell would have met a public relations man, let alone succumbed to his blandishments. Yet as part of the preparations for Big Bang the bank set up a Corporate Affairs Department and appointed the egregiously named Byron Ousey as its head. 'There is no longer a need for the mystique. We have to talk more vigorously,' said Ousey.[70] To general derision, he redesigned the stationery, circulating details of the new 'corporate logo' in a bemusing document entitled *Corporate Visual Identity*. He equipped each of the three divisions with a corporate colour – green for the bank, burgundy for asset management and blue for securities – and gave away umbrellas to match.[71] In apparent ignorance of an old adage in stockbroking – 'If there are pictures in the annual report, sell the stock' – the austere annual reports of old were discarded in favour of a new design filled with colours and pictures prepared by the Addison design consultancy. By September 1986 Ousey was circulating a glossy brochure advertising the bank's services intended, in his words, to highlight the bank's 'individualism'. It was illustrated with pictures of the directors in various improbable poses, usually surrounded by highly polished wooden surfaces but also exotic locations like the Sydney Opera House and the Raffles Hotel in Singapore. Pictures of directors posing in the halls of City livery companies like the Vintners' added to the pretentiousness of the document, rather than the historical authenticity of the bank. Each photograph was accompanied by a meticulous facsimile of its subject's signature, an imprudent gesture for a merchant bank which could sign away billions of pounds with a stroke of the pen.[72]

The change of tone testified less to the bank's powers of self-abnegation than to its immense confusion about the proper response of an 'undoubted' house to the events and opportunities unleashed by Big Bang. The result was an undistinctive me-tooism. 'You need to be a certain size or you are a boutique. We have said we do not want to be a boutique,' said Reeves.[73] 'There is much to be gained by remaining a specialist house with clearly defined and proven abilities and by avoiding the problems of managing multiple, and for the most part unfamiliar, risks,' said Ian Fraser, the then Chairman of Lazard's.[74] That banks must choose between being a super-market or a boutique was the received wisdom among merchant bankers in the Big Bang era. 'We intend to be in all the major markets and offer a waterfront service around the world,' added Reeves.[75] With most of the City's stockbrokers no longer independent, bankers worried that they would not be able to keep abreast of market sentiment during takeover bids or sell the shares issued by bidders to pay for acquisitions. Virtually everybody in the City in 1986 believed that banking could not afford to ignore any particular securities market because a presence in one necessitated, or led to, a presence in another. It was thought, for example, that companies would expect their bank to be able to sell their Eurobonds as well as their shares and also to trade them afterwards to ensure a liquid market for investors. This led banks into trading gilts and American Treasury bonds (for hedging risk) and into interest-rate swaps, to which many Eurobond issues were linked. These supposed 'synergies' were the principal argument of those who endorsed the Big Bang. At Morgan Grenfell, the most potent potential synergy of all was that between the highly successful Corporate Finance Department and the putative securities operations. The ordinary business of the Corporate Finance Department, such as takeovers and rights issues, generated large quantities of shares which in the past were placed with institutional investors by independent brokers like Cazenove or Rowe & Pitman. Now John Holmes was hoping they would be placed by Morgan Grenfell Securities:

Morgan Grenfell has a wonderful opportunity to turn itself into an investment bank on a US scale. You can only do that by integrating the operating divisions of the bank. Without the distribution side the corporate finance department cannot survive. And without the corporate finance side you won't make it as a big league player in this market – a broker needs the new issues, the underwriting, the placement.[76]

Holmes also hoped that Morgan Grenfell Asset Management would buy and sell securities on behalf of the funds it managed through Morgan Grenfell Securities and in particular that it would execute 'portfolio trades' – buying collections of shares at a discount for onward sale at higher prices – through them. Obviously, the strategy hinged on whether or not the Corporate Finance and Asset Management departments were prepared to help Morgan Grenfell Securities to grow by referring clients and business to them.

Coupled with 'securitization' – the fear that bank loans were being replaced by tradable securities – synergy was an unanswerable argument for involvement in the securities markets, but it took little or no account of the relative costs of entering them. Since virtually every bank in London had adopted the same strategy, the amount of capital and labour devoted to them all had multiplied many times. In the gilt-edged market the capital available had risen sixfold and the number of market-makers tenfold. By 1986 the Eurobond market was the most competitive capital market in the world, with Japanese banks prepared not just to make losses on underwriting Euro-bonds but actively to subsidize clients to win business. In the equity market, thirty-five well capitalized market-makers had replaced thirteen jobbers. Once fixed broking commissions were dropped on 27 October, commissions were likely to disappear altogether on large institutional orders, leaving the integrated brokers and market-makers simply hoping to pay less for the shares than they sold them for. Skill and space shortages added to costs as salaries and rents were bid up to record levels by the new entrants. The cost of the average Eurobond trader in 1986 was estimated at £300,000 a year including pay, screens, computers and office space at £50 a square foot.[77] It was reasonable to expect a share dealer to cost at least the same, if not more, and Holmes and Collier were working on a figure of £65 a square foot. Even Reeves was forecasting only 'adequate' returns on the investment in securities[78] but he expected publicly to make a profit even in the gilt-edged market.[79] Yet it is not clear on what evidence the profit projections in the flotation document were based. At the time of the flotation the directors had declared:

It is impracticable to calculate the exact profit contribution of each of the Group's activities owing to the interdependence and varying uses of capital and other resources from time to time of certain of those activities.[80]

The bank could measure the revenues and certain costs (such as salaries) of business areas but not their profitability. Capital was lumped together rather than assigned to particular busi-nesses, making it difficult to assess their return on capital and impossible to gauge their relative riskiness. Portfolio trading, for example, was much riskier than buying shares in takeovers with an indemnity against loss from the client. In October 1986, just ahead of Big Bang, Geoffrey Collier took a decision that Morgan Grenfell Securities International would buy a $100 million portfolio of French equities in a competitive tender against other houses. It took three days to sell them, Collier placing a lot of stock in the United States, but they netted a profit of £2.3 million. They could just as easily have been sold for a loss five times the size had the market turned, so there were enormous risks attached to owning $100 million of shares for three days. It was easy to mistake the £2.3 million trading profit for commission.[82] Without rudimentary tests of viability and riskiness, me-tooism was not so much a strategy as a syndrome. Arguably, their absence made the entire securities adventure possible: if Morgan Grenfell had worked out the likely risks and returns on the investments in Eurobonds, equities and gilts, they might never have been made.

Of course, it was almost impertinent to ask questions of management strategy or financial control of a man who had increased pre-tax profits at an annual compound rate of 36 per cent since 1981.[83] By mid-1986 it was as though Reeves believed what he read about himself in the newspapers. His gift, in the assessment of *Business* magazine, was 'to pick stars and keep them'.[84] The triumphs of Roger Seelig and George Magan seemed to vindicate his pleasure in 'entrepreneurial ability'[85] and his contempt for management other than by delegation. If there was a management adage at Morgan Grenfell under Christopher Reeves it was drawn from William Webb Ellis's public-school archetype: 'pick up the ball and run with it'. Or, as Reeves put it:

I don't go around sticking pins into people to get them going. We encourage them, give them personal motivation and satisfaction. They naturally come out ahead of the pack. Why employ talented people if you don't give them difficult decisions?[86]

It had worked well in the Corporate Finance Department, where the numbers involved were relatively small, the techniques, timetables and procedures were predictable, the market had not been penetrated to any significant degree by foreign competition and the fixed fees geared income automatically to the general rise in stock-market values. The same number of executives could handle a £1 billion takeover as a £1 million takeover but the fees, geared to the size of the deal, were much larger. Between 1981 and 1986 a thirteen-fold increase in the value of the business transacted by the department allowed productivity to rise despite a doubling of the number of transactions and of the staff involved. In 1981 56 staff handled 51 bids worth £1.2 billion. In 1986 110 staff handled 111 bids worth £15.2 billion.[87] True, Reeves had allowed Roger Seelig and George Magan to emerge as takeover 'stars', but this created little resentment within the department, where the number of executive staff was small and there were enough clients and fees to go round. In 1985 fifteen directors shared 163 clients and the department as a whole turned in a profit of £35 million. The demands of client confidentiality, by obliging the department to split into six or seven teams made up of eight or nine executives each, had even imposed a rudimentary management structure.[88] Above all, it was successful, making it easy to attract, retain and motivate staff. A young public school (and usually Oxbridge) educated accountant or solicitor could learn more about the takeover business in a fortnight at Morgan Grenfell than he could in years at another bank. Few corporate financiers would have considered a transfer to another department of the bank an accolade. Even travel was limited, as overseas offices were increasingly staffed with locals.[89] It was the only department of the bank which did not employ a single woman in an executive position. City gossip had it that Graham Walsh had told the board that he would not countenance females within his fief. In the Corporate Finance Department the business was profitable, the techniques were familiar, the culture was homogeneous, staff turnover light and morale high. It more or less managed itself.[90]

Irrespective of their highly competitive nature, the securities markets call for very different skills from those of corporate finance. One is dependent on fees earned by talented individuals; the other relies on capital commitment, keen prices, heavy turnover and careful attention to fundamentals like settlement (transferring securities from sellers to buyers in exchange for payment) and risk management (ensuring that the bank's capital is not lost when markets turn against it). The number of people employed by a securities business is also much higher. On the eve of Big Bang, the Eurobond Department alone employed more people (129) than the Corporate Finance Department. Another 353 were employed by Morgan Grenfell Securities.[91] With radically different cultures – bankers, brokers, jobbers, traders, research analysts, settlement clerks and secretaries – enmeshed for the first time the employees were also less homogeneous. As in all newly integrated securities houses, cultural conflict was endemic throughout Morgan Grenfell Securities. Accustomed to running their own outfit, measuring exactly their contribution to its capital and profits, and rewarding themselves accordingly, stockbrokers resented their relegation to the ranks of salaried employees. They were unfamiliar with the baser arts of corporate politics at which all the most successful merchant bankers excelled and despised what they learned of them. They were often bound to the jobbers only by their mutual detestation of the arrogance and snobbishness of the merchant bankers set over them. Otherwise, the friction between jobbers and brokers that characterized the old London Stock Exchange was reproduced exactly, and at closer quarters, in the new world. 'It's all these fucking jobbers,' was Basil Postan's explanation of the disgusting state of the gentlemen's lavatories at 20 Finsbury Circus, with neither irony nor *double entendre*. Morgan Grenfell's decision not to buy an established equity broker necessitated recruitment of staff from all manner of firms and backgrounds, denying Morgan Grenfell Securities even that elementary *esprit de corps* which S. G. Warburg and Barclay's Bank acquired free with their purchases.

These unfamiliar problems called for skilled and sensitive management, not the abrasive entrepreneurship Reeves had learnt from Kenneth Keith and the Rifle Brigade. Yet management was to most directors of Morgan Grenfell a despicable art. Stephen Syrett, a director in export finance, said, 'Very few of us are by instinct managers.'[92] A junior executive told the *Daily Telegraph* that staff were judged by the fees they earned and that management was not seen as fee-earning.[93] One director, Alex Catto, openly admitted that in the Eurobond Department promotion hinged on money alone:

We don't promote them because they're managers but because they make money for the bank.[94]

The enticements of wealth work only where profits are buoyant, responsibility clear and credit easily ascertainable. They work much less well in the securities markets, where responsibility is diffuse and the revenues of infant businesses are too meagre for everyone to take a satisfying cut of the profits. Brokers blame jobbers for overpricing their stock; salesmen blame bankers for failing to deliver new issues of stock. Transactions sometimes take years to develop and it is not always easy to apportion responsibility for success or failure very exactly.[95] This makes paramount the need to associate with success and dissociate from failure. At Morgan Grenfell, in the words of *The Economist*, 'it was often only the aggressive and bumptious who prospered in the tough environment'.[96] Though chance played a part in assignments, the more astute junior executives would make themselves indispensable to popular or successful directors, hoping to rise in their slipstream. Working for a successful director could double salaries, bonuses and fringe benefits like share options, subsidized mortgages and free motor cars. These naturally reached their apogee with elevation to the board, once a position of such esteem that it was virtually untouchable. As banks grew and the number of directors expanded, the currency was debased and many executives felt that they could do a better job than their director, who earned up to ten times their salary but often spent two hours at lunch, only to return well-oiled for a series of pointless committee meetings in the afternoon. It was an atmosphere which some were more adept at turning to their advantage than others, breeding destructive resentment rather than creative tension.[97]

All merchant banks lacked management. It was no use adjuring young merchant-banking directors to 'pick up the ball and run with it' in the securities markets, where they had not, as it were, yet learned even the rules of association football. Thus, as new markets erupted across the financial spectrum, banks impulsively pushed pawns into markets where kings were called for, rarely pausing to consider their qualifications for the job. At Morgan Grenfell, Martin Knight, with a high reputation earned solely in export finance, was appointed head of bond sales. Brokers and jobbers complained that merchant bankers submerged them in endless paperwork and meetings. They were appalled and distressed by the introduction of tape recording of all their telephone calls, intended to allow the terms of any sale made over the telephone to be checked later.

To all these difficulties were added the novel problems of 'Chinese Walls', the supposedly impenetrable barriers that prevented conflicts of interest within an institution engaged for the first time in underwriting, broking and jobbing the securities of its clients under a single roof. Directors of securities firms would be kept informed of, say, an impending takeover, lest they inadvertently fell foul of the various City watchdogs set up to police the integrity of the market. This privilege was called the 'need to know', and its effectiveness depended entirely on the probity of those who 'needed to know' and their willingness to subsume their personal interests in the success of the venture as a whole. It sometimes worked, as it did when Morgan Grenfell Securities sold shares in Boots just ahead of a placing of shares by the Corporate Finance Department.[98] A month later the Corporate Finance Department, acting for Coalite in a bid for Hargreaves, acquiesced in a Takeover Panel request to dissociate itself from a profit forecast and bid recommendation drawn up by the Coalite analyst at Morgan Grenfell Securities.[99] Yet when Roger Seelig stopped Morgan Grenfell Securities selling a block of shares to an important client, on the grounds that it would interfere with a deal he was contemplating, nobody questioned his right to intervene.[100] 'Chinese Walls', particularly when coupled with the 'need to know', were not particularly sturdy.

At 6.50 a.m. on Monday 3 November 1986 Geoffrey Collier picked up the telephone at 123 Home Park Road, Wimbledon, and dialled a number in Los Angeles. It was then 10.50 p.m in California. He spoke to Michael Cassell, a former colleague at Vickers da Costa still working for the same firm in Los Angeles and asked him to buy, before the formal opening of the London stock market at 9.00 a.m., as many shares as he could in AE, a troubled British automotive parts company then under siege from a hostile bidder, Turner & Newall. Collier told Cassell that he should buy as many as he liked at whatever price he could obtain them. The Wimbledon address was that of John Holmes's London house, where Collier had spent the night after a meeting with Holmes at the headquarters of Mirror Group Newspapers in Holborn, plotting with Philip Evans and others from the Corporate Finance Department a possible counter-bid for AE by Robert Maxwell's Hollis engineering group. Once Hollis moved, Morgan Grenfell Securities was to start buying AE shares in the market from the opening at 7.30 a.m. on Monday. Collier had not joined the all-day meeting until 5 p.m., and it was still in progress when he and Holmes had left at 10 p.m., with Evans promising to confirm the bid would go ahead by telephone early the following morning. With his house near Sevenoaks an hour or more's drive away and an early start likely, Collier had taken up an offer from Holmes of a bed for the night. Evans had rung at 6 a.m. to confirm that the bid was on at a price of £2.60 a share, leaving Collier no time to make the call to Cassell from the office before the news became public. Shortly after making it, he left for work, where there would be plenty to do.[101] Big Bang was just one week old.

At 8.10 a.m. London time Cassell executed Collier's order through Vickers in the City, by then part of the Citicorp Scrimgeour Vickers equity brokerage and trading combine. He managed to acquire 60,000 shares at a price of £2.39. At

8.30 a.m. Hollis Group announced its counter-bid for AE. The share price rose instantaneously from £2.39 to £2.65, netting Collier a gross paper profit of £15,600. Cassell rang Scrimgeour Vickers in London and, feigning surprise, sold the shares. He then telephoned Collier's home and left a message that the deal had been done. Unfortunately for Collier, the extraordinarily fortuitous timing of the purchase had alerted suspicious dealers at Chase Manhattan Securities, through which Scrimgeour Vickers had bought 35,000 of the 60,000 shares Cassell had ordered. They queried it with Scrimgeour Vickers, who queried it with Cassell, who tried to undo the order. The dealers at Scrimgeour Vickers refused to cancel the order, thinking it was a legitimate American client who would sue them for doing so just ahead of such a precipitate increase in value. Instead, they informed their chairman, Jeremy Paulson-Ellis. That night Cassell rang Collier to tell him what had happened and Collier asked him to try again to cancel the deal, but by then the matter was out of the hands of Cassell. Paulson-Ellis asked Cassell to meet him in New York on Wednesday 5 November. At that meeting Cassell confessed that the order had come from Geoffrey Collier, and that – without telling Collier – he had booked the purchase to Pureve, a Cayman Islands company jointly controlled by him and Collier.[102] By now extremely worried, Collier rang Paulson-Ellis in New York very early on the morning of Thursday 6 November and begged him to keep the transgression to himself, offering to repay any loss to Vickers or even to donate an equivalent sum to charity. Paulson-Ellis was sympathetic to Collier's plight, but adamant that he had no choice but to pass the details to Morgan Grenfell, on the grounds that knowledge of the illicit nature of the purchase was too widespread within Vickers for him to guarantee silence.[103] There was little love lost between Collier and the dealers at Scrimgeour Vickers, whose settlements team he had successfully poached.[104] Worse, his profit was equal to their loss. Paulson-Ellis said he would be returning to London on the Monday, and asked who he should contact at Morgan Grenfell, but Collier insisted that he would approach Christopher Reeves himself. Collier made an appointment to meet Reeves and Hardman in Reeves's office at 11 a.m. on the Friday morning, and penned a letter of resignation which he took with him. On entering the room he said to Reeves:

I've done a most terrible thing and made a terrible mistake. I've been insider dealing.[105]

He then proffered his letter of resignation.

Reeves had already been contacted by Paulson-Ellis's secretary to make an appointment. He had thought the invitation odd, since they had met only once, and that was for Reeves to apologize for poaching Collier, but he had nevertheless accepted a suggestion that they meet on the Monday. Picking up the letter of resignation, he said 'I'm not accepting this at the moment.' He then asked Collier if he had done anything like it before. Collier said that he had not. Reeves also asked how many people knew about it, and Collier said that he did not know. He suggested that Collier put the details of the transaction in writing, and submit them to him, which Collier duly did. Hardman then took Collier to lunch, at the Great Eastern Hotel, but Collier could not eat, and Hardman suggested that he went home early.[106] The senior management of the bank pondered the matter over the weekend, but when Reeves met Paulson-Ellis on Monday 10 November it was made plain to him that too many people knew about the deal to keep it quiet. A bowdlerized version of these events later circulated in the press, suggesting that the management of the bank was initially inclined to overlook the transgression, and that Collier was forced to sign a written confession for fear that he might be tempted to sue for unfair dismissal. Later on Monday, Collier met Reeves, the company secretary John Baylis and the head of personnel, George Miller. Reeves said: 'Your resignation has been accepted.'[107] He then asked Collier to sign a press release. It contained just a single sentence, which stated that he had dealt with an outside stockbroker in breach of the bank's requirement to direct all personal share transactions through the bank's own dealers. Morgan Grenfell then released it to the press. It said that 'following his admitted breach of staff rules Mr Collier has tendered his resignation . . . and that such resignation has been accepted with immediate effect'.[108]

It was a very pukka sentence, eschewing the dreaded term 'insider dealing'. News of the sacking was relayed to shocked staff in Morgan Grenfell Securities late on the Monday afternoon and the bank simultaneously passed the details provided by Collier to the Stock Exchange's four-man Professional Standards Panel.[109] The Exchange's surveillance team had already started a routine investigation of the price rise in AE shares just ahead of the Hollis bid, passing their findings to the Department of Trade and Industry on 13 November.[110] The Stock Exchange refused Collier's offer to resign his membership in order to retain jurisdiction over him in the event of disciplinary proceedings.[111] In almost the last great piece of showmanship of the Reeves regime, Morgan Grenfell's propagandists set about limiting the damage to the bank. In sharp contrast to the detailed revelations about Ivan Boesky made by the American authorities less than a week later, only sketchy details of what Collier had actually done appeared in dribs and drabs over the next two weeks. Until it was revealed that Collier had been shopped by Scrimgeour Vickers, Morgan Grenfell even tried to make capital out of him, suggesting that it testified to the excellence of the bank's compliance systems. Reeves over-compensated publicly for his private leniency:

Clearly Mr Collier breached staff rules. This is something we are not prepared to tolerate, however senior the man.[112]

George Law, although his compliance procedures had played no part in the revelation of the offence, added:

The decisiveness of our action demonstrates the seriousness of our commitment to compliance.[113]

For a time, the press was happy to agree. 'It is much to Morgan Grenfell's credit (and will do its reputation no harm) that it acted swiftly and without favour,' declared the *Econom-ist*.[114] 'Wholly laudable,' said *The Times*.[115] 'Morgan Grenfell has set everyone a good example,' cooed the *Daily Mail*.[116] Even Bryan Gould, the Labour Party Treasury spokesman, congratulated the bank on its prompt action.[117] There was no suggestion that Morgan Grenfell had hired an unreliable man or that the bank's 'need to know' provisions needed re-working, or that only Collier's co-operation had made the revelations possible. By Friday 14 November the bank could be pleased with the manner in which it had ducked any re-sponsibility for Collier's actions. It would be a very long time before the bank enjoyed such favourable publicity again.

At the close of trading on the New York stock market that night the Securities and Exchange Commission announced that Ivan Boesky, the man at the centre of virtually every takeover in the City and on Wall Street in the last five years, had agreed to hand back $50 million in illegal profits from insider dealing. Though Morgan Grenfell had decided not to say very much about Geoffrey Collier, Ivan Boesky had decided to tell the Securities and Exchange Commission in New York quite a lot about Morgan Grenfell.

Morgan Grenfell's successful attempt to distance itself from its former managing director made things infinitely worse for Geoffrey Collier, who seemed at times to be the object of an act of vengeance by society on the City. It was easy to forget that insider dealing had an exceptionally long pedigree in the City and that until the late 1970s it was regarded more or less as a perk of the job. As recently as March 1986 the London Stock Exchange had admitted that it could not catch organized rings of professional insiders dealing through offshore accounts, though it knew of their existence.[118] Insider dealing did not become a criminal offence in Britain until 1980 and in world-wide terms remains an Anglo-Saxon obsession. In Italy there are no laws against insider dealing, leading an Italian senator to describe the Milan bourse as 'more like a house of ill-repute than a market'.[119] In France fund management and broking are still not separated by a 'Chinese Wall' and the Pechiney insider-dealing affair has washed up at the gates of the Elysée Palace. In Japan insider dealing has been institutionalized by the excessive financial demands of pursuing a political career; there was no definition of insider dealing in Japanese law until the spring of 1988 and the laws introduced since have been feeble. The main Japanese banks and securities houses did not even introduce 'Chinese Walls' until late 1988. Japanese executives commonly – and legally – buy their own shares ahead of a major deal and advise their friends of the opportunity, as in the City of years ago. As the Lockheed and Recruit Cosmos scandals showed, even the Japanese Prime Minister is corruptible. In Switzerland, where until July 1988 banks could act as brokers to companies where they had board representation, laws prohibiting insider dealing are of very recent origin and were introduced only under relentless American pressure and in the face of fierce opposition from Swiss investors.[120] It is still not illegal in Hong Kong. Unfortunately for Collier, the monetary excesses of the Big Bang era had changed profoundly the climate in London. Vivid American examples like Dennis Levine and Ivan Boesky, who was uncovered at exactly the same time, had fuelled the common British perception that the City was populated by greedy parasites and sharpened the public appetite for some ritual humiliations of City cheats.

Bryan Gould wrote an almost bloodthirsty letter to the Secretary of State for Trade and Industry, Paul Channon, asking him to make an example of Collier and suggesting 'a couple of good prosecutions in the City would work wonders'.[121] In Parliament, Channon assured him that he took 'as serious a view of what Mr Collier is alleged to have done as you do'.[122] One of Channon's officials, ostensibly employed by an impartial government department, warned that 'people want blood. Public opinion must be satisfied. We are under some pressure to prosecute.'[123] On Friday 14 November Channon, anxious not to look soft on the City ahead of a widely anticipated General Election, equipped his department's inspectors immediately with draconian powers then proceeding slowly through Parliament. They included the power to examine witnesses under oath, impound documents and prosecute people who refused to co-operate, despite the fact that Collier had already confessed.[124] The maximum sentence for insider dealing was subsequently raised from two years to seven. He appointed two inspectors on Saturday 15 November, who rang Collier the same night and summoned him – on pain of arrest – to a meeting at the headquarters of the Department of Trade and Industry in London at 10 a.m. on Sunday morning, the day of his son's christening. When they learnt of this, the meeting was rearranged for 2.30 p.m., and it was clear that they were under intense political pressure to perform. But even with Collier's full co-operation, they still took two weeks to present sufficient evidence to charge Collier with an offence on the AE deal. Their victim was understandably aggrieved that he had been singled out for pillory by politicians and the press.[125] A senior executive at Merrill Lynch in London, Nahum Vaskevitch, was dismissed for insider dealing in the spring of 1987 with nothing like the righteous outrage which accompanied Collier's departure. Collier's solicitors, Winckworth & Pemberton, seriously considered an appeal to have the case dismissed on grounds that the outcome would be prejudiced by the hysterical press coverage and even the Department of Trade and Industry became concerned that their leaks to the media had got out of hand and might prejudice the case.[126] The hysteria was especially surprising in view of Collier's unconditional co-operation with the prosecution. His counsel, Robert Alexander, considered his confession the most complete admission of guilt he had seen in his professional life, and only agreed to take the brief if Collier pleaded guilty. No one anticipated the excitement the Collier case would arouse, least of all Collier himself. When he suggested to his wife, Barbara, that there might be some press interest, she had scoffed: 'You're not important enough.' Yet within days, there were journalists swarming through their garden, photographing their children at play, and the telephone rang almost incessantly. As Robert Alexander put it at Collier's trial:

He had a fall that was sudden, great, blazoned in the press and agonizing. He has brought disgrace on his family and he has suffered agony and remorse.[127]

Collier himself testified to the 'tremendous pressure' it put on him and his family. 'The attention I have received is totally out of proportion to what I am alleged to have done,' he said.[128]

Amid such a dreadful fall from grace, press speculation focused on the apparent idiocy of risking everything for £15,000. Collier himself was bemused. 'I cannot account for why I did it. I must have been mad.'[129] It was an immense risk for a minor sum in relation to the £95,000 he earned in his fifteen months at Morgan Grenfell, but justifiable as part of a pattern of similar deals. Collier told Reeves that the AE deal was 'a once only episode',[130] but when the existence of the Cayman Islands company, Pureve ('Everup', when the letters are transposed), was uncovered, it was assumed that Collier dealt habitually on the basis of inside information. Certainly the joke remains unexplained, and the establishment of a Cayman Islands company solely to invest ownership of a Cayman Islands condominium (Collier is a keen scuba diver, and the Cayman coral reefs are exceptional) stretches credulity, but other evidence suggests that the AE deal may even have been an isolated incident. A Cayman Islands company can be used as easily for legitimate, non-taxable transactions as for illicit deals. As a single-capacity broker with Vickers, Collier's opportunities for insider dealing, at least on the basis of hard information, were rather fewer than he enjoyed in his days of 'needing to know' at Morgan Grenfell, whereas his residence in New York must have increased the scope for minimizing his tax deductions. Similarly, the ease with which the deal was traced back to Collier suggests a naivety foreign to a hardened insider dealer. After trawling through all of Collier's personal dealings during his time at Morgan Grenfell, the DTI inspectors found only two cases which aroused their suspicions, only one of which led to charges. In this case, Collier confessed to dealing in Cadbury Schweppes while a Morgan Grenfell client, General Cinema, was building a stake in the company. It was less clear cut than the AE charges, and Collier agreed to plead guilty only in the expectation that full co-operation would reduce the severity of his punishment.

The ineptitude and apparent isolation of the AE deal makes it less, rather than more, explicable. It seems that he did not need the money. The family house, Oldbury Place, at Ightham near Sevenoaks, was sold for £900,000 after his disgrace, but a mortgage of only £250,000 was repaid, this being the limit up to which Morgan Grenfell subsidized the mortgages taken out by directors.[131] The house cost Collier £525,000, suggesting that he had raised £275,000 in cash to buy it. He loves fine wine, spending £15,000 on a cellar at Oldbury Place, and ran three cars, including a red Porsche he paid for himself. He could afford a pay cut on joining Morgan Grenfell, and did not baulk at hiring people at higher salaries than his own. 'You are always,' in the words of a stockbroker who knew him, 'ten grand short', but unlike many of the salaried City employees to which the jibe accurately pertains, Collier's lifestyle seems not to have been perpetually edging away from his means. Being 'ten grand short' was a common enough condition in the City, partially explaining why Christopher Reeves, himself a lover of Kenneth Keith's 'heavy metal' policies, took such an uncensorious view of Collier's transgression, but it was not what lay behind Geoffrey Collier's decision to buy shares in AE in November 1986. Even Reeves, the great fisher of men, failed to understand Collier's psyche completely.

Collier's origins were conventional enough. The son of a civil engineer in colonial East Africa, he was educated at King's School, Canterbury and Trinity College, Oxford, where he took a second in Politics, Philosophy and Economics and met his future wife. During and after Oxford he suffered from a resentment common to Oxford-educated Englishmen whose public school is relatively minor and whose parents are undistinguished. Encountering socially exclusive wealth and privilege at Oxford, he had dedicated most of his life since to acquiring its trappings. Significantly, he spent much of his working life outside the City, where the subtle gradations of class are probably more stifling even than those of Oxford. The social cultures of Hong Kong and New York are more generous to acquired, as opposed to prescriptive, status and in Hong Kong at least the authorities were completely indifferent to sharp practice. Collier even took to exaggerating the humbleness of his origins: if he could not belong, he could at least arrive from a long way off. At his trial Robert Alexander solemnly told the court that Collier was the son of a South Wales bricklayer who had paid his own way through Oxford. Though his father did once lay bricks, by the time Collier was born he had become a college lecturer, first at the Khartoum technical institute in the Sudan and then at Makerere University in Uganda. Though he went to preparatory school in Kenya, he was sent to King's, Canterbury at thirteen, in the normal way. He won a scholarship to Oxford, awarded by Automotive Products, not because he was especially poor but because his parents' expatriate status meant that he did not qualify for a local authority grant. There was similar artifice in much of Collier's public persona, for the bullying image of the office would be unrecognizable to his wife, friends and family. Ahead of his trial his lawyers, Winckworth & Pemberton, solicited testimonials to his character from 100 people, of which nearly three-quarters replied in his support. Nearly all of them commended his decision to adopt two children, Julia and Guy, on whom Collier must have felt that the burden of his disgrace would one day fall especially hard. Former colleagues at Vickers and Morgan Grenfell were debarred from writing in support of him on legal advice. In keeping with Morgan's instant relegation of Geoffrey Collier to an un-person, George Law wrote back on behalf of the Morgan's employees to say that Collier had proved himself unworthy of a responsible position. The paradox remains, however, and is soluble only in terms of Collier's own complex personality, which is at bottom a peculiarly English stereotype: that of the outsider clamouring at the gates of the establishment, whilst despising it all the while for its rank hypocrisy. Like many insider dealers, Collier did not buy shares in AE strictly because he needed the money. Paradoxically, he bought them both to fulfil and to expunge his social ambitions.

Geoffrey Collier appeared in court twice. A summons was served on him in early December alleging three offences under the Companies Securities (Insider Dealing) Act 1985. In a twenty-five-minute hearing at Wimbledon Magistrates Court on 23 February 1987 he was committed for trial at the Old Bailey and released on bail of £20,000, footed by his wife Barbara and Thomas Wyatt, a stockbroking friend. Three further charges, alleging insider dealing in shares of Cadbury Schweppes 'on or about 14 October 1986', were added. Morgan Grenfell had been assisting the American soft drinks company, General Cinema, to acquire an undisclosed stake in Cadbury Schweppes since September 1986.[132] Collier was involved in the purchases and took advantage of his knowledge. The fresh charges prompted a request from Cadbury Schweppes to the Stock Exchange that the stake-building exercise should be probed.[133] Collier seemed cheerful enough, joking with his lawyers and looking jaunty for the benefit of photographers before being driven from court by his wife. Seeing the pictures the following day, cynical Morgan Grenfell staff joked that he should have been convicted for wearing a coat with a fur-lined collar. Though Collier's choice of clothing that day can only have been an elaborate joke at the expense of his former colleagues, the culture gap remained as wide as ever. On 1 July 1987 Collier was sentenced at the Old Bailey to twelve months' imprisonment, suspended for two years, and fined £25,000 after pleading guilty on all charges. He was ordered to pay £7,000 towards the costs of the prosecution. The sentence was immediately denounced by Robin Cook, the Labour Party spokesman, as a 'mockery'.[134] Cook's colleague, Brian Sedgemore, was even more forthright:

The judge has effectively said to big City swindlers, 'carry on'. If a working-class person had obtained the kind of money he obtained by breach of trust and deception, he would have been inside for a few years.[135]

'City cheat walks free,' roared the headlines. Apparently compromised by his recent appointment as chairman of the Takeover Panel, Collier's counsel, Robert Alexander, wrote a letter to *The Times* warning that future culprits could not expect similar mercy.[136] It later emerged that Collier had dropped a charge of perjury against a Department of Trade and Industry official, whom he claimed had lied at the bail hearing, in exchange for a less aggressive approach by the prosecution.[137] This followed DTI attempts to prevent Collier returning to the United States to renew his 'green card' (work permit), fearing that any apparent leniency would have adverse political repercussions. In order to deny Collier the use of his passport as one of the conditions of bail, a DTI official told the court that Collier would be arrested by the Securities and Exchange Commission (SEC) as soon as he set foot in the United States, though the DTI had not contacted the SEC, which in any event has no powers of arrest. Robert Alexander had threatened to attack the DTI for perjury at Collier's trial, but dropped the charge in exchange for agreement that the prosecution would not press for the maximum sentence.

By July 1987 Morgan Grenfell was relieved to see the Government and the judiciary absorbing the brunt of public distaste for the City. Even the imperturbable Lord Catto, the author of the near-disaster of film finance, had conceded in April that year that the bank was enduring 'probably the most difficult passage in our history'.[138] The easy confidence of the days ahead of the flotation a year earlier had evaporated completely. Byron Ousey's glossy brochure, which featured Geoffrey Collier and John Holmes at opposite ends of a large leather sofa, had been discreetly pulped more than six months earlier.[139] Its paragraph on 'Group Compliance' would have made sorry reading:

The group is totally committed to ensuring that its high standards of integrity are scupulously maintained through the implementation of effective compliance procedures. A senior member of the Morgan Grenfell Group plc has been appointed Group Director of Compliance. One of his prime duties is to protect investors' interests and to ensure that potential conflicts of interest are always handled with complete professionalism so as to prevent them becoming actual.[140]

In many ways, the bank's astute handling of the Collier affair made it harder to comprehend the magnitude of the series of disasters which overwhelmed Morgan Grenfell from 1 December 1986, when two inspectors from the Department of Trade and Industry mounted the steps at 23 Great Winchester Street and asked to speak to Graham Walsh. Walsh, immersed in a meeting, sent another director, Donald Wells, in his stead.[141] They would not be so lightly dismissed in future, for within a year of their visit, 21 of the 48 directors of the bank featured in Ousey's brochure had resigned or been sacked. On Thursday 15 October 1987, one of them, Roger Seelig, was questioned for nine hours at Holborn Police Station, the headquarters of the Metropolitan Police Fraud Squad, where he was charged with 12 offences, including theft, and the fragile triumphs of the Reeves regime unravelled completely.

NOTES

[1] The phrase is quoted on the opening page of this book. In his Official Statement to a Committee of the United States Senate on 23 May 1933, J. P. Morgan Jnr said: 'If I may be permitted to speak of the firm, of which I have the honour to be the senior partner, I should state that at all times the idea of doing only first-class business, and that in a first-class way, has been before our minds.' The words were known to all members of Chappell's generation at Morgan Grenfell.
[2] James Saunders, *Nightmare: the Ernest Saunders Story*, Hutchinson, 1989.
[3] *The Economist*, 17 January 1987.
[4] *ibid.*

[5] *The Economist*, 12 November 1987.
[6] Morgan Grenfell Holdings Limited, Annual Report and Accounts, 1979; Morgan Grenfell Group plc, Annual Report and Accounts, 1986. Payroll costs multiplied eightfold in the same period, from £5 million to £42 million.
[7] Morgan Grenfell Holdings Limited, Annual Report and Accounts, 1983 and 1986.
[8] Morgan Grenfell Group plc, Offer of Ordinary Shares by Tender, June 1986.
[9] Ivan Fallon and James Srodes, *Takeovers*, Hamish Hamilton, 1987.
[10] *Wall Street Journal*, 4 August 1986.
[11] Morgan Grenfell Holdings Limited, Annual Report and Accounts, 1983 and 1986.
[12] Morgan Grenfell Holdings Limited, Annual Report and Accounts, 1983 and 1985.
[13] *Financial Weekly*, 9 January 1986.
[14] Fallon and Srodes, *op cit.*, Saunders, *op cit.*
[15] *Financial Times*, 19 March 1985.
[16] *Accountancy*, April 1986.
[17] *Asian Wall Street Journal*, 1 November 1984; *Standard*, 1 November 1984; *Financial Times*, 2 November 1984; *The Economist*, 10 November 1984.
[18] *Financial Times*, 8 November 1984.
[19] Morgan Grenfell Group plc, Offer of Ordinary Shares by Tender, June 1986.
[20] Estimates by David Pountney, banking analyst at W. Greenwell, *Standard*, May 1986.
[21] *The Economist*, 1 March 1986.
[22] William Kay, *Tycoons*, Piatkus, 1985.
[23] *Business*, July 1986.
[24] *Sunday Times*, 1 June 1986.
[25] *Financial Times*, 24 February 1986.
[26] *Euromoney*, April 1986.
[27] *Business*, July 1986.
[28] *Standard*, 24 February 1986.
[29] *Financial Times*, 25 February 1986; *Investors Chronicle*, 28 February 1986.
[30] *Financial Times*, 24 February 1986.
[31] Nick Kochan and Hugh Pym, *The Guinness Affair*, Christopher Helm, 1987.
[32] *Daily Telegraph*, 22 February 1986.
[33] *Guardian*, 1 March 1986.

313

[34] *Sunday Times*, 2 March 1986.
[35] *Daily Telegraph*, 10 March 1986.
[36] *The Times*, 25 February 1986; *Guardian*, 25 February 1986.
[37] *Financial Times*; 26 February 1986; *Guardian*, 26 February 1986.
[38] *Financial Times*, 6 March 1986.
[39] *The Times*, 18 November 1986.
[40] *Daily Mail*, 21 November 1986.
[41] *The Banker*, November 1986.
[42] *Financial Times*, 6 March 1986.
[43] *Standard*, 30 April 1986.
[44] *Daily Telegraph*, 3 November 1987.
[45] *Sunday Times*, 16 March 1986; *Guardian*, 18 March 1986.
[46] *Guardian*, 18 March 1986.
[47] *Financial Times*, 18 March 1986.
[48] *Daily Telegraph*, 16 May 1986.
[49] *Wall Street Journal*, 16 May 1986.
[50] *Daily Telegraph*, 16 May 1986.
[51] Morgan Grenfell Group plc, Offer of Ordinary Shares by Tender, June 1986.
[52] *Financial Times*, 16 May 1986.
[53] *Daily Telegraph*, 16 May 1986.
[54] *Guardian*, 16 June 1986.
[55] *Wall Street Journal*, 2 August 1986; *Guardian*, 2 August 1986; *Financial Times*, 2 August 1986; *The Times*, 2 August 1986; *Daily Telegraph*, 2 August 1986.
[56] *Financial Weekly*, 22 May 1986.
[57] Morgan Grenfell Group plc, Offer of Ordinary Shares by Tender, June 1986; Morgan Grenfell Holdings Limited, Annual Report and Accounts, 1985.
[58] *Financial Times*, 27 June 1986.
[59] *Acquisitions Monthly*, July 1986.
[60] Morgan Grenfell Group plc, Offer of Ordinary Shares by Tender, June 1986.
[61] *ibid*.
[62] *ibid*.
[63] Morgan Grenfell & Co. Limited, Accounts, 1986; Morgan Grenfell Group plc, Annual Report and Accounts, 1986.
[64] Morgan Grenfell Laurie Holdings Limited, Accounts, 1986.
[65] *Observer*, 12 October 1986; *Euromoney*, June 1988; *Financial Times*, 28 June 1986.
[66] Morgan Grenfell Group plc, Offer of Ordinary Shares by Tender, June 1986.
[67] *Standard*, 3 July 1986.

[68] *George Peabody & Co., J. S. Morgan & Co., Morgan Grenfell & Co., Morgan Grenfell & Co. Ltd, 1838–1958*, printed for private circulation by Oxford University Press, 1958.

[69] *Lombard Street, A Description of the Money Market*, by Walter Bagehot, Kegan Paul, 1888, cited in Anthony Sampson, *The Money Lenders*, Hodder & Stoughton, 1981.

[70] *PR Week*, 26 June 1986.

[71] *The Independent*, 28 July 1987.

[72] *Financial Times*, 23 September 1986.

[73] *Financial Times*, 18 June 1986.

[74] *Financial Weekly*, 19 June 1986.

[75] *Sunday Times*, 1 June 1986.

[76] *Financial Weekly*, 19 June 1986.

[77] *The Economist*, 16 May 1987.

[78] *Financial Times*, 18 June 1986.

[79] *Sunday Times*, 1 June 1986.

[80] Morgan Grenfell Group plc, Offer of Ordinary Shares by Tender, June 1986.

[81] Morgan Grenfell Group plc, Annual Report and Accounts, 1986.

[82] *Wall Street Journal*, 24 October 1986; Morgan Grenfell Group plc, Annual Report and Accounts, 1986.

[83] Morgan Grenfell Group plc, Offer of Ordinary Shares by Tender, June 1986.

[84] *Business*, July 1986.

[85] *ibid.*

[86] *Financial Times*, 18 June 1986.

[87] Morgan Grenfell Group plc, Offer of Ordinary Shares by Tender, June 1986; Morgan Grenfell Group plc, Annual Report and Accounts, 1986.

[88] *Acquisitions Monthly*, January 1986.

[89] *ibid.*

[90] *The Economist*, 12 November 1987.

[91] Morgan Grenfell Group plc, Offer of Ordinary Shares by Tender, June 1986.

[92] *Daily Telegraph*, 21 February 1987.

[93] *ibid.*

[94] *ibid.*

[95] *The Economist*, 25 June 1988.

[96] *The Economist*, 17 January 1987.

[97] Margaret Reid, *All-Change in the City*, Macmillan, 1988.

[98] *The Times*, 8 August 1986.

[99] *Daily Express*, 17 September 1986; *Guardian*, 17 September 1986.

[100] *The Economist*, 17 January 1987.

[101] *The Times*, 2 July 1987.

[102] *Financial Times*, 15 November 1986; *The Times*, 2 July 1987 and 15 November 1986.

[103] *Financial Times*, 12 November 1986; *The Observer Magazine*, 30 July 1989.

[104] *The Times*, 13 November 1986.

[105] *The Times*, 2 July 1987.

[106] *The Observer Magazine*, 30 July 1989.

[107] *Financial Times*, 14 November 1986.

[108] *Financial Times*, 11 November 1986.

[109] *The Times*, 11 and 12 November 1986; *Financial Times*, 11 and 12 November 1986.

[110] *Guardian*, 20 November 1986.

[111] *Financial Times*, 13 November 1986.

[112] *Financial Times*, 11 November 1986.

[113] *Financial Times*, 12 November 1986.

[114] *The Ecomomist*, 15 November 1986.

[115] *The Times*, 12 November 1986.

[116] *Daily Mail*, 12 November 1986.

[117] *Financial Times*, 12 November 1986.

[118] Fallon and Srodes, *op. cit.*

[119] *The Independent*, 8 September 1988.

[120] *Financial Times*, 2 June 1988.

[121] *Financial Times*, 14 November 1986.

[122] *Sunday Times*, 16 November 1986.

[123] *ibid.*

[124] *Financial Times*, 17 November 1986; *Guardian*, 11 December 1986.

[125] *Financial Times*, 14 November 1986.

[126] *Daily Mail*, 6 December 1986; *The Independent*, 12 January 1987.

[127] *The Times*, 2 July 1987.

[128] *Observer*, 25 January 1987.

[129] *The Times*, 2 July 1987.

[130] *The Times*, 2 July 1987.

[131] *Observer*, 4 January 1987.

[132] *Standard*, 23 February 1987; *Financial Times*, 24 February 1987.

[133] *Guardian*, 6 March 1987.

[134] *The Times*, 2 July 1987.

[135] *Daily Telegraph*, 2 July 1987.

[136] *The Times*, 3 July 1987.

[137] *Observer*, 11 October 1987.

[138] Morgan Grenfell Group plc, Annual Report and Accounts, 1986.
[139] *Investors Chronicle*, 28 November 1986. The picture was reproduced in *The Observer Magazine*, 30 July 1989.
[140] 'The Services of Morgan Grenfell', a publicity brochure published in 1986; also quoted in *Private Eye*, 6 March 1987.
[141] *The Observer Magazine*, 30 July 1989.

TEN

An Exceedingly Seedy Transaction

For Roger Seelig the journey that ended at Holborn Police Station on an autumn afternoon in October 1987 had begun nearly two years earlier, on 29 November 1985. That Friday he met Ernest Saunders, the chief executive of Arthur Guinness & Sons, for the first time. They chatted over lunch in one of the private dining-rooms at 23 Great Winchester Street for more than two hours. Distillers – the bid which was to humble them both – was not even touched upon. Instead, the discussion ranged freely over possible targets for a bid by Guinness in the retail sector.[1] Beecham and Boot's, both low-rated, were aired. Morgan Grenfell had arranged a £47 million agreed deal betwen Guinness and Martin's, the newsagent chain, in June 1984, and there was vague talk of new ventures with Underwood's and Paul Hamlyn at Octopus Books, both clients of Seelig's.[2]

At the time Britain's high streets were being reshaped by a new breed of entrepreneurial retailer. These men – Ralph Halpern, George Davies, Stanley Kalms, Terence Conran – were all known to Seelig, who had been close to most of the major retailing takeovers since the early 1980s. Even as he lunched with Saunders his team downstairs was finalizing the £1.52 billion merger of Habitat Mothercare and British Home Stores, the third act of a drama in which Seelig and his close friend, Terence Conran, had transformed Habitat, first through flotation and then the purchase of Mothercare, into a billion-pound retailing giant, Storehouse. The Dixon's bid for Curry's had given Seelig a reputation for getting his client's share price racing away, not just ahead of a bid but during and after it too, ostensibly as the market digested the unquestionable logic of the deal. Though the Curry's bid, and the Burton bid for Debenham's, had aroused the suspicions of the Takeover Panel, they had not found any evidence of wrongdoing. For his part, Seelig admitted that he found the Panel's interventions frustrating, accusing it of losing 'the respect of practitioners' and getting 'buried in its own bureaucracy'.[3]

'I was impressed with Roger Seelig. He struck me as a dynamic, forceful individual. I knew his reputation. Reeves had described him as the most entrepreneurial man in the bank and I could see him working out ideas as we were talking: he seemed to be able to think of several things at once,' was Saunders's memory of the lunch.[4] Seelig's obvious appetite for confrontation was a quality Saunders knew would be needed for the bid target – Distillers – that had been planted in his mind by Charles Fraser, the chairman of Morgan Grenfell Scotland.[5] For now he was content to stick to retailing. Here, he too had a record of sorts. In selling or closing 149 companies in the three years after his appointment to the top job at Guinness in October 1981, Saunders had recognized retailing as the one area of potential growth his predecessors had stumbled upon. Lavell's the newsagents, Drummond's the chemists and Clare's the shopfitters were carefully withheld from the most savage disposal programme in modern British management history and when he switched from retrenchment to acquisition his earliest targets were retailers. They were also Morgan Grenfell's first assignments for Guinness, after Christopher Reeves and Anthony Forbes, the senior partner of Cazenove's, had tempted Saunders to consider acquisitions over dinner at the Connaught in early 1985.[6] Saunders had been weaned away from the company's traditional bankers, Rothschild's, a year earlier and the company broker, James Capel, was also replaced in May 1984 by Wood Mackenzie, an Edinburgh firm well versed in the ways of the Scottish financial mafia. This helped when taking over Scottish companies like Distillers. Coupled with Morgan Grenfell's preferred broking house, Cazenove, whose clout Saunders respected, this was the team Guinness kept together until the end. Their first triumph was in

June 1984, topping a £36 million offer by W. H. Smith to capture the Martin's newsagent chain. Neighbourhood Stores followed, for £11.9 million. Over the subsequent twelve months Saunders created a retailing arm 1,200 stores strong, adding Lewis Meeson, R. S. McColl, and the British franchise of the Seven-Eleven convenience stores.[7]

Though the lunch at Great Winchester Street was the first time Roger Seelig had met Ernest Saunders (the Guinness account having so far been handled by Anthony Richmond-Watson, Lord Catto's nephew and one of the less flamboyant directors in the Corporate Finance Department) and the two men never became friends, there were enough similarities between them to suggest that they could work together instinctively. Saunders was just fifty, six feet two inches tall and greying, with a nose which invited comparison with a Roman senator. His habit of stooping eagerly, like some bird of prey, gave his nickname – 'Deadly Ernest' – a palpable form. It is hard to recollect now, but in November 1985 Saunders was acclaimed by Fleet Street and the City as a manager fit to compare with the giants of the bull market: BTR's Owen Green and James Hanson of Hanson Trust. He basked in the adulation accorded to him by pressmen anxious to present Big Bang to their readers in a popular form. Some financial journalists seemed to live in an almost marsupial relationship with Saunders. He was adept at handling them, learning early the value of feeding them stories for the barren Monday business pages and cultivating them so assiduously that they began to feel themselves part of a great personal rather than corporate drama. The press had also created Roger Seelig, still only forty but with some of the most spectacular deals of the merger wave behind him. He and George Magan were feted weekly in the Sunday press as the City's most inventive take-over tacticians, with the full approval of Christopher Reeves, who scoffed at suggestions that the two takeover stars over-shadowed him. 'The simple fact is that they like dealing with financial journalists and are rather good at it,' he said.[8]

Saunders and Seelig were both loners, preferring action to

teamwork. Ivan Fallon has described Seelig as 'much more of a free spirit than the others, working his own hours (which included most weekends) and tending his own clients and contacts. He would often disappear, out of contact except for emergencies, and return triumphant with the next deal planned.'[9] In the same way, Saunders consulted the full board of Guinness less and less during his time as chief executive. Unversed in financial intricacies, he preferred scything through the maze of business life using clever lawyers like Tom Ward, to involvement in the irksome give-and-take of corporate bureaucracy. Both Seelig and Saunders were outsiders, in companies packed with insiders. In October 1981 Saunders, the son of Austrian Jews who had fled Vienna after the *Anschluss*, came as a hired hand to a board which boasted an earl, a marquess, a viscountess and three Hons. Seelig had neither been to Eton or Oxbridge nor served in Her Majesty's Forces, in a bank where most of the directors had been schooled in at least one of these institutions. Instead, he had gone to Dulwich and shunned Cambridge for its indifference to cyber-netics in favour of the London School of Economics. Though he mimicked the pursuits of his peers, buying a country house in Gloucestershire, furnishing it at the London auction houses and riding to hounds, some suspected that these accoutrements were only an elaborate joke at the expense of Lord Catto. In business, he preferred to mix with his own kind – Terence Conran or Elliott Bernerd – rather than Anthony Richmond-Watson or Graham Walsh, with whom his relationship was poor. The institutional misanthropy of Saunders and Seelig meant that both men were unfamiliar with the hidden constra-ints of the caste, judging what little they knew of it as rank hypocrisy. In the events that followed, much hinged on this indifference to the ethics of English corporate warfare.

Saunders had never really been a retailer. The shops simply generated the cash Guinness needed to offset a corporation-tax regime which penalized companies (like Guinness) with high overseas earnings but low British turnover.[10] His heart, and his experience – at JWT, Beecham, Great Universal Stores and Nestlé – lay with international brand names, the signature of quality that cannot be counterfeited. This, as Saunders explained at the time, lay behind his first major takeover, the acquisition in 1985 of the Scotch whisky distiller, Arthur Bell & Sons:

A lot of people will tell you they are a worldwide business. They mean they have one bottle of their drink somewhere in every country. That does not mean worldwide. In bars, at events, parties, in aeroplanes you are subjected to brand names. The same groups seem to be appearing all over the place. We decided that to become a major player we had to make a major move.[11]

Raymond Miquel, the chairman of Arthur Bell & Sons, first heard that Guinness was bidding for his company in a Chicago hotel room in the small hours of Friday 14 June 1985. At 1.30 a.m. he was telephoned by the company's headquarters in Perth to be told that Guinness was offering £327 million for Bell's. The Guinness and Morgan Grenfell publicity machines later portrayed this – the chairman in America and the rest of the board scattered about the globe – as symptomatic of a bid in which the Bell's management seemed to be always on the run. In fact, after months of secret plotting, the bid had been flushed out by a sharp rise in the Bell's share price, clearly precipitated by some informed (and heavy) buying.[12] In the three days before the Guinness camp showed their hand the Bell's share price rose from £1.60 to £1.92, and on the day of the bid to £2.63, prompting a complaint by Saunders to the Stock Exchange surveillance unit.[13]

The probe threw up evidence of insider dealing, co-ordinated, apparently, by one man. Presented with it, Saunders chose not to pursue the matter, but he complained bitterly in private of a leak from inside Morgan Grenfell.[14] The accusation was corroborated by two other facts. First, secrecy ahead of the bid had been so intense that Guinness chose not to buy a single share in Bell's before the bid was announced. Secondly, two other deals handled by Morgan Grenfell around this time were also probed by the Stock Exchange surveillance unit: the bid for Matthew Brown by Scottish & Newcastle Breweries, which raged on and off throughout 1985, and the merger between Habitat Mothercare and British Home Stores, finally consummated in December 1985. In at least one of them, the Scottish & Newcastle bid for Matthew Brown, Guinness was involved, which may have persuaded Saunders to drop the matter.[15] Inspectors from the Department of Trade and Industry have since investigated whether or not Guinness was given an indemnity on the purchase. It was around this time that George Law, Morgan Grenfell's compliance officer, conceded publicly that he had discussed all three bids with Bob Wilkinson, the Stock Exchange surveillance chief.[16] The heaviest buying of Bell's shares came from Jersey nominee accounts controlled from Switzerland, where the Stock Exchange investigators initially drew a blank, being unable to identify a certain Brian Harris, the main Jersey buyer. Brian Harris later turned out to be a typographical error by a Stock Exchange secretary, who misheard it, for Brian Evans, the brother of a Morgan Grenfell executive working on the bid for Bell's, Philip Evans.[17] Normally based in South Africa, Brian was staying with Philip in London during the bid. His explanation – that he overheard a conversation between two Scotsmen in the Caledonian Club – stood up, though it seemed extraordinary to many observers at the time that a man should pledge £128,000 of his own money to buy 80,000 shares via a Jersey nominee account just four days ahead of a major bid solely on the basis of a conversation overheard in the bar of a club to which he does not even belong.[18] He is believed to have made a profit of £80,000 on the deal. Philip Evans was grilled by George Law and the Stock Exchange surveillance unit, after which the bank pronounced itself satisfied with Brian's explanation.[19]

In June 1985 all this lay in the future. For the present, flattering press coverage focused on the painstaking 18-month reconnaissance of Bell's carried out by Guinness, Morgan Grenfell and Bain & Co., the secretive Boston-based management

consultancy that furnished Saunders with much of his management team. Praise was lavished on the mesmerizing press and
public relations campaign directed by Brian Basham's Broad
Street Associates and on the exquisite timing of each new blow
to Raymond Miquel and Bell's. Later, the City learnt that
Morgan's apparently effortless counterpunching was based on
regular tip-offs from a mole in the Bell's camp. Throughout,
admirers contrasted the unflappable, meticulously prepared
Saunders with the irascible, no-nonsense Miquel, whose
manner antagonized journalists. Having refused to cancel further appointments in New York before flying home, Miquel
did not hold a press conference until Wednesday 19 June,
three days later. He held it late (4.00 p.m.) and in the West
End, a tiresome trek for City journalists whose deadlines were
approaching.[20] Miquel lost his temper with a television crew,
attacked Saunders personally and lambasted Morgan Grenfell,
accusing the bank of behaving 'unethically' in acting for
Guinness.[21]

Miquel had some justification for his anger. Morgan Grenfell
had acted for Bell's for over twenty years, though not in any
substantial capacity since early 1983, and it had continued to
put ideas for acquisitions to the Bell's board. In choosing to act
for Guinness in the bid for Bell's, Morgan Grenfell was simply
pushing its policy of seeking out and acting for acquisitive
companies to its logical conclusion, but in doing so it had not
only lost a loyal friend but acted in a manner unthinkable only
a few years before. Many observers, recalling the bank's honourable abstention from the great electrical takeovers of the 1960s,
have pinpointed this as the decision that propelled the Morgan
Grenfell Corporate Finance Department headlong into the
spiral of unprincipled greed which ended in the Guinness
affair. It was scandalous enough at the time to attract considerable attention. Pressed by journalists for a response, Graham
Walsh initially denied any 'significant business' with Bell's
since 1983 and insisted that the company had not contacted the
bank to help with its defence once bid rumours started to
circulate.[22] The denial infuriated Miquel, who had been

warned at the end of 1984 that Morgan's were preparing a bid for Bell's. He had asked Christopher Reeves quite specifically in December that year whether or not Guinness was – under Morgan's tutelage – stalking his company and had been assured by Reeves that they were not.[23]

Let down by his traditional merchant bankers Miquel contacted an old friend: Patrick Spens, the third Baron Spens of Blairsanquhar (his grandfather had been a Chief Justice of India) and head of corporate finance at Henry Ansbacher & Co. Ltd. To describe Spens as a forty-three-year-old chartered accountant does scant justice to a highly unorthodox character, whose feigned idleness, deceptive humour, love of gossip and faintly dishevelled appearance camouflage a highly creative talent. He had worked for over ten years at Morgan Grenfell, from 1969 to 1982, becoming in 1972 the bank's youngest director at the age of thirty. It was while working at Morgan's that he got to know Miquel, advising him on the company's flotation in 1971.[24] In 1982 Spens had surprised colleagues by moving to Ansbacher, an old but undistinguished name in merchant-banking circles, but the fussiness of Graham Walsh and the relentless expansion of Morgan Grenfell were not to his taste. He also felt acutely the shift in the balance of power towards the emergent superstars, George Magan and Roger Seelig. As he left in July 1982, a former colleague opined that he wanted to become 'a rather large fish in a small pond', but Spens was really looking for a return to the innovative deal-making he regarded as the essence of merchant banking.[25] For Spens is pre-eminently a deal-maker, willing to commit millions on a shake of the hand, given with an undeniable charm. One executive who worked with him at Ansbacher recalls his contempt for the technocrats who scoured tax and company statutes while there were deals to be done. He, by contrast, could be found in City wine bars riveting his staff and the adjacent drinkers with dramatic anecdotes of City life. Those who have worked with him testify to his ability to generate anticipation, excitement and loyalty and no one is surprised that both of the two executives he took with him from

Morgan Grenfell in 1982, Roger Cort and Peter Phillips, still work closely with him. Cort runs Amethyst Investments, which shares an office with Castlecrest Investments, the Mayfair corporate-finance boutique Spens opened after being fired by Ansbacher in January 1987. Though his decision to join Ansbacher was a mistake, in less than five years there he drove the bank's Corporate Finance Department from also-ran to a regular place in the takeover league tables, attracting clients like Robert Maxwell and Dr Ashraf Marwan who share his unorthodox approach to business. Now he has gone, Ansbacher has slipped back into obscurity.

Spens had advised Miquel on his two most recent acquisitions: the 1984 purchases of the Gleneagles Hotels group and of the US spirits distributors, Wellington's Importers. He had been warning Miquel for months that Morgan Grenfell was behind the persistent rumours of a Guinness bid, but Miquel refused to believe that Reeves would let him down. Now that the bid had come, his first advice was to seek a court injunction preventing Morgan's from acting for Bell's. The company's lawyers, Denton, Hall & Burgin, initiated proceedings, only to withdraw two days before the hearing citing a 'conflict of interest'. It later emerged that they were Ernest Saunders's personal solicitors. It was too late to draft in new lawyers, so Spens turned instead to the Takeover Panel. They went first to the Panel executive – the lowly administrators, rather than the City worthies that make up the full Panel – and rehearsed their case. Miquel explained that Morgan's betrayal had deprived them of their most important adviser at a crucial moment. Morgan's countered with a letter from Bell's dated November 1984, which apparently indicated that its services were no longer required. Spens produced evidence that Morgan's had earned a fee of £20,000 from Bell's in late 1984 and the company claimed that the bank had been advising it as recently as June 1985, but it did not count for much.[26] The Monday after the bid was launched, the Panel executive issued a meek rebuke to Morgan's but did not require it to abandon the account. Spens was staggered and asked immediately for a hearing by the full Panel.

This he was granted two days later, on Wednesday 26 June. The meeting, chaired by Sir Jasper Hollom, was held in the Council Chamber of the Stock Exchange building. A representative of the executive spoke first, explaining why they had absolved Morgan Grenfell. Spens spoke next, followed by Graham Walsh, who was addressing a body of which only four years earlier he had been the director-general. Walsh was mindful of the sums at stake if the Panel's judgement was an adverse one and was accompanied by Christopher Reeves. Anthony Richmond-Watson, the director in charge of the Guinness bid for Bell's, was deemed too junior to argue the bank's case with sufficient force and was debarred from speaking. At risk for Morgan Grenfell were millions of pounds in fees for underwriting and executing the bid. The costs of withdrawing from the sub-underwriting agreements which the bank had entered into with various institutional investors could have run to nearly £7 million. Shamelessly, Christopher Reeves told the Panel that the bank could earn more from a single deal with Guinness than it could hope to earn in a dozen transactions with Bell's, an argument to which the merchant bankers who served on the panel were naturally sympathetic.[27] Spens spoke last, and in an impassioned manner. The Panel, which usually deliberates for hours, took only three minutes to rule in Morgan's favour, not only clearing the bank of any misdemeanour but pointedly withdrawing the earlier rebuke by the executive. Sir Jasper Hollom made it clear to Spens that he considered the issue a frivolous one. Saunders, who was in the chamber when the verdict was delivered, was delighted, though he complained later that Morgan Grenfell should have told him more about its relationship with Bell's.[28] Spens, returning to Ansbacher's offices in Noble Street, was in no doubt that the Panel, reluctant to impose severe financial penalties on a mere matter of principle, had simply surrendered to the bigger, older and more venerable name. He reminded colleagues of 'the awesome power of Morgan Grenfell'. He was just as explicit with the press:

You have got to remember that the Takeover Panel was set up by merchant bankers for the good of merchant bankers. When they heard that Bell's had only spent £20,000 with Morgan Grenfell in the last two years and that Guinness had already spent £6 million that was the end of the case.[29]

It was a whitewash, presaging other equally weak-kneed decisions in the months that lay ahead. By 14 July Morgan Grenfell was confident enough to start making its own complaints to the Takeover Panel, following intemperate and inaccurate attacks by Miquel on the Guinness management and profit record. When the Panel rapped Miquel as a result, it seemed that Morgan Grenfell could mock its authority with impunity. Spens regretted his decision to drop the injunction, but he had not imagined that the Panel could be so feeble.

Bill Walker, the independent-minded Conservative MP for Perth, home of Bell's headquarters, tabled an Early Day Motion in Parliament calling for a debate on Morgan Grenfell's actions:

That this House notes with grave concern that the bankers, Morgan Grenfell & Co. Limited, were acting for both Arthur Bell & Sons plc and Guinness plc in the period immediately prior to the current takeover being launched; is further concerned at the consequence this may have for the Scottish financial institutions, the investors in Arthur Bell & Company plc and for the workers employed by that company; and believes this takeover should be referred to the Monopolies and Mergers Commission.[30]

He said that he had a copy of a letter from Morgan Grenfell to Bell's listing seven companies as suitable takeover targets:

To present these suggestions and offer advice on corporate strategy, they must have had access to highly sensitive material. The Takeover Panel has seen this evidence and still allowed Morgan's to act for Guinness. I am appalled.[31]

Graham Walsh at last conceded that the bank had continued to put ideas to Bell's during the time that it was plotting a takeover of the company by Guinness:

Since we parted company in 1983 we have been endeavouring to keep contact with them in the hope that they might want to use us again. We do not take being fired lightly. But perhaps on reflection it may have been a mistake to have carried on this relationship with them.[32]

Even Saunders concedes that Morgan Grenfell had told him they 'had information regarding Miquel's acquisition searches, which they felt would not impress the City'.[33] He had approached Bell's in 1984 about a friendly deal, presumably at Morgan Grenfell's prompting and, though he was initially reluctant to mount a hostile bid, Morgan Grenfell had egged him on.[34] Walker alleged dirty tricks, claiming his private life had been probed by detectives and that he had been followed around London, New York and Washington by secret agents.

To those working on the Bell's defence, the panel's decision was a dreadful setback. With hopes of salvation by the Takeover Panel or the Monopolies and Mergers Commission dashed, they resorted to more conventional methods of defence, and increased Bell's dividend forecast by a massive 66 per cent.[35] It was announced on Monday 5 August, along with a forecast of modestly increased profits but, with uncanny timing, Guinness effortlessly raised its offer from £327 million to £340 million the very next day, crushing with cash Bell's promise of income tomorrow. It was the last and hardest of a brilliant sequence of countermoves by Guinness. With its dividend increase capped, the Bell's board could do little more than fulminate. Miquel disagreed and, without consulting his board, retorted with a press release boldly entitled 'Bell's continues to reject Guinness'. That evening the mole declared himself. Peter Tyrie, a Bell's main board director, released his own statement publicly dissociating himself from Miquel and urging his five main board colleagues to recommend the Guinness bid, concluding that:

Until my colleagues come round to my point of view I shall be writing to Bell's shareholders giving the reasons for my decision in the course of the next few days.[36]

Any lingering hopes Miquel may have had of retaining his independence were extinguished with the revelation that the board was split. Ladbroke's, which had bought a 3.25 per cent holding in Bell's and had stated that it would not accept the offer, capitulated to Guinness immediately.

Tyrie had timed his defection to cause maximum damage to Miquel. Throughout the bid it had been suspected that Saunders had a mole on the Bell's board, because the timing of his punches and counterpunches had looked too immaculate to be entirely coincidental. Tyrie had plenty of reasons to loathe Miquel. He was a survivor from the Bell's takeover of the Gleneagles Hotels group in February 1984. Having tasted managerial independence, he resented Miquel's overbearing manner. Their differences of opinion were widely known in financial circles and Morgan Grenfell identified him as a weak link very early on. They introduced him to Saunders, who 'turned' him with promises of an unfettered hand in running the hotels if Guinness won.[37] Saunders denies this, claiming he told Tyrie only of his confidential plans for a hotel and leisure business, and that it was Peter Stevenson of Noble Grossart, Guinness's Scottish advisers, who persuaded Tyrie to defect.[38] Unknown to the Bell's board or the Bell's shareholders, Saunders had even agreed to pay Tyrie's legal costs. Morgan Grenfell supplied the list of the names and addresses of the Bell's shareholders to whom Tyrie wrote.[39] Shareholders were told, innocently enough, that Tyrie had acted because Miquel had refused to discuss the higher offer with the Bell's board. Suspicions of collusion between Saunders and Tyrie were confirmed in January 1987 when details of meetings between the two men became public.[40] After the bid the Guinness finance director, Olivier Roux, approved the payment of a bill for £50,979.61 (including £2,104 for the letter sent to Bell's shareholders) from Tyrie's merchant-banking advisers, Quayle,

330

Munro, a small Edinburgh firm that had worked with him during his early days with Gleneagles. It included the cost of the 'perusing of Bell's Board minutes of July 24' and reporting on them to Noble Grossart. This board meeting took place a full fortnight before Tyrie made his views known to Bell's shareholders on 7 August. Shaun Dowling, another Guinness director, queried the bill as unaccountably large, but it was cleared by Roux in unequivocal terms:

I have reviewed the charges and analysis provided. The full amount is a fair reflection of the work put in. Please organise for Bell to settle the invoice without delay.[41]

The fact that Quayle submitted its bill directly to Guinness rather than to its client, Tyrie, suggests that the arrangement was well understood by all the parties to it, except those Guinness directors insufficiently close to Saunders to appreciate his growing taste for pay-offs. In the event, three of the hotels – the North British, the Caledonian and the Piccadilly – were auctioned to the highest bidder between April and October 1986 for £54 million. The valuers and agents to the sale were Morgan Grenfell Laurie. The buyers included Norfolk Capital, a hotel group chaired by the Morgan Grenfell director who handled the bid for Bell's, Anthony Richmond-Watson. In the middle of the bid, Saunders had offered Alick Rankin, chief executive of Scottish & Newcastle Breweries, the right of first refusal over any hotels sold by Guinness.[42] Miquel was especially pained by the defection to Guinness of General Accident, a large shareholder based in Perth, Bell's home town, only minutes before the 3.00 p.m. deadline. On 23 August 1985, Sir Norman Macfarlane, a senior member of the board, took the decision personally without consulting his investment managers. Bill Walker, still battling, brandished copies of correspondence between Guinness and Sir Norman Macfarlane, showing that Saunders had offered Macfarlane the chairmanship of Bell's, a post he had declined only because one of his Macfarlane group of companies printed the labels for a rival whisky firm, Distillers.[43] (Ironically, Macfarlane later became chairman not just of Bell's but of all the Guinness companies, after the disgrace and dismissal of Ernest Saunders in January 1987. On the night of 23 August the Guinness camp hosted a victory dinner at the London showpiece of their vanquished adversary, the Piccadilly Hotel. The table had been booked the night before under an assumed name.[44] Among those who were there with Ernest Saunders was the shadowy American lawyer, Tom Ward. Over at Henry Ansbacher in the City, Roger Cort, a director who had worked on the Bell's defence, repaired to a nearby pub with a colleague. Patrick Spens, unable to bear the agonizing inevitability of the Guinness victory, had gone to Scotland to fish. The atmosphere was heavy with defeat. 'If we feel like this, just imagine how they must feel up there,' said Cort.

The Guinness bid for Bell's was among the most acrimonious the City had witnessed. Acclaimed at the time as a textbook example of how to conduct a hostile bid, it was in reality a tough and dirty battle with many of the characteristics now associated with the bid for Distillers. Saunders had sold a personal myth to credulous pressmen. He had made promises he was not able to keep. Morgan Grenfell had concluded that the Takeover Panel was spineless. Inside the bank a kind of megalomania had taken root. Those fainthearts who had expressed misgivings about the wisdom of abandoning loyal clients in pursuit of profit alone were marginalized. The Scottish mafia, once feared for its ferocious defence of Scottish industry, had not proved intractable. The team that fought the bid for Distillers – Morgan Grenfell, Cazenove, Wood Mackenzie – had been tested in battle. And, most important of all, the Guinness share price had held up.

The day after his lunch with Roger Seelig in the autumn of 1985, Ernest Saunders rang Christopher Reeves and told him that Guinness would be entering the bidding for Distillers and that he wanted 'the best man you have on my side'.[45] Reeves offered Seelig, whom he described to Saunders as 'a very powerful personality' who would 'want to do things his way'.[46]

Distillers was a target Saunders had been tempted by for some time, even raising the idea with Reeves at the time of the Bell's bid, but Reeves had scoffed at it then.[47] Reeves called Seelig to his office in the Partners' Room and told him the news.[48] It was the first job Roger Seelig had ever been asked to do at Morgan Grenfell. He had generated personally all the previous deals on which he had worked as a director. Seelig regarded the invitation with caution, but with the scale of fees likely to be generated by a £2 billion bid for Distillers, the biggest ever handled by the bank, he could hardly refuse a personal invitation from the bidder. Unlike the meticulously planned assault on Bell's, the bid for Distillers was an entirely opportunistic move by Saunders. At the time the prime contender for control of Distillers had been placed in baulk by the Takeover Panel. Guinness had until recently been preoccupied with the integration of Bell's, but with this process now under way, Saunders sensed a new target rich in his favourite commodity: brands.

By 1985 the Distillers company was a dinosaur awaiting extinction. Its share of the Scotch whisky market in Britain had slumped from 75 per cent in the early 1960s to 15 per cent by 1984. Worldwide, its share had fallen from nearly half in the 1970s to a third.[49] Production of its one-time brand leader, Haig, had shrunk from 1.5 million cases in 1973 to 300,000 in 1984.[50] In a dreadful blunder, the company's best-known brand – Johnnie Walker – was petulantly withdrawn from the British market altogether after a pricing row with the European Commission in 1979.[51] Across the corporate battlefield its whisky brands – which still accounted for four-fifths of profits – were retreating before brilliantly marketed labels like Bell's and Famous Grouse, a brand invented by Highland Distilleries for just that purpose. Its management had not grasped what its predators had: Distillers was a production and manufacturing business in an age of marketing and salesmen. The company, tainted by an aberrant venture into pharmaceuticals which ended in the scandal of thalidomide, a drug which led to terrible deformities among thousands of children born between 1959 and 1961, had shunned further diversification. The company's mean-minded four-year battle against the victims of thalidomide and their champion, the *Sunday Times*, won it no friends and sapped management morale. In the predatory environment of the 1980s, Distillers' days were numbered.

Among the people measuring Distillers for the drop was James Gulliver, the founder of a £300 million foods business called Argyll. He had long felt that his retailing skills could rejuvenate Distillers' jaded brands. He first tried to interest the City in a bid in early 1984 but Distillers, then capitalized at £750 million, was nearly twice the size of Argyll. At that time, the biggest takeover ever mounted in the City of London, BTR/Thomas Tilling, was worth only £600 million. Gulliver's merchant banker, Rupert Faure Walker of Samuel Montagu, advised him to wait, and he did not return to the idea until 1985, when Sir Arnold Weinstock offered to back a bid, using GEC's cash pile, then £1.5 billion high and attracting City criticism for not being put to more imaginative use. Weinstock had already started buying Distillers shares, in the hope of gingering up the management, and by the summer of 1985 had acquired 3.4 per cent. He openly despised John Connell, the newly appointed chairman of Distillers, and was highly receptive to suggestions for change. The use of Weinstock's name, coupled with an undertaking that GEC would under-write £350 million of any offer, made it easy for Gulliver to raise the balance for a serious bid.[52]

With hindsight, it is hard to understand why Gulliver felt he needed Weinstock's support, but in 1985 Britain had not yet matched the American appetite for bids using money borrowed from the banks, and the authorities were apparently discouraging attempts to emulate them. The £1.8 billion bank-financed offer for Allied Lyons by John Elliott's Elders IXL, a company a quarter the size of its intended victim, was eventually referred to the Monopolies and Mergers Commission not because it raised problems of competition but because of unease about the financing arrangements.[53] Gulliver's caution was fatal because Weinstock, by August preoccupied with his own impending £1.2 billion bid for Plessey, let him down. With leaks springing all over the market about an impending bid by Argyll, the Distillers share price was rising fast and threatening to put the company out of Gulliver's reach. Eventuaily, mounting speculation prompted an intervention by the Takeover Panel, which asked Lazard's, Gulliver's advisers, to clarify Argyll's intentions. Forced to choose between bidding or withdrawing, Gulliver unfortunately chose to do both:

Argyll, which has as its long-term business strategy the development of a major food business, has for some time regarded Distillers and a number of other companies as possible opportunities for growth by acquisition or association. The reports, however, of an imminent bid are inaccurate and the company does not intend to make an offer for Distillers at the present time.[54]

It was a terrible mistake. The panel interpreted 'at the present time' to mean three months, debarring Gulliver from bidding again until December. All Gulliver had done was arouse the slumbering Distillers, who began to prepare its defences, and signify to others that the company was 'in play'. Ernest Saunders, immersed during August in the integration of Bell's, was ready by December to enter the contest for Distillers. Unlike Gulliver, he and his advisers were daunted by neither size nor sentiment. In the autumn of 1985 Ernest Saunders was one of Britain's most popular and successful businessmen. In just four years he had transformed a family milch cow into a £1 billion international drinks conglomerate, bristling with brands. His advisers, Morgan Grenfell, had backed the bidder in half the biggest takeovers of 1985, itself a record year for size, and topped the mergers and acquisitions league table for the fourth year in succession, advising in 32 bids worth over £3 billion.[55] Once they were involved, Gulliver was unlikely to capture Distillers. Yet had he struck in August the Guinness bid for Distillers would never have happened, James Gulliver might now be running Britain's largest drinks company, and Ernest Saunders and Roger Seelig might not be facing criminal charges.

*

On Monday 2 December 1985 five apparently unrelated events took place. The terms of the £1.52 billion merger between British Home Stores and Habitat Mothercare were finally unveiled, freeing Roger Seelig for work on a Guinness bid for Distillers. Later the same day Imperial Group, the tobacco, beer and foods conglomerate, received the proceeds from the sale of a loss-making American motel chain, Howard Johnson ('Ho Jo'), which were rather less than it had paid for the chain in 1980. A disastrous acquisition, bought through Morgan Grenfell in New York, Ho Jo had dogged the company throughout the 1980s, exemplifying to its detractors in the City the problems the company had in integrating and managing its acquisitions. Earlier the same day the company's merchant bankers, Hambro's, unveiled a final solution to Imperial's problems: a £1.22 billion friendly takeover of United Biscuits (UB), intended to render both companies invulnerable to attack by trading Imperial's size for UB's management. Morgan Grenfell was advising United Biscuits. Almost simultaneously, Samuel Montagu finally launched Argyll Foods' long-awaited bid for Distillers, without Arnold Weinstock. Argyll was attacking a company three times its size. The £1.87 billion bid was so large that Gulliver had been unable to meet the costs of underwriting the shares he was using as currency if the bid failed or was stalled in the Monopolies and Mergers Commission. Instead, he persuaded underwriters for the first time to accept a success-related fee: £10 million if Argyll lost but £76 million if they won.[56] It was also the day that the quarterly board meeting of Hanson Trust, Britain's premier corporate predator, was held at the company's Knightsbridge headquarters. Lord Hanson and his partner, Sir Gordon White, had been toying with a bid for either Distillers or Imperial for over a year and now feared that both companies might escape them. They quickly ruled out going for Distillers, reckoning the Scottish lobby too hard to vanquish, and chose Imperial instead. That evening Lord Hanson instructed his merchant bankers, Rothschild's, to prepare a bid for Imperial. By Friday they had wrecked Imperial's cosy deal with UB with a £1.9

billion bid for Imperial. These were takeovers worthy of the epithet 'merger mania': all three bids easily dwarfed the largest takeover to date, the £968 million Morgan Grenfell had forced BAT to pay for Eagle Star. Bankers celebrated Christmas with no less than £9.56 billion chasing just six British companies.[57]

For Morgan Grenfell, the news of the Hanson bid for Imperial was devastating. Its workforce had not imagined any bidder would be bold enough to disturb an agreed deal, and now they faced the most feared corporate raider in the takeover arena. Nor had they anticipated what was to happen next. In February 1986 the new Industry Secretary, Paul Channon, referred the United Biscuits/Imperial Group merger to the Monopolies and Mergers Commission, simultaneously clearing the Hanson bid. Channon argued that the combined operations would have controlled 41 per cent of the £360 million-a-year snacks market in Britain, far above the 25 per cent at which a referral became mandatory. Hanson, imagining he was now in the clear, raised his offer to £2.3 billion.[58] Morgan Grenfell was forced into a desperate counter. In a remarkable display of verve and commitment the bank undertook to buy from Imperial Group its crisp-manufacturing subsidiary, Golden Wonder. The idea was that the combined group's share of the snacks market would then nudge below the 25 per cent threshold. No British bank had ever bought an industrial business on behalf of a client before, let alone in order to sidestep a monopolies reference. It marked a new departure in bid tactics: negotiation with the authorities, but it worked, and presaged a similar deal for Guinness. The merger was simultaneously turned on its head: if Imperial could not bid for UB, UB would bid for Imperial. UB topped Hanson's revised offer for Imperial with a £2.5 billion bid of its own.[59] In the event, boldness was not enough and Hanson won without a final stand-off, Morgan Grenfell's revised offer leaving UB shareholders with too few shares in the enlarged company to appeal to them at the meeting specially convened to win their approval. By 18 April 1986, Hanson controlled 64 per cent of the equity.[60] It was Morgan Grenfell's first major defeat, making victory in the concurrent battle for Distillers no longer just a matter of pride and money, but an act of redemption.[61]

Work on the Guinness bid for Distillers had progressed more slowly. Saunders wanted to avoid a hostile bid for, although aggressive tactics have the virtue of conviction, the cost of failure is high. As he put it, 'the scale of the whole thing was frightening'.[62] Furthermore, Distillers and Guinness controlled between them two-fifths of the Scotch whisky market and nearly half of total whisky production, making a reference to the Monopolies and Mergers Commission a distinct possibility.[63] With the underwriting of a £2 billion offer in place, a referral could cost Guinness £50 million for nothing. So on Thursday 9 January 1986 Roger Seelig rang Bay Green, then at Kleinwort Benson, the advisers to Distillers. He knew Green well, having worked with him on the recent Storehouse merger, and told him that Guinness was prepared to rescue Distillers from Gulliver, provided an amicable merger could be arranged along the same lines.[64] But in the BHS/Habitat Mothercare merger there had been no rival offer on the table, and the idea was ditched. Seelig then told Saunders that cash had to be countered with cash, not concepts, and it was agreed that Guinness would bid for Distillers, though Saunders was still anxious about the costs.[65]

The first unusual suggestion was now made: Distillers would offer to pay for the costs of its own rescue. Saunders says the idea was first advanced by Tom Ward, and that it was Ward and Seelig who persuaded Kleinwort Benson of its virtues.[66] Gulliver later construed this device as a 'poison pill' – an extra cost that he would have to pay if his bid succeeded – and it undoubtedly appealed to Ward, Saunders and Seelig on those grounds too. (At one point Saunders pressed Distillers for an undertaking to transfer two cognac brands to Guinness as well, irrespective of whether or not the merger was consummated, but even the beleaguered Distillers board baulked at this.[67]) Gulliver was faced with the possibility of paying not just for one bid but for two: his own costs of £76 million, Distillers' costs of probably £30 million and Guinness's costs of perhaps another £50 or £60 million. In all, the acquisition of control of Distillers might cost Argyll a sum equivalent to a third of the target's market worth.[68] When the news of the agreement became public, Gulliver protested to the Takeover Panel, arguing that Distillers should at least have asked its shareholders, but the panel, invoking memories of the bid for Bell's, dismissed the claim. Gulliver tried the law instead, issuing a writ against Distillers to nullify the costs agreement as a possible breach of Section 151 of the Companies Act, which forbids companies from aiding others to buy their shares. Seelig dismissed the claims as frivolous:

That's simply prudence on the part of Guinness. Why should Guinness shareholders finish up carrying the costs, when it's the Distillers' shareholders who will benefit?[69]

It later emerged that the Distillers directors had been indemnified by Guinness.[70]

By the beginning of the third week in January Seelig and Green had mapped out the rudiments of the deal. Guinness would cap Gulliver's £1.89 billion offer by a further £350 million and Distillers would pick up the tab. Only one detail was missing: a chairman for the merged boards. Initially, Saunders offered the job to John Connell, the chairman of Distillers, with himself as chief executive, but once Connell agreed to the terms of the Guinness takeover, he was dished. The job was offered instead to Sir Thomas Risk, the governor of the Bank of Scotland, who was put forward by Charles Fraser, the influential chairman of Morgan Grenfell Scotland, as someone who could placate the Scottish business lobby.[71] Roger Seelig was present at the meeting in Portman Square where Risk was formally offered the job, and his appointment was written into the takeover documents to which Morgan Grenfell lent its name.[72] Risk was reluctant to accept the post, and was only persuaded to take it after consulting with his colleagues at the Bank of Scotland. As it turned out, he need not have fretted, because once the bid was won, Saunders made sure he never took the chair at Guinness. He did not know it then but he had been duped.

Events moved quickly after Risk's appointment. Kenneth Fleet warned of the impending bid in *The Times* of Saturday 18 January. Gulliver rang Saunders to check the story's authenticity. Saunders was elusive but denied that he had any interest in a contested bid.[73] On Saturday evening Saunders was driven to John Connell's house in Walton-on-Thames, where Saunders toasted the merger with whisky and Connell with Guinness, but Saunders also broke the news to Connell that he would not be chairman of the merged companies. 'It was a miserable moment,' recalled Saunders.[74] The following day, Sunday 19 January 1986, at 4.30 p.m., 12 members of the Distillers board assembled at 6 St James's Square to enact their squalid corporate Jonestown. The agenda asked them to accept the Guinness bid, pay for it, dismiss nine of their number and appoint Sir Thomas Risk as chairman.[75] That morning's papers were full of speculation, orchestrated by Saunders, that the deal was as good as done, and so it proved.[76] Only the agreement to meet Guinness's costs proved really contentious, though resistance from one of the nine directors who lost their jobs, Bill Forrest, prolonged the discussion until 3 a.m.[77] Reassembling at 8 a.m. on the Monday morning, the board members signed the documents and moments later the waiting pressmen were told the terms of the Guinness bid. Within two and a half hours Morgan Grenfell and Cazenove had organized the underwriting of £1.6 billion of new Guinness shares, easily twice the sum Montagu had mustered for Argyll and blunt testimony to the incomparable power of the two houses. With the costs met by Distillers, they spurned Gulliver's device of a fee that altered with the fortunes of the bidder, guaranteeing the underwriters £15 million whether or not the bid succeeded. For Roger Seelig and Ernest Saunders the stakes had never been higher. With the UB/Imperial merger on its hands as well, Morgan Grenfell was now backing simultaneously two bids worth between them well over £3 billion. At stake were fees worth millions of pounds, immeasurable prestige and the reputations of three of Britain's most dynamic businessmen: James Hanson, James Gulliver and Ernest Saunders. The bank once mocked for timidity was reshaping the face of corporate Britain.

Unfortunately, Morgan Grenfell's expectation that the bid would not be referred by the Office of Fair Trading (OFT) to the Monopolies and Mergers Commission (MMC) proved mistaken. It knew the combination of Bell's and Distillers' whisky brands would give the new grouping two-fifths of the British whisky market, but Saunders and Seelig reasoned that, since nine-tenths of Distillers' production was exported, the OFT would overlook its usual rule that bids for any company controlling more than a quarter of a market should be referred. Seelig had even encouraged Saunders to raise the matter with the OFT in search of informal assurances: [78]

We clearly would not have embarked on this course without taking full benefit of the informal guidance procedures of the OFT.[79]

The OFT felt pressurized. The next morning it replied frostily to Seelig's assertion:

There is no, repeat no, question of any bidder having been told at any time that any bid other than that by Argyll for Distillers would not be referred to the Monopolies and Mergers Commission for full investigation.[80]

Three weeks later the bid was referred, on grounds that the combined market share of the two companies was 38 per cent, thus above the 25 per cent threshold for referral.[81] Saunders could not believe it and remonstrated with both Sir Godfray Le Quesne, the chairman of the Monopolies and Mergers Commission, and officials at the Department of Trade and Industry, but to no avail. He then rang Charles Fraser, the chairman of Morgan Grenfell Scotland.[82] Morgan Grenfell provided a ready-made solution. Officially, its executives working on the plan to warehouse Imperial Group's Golden Wonder Crisps subsidiary could not pass information about it to the team working on the Distillers bid, but Charles Fraser, who

341

was also deputy chairman of United Biscuits, knew about it and he contacted the barristers who had devised it. Over the weekend of 15–16 February they hatched a similar scheme in which five Distillers whisky brands would be parked with Morgan Grenfell for later sale to a third party. This scheme, which reduced the combined market shares of Guinness and Distillers to below 25 per cent, was put to Le Quesne.[83]

Most bidders would have walked away from a referral. It is a measure of Morgan Grenfell's cockiness that it did not, and not once but twice. Sir Peter Carey, the former Permanent Secretary at the Department of Industry, who joined the board of the bank in 1983, was glad to roam his old haunts in Whitehall, smoothing Saunders's path.[84] Alex Fletcher, a former Tory Industry Minister then advising Argyll, claims that Seelig and Saunders bulldozed Le Quesne at a series of relentless meetings on 17, 18 and 19 February:

Guinness and Morgan's very skilfully knew their man. There's no break for coffee, or lunch, or dinner with Saunders. He's the general on the field. It's attack, attack, attack. He did it with the OFT and he did it with Le Quesne.[85]

Whatever the method, the results were gratifying. Le Quesne claims that he was ultimately persuaded by the argument that the referral had denied Distillers shareholders a choice of new management. He allowed the first bid to lapse, shunting the issue out of his domain and back to Sir Gordon Borrie, the director-general of the OFT. Saunders says he was reluctant to renew the assault, and only agreed to do so after relentless encouragement from Seelig, but especially Reeves. 'The bank could no doubt see the millions of pounds in fees disappearing. He said it would ruin my reputation. Nobody in the City would ever listen to me again. We would never have the credibility to make another major bid. My reputation was at stake, so was the company's, so was Morgan's,' recalled Saunders.[86] On 20 February Guinness submitted a new, increased bid of £2.35 billion and went back to Borrie for clearance. He did not like the plan to sell the brands to Morgan Grenfell, so

Saunders asked his friend Tiny Rowland to buy them instead. The Lonrho subsidiary, Whyte & Mackay, formally acquired all five for just £3.5 million a month later. The decision to sell a former Bell's brand, The Real Mackenzie, was vehemently attacked in a letter to the *Financial Times* from Patrick Spens:

The present proposal announced this week, to increase the Guinness offer for Distillers and in the process to get rid of the UK rights to The Real Mackenzie brand would appear to belie all the reassurances given by Guinness in its offer documents [for Bell's] and in discussion with shareholders of Bell's . . . As the principal advisor to Bell's in its struggle to retain its independence, I am concerned that assurances, and in the case of employees, unconditional guarantees, freely given by Guinness, which to Guinness can be so flagrantly abandoned in the pursuit of naked ambition so soon after the event . . . Should assurances and undertakings given in a takeover battle count for nothing so soon after the event? I believe that the Office of Fair Trading must consider this part in its further deliberations on the merits of the present Distillers/Guinness situation . . . Ernest Saunders accused me at the height of the battle, when I refused to recommend his offer, of 'deliberate industrial sabotage'. I wonder who the real saboteur might be now.[87]

It was a prescient judgement, though not one that precluded Spens's subsequent involvement in the bid on behalf of Guinness.

Le Quesne's decision sent Gulliver scurrying to the courts. On 25 February Argyll pleaded in the High Court for a judicial review of Le Quesne's decision simply to 'lay aside' the first bid as if it had never been mounted, without even consulting the other members of the Monopolies and Mergers Commission. Gulliver felt, not unreasonably, that the first bid had been modified rather than abandoned. The judicial review was held on 7 March and was characterized by petty bickering between the two sides as to the authenticity of a Department of Trade and Industry press release, but the ruling went against Argyll, with costs awarded to Guinness.[88] On 10 March Gulliver moved to the Court of Appeal to question the findings of the judicial review. The Master of the Rolls, Sir John Donaldson, queried only Le Quesne's powers to act without consulting his colleagues. Even then, Argyll did not give up, and went to the Scottish Faculty of Advocates in search of a ruling that the bid was monopolistic under Article 26 of the Treaty of Rome. They found it was not, but the increasing resort to litigation testified to the ferocity of the battle for Distillers and the increasing ill-will between the two contenders.

Much anger was vented in the most uncompromising advertisements yet seen in a British bid. In January alone Guinness and Distillers spent £1.9 million pressing their case with full-page advertisements in the newspapers, and Argyll spent another £820,000.[89] One of Argyll's advertisements, picturing a plate of Guinness products, one drawn from each of the company's eleven acquisitions since 1984, was accompanied by the question: 'After consuming all this, are Guinness in any state to swallow 150 Scotches?' It was described by Saunders as 'absolutely foul', and writs were issued against Argyll, Gulliver and their advertising and public relations advisers, Saatchi & Saatchi and Broad Street Associates, accusing them of injurious falsehood and defamation.[90] Once Argyll refused to stop using the advertisement, nothing more was heard of the case. In Washington Thomas Ward, Saunders's freebooting legal confidant, filed for damages of $200 million on behalf of a Guinness subsidiary, Wellington's Importers, for unlawful use of the Bell's trademark in Argyll advertisements in British newspapers circulated in the United States. This case, too, was quietly dropped.[91] The increasing venom of the copy eventually provoked even the Takeover Panel, which barred the use of material designed to discredit the opposition.

It was not, however, just a war of words and writs, for Morgan Grenfell was carrying the battle to the enemy in the market too, stockpiling the shares of its clients with unparalleled ferocity. Doubts were beginning to creep in about Morgan's style and methods, and the day after the Guinness bid was re-launched, Rothschild's and Schroder Wagg (acting for Hanson Trust) and Montagu and Charterhouse (acting for Argyll) complained to the Stock Exchange that Morgan Grenfell had breached Stock Exchange regulations during its share-buying spree. Stock Exchange rules did not allow listed companies to spend sums which amount to more than a quarter of their share capital and reserves without asking shareholders for approval, and Morgan Grenfell had spent £360 million buying shares in Imperial and another £70 million buying shares in Distillers, apparently on its own account but in fact with indemnities against loss from both United Biscuits and Guinness.[92] Rothschild and the others argued that the indemnities put United Biscuits and Guinness, not Morgan Grenfell, at risk. The £70 million spent on Distillers shares easily exceeded a quarter of Guinness's share capital of £264 million, and £360 million accounted for nearly the whole of United's share capital of £410 million.[93] It was undoubtedly just a clever way round the rules but, ever the willing accomplice, the Stock Exchange Council dismissed the claim, distinguishing between the acquisition of assets (which would require shareholder approval) and the assumption of liabilities (which would not). The Exchange added lamely that in future it would like to see banks assume the full liability for share purchases on behalf of clients. It was another whitewash, and the bank's detractors were not satisfied. Russell Edey of Rothschild's, advising Hanson, told the press:

We find this unacceptable. Morgan has made a nonsense of the rules.[94]

He was not alone in this view. Writing in the *Daily Mail*, City Editor Andrew Alexander considered that

It would seem to drive a very large coach and horses through the regulation.[95]

In fact press hostility became so intense that Morgan Grenfell decided to explain itself. The value of the shares, it said, could never fall to zero whilst a rival bid placed a natural floor on the price. Thus, the risk was only the difference between the price it paid for the shares and the value of the rival cash offer, far below the 25 per cent threshold. This argument was clearly an abuse of the spirit, if not the letter, of the regulation but Morgan Grenfell went further in its indignation and explained that the bank had bought 22.8 million Distillers shares (6.3 per cent of the company) but that only 8.8 million of these were subject to the Guinness indemnity, which was in any event limited to shares worth £66 million, or exactly a quarter of Guinness's capital. In the case of the Imperial purchases no explanation was offered, beyond an imperious assertion that £360 million was £50 million less than United's share capital.[96] As Andrew Alexander told his readers the following day:

> In response to expressions of Stock Exchange concern what does Morgan Grenfell do? It puts on a contrite air and explains that in the case of Guinness it will not breach the 25 per cent rule. It will not require the company to indemnify its purchases above that level. From the same address and at the same time, however, it says of the shares bought on behalf of UB that, yes, it is indemnified for any losses on the massive chunk of shares it has bought so far. All that is missing from this statement is a concluding 'and sucks to you!' . . . This will not do. Regulations must not be interpreted in this hap-hazard and casual way. The regulations are designed to safeguard shareholders, not to be made sport of by merchant bankers making a lot of money by masterminding takeover bids.[97]

Guinness had of course been giving other indemnities at the same time, but these would not be discovered until after the bid was over.

On 1 March the Bank of England, clearly tiring of the spineless performance of the Stock Exchange, announced measures to curb the direct financial involvement of banks in supporting their clients. Banks now had to submit advance notice to the Bank if they intended to assume major risks. Any share purchases which exceeded a quarter of a bank's capital were now ruled 'imprudent', and would lead to a commensurate deduction from the bank's capital base. Worse, all outstanding transactions were to be 'regularized' at once.[98] Nobody doubted that the changes had been prompted by Morgan Grenfell's aggressive tactics. The *Guardian* described them bluntly as a 'slap in the face to Morgan Grenfell', and the incident wrecked the bank's efforts to persuade the Bank of England to approve its merger with Exco.[99] The Conservative Government, then piloting the Financial Services Bill through the House of Commons, was dismayed. Michael Howard, the minister responsible for the Bill, called on banks to ensure 'that the spirit and not just the letter of the rules are obeyed'.[100] The authorities would later regret that they had not been harder, for now Morgan Grenfell was scornful. Questioned about the bank's bully-boy tactics a few months later Christopher Reeves offered an explanation which must haunt him still:

Some say we got round the rules. I think we innovated. Clients want to deal with people with original ideas, so new rules have to be created. We must not believe that rules are written in tablets of stone.[101]

Graham Walsh promised 'different ways of meeting the Bank's requirements which would not damage the interests of our corporate clients'.[102] In an astonishing snub to the Bank of England, Morgan Grenfell arranged for a consortium of banks – British Linen Bank, Allied Irish and ANZ – to acquire £111 million of the bank's stake in Distillers, which had now swollen to £180 million.[103] Guinness indemnified the banks for any losses, allowing Morgan Grenfell to carry on buying on behalf of Guinness much as before. As Rupert Faure Walker, advising Argyll, commented:

You might as well rip up the Stock Exchange agreements.[104]

A few days later the Stock Exchange introduced a new rule forbidding companies to indemnify others against loss without consulting shareholders. The rules, it seemed, were following Morgan Grenfell, rather than vice versa.

Morgan's had also begun to fall out with the institutional investors underwriting the bid, some of whom were dismayed when it became known, probably through a sacked or disgruntled Distillers director, that Distillers had agreed to meet the costs of the Guinness bid. One fund manager, David Thomas of Equitable Life, spoke for many when he expressed surprise that Morgan's had ignored their disquiet over the arrangement when shaping the second bid:

I must say this upset me and led to something of a row. What I object to is not so much Distillers paying Guinness's costs or the amount of money involved but the principle of disclosure. The second bid was supposed to be a totally new bid. Yet there was no disclosure of the payment of costs in the sub-underwriting papers and we were told that it was all in the huge legal contract which we as sub-underwriters never see.[105]

Later, the investing institutions' representatives, the National Association of Pension Funds and the British Insurance Association, forced Morgan Grenfell to alter the terms of a share placing for Boots, after complaining that the bank had not given existing Boots shareholders the chance to participate.[106] In its drive to win the best possible terms for its clients, Morgan Grenfell was becoming increasingly cavalier in its treatment of investors. Morgan's was now at war with every form of authority in the City: the Monopolies Commission, the Stock Exchange, the Takeover Panel and the investment institutions. 'If you want to win your bid no matter what price you pay, then Morgan's are the bank for you. But if you want a more reflective view, try somebody else,' said John Gillum, a director at Rothschild's.[107]

Tactics degenerated accordingly. The *Sunday Times* revealed that Gulliver's *Who's Who* entry implied that he had attended the Harvard Business School, when he had only attended a few odd weeks there while studying at Georgia Institute of Technology.[108] Gulliver had to confess that his academic credentials had been 'incorrectly stated'. The story was leaked by a public relations adviser to Distillers.[109] A private detective, former SAS man Nicholas Vafiadis, of Tempest Consultants, Malvern, Worcestershire, probed Gulliver's past for 'dirt', but it is not clear that he was in the pay of Distillers.[110] Stories of Gulliver's sexual athleticism were regularly reported in *Private Eye*.

Once the second Guinness bid was cleared by the OFT on 21 March, all that remained was for the Distillers shareholders to choose between their two suitors. Billions of pounds were pledged on Distillers by both Argyll and Guinness, whose winning bid was over £2.5 billion, but neither Guinness nor Argyll was offering to spend sums of this magnitude in cash. Instead, they were offering to exchange their shares for Distillers shares. This is a feature of takeover bids peculiar to Britain (unlike the United States, where companies are usually acquired with a mixture of bonds and cash) and it poses a particular problem. The laws of supply and demand dictate that if the amount of any commodity is increased its price will tend to fall, unless demand increases commensurately. In this respect shares are no different from bananas. The trick is to increase demand and it was in increasing the demand for the shares of its clients that Morgan Grenfell excelled.

Both bidders offered a 'cash alternative'. This involves a group of institutions agreeing for a fee to place a floor on the value of a bid by undertaking to buy unwanted shares for cash. Bidders like to offer a cash alternative because they can pay for most of a company in shares but do not have to find or borrow money to pay those shareholders that want cash. It also conveys an impression of substantial institutional support for the bid, while in bull markets like that of 1986, it usually goes unused because cash is worth less than the offer of shares, giving institutions a fee for nothing. Because cash is less risky than shares, the cash alternative is always priced at a discount to the share offer. In early 1986 most Distillers shareholders were likely to opt for Guinness or Argyll shares rather than cash, in the expectation that they would go on rising in the aftermath of the bid. In defiance of the laws of supply and demand, if not of gravity, the clients of Morgan Grenfell had grown used to seeing their share price carry on rising in the wake of a successful bid despite huge increases in their share capital. The BTR share price flew up at the end of the bid for Tilling's. The

Dixon's share price doubled during the course of the bid for Curry's. The official explanation is that new management can breathe fresh life into under-exploited assets, but the bank's more scrupulous opponents suspected a more prosaic explanation. Anthony Parnes, since charged with nineteen offences in relation to the Guinness bid for Distillers, explained it thus to the police:

I would be under the impression that in a number of bids, Morgan Grenfell could arrange support.[111]

In the bid for Distillers it just went over the top.

NOTES

[1] Ivan Fallon and James Srodes, *Takeovers*, Hamish Hamilton, 1987.
[2] James Saunders, *Nightmare, The Ernest Saunders Story*, Hutchinson, 1989.
[3] Fallon and Srodes, *op. cit.*
[4] Saunders, *op. cit.*
[5] *ibid.*
[6] *ibid.*
[7] Nick Kochan and Hugh Pym, *The Guinness Affair*, Christopher Helm, 1987.
[8] *Business*, July 1986.
[9] Fallon and Srodes, *op. cit.*
[10] *ibid.*
[11] Peter Pugh, *Is Guinness Good for You? The Bid for Distillers – The Inside Story*, Financial Training Publications, 1987.
[12] *Acquisitions Monthly*, January 1986.
[13] *The Times*, 23 April 1988; *London Daily News*, 9 July 1987.
[14] *The Times*, 23 April 1988.
[15] In December 1985, a Guinness subsidiary purchased 200,000 shares in Matthew Brown at a cost of over £1 million, which were registered in the name of a third party. The shares were bought by the stockbroker, Anthony Parnes, acting on instructions from Olivier Roux, the Guinness finance director. The purchase was raised in the House of Commons on 27 April 1988 by John

Marshall, MP for Hendon South (*The Times*, 18 and 27 April 1988).

[16] *Mail on Sunday*, 22 December 1985 and 5 January 1986.

[17] *Financial Times*, 8 July 1987.

[18] *The Times*, 9 July 1987.

[19] *ibid.*; *Daily Telegraph*, 9 July 1987.

[20] Kochan and Pym, *op. cit.*; Pugh, *op. cit.*; *Acquisitions Monthly*, January 1986.

[21] *The Times*, 21 June 1985.

[22] *Financial Times*, 21 June 1986.

[23] Kochan and Pym, *op. cit.*; Pugh, *op. cit.*

[24] Kochan and Pym, *op. cit.*

[25] *Financial Times*, 9 July 1982.

[26] Kochan and Pym, *op. cit.*

[27] Saunders, *op. cit.*

[28] *ibid.*

[29] Pugh, *op. cit.*

[30] *Hansard*, 4 July 1985.

[31] *The Times*, 5 July 1985.

[32] *ibid.*

[33] Saunders, *op. cit.*

[34] *ibid.*

[35] *Acquisitions Monthly*, January 1986.

[36] Kochan and Pym, *op. cit.*

[37] *Sunday Times*, 11 January 1987.

[38] Saunders, *op. cit.*

[39] Pugh, *op. cit.*

[40] *Sunday Times*, 11 January 1987.

[41] *Sunday Telegraph*, 27 March 1988.

[42] Pugh, *op. cit.*

[43] Kochan and Pym, *op. cit.*

[44] Pugh, *op. cit.*

[45] Saunders, *op. cit.*

[46] *ibid.*

[47] *ibid.*

[48] Fallon and Srodes, *op. cit.*

[49] *ibid.*

[50] Pugh, *op. cit.*

[51] *ibid.*

[52] Fallon and Srodes, *op. cit.*

[53] *Acquisitions Monthly*, December 1985.

[54] Fallon and Srodes, *op. cit.*

[55] *Acquisitions Monthly*, January 1986.

[56] Fallon and Srodes, *op. cit.*; Peter Osborne, 'Paying the Piper, Fees Paid for UK Acquisitions', in *Acquisitions Monthly*, January 1986; *Evening Standard*, 21 January 1986.

[57] Fallon and Srodes, *op. cit.*

[58] *ibid.*

[59] *ibid.*

[60] *Acquisitions Monthly*, May 1986.

[61] Saunders, *op. cit.* Saunders said 'Seelig was very excited and pushy. Morgan Grenfell had lost a number of bids lately, and he was sure that we could do this, we had to do it, now was the time, we would never forgive ourselves if we didn't, and so on.'

[62] *ibid.*

[63] Pugh, *op. cit.*

[64] Kochan and Pym, *op. cit.*

[65] Fallon and Srodes, *op. cit.*

[66] Saunders, *op. cit.*

[67] *ibid.*

[68] *ibid.*

[69] *Wall Street Journal*, 14 January 1987.

[70] Kochan and Pym, *op. cit.*

[71] Saunders, *op. cit.*

[72] Kochan and Pym, *op. cit.*; Saunders, *op. cit.*

[73] Fallon and Srodes, *op. cit.*; Saunders *op. cit.*

[74] Kochan and Pym, *op. cit.*; Saunders, *op. cit.*

[75] Fallon and Srodes, *op. cit.*

[76] Pugh, *op. cit.*

[77] Kochan and Pym, *op. cit.*

[78] Saunders, *op. cit.*

[79] *Financial Times*, 22 January 1986.

[80] Pugh, *op. cit.*

[81] Kochan and Pym, *op. cit.*

[82] Saunders, *op. cit.*

[83] The two barristers were Jeremy Lever and John Swift. In Fallon and Srodes, *op. cit.*; Kochan and Pym, *op. cit.*; Pugh, *op. cit.*

[84] Kochan and Pym, *op. cit.* Saunders, *op. cit.*

[85] *ibid.*

[86] Saunders, *op. cit.*

[87] *Financial Times*, 21 February 1986.

[88] Kochan and Pym, *op. cit.*; Fallon and Srodes, *op. cit.*

[89] Fallon and Srodes, *op cit.*

[90] *ibid.*

[91] *ibid.*

[92] *Observer*, 23 February 1986.

[93] *Financial Times*, 22 February 1986; *Daily Telegraph*, 22 February 1986; *Daily Mail*, 22 February 1986.
[94] *Daily Telegraph*, 22 February 1986.
[95] *Daily Mail*, 22 February 1986.
[96] *Financial Times*, 25 February 1986.
[97] *Daily Mail*, 25 February 1986.
[98] *Financial Times*, 1 March 1986; *Guardian*, 1 March 1986.
[99] *ibid.*
[100] *Sunday Telegraph*, 2 March 1986.
[101] *Financial Times*, 18 June 1986.
[102] *Financial Times*, 1 March 1986.
[103] *Daily Telegraph*, 4 March 1986.
[104] *ibid.*
[105] *Financial Weekly*, 6 March 1986.
[106] *Daily Telegraph*, 7 August 1986.
[107] *Financial Weekly*, 6 March 1986.
[108] Fallon and Srodes, *op. cit.*
[109] Kochan and Pym, *op. cit.*
[110] *ibid.*
[111] *Observer*, 27 March 1988.

ELEVEN

The Inspectors Call

By the early 1980s, countering the natural tendency of a share price to fall during the course of a bid had become the central concern of the aggressor. Informal 'fan clubs' who could be relied upon to support a bidder's share price were an unspoken feature of contested bids. Defensive tactics had also developed. Defenders were persuaded to sell or to 'short' the shares of the bid target or even of rival suitors, but as the value of bids multiplied so did the risks. 'Fan clubs' began to ask for danger money. At first they got indemnities, but later they collected 'success fees' too, taking 'fan clubs' beyond the normal give and take of the bid arena and into the realms of criminal activity. The earliest sign that the scale and nature of support operations had changed came in September 1986, when the Takeover Panel overturned a successful defence by AE against a bid by Turner & Newall, on the grounds that AE's advisers, Hill Samuel, had indemnified buyers of AE stock.[1] Saunders claims that the fragility of the Guinness share price was his principal preoccupation during the bid for Distillers, that the threat of an Argyll shorting operation represented the biggest danger to its continued buoyancy and that any buying of Guinness shares was intended only to counter downward pressure exerted by Argyll. It has long been rumoured that the Wall Street arbitrageur, Salim B. 'Sandy' Lewis, was recruited to the Argyll cause by Angus Grossart of Noble Grossart, joint advisers to Gulliver. It has also been alleged that an operation to 'short' Guinness shares was co-ordinated by Nahum Vaskevitch, a former managing director of Merrill Lynch, one of the underwriters of the Argyll bid for Distillers.[2] Though the allegations (and the AE defence) suggest that his fears were justified, they were also absurdly exaggerated. Shorting is notoriously difficult to do profitably at the best of times, and in a takeover battle, especially a three-cornered fight where the opposition might up the price at any time, it is the riskiest tactic of all. The evidence suggests that shorting by Argyll was only one fear among many and that every element of the Guinness share price support operation was deliberately contrived and executed by at least one of the important figures involved in the bid for Distillers, however little he may have known or understood of the actions of others. The operation was not orchestrated by one man or group, but organized spontaneously among a group of individuals, each of whom understood instinctively the nature of what was being done, having known and worked with or against each other for very many years.

Rupert Faure Walker, advising for Argyll, first noticed something unusual in late March 1986. Aware that once the second Guinness bid was cleared by the OFT on 21 March Argyll could not go on trading punches with a more powerful opponent, he advised one last raid in a desperate bid to win control. Within 36 hours Montagu raised £700 million from a group of banks including Midland, Citicorp and Royal Bank of Scotland to buy 115 million Distillers shares at prices up to £6.60, the value of the Argyll cash alternative – the highest price permitted by Rule 11(1) of the Takeover Code, which stipulates that any bidder controlling less than 15 per cent of the target company, or any buyer acting in concert with a bidder controlling less than 15 per cent, cannot pay some shareholders in the target company a higher price than others. It enshrines one of the central precepts of the code: equality of treatment for all shareholders. Faure Walker tells what happened next:

It was from that morning onwards that suddenly this massive buying of Guinness shares started. The Guinness share price really took off with massive buying from every direction. That pulled the Distillers price up and it went beyond the level at which we could buy them so we couldn't get them. I think we only got a million or so . . . From this moment onwards we saw this massive buying of Guinness shares and we found it very hard to accept that it was traditional investment buying.[3]

It was not. On the penultimate day of the bid – Thursday 17 April 1986 – Morgan Grenfell flagrantly breached Rule 11(1). Mercury Investment Management (MIM), the fund-management arm of S. G. Warburg, put up for auction a block of 10.6 million shares in Distillers and buyers were asked to settle in cash that day. Whichever camp acquired the stake would probably win the bid. At the time Argyll was 50p behind Guinness on the paper offer but 30p ahead on the cash alternative. Theoretically Guinness, whose cash offer was marooned at £6.30, stood no chance at all of winning the auction and Montagu's duly bid £6.60, confident they would win. But to Faure Walker's astonishment, Cazenove outbid them, paying £7.05, 75p more than Guinness was entitled to pay under Rule 11(1). Of course, Faure Walker could not be sure that Cazenove was buying on behalf of Guinness or even of buyers acting in concert with Guinness, but there could be few disinterested investors prepared to spend £76 million on a share inflated to bursting point by a three-cornered takeover battle hours from its denouement, and Cazenove were joint brokers to Guinness. Faure Walker asked the Takeover Panel to find out whether or not the buyer had been acting in concert with Guinness. After desultory enquiries of Morgan Grenfell, Guinness and Cazenove, it was ruled that the buyer had not. Had the panel probed further it would have discovered that its conclusion was the exact opposite of the truth.

What really happened that extraordinary Thursday was rather different from what the Panel was told at the time. The previous day – Wednesday 16 April – a committee of three at MIM, a shareholder not noted for a sentimental attachment to the companies it invested in, decided that it would auction the shares to the highest bidder. With Distillers under siege from two rival bidders, buyers were not hard to find. Rowe & Pitman, brokers to Argyll, and Cazenove, brokers to Guinness, were contacted by Fielding Newson-Smith, brokers to MIM.[4] David Mayhew, the Cazenove partner handling the Guinness bid, rang Roger Seelig at Morgan Grenfell early on Thursday morning, stressing that should Guinness be able to find a buyer Mercury wanted the money in cash by 3 p.m. that day. He added that if Guinness was serious Cazenove needed the cash immediately, emphasizing to Seelig that 'there should be no messing about'.[5] Seelig briefly explored the idea of Morgan Grenfell advancing the money to Cazenove but quickly rejected it.[6] Instead, he rang Tom Ward at Guinness.[7]

Ward, the *eminence grise* of the Guinness affair, is a partner in the Washington law firm of Ward, Lazarus, Grow & Cihlar. Saunders had known him since his days as president of Nestlé Nutrition, when they had worked together on a widely criticized campaign to discredit a threatened US boycott of Nestlé products. The World Health Organization had criticized Nestlé for its heavy marketing of powdered milk in the Third World. Less nutritious than breast milk and frequently mixed with contaminated water, it had led to thousands of infant deaths.[8] In combating the adverse publicity, Saunders and Ward had stooped to tactics – like subventions to right-wing think tanks – that presaged a later obsession with winning at all costs.[9] The two men forged a close relationship and, when he took over at Guinness in October 1981, Saunders appointed Ward a non-executive director. At the outset of the Guinness bid for Distillers he installed Ward at his family house in Penn, using him as a freelance troubleshooter.[10] Throughout his time at Guinness Ward was aide-de-camp to Saunders, assisting in the merger talks with Distillers, deflecting awkward questions from Gulliver before the Guinness bid, renegotiating the bid with Sir Godfray Le Quesne and Sir Gordon Borrie, and firing the unwanted Distillers directors.[11] Saunders called him 'the man who did more, in my opinion, than any other to bring about the success of the bid'.[12] He was described by a fellow director as 'not wholly trustworthy' and by a partner of a law firm as a man with 'a penchant for decoration and concealment'.[13]

Seelig asked Ward to send money to Cazenove. It would be

too obvious if Guinness supplied it itself, so Ward rang the Bank Leu in Switzerland, whose chairman, Dr Arthur Furer, had once been Saunders's boss at Nestlé and had now been appointed a non-executive director of Guinness. Saunders described this as 'very much a personal appointment of mine. He is a man I very much respect.'[14] The three of them – Ward, Saunders and Furer – were not just co-directors, but close personal associates, who had fought the baby-milk scandal together a few years earlier. For a fee of £47,250, an indemnity against loss and a commitment to repurchase the shares within 60 days Ward arranged for a Leu subsidiary, Pipetec AG of Lucerne, to advance £76 million to Cazenove in London to buy the 10.6 million shares at £7.05. Ward rang Seelig with the news, and Seelig told Mayhew to expect a call from a Mr Baumann at Bank Leu.[15] The arrangement was confirmed in a letter sent the next day by Pipetec to Ward, who countersigned it.[16] There is no evidence to suggest that Ward at any time consulted the full Guinness board about the arrangement which, as a non-executive director, he should have done.[17] The money reached Cazenove just after 1 p.m. the same day. Having heard nothing from Mayhew and worried that Leu would not get the money to Cazenove before the 3 p.m. deadline, Ward rang Mayhew at 2.45 p.m. to check whether Cazenove still needed the money but Mayhew was busy, and a colleague, unaware that it had arrived from Switzerland nearly two hours earlier, said that they did. Anxious, Ward sent a further £76 million of Guinness's money to Cazenove. Realizing what had happened, Mayhew tried to stop the Guinness money, but was too late. It was placed on deposit overnight, and returned to Guinness on Friday morning.[18] The first bid, at £6.60, came from Rowe & Pitman, on behalf of Argyll. It did not stand for long. Cazenove bid £7. Argyll hit back, offering £7.05, but for only 2 million shares, the Takeover Code preventing it buying any more at the higher price. Within an hour Cazenove had returned with what proved to be the winning bid, offering £7.05 for all the shares.[19]

When Argyll complained, the panel rang Mayhew, who told

it that his instructions to buy had come from Bank Leu, who he felt were acting as agent rather than principal. He did not tell the panel about the Guinness money, referring it instead to Mr Baumann at Bank Leu in Switzerland, who in turn referred it to Dr Werner Frey, the managing director of Pipetec. Frey denied any connection with Guinness or Distillers. The panel then asked Roger Seelig for written assurances that there had been no deals between Guinness and Pipetec, and he said he would be happy for Guinness to give the assurances.[20] Anthony Salz, a partner at Freshfields, the firm of solicitors advising Guinness on the bid, was instructed to draft a letter from Guinness to the director-general of the Takeover Panel.[21] The letter, which has been described as 'misleading', was approved by Tom Ward, David Mayhew, Anthony Forbes (also a partner of Cazenove) and Roger Seelig.[22] Signed by Olivier Roux, the Guinness finance director, it read as follows:

Dear Sir,
You have asked us to write to you with respect to the reported purchase today of approximately 10 million shares of Distillers through Cazenove & Co. We have spoken to Cazenove's and can confirm that the purchaser is not a subsidiary or associated company of Guinness, that such shares were not bought for our account and that we have made no financial arrangements with the purchaser with respect to such shares (including any arrangement linked to the sale of Distillers listed investments).
Yours faithfully,
Olivier Roux,
For and on behalf of Guinness PLC.[23]

For Morgan Grenfell, as for Guinness, the pursuit of victory had long since superseded honour. The Argyll bid was now defeated and by 7 p.m. that night Morgan Grenfell could boast that its client controlled 46 per cent of the shares in Distillers. When Faure Walker told Gulliver of the Panel's decision the Argyll chief knew he had been defeated. 'That's it; it's all over now,' he said.[24] At just after 1 p.m. on the afternoon of Friday 18 April, Morgan Grenfell announced that

Guinness spoke for 50.74 per cent of Distillers and that the bid was now unconditional. Officially, Distillers cost Guinness £2.5 billion and another £110 million in underwriting fees, stamp duty and advertising, but there were also hidden debts to those who had helped along the way.[25]

Saunders and Gulliver politely exchanged letters of congratulation and commiseration, but Saunders immediately set about abandoning pledges, once expedient in battle, now expendable in victory. It marked the final repudiation by Morgan Grenfell of Jack Morgan's injunction to do only 'first class-business', for in agreeing to advise on and underwrite the bid, it lost not just its financial muscle but its reputation and with this, its most valuable asset, the bank was becoming increasingly careless. Morgan Grenfell's name appeared on a series of documents in which Saunders had given undertakings, most of them designed to placate the Scottish lobby, whose power he had first encountered during the bid for Bell's. He had pledged that the Distillers board, including John Connell, would remain intact; that the headquarters of the merged companies would be moved to Scotland; and that Sir Thomas Risk, governor of the Bank of Scotland and doyen of the Scottish business establishment, would be chairman. Morgan Grenfell was unable to ensure that Saunders honoured these undertakings. John Connell was denied any executive role on the Monday following the bid. Six Distillers directors went with him and the company's headquarters were never moved to Scotland, an omission which attracted the attention of the Scottish Secretary, Malcolm Rifkind, who formally complained to Saunders.[26]

Sir Thomas Risk was eventually denied the chairmanship. It seems Saunders did not understand the implications of what he had agreed to do: 'He [Risk] kept banging on about the fact that the listing particulars were legally binding.'[27] Though he met Saunders three times, with Ward in attendance, Risk was not formally told that he would not get the job until Thursday 10 July, nearly three months after the bid.[28] The news was imparted to him by Lord Iveagh, the Guinness chairman.[29]

The same day a meeting was held at 23 Great Winchester Street attended by David Mayhew of Cazenove, Bay Green of Kleinwort, Christopher Reeves, Roger Seelig, and John Chiene of Wood Mackenzie, joint brokers to Guinness.[30] The breach of promise was especially embarrassing for Wood Mackenzie, which was close to the outraged Scottish financial establishment, but Chiene had anyway become increasingly disenchanted with the Morgan Grenfell–Guinness axis. Throughout the bid he had played second fiddle to Mayhew. Now he felt that they were going too far, and told Seelig that unless the undertaking to appoint Sir Thomas Risk as chairman was honoured, his firm would resign the account. The following day he repeated this message to Saunders and Tom Ward in meetings at Portman Square[31] and offered to discuss a compromise candidate, but Saunders simply walked out of the room.[32] Saunders, Ward and Iveagh were reprimanded by the governor of the Bank of England, Robin Leigh-Pemberton, on 14 July. The next day Reeves and Walsh advised submission of the issue to an extraordinary general meeting of shareholders, which Saunders agreed to do. At the end of the month Saunders was summoned to the Department of Trade and Industry, where Michael Howard threatened him with an inquiry if he did not implement the provisions of the offer to Distillers to the letter.[33]

Saunders's conduct was becoming increasingly arrogant. He raised his own salary and began to run the company singlehanded, using Ward, Roux and swarms of Bain management consultants ('the Bainies') to do his bidding.[34] On 28 May Saunders, Ward and Roux invested $100 million (£69 million) in an Ivan Boesky fund in New York, but did not tell the rest of the board for five weeks. Saunders claims that Ward was the 'originator and architect' of the investment, and that it was 'a means of having a high-level financier taking an interest in the company: he could put us in touch with key people and help us with our eventual US acquisition programme.'[35] The only director to query it, Jonathan Guinness, was told by Thomas Ward that

The main point of the investment was strategic, namely that Boesky would be on our side in any American takeover. He would also be available in defending against any predator.[36]

Roux said that they were 'following the advice of Thomas Ward that Ivan Boesky would be a good person to have on the side of Guinness'.[37] Nobody seems to have thought to ask whether or not Boesky had already been on Guinness's side in a takeover.

The truth of the matter was staggering. Ward had admired Boesky's leading role in the Nestlé bid for Carnation in 1984, in which Ward himself had been involved.[38] Boesky had bought Distillers shares very early in the battle and had approached Gulliver hoping to trade support for information, but was not welcomed.[39] Once Guinness entered the bid, he seems to have bought both Guinness and Distillers shares heavily and shorted Argyll shares. There is evidence from a memorandum submitted to a New York district court that people representing Guinness asked him to 'purchase large amounts of Guinness stock to artificially affect its market price and make the Guinness offer more attractive', indemnified him against loss, guaranteed him a profit and promised to invest $100 million in one of his funds.[40] Boesky was arrested in November 1986 and Guinness has been trying to recover the $100 million ever since.

The Saunders version of the news that Risk would not be chairman broke publicly in an article by Ivan Fallon in the *Sunday Times* of 13 July:

Ernest Saunders, as the world now knows, has performed one of the great wonders of the modern commercial world . . . Saunders needs an unfettered hand and there is just a possibility he won't get it. The key man was to be the august Sir Thomas Risk, Governor of the Bank of Scotland and Distillers' principal banker. On paper and in the heat of battle that sounded fine. Events since have changed the perspective, however.[41]

Saunders also let it be known that Risk was demanding an unreasonable share of Guinness's banking business for the Bank of Scotland, but his real objection was to the presence of an active chairman, unlike the compliant Lord Iveagh, under whom he had served so far. Alone at Morgan Grenfell, Charles Fraser was prepared to speak out. He was deeply uneasy about his role in the recruitment and betrayal of Risk, but when he mentioned this publicly, Ward threatened to sue him for the damage it had done to the Guinness share price. Once the row spilled into the newspapers, Chiene decided that enough was enough. On Tuesday 15 July Wood Mackenzie resigned as brokers to Guinness in a message sent by facsimile machine. Cazenove told Guinness that they would not resign, but would not act either.[42] Charles Fraser resigned as Scottish legal adviser to Guinness, but Morgan Grenfell made no public protest. In the House of Commons Labour's Scottish trade spokesman, John Smith, pressed for a statement, arguing that a 'coach and horses [is] being driven through the regulations'.[43] Though the Government supported Risk, the governor of the Bank of England, Robin Leigh-Pemberton, favoured compromise. At the time belief in Saunders's marketing genius was widespread. 'Riskless Guinness is good for you,' as Robert Maxwell put it. Sir Nicholas Goodison, chairman of the Stock Exchange, was merely unconcerned:

There are occasions, however rare, when a Board finds it necessary to depart from the precise terms of intentions stated in Listing Particulars.[44]

He, like Morgan's, advised submission of the issue of the composition of the board to an extraordinary meeting of shareholders. This was duly scheduled for 11 September. Reasoning that Morgan's was too tainted to become involved searching for alternatives to Risk, Saunders appointed Lazard's to supply a list of suitable non-executive directors.[45] It included Sir Norman Macfarlane, who within months became chairman. Anxious not to lose an extremely profitable client, only Morgan Grenfell stayed on the Guinness payroll and, at the extra-ordinary general meeting, Roger Seelig used Morgan Grenfell's holding in Guinness to support Saunders. (When the question of whether Morgan Grenfell should follow Wood Mackenzie's honourable resignation was raised at a Morgan Grenfell board meeting, Christopher Reeves explained bluntly that the bank had too much money tied up in Guinness to consider it seriously.)

In the aftermath of the victory over Argyll on 18 April, the Guinness share price was under severe downward pressure. Institutional investors were taking their profit from a share price hugely inflated by the recently concluded bid, hoping to escape a market about to be flooded with the Guinness shares used to pay for it. They also knew that Argyll's £360 million shareholding in Distillers was about to be put up for sale and that the 15 per cent stake in the company held by Morgan Grenfell and its associates could not be held off for long. What the market did not know was that members of the 'fan club' would also want to sell their shares. Because they had been indemnified against loss, the cost of the indemnities to Guinness rose with every drop in the share price. Seelig, realizing that the costs of the support operation could spiral out of control, worked fast. On 22 April Guinness bought and cancelled the 15 per cent stake held by Morgan Grenfell, relieving some of the pressure on the share price. This was an unusual tactic: Guinness's borrowings were already high in relation to its share capital, suggesting that in the longer term it would have been better to place the shares with a group of institutional investors rather than cancel them, but with all the immediate threats to the share price it was hard to think strategically. Preventing the 'fan club' flooding the market was rather harder. The plan, devised by Seelig and David Mayhew, was to postpone the emergence of 'fan club' shares in the market-place until the announcement of the first set of results of the newly merged companies, when the price would, it was hoped, start to recover, reducing the cost of the indemnities.[46] A massive mopping-up operation began, using Bank Leu. All the parcels of shares would be purchased at cost by Leu, adding them to the 10.6 million Distillers shares it had bought on the penultimate day of the bid, which had, in accordance with the terms of the bid, been exchanged for Guinness shares. Ward had promised to repurchase the shares from Leu within 60 days, but an extension was granted in return for an interest-free deposit of £50 million by Guinness with Leu as security against loss on their holding of Guinness stock, swelled by the mopping-up operation to over 41 million shares by the beginning of June 1986.[47] Bank Leu and its former chairman, Dr Arthur Furer, have said that Saunders intended eventually to sell the shares to overseas investors once the price had recovered, to 'broaden the shareholder base'. Saunders claims that this was his eventual goal[48] but, while this may have been the ultimate intention, the immediate need was to keep stock off the market.[49] It was not long before the first member of the 'fan club', Patrick Spens, the head of corporate finance at Henry Ansbacher, asked to sell.

Spens had joined the support operation during the closing stages of the bid. While lunching with Roger Seelig on other matters in April 1986, he had offered to help Guinness, providing Morgan Grenfell indemnified any supporters he could muster. It was a somewhat surprising offer, given the bitter skirmishes between Saunders and Spens during the bid for Bell's, only recently reopened by Spens's letter to the *Financial Times* in late February, after which Saunders had threatened to sue. Yet arbitrage, 'fan clubs' and indemnities were so much a part of orthodox bid-making by 1986 that by the time of his lunch with Seelig, Spens had already bought some Guinness shares on behalf of Ansbacher. Just a month earlier – March 1986 – Ansbacher had arranged for a client to hold 768,000 Extel shares owned by three Robert Maxwell companies, in exchange for an indemnity.[50] This was regarded as a normal banking transaction, and was initiated by the Ansbacher chief executive, Richard Fenhalls. Clients often placed portfolios or single shareholdings with other investors on the understanding that they would be repurchased without loss. After his lunch with Seelig, Spens had discussed with Fenhalls, whether or not the Ansbacher holding in Guinness should be enlarged. Fenhalls did not wish Ansbacher to become directly involved in the bid, however, and the bank's existing shareholding was sold, but he freed Spens to advise his clients to buy. A Guinness victory was the outcome most favoured by Spens, not because he admired Ernest Saunders, but because he had great respect for the management at Bell's, and felt that they would make a much better fist of running Distillers than James Gulliver. He duly arranged for some clients of his to buy Guinness shares, on the understanding that Morgan Grenfell would indemnify them against loss. The Takeover Code did not then specify that this indemnity should be disclosed, and it was not.

The clients that Spens induced to support Guinness were Dr Ashraf Marwan, an Egyptian financier, and TWH Investments, a company associated with him which acts for Arab investors.[51] Marwan is a son-in-law of the late President Nasser and was a former adviser to his successor, Anwar Sadat. He has been close to many of the less salubrious deals of the 1980s, including the battle for control of Harrod's, where he was a member of the Rowland concert party buying shares in House of Fraser in a bid to thwart his fellow countrymen, the Al-Fayeds.[52] In May 1986, Marwan wanted to sell his shares in Guinness. Olivier Roux, then Guinness finance director, explained what happened next:

Roger Seelig told me that one of the supporters, Ansbacher, intended to sell their Guinness shares. He did not tell me why but we both realized the sale might result in depressing the market in Guinness shares. Roger Seelig suggested that Ansbacher would only consider holding onto the shares if Guinness placed an amount equivalent to the total paid for the shares with them. This would be a short-term interest-free deposit. This suggestion was put to me by a reputable banker from a reputable bank, Morgan Grenfell.[53]

So he fell in with it. On 6 May 1986 £7,614,682.10 was deposited by Guinness, via Morgan Grenfell, with Henry Ansbacher.[54] Seelig had assured Roux that it was an interest-free deposit to dissuade Spens from selling, but the shares were not Spens's to sell. The deposit in fact represented the price of purchasing the shares from Marwan and it included the value of his indemnity, since £7.6 million implied a price of £3.55 a share, considerably above the then value of just over £3. The very exactitude of the sum involved bears this out, as does their subsequent sale to Down Nominees, an account controlled not by Marwan but by Ansbacher. In providing money for the purchase of its own shares Guinness had committed an offence under Section 151 of the Companies Act, which prohibits companies buying their own shares.

There is no evidence to suggest that Spens knew the money had come from Guinness. His assumption that it had come from Morgan Grenfell, and therefore did not contravene Section 151, was at the core of his later public dispute with Seelig. For the time being, however, it was only one among several deals they concluded together. Later in the year Roger Seelig asked Spens to repeat the favour in another deal where he was involved: the Next merger with Grattan, the mail-order house, where Morgan's was advising Next.[55] In this case, the circumstances were slightly different. News of the takeover was leaked by the *Evening Standard*, and the jobbers began to sell their holdings of Next shares, depressing the price and making it difficult for Cazenove, the brokers to Next, to establish a level at which institutional investors could be persuaded by them to underwrite the cash alternative.[56] In this case Spens asked TWH investments to buy Next shares from the jobbers, with an indemnity against loss, in order to stabilize the price ahead of the underwriting exercise, illustrating the diverse applications of the indemnity technique. Writing to Seelig to ask for repayment of £177,652.30, being the size of the loss and funding costs incurred by TWH on holding the Next shares, Spens said that:

It would be nice if you felt that you could charge Next a rounded up figure of £200,000 as a small reward for these people [TWH] for assisting us, as I am sure they will be available to do it again when necessary and indeed they made absolutely nothing out of the Guinness transaction.[57]

Spens was hoping that by rounding up the figure, Ansbacher themselves could collect a small fee. To avoid a contravention of Section 151, it was decided that the indemnity should be paid by Grattan, though it was by then a subsidiary of Next. £180,000 was eventually paid by Grattan, of which

£177,652.30 was paid to TWH, and the balance was retained by Ansbacher. An internal Ansbacher report later concluded that 'a false market in the price of Next shares was created' and the Takeover Code was 'widely ignored in respect of false markets and indemnities ... Indeed, the markets, led by Morgan Grenfell, were continually stretching the Code to and beyond limits.'[58] It was exactly what happened in the aftermath of the Guinness bid for Distillers.

None of these transactions would have emerged, were it not for Ivan Boesky. On Friday 14 November 1986 – the end of the week in which Geoffrey Collier, managing director of Morgan Grenfell Securities, had resigned after admitting insider-dealing offences to his superiors – the Securities and Exchange Commission in New York announced that Boesky had agreed to return $50 million in illicit profits from insider dealing and to pay a $50 million fine. For six weeks he had attended meetings wearing a hidden tape-recorder, putting all his contacts in jeopardy.[59] Among the deals he had told the investigators about was his role in the Guinness bid for Distillers. The Securities and Exchange Commission then told the Department of Trade and Industry in London. Gary Lynch, chief of its enforcement division, said he thought 'we were pretty helpful on Guinness'.[60] Certainly they supplied enough information for the Department of Trade and Industry to move against the main protagonists.

At 9.30 a.m. on 1 December 1986 two inspectors appointed by the DTI arrived at 23 Great Winchester Street. It was one of seven addresses they and their like had visited that day: the London and Edinburgh offices of Wood Mackenzie, formerly brokers to Guinness; the London headquarters of Guinness; Cazenove, brokers to Guinness; and Robert Fleming and Kleinwort Benson, formerly bankers to Distillers.[61] From the moment they arrived, the hitherto irrepressible Morgan Grenfell publicity machine began to malfunction. George Law, the group compliance officer, still flushed with his success in excising Geoffrey Collier, conceded to waiting pressmen that what they wanted was to look at all files or other records that in any way related to dealings in Guinness shares from the start of the bid for Distillers.[62]

Within days, the bank was having to deny rumours that Roger Seelig had resigned.[63] In the House of Commons Labour's trade spokesman, Robin Cook, described the Distillers bid as 'an extremely seedy transaction'.[64] Coming so soon after the Collier crisis, Christopher Reeves could be forgiven a sense of incredulity. He told the *Guardian*:

It is absolute nonsense. I know of no resignations from Morgan Grenfell and there are certainly none contemplated as far as I am aware. People must come to their senses. It's not an investigation into Morgan Grenfell. It's an investigation into Guinness.[65]

Rivals, often bloodied in their encounters with the bank's ruthless takeover tacticians, were not slow to seize upon the bank's discomfiture. Schroder Wagg, then advising LCP Holdings against a hostile bid from Ward White, which was being advised by Morgan Grenfell, asked the Stock Exchange to probe suspicious purchases the day ahead of the announcement of the bid on 20 October. Schroder's had in fact known about a suspect purchase of 25,000 LCP shares since at least mid-November, when it had asked for – and received – assurances from George Law that Geoffrey Collier was not the buyer.[66] Philip Evans, the Morgan director handling the Ward White bid, did not like the taste of his own medicine:

For them to use this particular time on the back of the DTI investigation to announce what they have done today is down to the dirty tricks world.[67]

For a few days the City was simply bewildered. The most likely explanation for the official raids was that Boesky had grassed on someone, and Seelig was the obvious candidate. He denied vehemently anything beyond a vague acquaintanceship with the disgraced arbitrageur:

Of course I know him. He knows me. That is his job. But there were no transactions, dialogues or anything else between us and him . . . I can remember a cocktail party hosted by Boesky at the Savoy about a year ago which was attended by virtually the whole City.[68]

The denial began to look implausible. The week before Christmas, on Thursday 18 December, the news leaked out about the $100 million investment by Guinness in an Ivan Boesky arbitrage fund.[69] By 20 December both Roger Seelig and Graham Walsh were conceding that Morgan Grenfell's solicitors, Slaughter & May, were advising rapid dissociation from the burgeoning scandal, though they still denied any connection with Boesky.[70] Few believed them. It was common knowledge in the City that Boesky had been highly active in the London takeover boom through his London vehicle, the Cambrian & General Investment Trust. Piers de Montfort, a junior executive who worked with Seelig on the Guinness bid for Distillers, was overheard at a City cocktail party boasting that 'Boesky always delivers the stock'. Within a fortnight of the scandal breaking, Morgan Grenfell was making it known publicly that it was no longer acting for Guinness in a major capacity, but still refused to resign the account. The bank's reluctance to abandon Guinness reflected the knowledge that some of the fees from the Distillers bid were still unpaid. Roger Seelig was submitting invoices to Guinness more than a fortnight after the inspectors' raids and Morgan Grenfell Laurie's sale (for £30.5 million) of the former Distillers headquarters in St James's was not completed until the middle of the month.[71]

On 12 December the plot thickened. Schenley Industries admitted that it had contravened Companies Act requirements in failing to disclose to the Takeover Panel a stake of over 5 per cent in Guinness, which the company had acquired during the bid for Distillers.[72] In other words, Schenley's support for the Guinness share price had been so heavy that it had breached takeover disclosure rules. In this case Guinness seems to have paid for the support in kind, not cash. The shares were bought through Cazenove and Wood Mackenzie, the brokers to Guinness, via an anonymous account, Atlantic Nominees.[73] In an internal investigation into their role in the Guinness scandal prepared by their solicitors, Simmons & Simmons, Cazenove pleaded ignorance of the connections between Guinness, Distillers, Schenley and Atlantic Nominees, though it regretted publicly its involvement with Schenley:

It would have been better if Cazenove had not relied on the assurances it received that there was no association between Guinness and Schenley Industries, a US distributor of Distillers whisky, for whom Cazenove bought shares in both Guinness and Distillers, but had made its own enquiries of Schenley.[74]

Schenley, for its part, pleaded ignorance of the law and argued that, diluted in the wake of the bid, it amounted to only 3.5 per cent anyway.[75]

Schenley was owned by the Rapid American Corporation, a conglomerate run by the colourful Israeli-American businessman Meshulam Riklis, one of the most feared corporate raiders of the 1970s. Schenley had distributed a Distillers brand, Dewar's scotch whisky, in the United States since 1936.[76] During the battle for Distillers he had become anxious that he did not lose the franchise if the company fell to an ill-disposed predator though, given Distillers' dilapidated state, he also scented the possibility of a lucrative arbitrage. In December 1985, Riklis initially approached Gulliver, who was left with the impression that Riklis would back the Argyll bid if the Dewar's dealership stayed with Schenley. Gulliver gave no assurances, so Riklis tested Guinness instead.[77] It was more receptive, and during the bid Riklis spent £30 million buying Distillers shares and £60 million buying Guinness shares, for which he was duly rewarded with not only the retention of the Dewar's distribution rights but Gordon's gin as well. The deal, as usual, appears to have been the work of the ubiquitous Tom Ward, in whose Washington office it was signed.[78] At the Guinness shareholders' meeting on 11 September Schenley's Guinness shares were voted for Saunders's controversial plans to reshape the board.[79] Riklis even became a co-investor in the Boesky fund, albeit injecting a relatively paltry $5 million. He retained his 3.5 per cent stake (29.3 million shares) in Guinness until long after Saunders left. It was finally placed with a group of City institutions in May 1988.[80] In September 1987 the new Guinness management, appalled by Saunders's willingness to deal with a man who boasted of being the 'most sued executive in American business history', bought Schenley from him.

Seelig had to deny involvement with the Schenley deal:

Neither I nor anyone at Morgan Grenfell knew of, or had any contact with, Schenley or with Boesky over any special arrangements or sweetheart/support deals. We were not party in any way to any improper deals with Boesky, Riklis or Schenley.[81]

This much was true, but his position was fast becoming untenable. *Private Eye* carried a more or less explicit suggestion that he had all but resigned.[82] A New York journalist, alerted by the *Eye* story, rang Morgan's in New York for confirmation but was referred instead to Byron Ousey, the bank's public relations director in London. Tormented by a crisis best left to lawyers rather than public relations men, and denied the truth by his superiors, Ousey was developing a reputation among curious journalists for belligerence. He angrily warned the reporter that any suggestion that Seelig would have to resign would be regarded as actionable, and the story was dropped.

On 28 December 1986 the Sunday papers carried the news that Morgan Grenfell had retained its title at the top of the annual mergers and acquisitions league table, but the *Sunday Telegraph* also contained the less pleasing revelation that Henry Ansbacher had furnished the DTI inspectors with the details of the Guinness share-repurchase deal between Seelig and Spens.[83] It was the first time Morgan's name had been explicitly linked with any skulduggery and emerged only because of a curious incident involving a dividend on the shares. On 17 August 1986 Guinness issued a dividend cheque of £48,000 to the shareholders in the Down Nominees account, where Spens had parked the shares once owned by Ashraf Marwan. By August, of course, Morgan Grenfell controlled the account on behalf of Guinness, who had effectively repurchased the shares from Dr Marwan with the cheque for £7,614,682.10 issued in

May. Morgan Grenfell had paid the stamp duty of £23,940 on the sale to Down Nominees in early June and at the Guinness shareholders' meeting on 12 September Seelig controlled the way the shares were voted. When Ansbacher received the dividend cheque it remitted the sum, on Morgan Grenfell's instructions, to 23 Great Winchester Street, where it was credited to Morgan Grenfell. By November 1986 Ansbacher was uneasy about the arrangement and asked Seelig for an indemnity to cover the risk of the Down Nominees holding, but Seelig was reluctant and agreed only to repurchase the shares by the end of the year. If he did not, he would then sign a letter of indemnity.[84]

In the event he did neither, for on 1 December the inspectors called. George Law, Morgan's compliance officer, returned the £48,000 to Ansbacher, stating that the dividend had been forwarded in error four months earlier.[85] Richard Fenhalls, the Ansbacher chief executive, had ordered an internal inquiry into the £7.6 million 'interest-free deposit' as soon as the Guinness inquiry began on 1 December.[86] Once apprised of the facts he wrote to Ernest Saunders, citing two letters prepared by Morgan Grenfell and sent by Ansbacher to Guinness in May and June 1986. That they both referred to the £7.6 million as 'an interest-free deposit' was, Fenhalls alleged, 'a mistake of fact', namely that the sum reflected not a deposit but the price of purchasing the shares from Dr Marwan plus the cost of his indemnity.[87] On 5 December he told the Bank of England about it.[88] The Bank pressed him into telling the Department of Trade and Industry, whence the story leaked into the *Sunday Telegraph*. Morgan's feigned ignorance was instantly transparent. It had handled the funds for Guinness, paid the stamp duty on the sale, issued voting instructions and even cashed the dividend cheque, but Morgan Grenfell continued to stall. With Seelig denying any indemnity had been given and Spens averring exactly the opposite, Morgan Grenfell did eventually concede that it could not rule out a less formal arrangement of some kind. 'It is now just a matter of one merchant banker's word against another's,' remarked Spens on 29 December.[89]

Spens did not have long to wait for an answer. Roger Seelig resigned the following morning after a perfunctory meeting with Christopher Reeves and the bemused Lord Catto, in Reeves's office.[90] Guinness had paid its outstanding invoices the same day.[91] Only then did Morgan Grenfell resign as advisers to Guinness, who simultaneously dismissed the bank. 'Our letters will probably cross,' said a Guinness spokesman. The Morgan Grenfell share price plunged 16p on news of Seelig's dismissal, reflecting how far the bank had come to rely on his deal-making skills. Adjured to be so by Reeves, Catto and the bank's solicitors, Slaughter & May, Seelig was stoic, at least in public:

Throughout my time at Morgan Grenfell I have sought to serve to the best of my ability the interests of the house and its clients. I shall await the outcome of the Guinness enquiry and make no further comment until then.[92]

He resigned no other board positions, but privately he was bitter and felt he had been made a scapegoat. He told journalists that he had been duped by Saunders and Ward who, he claimed, had initiated the share-support operation on their own initiative. He told friends that if he wrote a book about the City it would be called 'Hypocri-City'.[93] And he told Ivan Fallon:

You can't take a taxi without getting authority for it in this bank. Anyone who thinks I acted on my own must think I'm six feet taller than I am.[94]

The bank hoped to repeat its successful handling of the Collier affair by suggesting that Seelig had 'breached the bank's rules' and exceeded his authority, but this was scarcely credible. That weekend a spokesman for Morgan Grenfell told the *Sunday Times*:

All we are saying is that we do not own the shares and we never paid for the shares. We are not saying that Guinness, or anybody else, owns or paid for them. But what I can say is that Roger is surrounded by a clutch of lawyers and so are we.[95]

There was room for doubt about exactly how much Seelig had told his superiors of what was going on in the bid for Distillers, or even how much he knew himself, but the conviction was growing that even if Christopher Reeves, the chief executive, and Graham Walsh, the head of Corporate Finance, did not know what was going on they ought to have done.

On 13 January Lord Catto agreed to chair a committee of non-executive directors to probe the bank's 'organizational structure and management-reporting systems' or, in his own less discreet phrase, to 'look at what happened and why it happened without the knowledge of senior management' and report their findings to the Bank of England.[96] Students of Catto's absentee chairmanship relished the irony of his statement. To outsiders, it smacked of complacency to appoint the chairman and the non-executive directors to ask the questions they were paid to ask anyway. Most concluded it had an unwritten but squalid and ultimately unsuccessful brief: to save Christopher Reeves and Graham Walsh, who were still clinging to office. As if to affirm this, an unnamed spokesman said it 'will not be a witch hunt and will not be a whitewash'.[97] Efforts were made to sell the committee's dynamism, but the contribution of one member, David Palmer, the chairman of Willis Faber – 'if we have to work at weekends we will do it' – was merely ridiculous.[98] 'I don't think we have ever had a problem of public exposure of this type,' mused Reeves, still apparently unable to grasp the responsibility which went with his £310,000 a year salary. 'We have had difficulty knowing what to say and when to say it,' added Lord Catto, hoping news of an internal investigation would suffice.[99] He circulated a memorandum to staff the following day explaining that the board had

identified certain actions taken by Roger Seelig during the course of the Guinness bid, including an involvement in the Ansbacher affair. These actions were not in accordance with our established policy and consequently Mr Seelig offered his resignation, which was accepted.[100]

It was a shameful repudiation of a man on whom the bank had been content to rely during his years of triumph, which owed more to the legal fastidiousness of Slaughter & May than to any wider conceptions of corporate responsibility. A similar letter was sent to shareholders assuring them, by way of omission, that Seelig was to blame for everything and that the crisis has been tamed, but by now events were out of even the Bank of England's control.[101]

After Fenhalls had informed the Bank of England on 5 December that Spens had secured indemnities from Seelig, Bank officials had threatened him with a full-scale investigation of Ansbacher if he did not pass the details of the Marwan deal to the Department of Trade and Industry. This he did, assuring the Bank that Spens would resign as soon as this could be effected with minimum damage to Ansbacher.[102] There matters rested until the weekend of January 17–18 1987, when the Bank came under heavy pressure from 10 Downing Street to stage some exemplary sackings.[103] With a spring or summer election looming, the Guinness scandal was fast becoming an electoral liability to a Conservative Party already hamstrung by the fact that the Cabinet Minister responsible, Paul Channon, was precluded from any involvement because he was a member of the Guinness family. The Labour Party trade spokesman, John Smith, was skilfully exploiting Channon's discomfiture, not least by pointing out that Morgan Grenfell had given £25,000 to Tory Central Office in 1986. 'Get the handcuffs on quick,' was the advice of John Wakeham, the Leader of the House, and the Prime Minister made it clear to the Chancellor, Nigel Lawson, that heads must roll:

I want Reeves and Walsh out today, not next week or next month but by lunchtime today.[104]

Lawson passed the news to the governor of the Bank of England, Robin Leigh-Pemberton. George Blunden, the deputy governor, explained to a former governor, Lord O'Brien of Lothbury, who was now a non-executive director of Morgan Grenfell and an *ex officio* member of the Catto committee, that he would invoke Section 17 of the Banking Act, which requires banks to be prudently managed, if Reeves and Walsh did not resign.[105] This circuitous message does not seem to have been interpreted literally by Lord Catto, himself the son of a former governor of the Bank, and the man who had hired Christopher Reeves. On the Monday morning Catto was summoned to Threadneedle Street and told bluntly that an internal inquiry was not enough, that Reeves and Walsh would have to take responsibility and resign and that the Bank was prepared to suspend Morgan's banking licence if they did not comply. On the Tuesday Catto returned to concede the heads of Reeves and Walsh.[106] They resigned the same day, taking with them compensation totalling £562,500 and senseless, if defiant, assurances of the bank's goodwill.[107] Lord Catto, whose letters to staff and shareholders now looked distinctly foolish, issued a statement saying that – unlike Seelig's departure – the resignations were a 'matter of deep personal regret'.[108] That afternoon Nigel Lawson told the Commons that the decision had been his. Next the Bank turned to Ansbacher. On the evening of 20 January Fenhalls and David LeRoy-Lewis, the chairman of Ansbacher, were summoned to Threadneedle Street by Rodney Galpin, head of the Bank's supervisory department and told that if Spens did not resign immediately the Bank would withdraw Ansbacher's banking licence. At a board meeting the following morning Spens was told that the board was unanimous in wanting to keep him, but that the Bank wanted his head. Fenhalls, the chief executive, did not demur from the board's opinion, though it was known that he and Spens had a poor personal relationship. Spens resigned the same day, receiving compensation of £79,000.[109] It was in one way an unexpected bonus – Spens had been planning to leave anyway, to set up Castlecrest Investments.

The Ansbacher revelations had also put the incumbent regime at Portman Square under pressure. Both the new non-executive directors and the major shareholders were wondering just how much their chief executive had known, especially after the correspondence between Fenhalls and Saunders disputing the nature of the £7.6 million payment was published.[110] With Seelig's resignation accomplished the spot-light began to play on Saunders. He returned from his annual skiing holiday on Sunday 4 January 1987 to newspapers filled with speculation about his imminent resignation.[111] The same day Olivier Roux made a long statement to Sir David Napley, who had been appointed solicitor to Guinness by Saunders on Boxing Day. Roux told of some £25 million which Guinness had paid out to supporters of its share price during the bid for Distillers, insisting that Saunders had full knowledge of all the arrangements.[112] A copy was given to Saunders the following day. 'This all came as a complete surprise and terrific shock to me,' Saunders claims.[113] The statement was discussed at a Guin-ness board meeting on 9 January, which both Roux and Saunders attended. Though Saunders denied each allegation in turn he was asked by the board to stand aside whilst they completed their investigations. On 11 January Sir Norman Macfarlane, who had led the group of five non-executive directors appointed after the Risk affair, became chairman. Price Waterhouse, the company's auditors, was instructed to find out what had happened to the £25 million which Roux had told the board about. Roux resigned on 12 January and two days later Saunders, Ward and Furer were fired. Napley was replaced as the company's solicitor with the City firm of Herbert Smith.[114]

On Wednesday 21 January the newspapers were treated to some hard copy at last. The previous day the *Financial Times* had revealed that Gerald Ronson had been a heavy buyer of Guinness shares in the dying days of the Distillers bid and that his Heron Corporation had been rewarded for this support with the contract for the management and maintenance of the Guinness car fleet.[115] The following day Ronson confessed in an open letter to Sir Norman Macfarlane that he had received £5 million from Guinness for buying shares during the bid and a further £800,000 for losses sustained. On the BBC evening news of Thursday 22 January the results of the Price Water-house probe into the whereabouts of the £25 million became public for the first time. They had found eleven unexplained invoices documenting payments to Marketing and Acquisitions Consultants (£5.2 million), J. Lyons Chamberlayne (£300,000), Konsultat S.A. (£3 million), Heron Managements (£2.5 million), Pima Service Corporation (£3.413 million), CIFCO (£1.94 million), Erlanger (£1.495 million), Zentral-sparkasse und Kommerzialbank (£254,000), Consultations et Investissements S.A. (£3.35 million), Rudani Corporation N.V. (£1.953 million) and Morgan Grenfell (£1.65 million).[116] Seven and a half weeks and seven resignations after the Department of Trade and Industry inspectors had first arrived at the offices of Morgan Grenfell, outside investigators had at last reached the core of the Guinness affair.

At the time it was widely assumed that the Guinness share-support operation had been hastily cobbled together in the closing weeks of the Distillers bid to counter short-selling by Argyll, which had a share-support operation of its own in place too. Olivier Roux, in his statement to David Napley, said as much:

Argyll began to employ strange tactics in order to affect the market price of Guinness – for example, by giving late orders to jobbers and selling the shares at night.[117]

Gerald Ronson, in his letter to Macfarlane, explained that he became involved for the same reason:

It was, in effect, as I understood it, designed as a legitimate corrective to the tactics of the other side.[118]

In fact the support operation was an integral part of the bid from the outset, just as it had been during the Guinness bid for Bell's. In his evidence to the Department of Trade and Industry inspectors Roux recalled a meeting between Saunders, Seelig and Anthony Salz of Guinness's solicitors, Freshfields, on 19 December 1985 – a full month ahead of the bid – at which they discussed tactics for subverting the Argyll bid for Distillers, which was already well advanced when they resolved upon their own. Techniques surveyed included:

sabotaging the[Argyll] bid by investing in Argyll and then unsettling the share price to prevent Argyll underpinning an increased bid.[119]

He added that it was Seelig, a month later, who first suggested that if the Guinness share price weakened on the announcement of the bid,

it would be important to plan for the share price to recover as quickly as possible . . . It was in this context that names of possible supporters began to emerge . . . Gerald Ronson, Rothschild and Goldman Sachs were discussed . . . [such discussions] led me to believe that these practices were entirely normal and part of accepted bid tactics.[120]

Anthony Parnes also told the inspectors that such ruses were part of Morgan Grenfell's stock-in-trade. He told them a similar scheme of support had been in place during the bid for Bell's and that for his role in it he received £350,000, paid into a Swiss bank account, codenamed Loganberry, at Pictet & Cie.[121] The client he had introduced was Gerald Ronson.

Ronson, born in Paddington in 1939, is the grandson of Russian Jews who fled the pogroms in the early part of this century. His father, Henry, was a useful light heavyweight in the 1930s, and ran a furniture business which Gerald joined after leaving school at fourteen and a half. In the 1950s he discovered property when he and his father built a new factory for £100,000 and sold it instantly for £198,500, making more on a single deal than in years of furniture manufacture.[122] In 1957 Ronson sold the family furniture business and invested the proceeds in house-building. He established then a pattern of work – twelve hours a day, six days a week – to which he still adheres. In the mid-1960s he moved into self-service petrol stations sooner than anyone else in Britain and, by spotting likely sites, buying them cheaply and converting them into filling stations he generated the cash flow and the asset backing which enabled him to finance major property deals. He moved on to other activities, notably the H. R. Owen Rolls-Royce franchise, and today the Heron Corporation, named after his father Henry Ronson, now spans financial services, video distribution, private house building and commercial property interests in Spain, Switzerland, Belgium and France. The company is probably worth over £1 billion but Ronson has never contemplated going public, since it would mean forfeiting control of a company held exclusively by his family and the Ronson Charitable Foundation, which is one of the most generous corporate charities in Britain.[123]

This is a benevolent dictatorship. I'm not responsible to outsiders and I don't want to be. That's why this is a private company and why it is going to remain one.[124]

Anthony Parnes had been Ronson's private stockbroker for years.[125] At the time the Guinness bid was launched in January 1986 he was a 'half-comm' broker at Alexanders Laing & Cruickshank. Half-commission brokers (the correct term is 'associate') were a familiar aspect of the pre-Big Bang City. For the most part highly individualistic, they combined independence with economic expedience by 'renting' a desk at a firm of stockbrokers, usually halving commission with the partners. The partners liked it because half-comm men brought major clients, and Parnes's list included not just Gerald Ronson but Robert Maxwell, Sir Phil Harris and Ephraim Margulies, chairman and chief executive of the commodities house S & W Berisford. (He has also dealt for some dubious clients, notably Gerald Caplan, who fled to California after stealing millions from his company, London & County.[126]) Dubbed 'The Animal' – a reference to his habit of prowling across the dealing-floor with a telephone at each ear – Parnes was the City's premier half-commission stockbroker. He had become extremely rich, with a house in Frognal Green, Hampstead which was recently sold for £4.5 million.[127] He is also a cousin of the late Larry Parnes, the impresario behind the 1960s rock stars Tommy Steel and Billy Fury.

On the evening of Wednesday 22 January 1986 Parnes, who lived near by, arrived at Gerald Ronson's mansion in Winnington Road, Hampstead.[128] The Guinness bid for Distillers was two days old. In his letter to Sir Norman Macfarlane almost exactly a year later, Ronson described the encounter as an approach from 'a representative of eminent stockbrokers'. (This led initially to speculation that it had been David Mayhew not Anthony Parnes.) Ronson explained to Macfarlane what happened next:

It was explained to me that the general opinion (which I must say I shared) was that it was in Distillers' as well as Guinness's best interests that the bid should succeed. I understand that with the approval of the Guinness senior management (and Ernest Saunders in particular – whose skill and integrity were always regarded as of the highest) efforts were being made to support the Guinness share price by persuading Guinness's friends to buy in the market. I was told that in the event that Heron suffered any loss it would be covered by Guinness. This did not seem to me at the time to be in any sense unusual or sinister, particularly as it was public knowledge that Distillers itself had agreed to cover the expenses of Guinness in rescuing it from the Argyll bid. It was also agreed that in the event of the Guinness bid being successful we would receive a success fee of £5 million. These arrangements were expressly confirmed to me by Mr Saunders. In due course our invoices were rendered in the total funds mentioned . . . and these were paid.[129]

'When you shake hands with Gerald Ronson, the deal is done,' said Gerald Ronson in another context and, accordingly, after the bid was over, Heron submitted two invoices to Guinness.[130] The first, from Heron Managements, was for £2.5 million plus VAT of £375,000 for 'services rendered year 31/3/86'.[131] The second, for $4.8 million (£2.5 million), came from Pima Service Corporation, the Arizona Savings & Loan Association Ronson then owned but later sold.[132] Alan Goldman, then a Heron director, now deputy chief executive, had wanted the indemnity part paid in dollars. He even tried to round it up to $5 million.[133]

Saunders denied that he confirmed the arrangement with Ronson,[134] but Parnes told the Department of Trade and

Industry inspectors that the two men had met and that Ronson had agreed to support the brewer provided he was indemnified. Olivier Roux, who cleared the payment of the Heron invoices, told the inspectors that Saunders had gone further and promised to award Heron property consultancy contracts if the bid succeeded.[135] Ronson then agreed to spend up to £25 million buying Guinness shares in exchange for an indemnity and a £5 million success fee, the details of which (according to Parnes) were finalized at a second meeting between Ronson, Roux and Parnes in February 1986.[136] Parnes's role in involving Ronson is confirmed by Roux:

Parnes controlled the way in which Gerald Ronson's support would be used ... Parnes told me he would use Gerald Ronson's funds only after he had cleared this directly with Gerald Ronson.[137]

Parnes began buying on behalf of a Heron company, National Insurance & Guarantee Corporation, on 23 January, the fourth day of the Guinness bid. To achieve the greatest effect he bought through a range of brokers, including Quilter Goodison, James Capel, Wood Mackenzie, Phillips & Drew and Chase Securities, and by 3 April he had spent up to the £25 million limit.[138] A year later, on 21 January 1987, Ronson repaid Guinness the £5 million success fee and the £800,000 indemnity he received, apologizing profusely and blaming his actions on others:

I did not focus on the legal implications of what had occurred, nor did it cross my mind that City advisers and business people of such eminence would be asking us to join in doing something improper. I am very upset to have been involved, albeit in good faith, in these transactions in support of the Guinness endeavour.[139]

Friends report that Ronson can no longer exchange a civil word with Parnes. At a party given by Sir Phil Harris for his son Martin's eighteenth birthday, Ronson pointedly insisted on being placed at a different table.[140]

A day after Ronson repaid his winnings, another Parnes client, Ephraim Margulies, chairman and chief executive of the commodities and property house S & W Berisford, admitted that a subsidiary had received a fee from Guinness and also offered to return it. In a letter to Sir Norman Macfarlane dated 22 January 1987, Margulies explained that Howard Zuckerman, a New York attorney who became joint chief executive of Berisford US in 1985, had been introduced to Thomas Ward, with whom he had discussed 'parallel trading', or the exchange of goods in countries where the two companies were experiencing payments difficulties.[141] Or, as Margulies put it:

Proposed co-operation between our two companies in relation to international trade, and in particular the provision by us of a stand-by facility for the purpose of conducting counter-trade and barter transactions on your behalf.[142]

In the same letter Margulies admitted that another Berisford subsidiary in the United States, Berisford Capital Corporation, did acquire 2.8 million Guinness shares during the bid but had done so 'entirely on its own initiative'.[143]

Anthony Parnes tells a somewhat different story. He claims to have recruited Margulies to the support operation in February or March 1986 and that he met Ernest Saunders to agree the details.[144] At the time Berisford was under threat from two bidders, Ferruzzi of Italy and Harry Solomon's Hillsdown Holdings, both of whom were principally interested in acquiring British Sugar, the Silver Spoon sugar-beet processor Margulies had bought in 1982. His defence involved the sale of British Sugar to arch-rival Tate & Lyle, accompanied by a management buy-out of the rest of the business. Parnes claims that when Margulies met Saunders he attempted to trade support for Guinness for a pledge from Saunders to back his proposed buy-out.[145] With this agreed, a full indemnity and a success fee of £3.5 million were pledged by Saunders. Once the Distillers bid was over, Olivier Roux, as Guinness finance director, received two invoices from Berisford, via Parnes. The first, for £1.94 million, was from a mysterious Swiss entity, Compagnie Internationale de Finance et de Commerce

(CIFCO) and referred to 'advisory service re: Distillers PLC'.[146] The second, for £1.495 million, was from Erlanger, a Berisford subsidiary. It referred to 'work in connection with the acquisition of Distillers'.[147] Roux told the Department of Trade and Industry inspectors that he had no idea who CIFCO represented and the ultimate beneficiaries of the £1.94 million are still unknown. Recently £1.2 million paid to CIFCO was repaid to Guinness through a firm of London solicitors, thereby shielding the identity of the source. The most likely explanation is that it was a cover for purchases made via Rahn & Bodmer, a Zurich bank which has connections with Berisford.[148]

Margulies still denies any knowledge of either CIFCO or any indemnity payments.[149] As if to corroborate this, he has returned only the £1.495 million paid to Erlanger. Yet his son, Ari, confirmed in June 1987 that he had arranged for CIFCO to buy Guinness shares worth £4 million during the bid for Distillers. Charles Rosenbaum, a family friend of Margulies, runs CIFCO in Geneva.[150] He has written to Guinness twice, claiming that CIFCO arranged with Saunders to research marketing possibilities in the Third World for Distillers products, for which a fee of £1.8 million plus expenses was agreed.[151] Parnes contends that he personally delivered the £1.94 million CIFCO cheque to Ephraim Margulies and that it was only when the Department of Trade and Industry inspectors began to probe that Margulies tried to dissociate himself from it.[152] A cover-up certainly seems to have been attempted. When Margulies repaid the £1.495 million paid to Erlanger, he told Macfarlane that it was for 'services we are to provide related to Distillers products and therefore arose by reason of your acquisition of that company' and that the original wording of the invoice – 'work in connection with the acquisition of Distillers' – had been suggested by Guinness. Yet he pointedly ignored the £1.94 million paid to CIFCO, denying any connection with the company. Parnes has also testified that he feared Margulies would 'frame' him and that he had been expected to lie about what he knew of the CIFCO payment.[153] He claims that in meetings at his home and that of Margulies the two men had discussed fabricating evidence about the CIFCO payment which could be given to the inspectors. Parallel trading was one possibility but the preferred alternative was blaming it all on Parnes. At his first meeting with the inspectors on 22 January 1987 Parnes said he felt threatened but would not explain by whom.[154] He told them on 27 January 1987, in a reference to Margulies and his cronies:

People who were sticking together, who are working together, who are close, they will say they don't know each other. They do. They can do this or that, people can change records. To my mind they could do anything and I was frightened of that, not knowing what they were capable of.[155]

Margulies insisted that Parnes take £340,000 of the CIFCO money and alter the invoices accordingly.[156] Asked by the inspectors what he was expected to do in return, Parnes said: 'Lie.' 'To whom?' they asked. 'To you,' he replied.[157] That Parnes was pushed into taking some of the CIFCO cash is corroborated by Roux, who recalls a dinner party at Parnes's Hampstead mansion on 10 December 1986, nine days after the raid on Guinness by the inspectors:

I think it was after dinner that he took me to one side and told me that he had unwisely accepted from CIFCO a commission of about £350,000.[158]

Roux says Parnes tried to return it but was refused and had become 'frightened'.[159]

The £340,000 from CIFCO was not the only money Parnes received from the Guinness affair. On 5 October Guinness issued a writ claiming £3.69 million from him in all. He had invoiced Guinness twice in 1986. The first, dated 4 June, was from a Swiss company called Consultations et Investissements S.A. and referred to a 'corporate finance success fee' of £3.35 million.[160] This was paid by Guinness on 1 July into an account at Pictet & Cie in Geneva and included £350,000 for his work on the Guinness bid for Bell's. It seems that Consultations et Investissements was a company invented by Ari Margulies.[161] Parnes split the £350,000 Bell's payment with Sir Jack Lyons, the man who had introduced him to Guinness and to an extremely profitable line of work.[162] Interestingly, Ernest Saunders maintains an account at Pictet & Cie.[163]

Sir Jack Lyons was a London director of Bain & Co., the Boston management consultancy which supplied Saunders with much of his management workforce, including Olivier Roux. Then aged 71, he had enjoyed a successful business career at the retail chain founded by his father, United Drapery Stores (UDS), which used to run John Collier and Richard Shops. He resigned in March 1980 amid allegations of insider dealing and he is currently under investigation by the DTI for suspected insider dealing in the shares of Grosvenor Group, a small electronics company taken over by Robert Maxwell in late 1986.[164] He knew and was known by most of the major participants in the Guinness share-support operation. Lyons owns a private company, J. Lyons Chamberlayne, of which Anthony Parnes was a director. Maxwell was a client of Parnes's and is known to have bought 100,000 shares in Guinness during the Distillers bid through him.[165] He is married to Rosalyn Rosenbaum, who is related to Charles Rosenbaum, the friend of Ephraim Margulies in Switzerland.[166] He also knew Ronson, having served on the board of First Computer, a high-street computer retailer run by Heron Corporation.[167] In 1983, Gerald Ronson bid for UDS, but was defeated by a rival bid from Hanson Trust, who in turn sold Richard Shops to Terence Conran, who was advised by Roger Seelig, and for some time Morgan Grenfell owned half of Richard Shops.[168] It is a small business world, in which the participants are all well known to each other.

According to Roux, Lyons was engaged by Guinness in late 1984 to advise on the retail businesses, for which he was paid a retainer of $3,000 a month. Roux also claims that Saunders gave Lyons £5 million of the company's money to manage on a discretionary basis.[169] According to Saunders, Lyons was put forward by John Theroux, of Bain, because he 'apparently knew everybody' in government, the City and Whitehall.[170] His political connections were certainly impeccable. On 7 January 1987, only days before being fired by Bain for his involvement in the Guinness scandal, he entertained Mrs Thatcher to lunch at their Connaught Place offices. After the Distillers bid closed he and his wife Rosalyn had co-hosted a Leonard Bernstein evening at the Barbican attended by the Queen and Prince Philip. He received two payments for his purchases of Guinness shares during the bid. One, for £300,000, went to J. Lyons Chamberlayne. Another £2.8 million was paid to Konsultat S.A., a Swiss company run by a friend. In February 1987 Lyons explained to Sir Norman Macfarlane that £750,000 of the payment to Konsultat covered the purchase from him of an apartment in the prestigious Watergate complex in Washington, which Thomas Ward claims he purchased using his personal account.[171] This transaction is currently subject to litigation in the United States.[172] In November 1987 Sir Jack repaid an undisclosed sum to Guinness.[173]

Thomas Ward, the Washington lawyer eulogized by Saunders as the man who did more than any other to fell Distillers, was rewarded accordingly. In May 1986 a Jersey company controlled by him, Marketing and Acquisitions Consultants (MAC), submitted an invoice for £5.2 million to Guinness. It was this payment which was described by the Vice-Chancellor in the High Court in April 1987 as one which 'could not have been lawfully made' under the Companies Act, a view upheld by the Appeal Court in May 1988 on the grounds that it needed board approval.[174] Ward personally retained 60 per cent of all Ward, Lazarus, Grow & Cihlar's income from Nestlé and Guinness, the partnership's two biggest clients.[175] Though American lawyers are usually more commercial than their British counterparts, Ward took the go-for-it mentality to extreme lengths. City old-timers were frequently shocked by his outrageous suggestions and circuitous reasoning but Saunders liked him, preferring quick legal bypasses to financial mumbo-jumbo, which he left largely to Roux, who claims Saunders was virtually innumerate. Because his relationship with Ward was so close, it was initially thought that Saunders might have taken a cut of the £5.2 million. Certainly £3 million was transferred to a Swiss bank account controlled by Saunders but it transpired that Ward had merely borrowed the account temporarily. This explanation has certainly been accepted by Guinness, which has not implicated Saunders in its legal battle to recoup the money from Ward.

Ward set up MAC in 1981 as a conduit for his European earnings. It received a fee of $100,000 from Guinness in March 1985 for work he did in 1983 and 1984 and the company's administrator, Michael Dee, dealt in both Bell's and Argyll shares in 1985 and 1986.[176] The £5.2 million arrived via five different banks on the island – National Westminster, Midland, Charterhouse, Charterhouse Japhet and Standard Chartered – and it was from the account at Charterhouse that £3 million was shifted to the Saunders account at Union Bank in Switzerland, before being moved, at Saunders's request, to Ward's account at Finterbank. It is likely that using the Saunders account was part of an elaborate web of deception. In steering the £5.2 million into his own bank account, Ward laundered the money through 300 separate transactions which it took a team of accountants to unravel.[177]

Neither Ward nor Dee has conceded much to the Guinness lawyers. On hearing of the first writs issued against him on 19 March 1987 Ward dismissed the claim, insisting that the £5.2 million were his rightful earnings and that after deductions for American taxes and 'certain expenditures' the balance remained in his possession on deposit.[178] After he was dismissed as a Guinness director in January 1987 twelve car-loads of documents were shipped from his office to the Watergate apartment that Ward claims he bought using a loan from Lyons. Many have not been seen since.[179] Lyons claims that £750,000 of the £3 million he received from Guinness represented the purchase of the apartment by Guinness rather than Ward and that Ward's name was used purely as a convenient way to bypass restrictions on corporate ownership of apartments in the Watergate complex. Guinness now intends to sell it and keep the proceeds.[180] It has offered Ward $60,000 in compensation.[181]

Meanwhile, Ward has become involved in another scandal in the United States described by the US Attorney General as a 'story of corporate greed and irresponsibility'. In early 1988 he was subpoenaed as a witness by Niels Hoyvald, the former president of the Beech Nut Nutrition Company, a Nestlé subsidiary, who was facing charges of conspiracy, fraud and 449 violations of the Food and Drugs laws for selling as 'pure apple juice' a fluid described by the prosecution as a 'chemical cocktail', but mostly made of sugar and water. Uncovered in 1982, Hoyvald had shifted 25,000 cases of the offending product to Puerto Rico in the hope of avoiding detection. Hoyvald claims that he was advised in these decisions by Ward who, fearful that a court appearance might jeopardize his case against Guinness, exercised his right not to incriminate himself under the Fifth Amendment to the United States constitution. Hoyvald and another executive were found guilty, fined $2 million and ordered to pay compensation of $7.5 million to retailers and their customers.[182] Hoyvald was recruited by Ernest Saunders when he was president of Nestlé Nutrition. Apple juice is Saunders's favourite drink.[183]

The two other payments listed by the BBC on 22 January remain relatively mysterious. But the £1.953 million paid to the Rudani Corporation, a Netherlands Antilles company, as a 'fee for advising on the acquisition of Distillers' is the only payment where there is evidence of direct involvement by employees of Morgan Grenfell.[184] During the Guinness bid for Distillers, Roger Seelig's friend and colleague, Elliott Bernerd, then chairman of Morgan Grenfell Laurie, advised the Swiss-based Violet Seulberger-Simon, the sister of his former business associate, the property dealer and Keyser Ullman secondary banking tycoon, 'Black' Jack Dellal, to buy shares in Guinness. She bought, through Cazenove, some £17 million of Guinness shares, using two Swiss bank accounts, one at Trade Development Bank and the other at Union Bank of Switzerland, on the basis of assurances from Bernerd that she would be indemnified against loss. Seelig subsequently 'requested that Guinness make good the losses of a confidential third party who had supported the Guinness share price during the Distillers Bid' and submitted an invoice from the Rudani Corporation.[185] Rudani has since repaid the money to Guinness[186] and Morgan Grenfell claimed that 'we have no knowledge of any employee having any interest in Rudani . . . This includes Mr Bernerd.'[187] Further investigation of the Rudani deal by the Fraud Squad has been hampered by Swiss banking secrecy and the lack of an agreement between Britain and Switzerland on the pursuit of criminal investigations.[188] The ultimate beneficiaries of the other payment, of £254,000 to a little known Austrian bank, Zentralsparkasse und Kommerzialbank, may never be known. According to Guinness director Shaun Dowling, the documents relating to this transaction, which was completed in May or June 1986, were tampered with in November that year.[189]

The Department of Trade and Industry inspectors, who have no powers to charge criminals, called in the Fraud Squad in April 1987 and the arrests began shortly afterwards. Ernest Saunders was arrested on 6 May and charged with three offences involving the destruction of documents. Thirty-seven additional charges, covering the theft of virtually the entire £25 million, were added at a second hearing on 13 October.[190] 'He had about as much idea of what he was being charged with as I did,' says his son, James.[191] Anthony Parnes was arrested by FBI agents at Los Angeles airport on 30 September, whence, in conscious emulation of his former client, Gerald Caplan, he had fled as the Fraud Squad closed in. He spent the next six months at the Terminal Island Detention Center outside Los Angeles, fighting extradition to the United Kingdom. In March 1988 he agreed to return to London to face nineteen charges, including the theft of more than £13 million. Rumours that he had traded co-operation for leniency, Boesky-style, and would be a star witness for the prosecution, along with Olivier Roux, are probably unfounded.[192]

Sir Jack Lyons was arrested on 8 October 1987 and charged with the theft of £3.25 million. Gerald Ronson was arrested on 13 October and charged with eight offences, including falsifying invoices, creating a false market in shares and stealing £5.8 million.[193] Roger Seelig was arrested on 15 October 1987 and charged with twelve offences. Three related to dishonestly procuring payment for Rudani, others to the submission to Guinness of invoices that bore no relation to the commercial value of the work undertaken. One referred to an indemnity given to L. F. Rothschild 'on a day unknown between March 15, 1986 and June 30, 1986'. Little is known about Rothschild's participation in the share-support scheme, but the New York investment bank bought six million shares for about £20 million during the Guinness bid for Distillers, apparently with the usual indemnities. L. F. Rothschild was then controlled by Seelig's friend, Jacob Rothschild.[194] Seven fresh charges against Seelig were added on 5 July 1988, all of which related to the Ansbacher and Pipetec deals.[195] Patrick Spens was arrested at his Kent home early on the morning of 10 March 1988. He faces four charges of aiding and abetting Guinness in spending £7.6 million of the company's money on its own shares by agreeing to deposit them with Down Nominees and conspiring to create a false market in shares.[196] David Mayhew was arrested on 7 April 1988 and charged with three offences, all relating to the Pipetec transaction on 17 April two years earlier. A fourth charge, also stemming from the Pipetec deal, followed on 4 July 1988, but none of the charges he faces arise from criminal offences.[197] Thomas Ward was arrested on 5 October 1989 in the United States at the request of the Serious Fraud Office, and charged with Theft Act offences.[198]

Of the central figures, only Ephraim Margulies remains untouched. Ward may prove beyond the reach of British justice since extradition treaties with the United States are limited to criminal offences, though Scotland Yard issued a warrant for his arrest in March, accusing him of the theft of £5.2 million.[199] Margulies is still at work at Berisford, the evidence of the truth hidden from view by Swiss banking laws. To many in the City, of course, none of those involved in the Guinness affair did very much that was not common practice in the overheated takeover market of the mid-1980s. The dividing line between legitimate indemnification and a breach of Section 151 is perilously thin. Bankers and brokers in the City of London have managed their affairs for years on the assurance of indemnities of one sort or another, though few would judge them blessed by their lawyers. Of course, some activities, like theft, are not made legitimate by virtue of longevity or complexity of practice, but the onus of proof is on the prosecution to prove that the Guinness indemnities were not in the wider interests of the shareholders of the company, but in the narrow service of a group of greedy men. Deal-makers like Roger Seelig, Patrick Spens and Elliott Bernerd are not inattentive to legal niceties, but have chosen to lead their business lives where legal history is made, not imitated. 'No lawyer will give you a clean opinion, but life has to go on. You have to form your view,' says one such deal-maker. Their instinctive urge to transact must be restrained by a management removed from the fray. It was this safeguard that was missing at Morgan Grenfell, where Christopher Reeves had got caught up in the excitement, and so unleashed the deal-makers. Even now, they seem undaunted. Roger Seelig, driving back to his country house at Tetbury on the evening of his first court appearance, was stopped by the police for speeding. 'You're a lucky man,' said Seelig to the policeman. 'You've got the thirteenth charge.' Once he had explained himself, the policeman let him off.[200] As Patrick Spens left Bow Street Magistrates Court on bail of £500,000 the day after his arrest, a mackintoshed journalist from the *News of the World* tugged at his arm and told him that the paper had discovered the whereabouts of his longstanding mistress, who had borne him a son. The reporter told him they would be running the story in Sunday's paper. Spens knew his wife was unaware that he even had a mistress. 'Must you do that? I need it like a hole in the head,' he pleaded. When the journalist insisted that they would run the story anyway, Spens reflected that his wife would be furious at the discovery, but it was not in his nature to deny a man the benefits of good information. 'Fine,' he said laconically.

NOTES

[1] *Private Eye*, 3 October 1986; *Sunday Times*, 26 October 1987; and *The Independent*, 26 October 1987.

[2] Ivan Fallon and James Srodes, *Takeovers*, Hamish Hamilton, 1987; Nick Kochan and Hugh Pym, *The Guinness Affair*, Christopher Helm, 1987; *The Observer*, 16 July 1989. Lewis was indicted in November 1988 for manipulating the shares of the Fireman's Fund during 1986 to help American Express sell its stake at a higher price. Vaskevitch was dismissed by Merrill Lynch in 1987 after being named in a $4 million insider-dealing suit brought by the United States Securities and Exchange Commission.

[3] Kochan and Pym, *op cit.*

[4] *The Times*, 20 January 1988.

[5] *ibid.*; *The Independent*, 20 January 1988.

[6] *ibid.*

[7] *The Independent*, 19 November 1987.

[8] Fallon and Srodes, *op. cit.*

[9] Kochan and Pym, *op. cit.*

[10] Fallon and Srodes, *op. cit.*

[11] Fallon and Srodes, *op. cit.*; Kochan and Pym, *op. cit.*

[12] *ibid.*

[13] The fellow director was Shaun Dowling (*The Independent*, 22 January 1988). The other comment was made by a partner of Herbert Smith at a Takeover Panel hearing on 25 August 1987 (*The Times*, 21 January 1988).

[14] *Financial Times*, 21 October 1983.

[15] *The Times*, 20 January 1988.

[16] *The Times*, 19 January 1988.

[17] *The Independent*, 25 January 1988.

[18] *The Times*, 20 January 1988; *The Independent*, 20 January 1988.

[19] *The Times*, 20 January 1988.

[20] *The Times*, 19 January 1988.

[21] *The Times*, 14 April 1988.

[22] Salz had written on a draft of the letter that it was 'read and approved' by these four (*The Times*, 22 January 1988).

[23] *The Times*, 19 January 1988.

[24] Kochan and Pym, *op. cit.*

[25] *Aquisitions Monthly*, May 1986.

[26] Kochan and Pym, *op. cit*; James Saunders, *Nightmare, The Ernest Saunders Story*, Hutchinson, 1989.

[27] Saunders, *op. cit.*

[28] Kochan and Pym, *op. cit.*

[29] Saunders, *op. cit.*

[30] Peter Pugh, *Is Guinness Good for You? The Bid for Distillers – The Inside Story*, Financial Training Publications, 1987; Saunders, *op. cit.*

[31] Saunders, *op. cit.*

[32] Pugh, *op. cit.*

[33] Saunders, *op. cit.*

[34] *Private Eye*, 5 September 1986.

[35] Saunders, *op. cit.*

[36] *The Times*, 19 March 1988.

[37] Kochan and Pym, *op. cit.*

[38] Fallon and Srodes, *op. cit.*

[39] *ibid.*

[40] *The Times*, 17 December 1987.

[41] *Sunday Times*, 13 July 1986; Saunders, *op. cit.*

[42] Saunders, *op. cit.*

[43] Kochan and Pym, *op. cit.*

[44] *ibid.*

[45] Saunders, *op. cit.*

[46] Kochan and Pym, *op. cit.*

[47] Letter sent by Bank Leu to Sir David Plastow, a non-executive director of Guinness, on 7 January 1987, listing arrangements entered into by Guinness without the knowledge of the Guinness board (*The Independent*, 27 January 1988).

[48] Saunders, *op cit*. At a meeting with Furer at Christmas 1985, Saunders says Furer suggested Guinness seek international quotations for its shares (p. 145) and at a similar meeting a year later asked if the DTI inquiry 'might prejudice the timetable for the planned introduction of Guinness shares in the US, Japanese and European stock markets' (p. 213).

[49] *Sunday Times*, 10 April 1988.

[50] *The Independent*, 24 March 1988.

[51] *Private Eye*, 4 and 18 March 1988.

[52] Jeffrey Robinson, *The Risk Takers*, Unwin, 1986; Richard Hall, *My Life With Tiny*, Faber & Faber, 1987.

[53] *Sunday Times*, 25 January 1987.

[54] *The Scotsman*, 8 January 1987; *Financial Times*, 8 January 1987.

[55] *Sunday Telegraph*, 10 January 1988; *The Times*, 11 January 1988; *Private Eye*, 30 October 1987.

[56] *The Times*, 18 March 1988.

[57] *The Times*, 18 March 1988; *Private Eye*, 30 October 1987.

[58] *The Times*, 18 March 1988.

[59] Fallon and Srodes, *op. cit.*

[60] *The Independent*, 29 July 1988.

[61] *Financial Times*, 3 December 1986.

[62] *The Times*, 3 December 1986.

[63] *Guardian*, 4 December 1986.

[64] *The Times*, 3 December 1986.

[65] *Guardian*, 4 December 1986.

[66] *The Times*, 5 December 1986.

[67] *Guardian*, 5 December 1986.

[68] *Observer*, 7 December 1986.

[69] Kochan and Pym, *op. cit.*

[70] *Observer*, 21 December 1986.

[71] *The Times*, 16 October 1987; *Daily Telegraph*, 20 December 1986.

[72] *Financial Times*, 13 December 1986.

[73] Kochan and Pym, *op. cit.*; Pugh, *op. cit.*

[74] Kochan and Pym, *op. cit.*

[75] Pugh, *op. cit.*

[76] Fallon and Srodes, *op. cit.*

[77] Kochan and Pym, *op. cit.*

[78] Fallon and Srodes, *op. cit.*

[79] *The Independent*, 2 December 1986, cited in Pugh, *op. cit.*

[80] *The Times*, 7 May 1988; *Financial Times*, 7 May 1988.

[81] *Observer*, 7 December 1986.

[82] *Private Eye*, Christmas 1986.

[83] *Sunday Telegraph*, 28 December 1986.

[84] *The Scotsman*, 8 January 1987; *Financial Times*, 8 January 1987.

[85] *ibid.*

[86] *The Times*, 21 March 1988.

[87] *Financial Times*, 8 January 1987.

[88] *The Times*, 21 March 1988.

[89] *The Times*, 30 December 1986.

[90] *Financial Times*, 31 December 1986.

[91] *The Times*, 19 October 1987.

[92] *The Times*, 31 December 1986.
[93] *Observer*, 28 October 1987.
[94] Fallon and Srodes, *op. cit.*; *Sunday Times*, 4 January 1987.
[95] *Sunday Times*, 4 January 1987.
[96] *Wall Street Journal*, 14 January 1987. The committee consisted of Lord Pennock, formerly chairman of BICC; Sir Peter Carey, formerly Permanent Secretary at the Department of Industry; Sir Kenneth Durham, chairman of Woolworth and former chairman of Unilever; and David Palmer, chairman of Willis Faber. It consulted J. E. H. 'Tim' Collins, the former chairman of the bank, and Lord O'Brien of Lothbury, the former governor of the Bank of England.
[97] *Financial Times*, 14 January 1987.
[98] *Financial Times*, 21 January 1987.
[99] *Wall Street Journal*, 14 January 1987.
[100] *Daily Telegraph*, 14 January 1987.
[101] *Financial Times*, 19 January 1987.
[102] *The Times*, 21 March 1988.
[103] *ibid*.
[104] *Business*, June 1987.
[105] Stephen Fay, *Portrait of an Old Lady*, Penguin, 1988.
[106] Fallon and Srodes, *op. cit.*
[107] Morgan Grenfell Group plc, Annual Report and Accounts, 1986; *Observer*, 16 July 1989.
[108] *Birmingham Post*, 21 January 1987.
[109] *The Times*, 21 March 1988.
[110] *The Times*, 6 January 1987.
[111] Kochan and Pym, *op. cit.*
[112] *Sunday Times*, 25 January 1987. The story was published as a statement by Roux, rather than as a leaked testimony to Napley, leading Roux to complain that it was a 'largely misleading and inaccurate version' (*Financial Times*, 27 January 1987).
[113] Saunders, *op. cit.*
[114] Kochan and Pym, *op. cit.*
[115] *Financial Times*, 20 January 1987; Pugh, *op. cit.*
[116] *The Times*, 23 January 1987.
[117] *Sunday Times*, 25 January 1987; Fallon and Srodes, *op. cit.*
[118] *ibid*.
[119] *Observer*, 27 March 1988.
[120] *ibid*.
[121] *Sunday Times*, 13 March 1988.
[122] William Kay, *Tycoons*, Pan, 1986.
[123] Robinson, *op. cit.*

124 *The Times*, 14 October 1987.

125 Fallon and Srodes, *op. cit.*

126 Margaret Reid, *The Secondary Banking Crisis 1974–75: Its Causes and Course*, Macmillan, 1982.

127 *Observer*, 16 August 1987.

128 Fallon and Srodes, *op. cit.*

129 *ibid.*

130 Robinson, *op. cit.*

131 *Sunday Times*, 13 March 1988.

132 *The Times*, 29 March 1988.

133 *Sunday Times*, 13 March 1988.

134 Saunders, *op. cit.* 'My father has always denied this,' wrote James Saunders (p. 227).

135 *Sunday Times*, 13 March 1988.

136 *ibid.*

137 *Observer*, 27 March 1988.

138 *ibid.*

139 Kochan and Pym, *op. cit.*; Pugh, *op cit.*

140 Fallon and Srodes, *op. cit.*

141 *Sunday Times*, 13 March 1988.

142 Fallon and Srodes, *op. cit.*

143 *Sunday Times*, 13 March 1988; Fallon and Srodes, *op. cit.*

144 *Observer*, 13 March 1988.

145 *Sunday Times*, 13 March 1988.

146 *The Independent*, 14 March 1988.

147 Fallon and Srodes, *op. cit*; *Sunday Times*, 13 March 1988.

148 *Observer*, 20 March 1988, 27 March 1988.

149 *Guardian*, 14 March 1988.

150 *Observer*, 13 March 1988.

151 *Observer*, 17 April 1988.

152 *Observer*, 13 March 1988.

153 *Observer*, 20 March 1988.

154 *ibid.*

155 *ibid.*

156 *Private Eye*, 5 February 1988.

157 *Observer*, 20 March 1988.

158 *The Independent*, 14 March 1988.

159 *ibid.*

160 *ibid.*

161 *Sunday Times*, 13 March 1988.

162 *ibid.*

163 *Private Eye*, 29 April 1988.

164 *The Independent*, 18 April 1988.

[165] *Private Eye*, 13 May 1988.
[166] *Private Eye*, 13 November 1987.
[167] Pugh, *op. cit.*
[168] *Financial Times*, 1 October 1983; Morgan Grenfell Holdings Limited, Annual Report and Accounts, 1983; Robinson, *op. cit.*
[169] *The Times*, 22 March 1988.
[170] Saunders, *op. cit.*
[171] *The Times*, 17 November 1987.
[172] *Observer*, 24 April 1988; *The Independent*, 1 March 1988.
[173] *The Times*, 17 November 1987; *The Independent*, 17 November 1987.
[174] Kochan and Pym, *op. cit.*; *The Times*, 11 May 1983; *The Independent*, 11 May 1988.
[175] *Financial Times*, 6 August 1988.
[176] *The Independent*, 2 June 1988.
[177] *The Independent*, 25 February 1988.
[178] Pugh, *op. cit.*
[179] *Financial Times*, 6 August 1988.
[180] *Observer*, 17 April 1988.
[181] *Financial Times*, 6 August 1988.
[182] *Observer*, 28 February 1988; *Guardian*, 17 June 1988.
[183] *The Spectator*, 11 June 1986.
[184] *Observer*, 17 April 1988.
[185] *ibid.*; *The Times*, 16 October 1987.
[186] *ibid.*
[187] *The Times*, 14 July 1987.
[188] *Observer*, 10 July 1988; *The Independent*, 24 February 1989.
[189] *The Independent*, 22 January 1988.
[190] *The Times*, 14 October 1987.
[191] Saunders, *op. cit.*
[192] *The Times*, 24 March 1988.
[193] *The Times*, 14 October 1987.
[194] *Private Eye*, 18 September 1987; *Private Eye*, 17 March 1989.
[195] *Financial Times*, 6 July 1988.
[196] *The Independent*, 11 March 1988.
[197] *The Independent*, 5 July 1988.
[198] *Observer*, 8 October 1989; *The Independent*, 9 October 1989; *The Independent*, 21 October 1989; *Observer*, 22 October 1989.
[199] *The Times*, 23 March 1988.
[200] *Business*, December 1987.

TWELVE

Whitewash

On the evening of Tuesday 13 January 1987, music-loving directors of Morgan Grenfell gathered at Covent Garden for a bank-sponsored performance of Verdi's *Otello* with Placido Domingo in the title role. The unfolding of the tragedy of the gullible Moor must have seemed as inexorable as their own. Earlier that day the Catto committee of non-executive directors had been appointed, in a last attempt to save Christopher Reeves and Graham Walsh from resignation. It was left, of course, to the Bank of England to spell out what they could both have read in any newspaper: if Reeves and Walsh had known what was going on, they were accomplices and ought to go; if they had not, they were incompetent and should not stay. 'They have done the honourable thing,' said Sir Peter Carey, the new head of Morgan's, of Reeves and Walsh after their departure, omitting to mention that they had been prised out and adding for good measure that there was 'no evidence' of any wrongdoing by them.[1] Their departure catapulted Carey, a 63-year-old ex-civil servant, up to the hierarchy. Suddenly, he found himself running the bank.

Carey was the only internal candidate sufficiently unthreatening and untainted to appeal to both his colleagues and the Bank of England as a replacement for Reeves, though not as chief executive ('Not a role I purport to fill,' he said).[2] The Bank seems from the outset to have favoured the appointment of Reeves's successor from outside Morgan Grenfell and, though Carey claimed to be considering internal as well as external candidates, the real search was being conducted around the globe by Norman, Broadbent International, the headhunters Carey had known at the Department of Industry and who had recruited Ian MacGregor to run British Steel in 1980.[3] To placate those who might suspect a cover-up, the Chancellor of the Exchequer, Nigel Lawson, told the Commons that the Bank of England had also insisted on the addition to the Catto committee of an independent auditor.[4] Carey tried to dampen the air of crisis by conceding that while the Bank of England had 'intimated to us the concern being felt'[5] Morgan Grenfell's affairs were not being orchestrated from Threadneedle Street:

No decisions were imposed by the Bank of England. The decisions taken represented a consensus of our views and of government's. The suggestion just came about that I might be the right person to do this interim business.[6]

This was stonewalling of the kind that Carey had perfected in countless appearances before committees of the House of Commons. Indeed, it was as if he were describing his emergence as leader of the Tory Party. In reality, of course, the Bank of England was taking as close an interest in implementing change at Morgan Grenfell as it could without endangering the stability of the bank, especially in urging the dismissal of all of those associated with Guinness. In an obvious attempt to spread the burden of public dismay weighing upon Morgan Grenfell, the Bank of England sent a warning to the twenty-four other merchant banks, to ensure that, in the words of Kenneth Fleet, 'those most successful at bringing in the fees do not suppose they have 007 designation'.[7] Pending the publication of the Catto committee's report, Carey appointed himself chairman of a temporary executive committee made up of representatives of all the main businesses. They were Blaise Hardman (Morgan Grenfell Securities), Charles Rawlinson (Banking), Christopher Whittington (Overseas Offices) and Sir John Sparrow (Morgan Grenfell Asset Management).[8] Richard Webb, a reassuringly uncontroversial figure, was added a day later as the Corporate Finance representative.[9] They were all men who had prospered under Christopher Reeves, but Carey could scarcely recast the management completely ahead of the Catto committee's report.[10]

As in the Collier affair, Carey's first task was to distance the bank as far as possible from the unseemly revelations being disgorged daily by the quality press. Seelig and those who worked with him were an appropriate starting-point:

We had developed an over-eagerness which led perhaps to a bit of arrogance but this was confined to a few people . . . I am confident we know what happened. But if any other persons did emerge as having been involved in this affair, we shall deal with them in the same way. It is conceivable that one or two people were involved at a junior level and we shall deal with this. We are quite determined to clean ourselves.[11]

A partner of Slaughter & May, Michael Pescod, was on almost permanent duty at Morgan Grenfell once the Guinness affair erupted, and he joined the Bank of England in advising Carey to rid the payroll of all those even remotely associated with the Guinness account. This was done as slowly and surreptitiously as possible. One Saturday morning in the summer of 1987 Carey even assured a crisis meeting of directors at the Hyde Park Hotel that the Bank of England was not applying pressure for anyone else to go as a result of the Guinness affair, but fresh departures started almost as soon as he spoke. Elliott Bernerd, who had been linked with the Guinness share purchases by Violet Seulberger-Simon, was the first of a new batch of departures. He resigned as chairman of Morgan Grenfell Laurie in August 1987 to 'go back to being a principal' in the property market, denying any involvement in the illicit purchases.[12] Piers de Montfort, a junior executive believed to have dealt on Seelig's behalf with Boesky and L. F. Rothschild, went next, resigning 'by mutual agreement' in September 1987 to take up a job the bank had found for him at Morgan Stanley.[13] Philip Evans, the other main assistant to Seelig in the bid for Distillers, who by July had the additional disadvantage of association with his brother's extraordinarily timely purchase of shares in Arthur Bell, went last, in April 1988. At the time of de Montfort's exit he had to deny rumours that the bank had also asked for his resignation. Morgan Grenfell insisted that he kept a low profile, denying him access to clients, until it was safe for him to leave inconspicuously and take up a job at the French bank, Paribas.[14]

These departures followed swiftly on the news of an attempt by Michael Pescod, a partner at Slaughter & May, to clarify the terms on which past and present Morgan Grenfell staff associated with the Distillers bid, including Seelig, Evans and de Montfort, would be interviewed.

Until then, they had been interviewed only by the Department of Trade and Industry inspectors. Pescod was concerned that the bank might be vulnerable to possible prosecution under Section 151 of the Companies Act, the clause which makes it unlawful for companies to offer financial assistance to buy shares in takeovers.[15] By early September he had received informal assurances from the Crown Prosecution Service that no current employees would be prosecuted as a result of the Guinness affair.[16] This was a material reassurance, because both the new Guinness board and the Fraud Squad alleged that around a third of the £2.9 million Roger Seelig is charged with stealing stemmed from overcharging by the bank, the surplus funds being diverted to those members of the 'fan club' – Henry Ansbacher, the Rudani Corporation and L. F. Rothschild – recruited by Morgan Grenfell.[17] 'When a customer is unhappy with the level of fees for any reason, it's something one is prepared to talk about,' said George Law.[18] Some think that Morgan Grenfell could not fire Evans and de Montfort – and so relinquish control over them – until Pescod had received assurances that the Crown Prosecution Service would prosecute only individuals and not the bank. Certainly their interviews with the Fraud Squad, which Morgan Grenfell also wished to monitor, were postponed until he had completed the negotiations.[19] Reports later circulated that 10 to 15 employees of Morgan Grenfell were questioned by the Fraud Squad in late September and that de Montfort had been approached to act as a witness for the prosecution.[20] Though both Evans and de Montfort were compensated with jobs elsewhere and, in Sir Peter Carey's words, 'We do take the advice of our solicitors',

Morgan Grenfell's eagerness to avoid corporate responsibility for the actions of its staff looked distinctly shabby.[21] Within a few weeks it was able to say that it would be 'amazed' if any current employees were prosecuted as a result of the Guinness enquiry.[22] The dispute with the new Guinness management over the exorbitant size of Morgan Grenfell's fees for the Distillers takeover was settled separately by the repayment of about £1 million.[23]

Clearly, the bank's explanation of its involvement in the Guinness affair – that Seelig had exceeded his authority – was implausible unless Morgan Grenfell admitted that management controls had failed to restrain him. The Catto committee was an obvious expression of this confessional necessity. 'What we must do is establish adequate self-restraint without damaging our flair,' said Carey.[24] There was much worthy discussion on how to meet the mundane demands of man and risk management, cost control, training and the like. The management consultancy arm of the bank's auditors, Spicer & Pegler, were invited to make recommendations. Directors of planning and personnel, stricter financial controls and a training course for graduate staff were introduced, but the main novelty was committees.[25] The Catto report, submitted to the Bank of England at the end of January, resulted in the formation of seven.[26] The one that mattered most was the Group Executive Committee, chaired by Sir Peter Carey, because it incorporated the chairmen of all the other committees. One of these – the Supervisory Committee – addressed the danger of another Seelig. Chaired by Christopher Whittington, it was charged, in a passage worthy of Sir Humphrey Appleby, with 'preserving the integrity of the bank as a corporate entity as distinct from day-to-day management', Day-to-day management was handed to four 'Operating Committees', one for each of Corporate Finance (chaired by Richard Webb), Asset Management (Michael Dobson), Equity Securities (John Holmes) and the newly renamed Eurobond and International Banking Department, Debt Securities and Banking (Christopher Whittington again). Each of these areas was called a 'business stream', in the expectation that this elliptical phrase would somehow lend coherence to the hectic growth of recent years.

The committees were intended to involve the younger directors, many of whom felt excluded under the cabalistic management of Reeves, more intimately in the decision-making process. Anxieties that staff further down the line had become restless and alienated as their numbers had grown were addressed by a new Administration Committee chaired by Lord Pennock. The old guard still lingered on, albeit in truncated roles. Charles Rawlinson, retiring on health grounds, stayed on as a vice-chairman. Sir John Sparrow became a roving finance director and Blaise Hardman the chairman of Morgan Grenfell Securities. Jon Perry was on the Group Executive Committee in Whittington's old role of group director of overseas companies. The most extraordinary newcomer was John Rawlings, the director in charge of interest-rate and currency swaps, who had somehow muscled on to the Group Executive Committee with, oddly enough, the same responsibility for Debt Securities and Banking as Christopher Whittington.[27] As subsequent events showed, his arrival in the highest echelons of the bank reflected a fundamental shift of emphasis within the Eurobond Department. Though all the changes were sold to the press as a radical departure from the *laissez-faire* management philosophy of Christopher Reeves, it matched exactly what Reeves had been planning to do before he was despatched by the Bank of England:

Our objective for 1987 is to delegate decision-making and policy to the younger chaps in the business streams . . . We must have another look at making our structure reflect our business streams more closely.[28]

It was not surprising. Continuity and committees came naturally to a former Permanent Secretary. A complete break with the past awaited the appointment of a new chief executive.

Bemused staff and journalists ransacked the gobbledygook for its real meaning. It was clearly a defeat for the acolytes of Christopher Reeves. Blaise Hardman had been kicked upstairs and replaced by John Holmes. Charles Rawlinson and Sir John Sparrow (replaced by Michael Dobson) were in that state of suspended animation by which Morgan Grenfell chose to retire its senior members: the gradual stripping of functions. As the technique became increasingly popular, the syndrome became known as 'the departure lounge'.[29] Jon Perry had lost control of the Eurobond Department, now augmented by the fusion of Eurobond, gilt and treasury trading. Only one of Reeves's close associates, Christopher Whittington, had prospered from the management reshuffle, and this proved temporary. The decision not to appoint him chief executive finally scotched any suggestion that an internal appointment was likely.[30] Yet it was not an unqualified victory for the faction within the bank popularized in the press as the 'Young Turks'. The *ancien-régime* Richard Webb had been confirmed as head of Corporate Finance, if only because Young Turks were temporarily unfashionable in the takeover business. George Magan, who had rivalled Seelig in conducting aggressive and public takeovers, had miraculously rediscovered the virtues of a low profile and Anthony Richmond-Watson, who had handled the Guinness bid for Bell's, was similarly tainted. For the driving Michael Dobson – 'I suppose you needed drive,' he said of his early successes[31] – the promotion was an unmitigated triumph. The undoubted success of the Asset Management Department probably owed less to his gladhanding approach and more to the orthodox and painstaking efforts of James Norton, Patrick Dawnay, Philip Douglas and Piotr Poloniecki. Norton, however, was drawn upwards into the hierarchy as group personnel director[32] by the vacuum which followed the departure of Reeves and Walsh, and Dawnay, Douglas and Poloniecki had all departed for fresh challenges.[33] Dobson had ascended within his own department, and thence within the bank, without serious challenge. John Holmes had leapfrogged Blaise Hardman to assume full control of the securities operation. In a significant appointment, John Rawlings was elevated to the committee from running swaps.[34]

A new chief executive, the forty-six-year-old John Craven, was not appointed until April 1987 and did not start work until May. He was an odd, if cosmopolitan, choice. Educated in South Africa, he had a law degree from Cambridge and an accountancy qualification from Canada. He was then chairman of Phoenix Securities, a tiny merchant-banking concern with just four partners. His career to date, though not dilettantish, suggested an aversion to large organizations like Morgan Grenfell. He was, in the words of one observer, 'the best financial negotiator in the City, but the worst financial manager', which was rather the reverse of Morgan Grenfell's current requirements. Once Warburg's youngest director, in 1973 he became, at the age of thirty-one, chief executive of the Eurobond house Credit Suisse White Weld, staying for eight of the market's formative years before rebelling against the merger with First Boston in 1978, which he felt created 'a machine to pump out ever increasing volumes of Eurobonds'.[35] He returned to Warburg's as a vice-chairman a year later, where myth holds it that he lost a succession battle to David Scholey but Craven claims simply that 'the personal relationships had become more formal in my absence'.[36] He rejected Scholey's offer to run their Eurobond operation. Instead he set up Merrill Lynch International in London in 1980, but stayed only a year, describing it as 'a very unhappy experience', in which the American giant refused to delegate, giving him only 'responsibility without authority'.[37] In 1981 he went to Merrill Lynch's chairman in New York, Donald Regan, later President Reagan's Treasury Secretary, and resigned, but they generously bought out his three-year contract.[38] At Phoenix Securities, which he founded in his Chelsea house in 1981 with £75,000 of Merrill Lynch's money, Craven seemed finally not only to have rejected the City establishment but to have returned to a classic, but then unfashionable, type of merchant banking: advising disinterestedly in exchange for fees. Early successes in restructuring Mexican debts and backing a C$2 million share offering for two Canadian gold-mining companies, added to his already considerable wealth.[39] The creation of Phoenix also coincided with the preparations for Big Bang, when disinterested advisers were in short supply. Though its role as a marriage broker between jobbers, brokers and bankers has been exaggerated, Phoenix did act for Wedd Durlacher in the creation of one of the monuments to Big Bang, Barclay's De Zoete Wedd (BZW), and advised Orion Royal Bank during its merger talks with Pember & Boyle, so Craven knew the weaknesses of Morgan Grenfell's broking arm.

Craven came to Morgan Grenfell with a loathing for the politics of large organizations, an entrepreneurial flair ideally suited to small ones, proven limitations as a manager, a distaste for Eurobonds and a belief that the securities business in general was an 'unsound policy' for a merchant bank.[40] Since Morgan Grenfell exhibited most of the facets of banking he professed to dislike, some wondered why he had taken the job at all. The main reason was probably money. Morgan Grenfell agreed to buy not just John Craven but his entire firm as well. The total consideration was £15 million, £1.26 million paid in cash and £13.74 million in convertible bonds. It was a sizeable sum for a five-year track record, pre-tax profits of just £2.5 million, four partners, three associates and five to seven support staff.[41] Craven controlled 39.5 per cent of Phoenix Securities, so the deal netted him and his interests £740,825 in cash and £5.2 million in bonds.[42] For Morgan Grenfell, it was doubtless part of the price of having Craven at all. Cynics noted that the high proportion of convertible bonds in the consideration gave Craven a strong incentive to cash in quickly by selling the bank to the highest bidder, rather than cash in slowly (or maybe not at all) by the tedious processes of profit-making. With its valuable independence compromised, cynics assumed that Phoenix would be starved of business unless it could arrange the sale of Morgan Grenfell, pocket the proceeds and move on. The takeover speculation that had dogged Morgan Grenfell almost from the moment it went public fuelled expectations that Craven would find deliverance from outside the bank. This increased when he finally dislodged the tenacious Lord Catto and replaced him as chairman with the deferential

Sir Peter Carey, though Catto travelled only as far as upstairs. The honorary post of 'President' was specially created for him at that year's Annual General Meeting.[43]

On the morning of Thursday 3 July 1986, the first day of dealings in Morgan Grenfell's shares, a premium of 16p to the £5 sale price had developed. By the evening it had turned into a discount of 15p and did not recover, settling at around £3.60–£3.70 in the autumn of that year. The anticipated decline in mega-bids after the Guinness affair and the fierce competition of the Big Bang era were mainly responsible, but errors were creeping in. In December 1986 the bank's role in the Channel Tunnel financing was downgraded after difficulties in raising £206 million in the initial share placing at the end of October.[44] The first company flotation handled by Morgan Grenfell Securities – the offer for sale of the European operations of the Avis car-hire company – was a flop.[45] In the spring of 1987, Morgan Grenfell's Jersey office was implicated in the Irangate scandal. The four directors of Morgan Grenfell Jersey turned out to be also the directors and shareholders of KMS ('Keeny Meeny Services'), the company used by Colonel Oliver North to ship arms to the Contras.[46] With the share prices low, the bank began to attract speculators.

The Collier and Guinness affairs, by making Morgan Grenfell more vulnerable, added to the takeover speculation which sustained the share price of most of the London merchant banks for the year between Big Bang and the Crash. In the autumn of 1986 the American arbitrageur, Saul Steinberg, built up a near 15 per cent holding in Morgan Grenfell's before it was safely passed in 1987 to a friendly investor. In January 1987 the Australian insurance magnate, Larry Adler, emerged with a speculative 7.4 per cent stake in Hill Samuel. He was quickly joined by two other antipodean entrepreneurs, Kerry Packer and Ron Brierley, and between them they accumulated a stake of 26 per cent. In the summer of 1987 Union Bank of Switzerland came close to an agreed merger with Hill Samuel and, though the Swiss pulled out in August, they and Adler put Hill Samuel 'in play', a feeling which rubbed off elsewhere. Morgan Grenfell's own share price rose 63p the day Union Bank announced it was talking to Hill Samuel,[47] whose corporate finance chiefs were later sacked – at the behest of the Bank of England – for trying to sell their department to BZW. Hill Samuel eventually succumbed to the Trustee Savings Bank for £777 million in November 1987.[48] Many people inside Morgan Grenfell shared the received opinion in the City that merchant banks were vulnerable to foreign predators, Philip Evans saying as much to a national newspaper.[49] Takeover fever gripped all the staff for much of 1987 and it was no surprise to find that it was Morgan Grenfell, via its Australian office, who first advised Larry Adler to buy shares in Hill Samuel.[50]

The earliest suitor for the hand of Morgan Grenfell seems to have been Drexel Burnham Lambert, the modern incarnation of the Philadelphia investment bank founded by Francis Drexel, the father of one of J. P. Morgan's earliest partners in New York, Anthony Drexel.[51] It tried at first just to tempt away Roger Seelig, approaching him several times up to September 1986. Seelig was then widely understood to be on the verge of detaching himself from Morgan Grenfell anyway, and setting up a corporate-finance boutique with George Magan. As Morgan Grenfell's share price plummeted, Drexel pondered buying the entire bank instead, though it is unlikely that the Bank of England would have approved.[52] Drexel was probed by the American authorities as part of the Boesky investigation and was itself later linked with the investigation into Guinness.[53] After the Guinness affair, Hong Kong & Shanghai, Lloyd's Bank, Barclay's Bank and Deutsche Bank, not all of whom would be much more acceptable to Threadneedle Street, were variously rumoured to be looking at a bid for Morgan's.[54] Lloyd's admitted that Morgan Grenfell would be 'a good short cut to expanding our activities' and Sir Peter Carey, presumably with the implicit support of the Bank of England, was not entirely discouraging:[55]

We would definitely prefer to remain an independent force. But other banks live very well as part of a larger group. There might be a price at which it would be in the best interest of our shareholders to accept.[56]

In April 1987 a mysterious 4.4 per cent stake in the bank was uncovered, hidden behind a nominee company owned by the Bank of England itself. Though Morgan Grenfell asked the Bank to identify the ultimate shareholder, it proved exempt from laws requiring disclosure.[57] It later turned out to be the secretive and powerful Kuwait Investment Office, which has a penchant for taking stakes in vulnerable companies.[58] It was understood to have bought the shares from GEC, which had acquired them in the expectation of a rapid increase in their value. That spring Carey admitted that the bank had received a number of 'tentative' and 'goodwill' approaches since January, though 'not from the expected sources'.[59] They were probably from Lloyd's Bank, still looking for a late re-entry to the securities markets, and Shearson Lehman and Kidder Peabody, two American investment banks looking for a friendly merger with a strong corporate finance team.[60] Kidder is certainly known to have made firm overtures. Shearson, which had already devoured the prestigious Wall Street firm of Lehman Brothers, emerged in July with a 2.7 per cent stake in Morgan Grenfell, apparently acquired via seven nominee accounts in just two weeks in January.[61] Presumably rebuffed, it had sold its stake by August.[62] Just a few days later Robert Holmes à Court, chairman of the Australian Bell Group, disclosed a 5.2 per cent stake in Morgan Grenfell acquired for £34 million via his British insurance company, Dewey Warren. He had bought the bulk of it from the Kuwait Investment Office, until then thought to be helping the Bank of England protect Morgan Grenfell.[63] For the first time since the flotation over a year before, the Morgan Grenfell share price cleared £5.[64]

Holmes à Court, the most brilliant stock-market operator of the bull market of the 1980s, was clearly not interested in buying Morgan Grenfell. Much thought was devoted both in and outside the bank as to his likely motives. Speculation suggested that he would merge Morgan's with the Standard Chartered Bank, where he was deputy chairman and a 15 per cent shareholder, or somehow use Morgan Grenfell and Willis Faber to build a vast financial empire in London. Craven later confessed that Holmes à Court did suggest a merger with Standard Chartered.[65] Sir Peter Carey, deputizing for John Craven, who was away in Canada, assured the press that it was merely an arbitrage because all the staff would leave if Holmes à Court took over. He then added to the air of unease by offering to meet the bank's latest tormentor.[66] In fact, all Holmes à Court had done was put Morgan Grenfell 'in play' as a takeover candidate and the arbitrageurs duly descended on the shares. Alan Bond, chairman of the aggressive Australian beer and television company, Bond Corporation, and a client of the bank, acquired 2 per cent.[67] 'He is a friend of the bank,' claimed a spokesman. Lord Hanson, Britain's leading takeover practitioner, then emerged with 3.3 per cent. His intentions were unknown, but assumed to be hostile, since Hanson was a former director of Lloyd's Bank and had just taken a sizeable interest in the Midland Bank. Seelig's friend, Jacob Rothschild, bought 1 per cent.[68] Morgan Grenfell was starting to conform to the pattern established by Hill Samuel. 'We do not find it satisfactory that some of our shares have been bought by people with such a short-term attitude,' moaned John Craven, without ruling out an agreeable merger.[69] The bank's largest shareholder, Willis Faber, was strapped for cash after merging with another insurance broker, Stewart Wrightson, and increasingly nervous about the present and prospective costs of maintaining a sizeable stake in a vulnerable and scandal-prone merchant bank which had only recently embarked on a massive experiment in the securities markets.[70] As David Palmer, Willis Faber's chairman, put it on the eve of the stock-market crash of 1987:

We would not be an unwilling seller if an acceptable offer came along. We have to listen to any approach that comes to us . . . It could never have been said that it was not for sale.[71]

Unfortunately, the timing was not propitious. Even Hill Samuel's pathetic tryst with the Swiss was outshone by the cheek of the Saatchi brothers' offer to buy the Midland Bank. In September Equiticorp, an over-borrowed and ramshackle banker and carpet manufacturer from New Zealand, won control of Guinness Peat, owners of the Guinness Mahon merchant bank, despite protests from the Bank of England. With the Johnson Matthey Bankers scandal still fresh in public minds, the Bank began to fret. The governor, Robin Leigh-Pemberton, said he would not allow banks 'at the core of our financial system' to succumb to industrial, commercial, or foreign bidders without being passed 'fit and proper' by him, though he let it be known that his protection did not necessarily extend to merchant banks.[72] A Banking Act giving effect to these powers had just come into force. In the end, Leigh-Pemberton was never challenged. Five days after he spoke the Stock Market crashed and Robert Holmes à Court was all but ruined, the value of his 5.6 per cent stake in Morgan Grenfell falling by £19 million.[73] The share price wilted from £5.50 to only £3 in the crash itself and carried on falling until the spring of 1988. For the time being, Morgan Grenfell was left to work out its own destiny.

From the moment that the Guinness scandal broke, Morgan Grenfell's competitors watched eagerly for signs that the bank's Corporate Finance Department was losing business or clients or perhaps just its touch. There was plenty of further gloating over the humiliating abandonment of the £1 billion BTR bid – via Morgan Grenfell – for the St Helen's glassmaker Pilkington Brothers, which had suddenly become much loved. 'BTR's decision is a manifestation of the workings of the free market, whose judgement they may not always respect but whose verdict they will always accept,' said BTR's chairman, Sir Owen Green, in a pithy phrase that must have been composed by George Magan.[74] In fact, the market had little to do with the outcome. Once the Guinness scandal broke and Seelig had gone, even Reeves recognized this. 'The goalposts have moved,' he told the Board but, for once, valour got the better of discretion and George Magan ploughed on with the £1.2 billion bid for Pilkington. Its abandonment was delayed until within a few hours of the departure of Reeves and Walsh. Dispassionate observers wondered aloud why Green and George Magan had been so foolhardy as to pursue the bid at all, let alone for so long, given the circumstances of its initiation.

The assault on Pilkington was launched on 20 November, less than a week after Boesky had confessed publicly and only ten days after Collier's resignation. Within less than a fortnight, Morgan Grenfell was engulfed in the Guinness scandal. With its profits recovering and its investment in research and development paying off, Pilkington was not an easy target anyway. Now its long-range thinking and paternalistic management of the only major business in a northern town became symbols of industrial virtue. BTR and Morgan Grenfell, lampooned as venal accountants, asset-strippers and insider-dealers, were its City antonyms. Pilkington's advisers, Schroder Wagg, had the company's auditors, Coopers & Lybrand, prepare a report detailing BTR's obsession with short-term performance. Though it was later denounced by the Institute of Chartered Accountants' Disciplinary Committee for what BTR called 'substantial inaccuracies', Schroder's had understood the political climate rather better than its opponents. Already debarred by his membership of the Guinness family from full involvement in a scandal being probed by his own department, the continuation of the BTR bid for Pilkington forced the Secretary of State for Trade and Industry, Paul Channon, to choose in an election year between capitulating to the growing furore and adding to it. He bravely chose the latter, deciding not to refer the bid to the Monopolies and Mergers Commission on grounds that the implications for competition did not warrant it. It was a major embarrassment to a Government which had invested its prestige in popular capitalism, exposing it to charges of cronyism in the City and fitting Labour's depiction of a country divided between northern destitution and southern privilege. Thereafter, the bid was simply howled down by an unlikely alliance of journalists, trade unionists, bankers and politicians from all the major parties. 'Big contested bids are not flavour of the month just now, particularly in the run-up to an election. No client should be under any illusion about the possible political reaction if he launches one,' said Richard Webb.[75]

Pilkington was only the most obvious of Morgan Grenfell's difficulties in the post-Guinness environment. The principal threat was the defection of clients. MEPC, one of the bank's oldest clients, used Warburg instead in 1987 and so did Legal & General.[76] Terence Conran, who stood bail for Roger Seelig, said he was concerned that 'someone who did a first-rate job for us and helped Guinness win the battle for Distillers is no longer there' but has not used the bank in the defence of Storehouse against a range of actual and assumed bidders since then.[77] The Dee Corporation, latterly renamed Gateway, defected to Lazard's.[78] By Morgan Grenfell's own estimation, the number of active clients dropped from 84 in 1986 to 62 in 1987, though bids, especially hostile ones, tailed off anyway in a year which included the Guinness affair, Pilkington, a General Election and the October stock market crash.[79] In fact, the effects of the Guinness affair were felt much more slowly than anybody could have anticipated. *Crawford's Directory*, which recorded 143 clients for Morgan Grenfell in 1986, recorded 131.5 in 1987, 117.5 in 1988 and 95 in 1989, suggesting a slow attrition rather than rapid losses. Some clients were fiercely loyal. 'Why shouldn't we use them? We think they're both very good, well organized businesses that have helped us over the years,' said Stanley Metcalfe, the RHM chief executive, when the press suggested he might drop Morgan Grenfell and Cazenove.[80] Rivals started a whispering campaign, letting it be known that they thought Morgan Grenfell was losing more often than it was winning and that the bank's increased prominence in defence rather than attack testified to intellectual atrophy. Certainly the loss of Roger Seelig deprived it of a fertile source of ideas for deals, and what clients he and the bank might have attracted without Guinness will never be known.

Yielding to the obvious, Carey pledged the bank to a less 'robust and aggressive' approach:

Guinness was the apogee of hostile bids. I think it was pretty distasteful and I regret the part we played in going over the top on that. I want to draw a line under what has happened and make a new start.[81]

As Webb pointed out, even without Walsh and Seelig the bank still had '14 corporate finance directors other than Roger Seelig'.[82] In 1987 Webb himself guided Scottish & Newcastle Breweries to victory over Matthew Brown at the third attempt, which was a triumph of sorts.[83] Belated attempts were made to drum up business abroad. New York was successful enough, the bank ranking second only to Lazard's in the value of its transatlantic takeover business in 1986, including Boot's $555 million takeover of Flint Laboratories, but the United States was almost the only market trawled by British predators, and the bank could not rely for continuing success there on domestic clients.[84] In the spring of 1987 the New York mergers and acquisitions team began to disintegrate in the face of insensitive management by Geoff Hill, the abrasive Australian despatched from Sydney only four months earlier.[85] He left abruptly to run his own business again. (Called Overseas Corporate Funds, it invests in New York for Hill's former Australian clients, like Alan Bond.)[86] Three senior American executives left at the same time to join Prudential Bache.[87] The results from elsewhere were desultory, mainly because few countries other than Britain and the United States have much of a takeover market. Phoenix Securities won some advisory roles in France, arranging financial mergers ahead of the deregulation of the Paris *Bourse* and a corporate finance team, headed by a Japanese-speaking recruit from Baring's, was despatched to Tokyo to whet the muted Japanese appetite for acquisitions in Europe, without much immediate success.[88]

Despite these problems, the wider effects of the Guinness affair were ultimately felt most keenly not in the strongest parts of the bank, like Corporate Finance, but in its newest and weakest. There, the irruption of the crisis laid bare the problems all the excitement of recent years had so helpfully concealed and rendered them even harder to resolve. To this extent, it was misleading to suggest that the Guinness scandal was purely the work of individuals exceeding their authority or of management controls breaking down in one area of the bank. Rather, it was the failure of the entire corporate culture of the Reeves regime to adapt to fundamental changes in the nature and scale of the business. It mattered less that the Guinness scandal could not have happened at S. G. Warburg – where no director would ever have been accorded the leeway given to, say, Roger Seelig or George Magan – than that the decision to give them a free rein was passed off under Reeves as a form of management for a business increased vastly in size and tackling almost for the first time the unfamiliar risks of the securities business.[89] 'Picking up the ball and running with it' had ended in scandal for the Corporate Finance Department, but it ended in commercial disaster for the securities businesses, where bankers, brokers, jobbers, Eurobond traders and research analysts, many of them drawn from a wide variety of firms and backgrounds, commingled.

NOTES

[1] *Financial Times*, 21 January 1987; *The Independent*, 21 January 1987.
[2] *Financial Times*, 3 February 1987.
[3] *Sunday Telegraph*, 25 January 1987; *Financial Times*, 27 April 1987.
[4] *The Independent*, 21 January 1987.
[5] *ibid.*
[6] *Observer*, 25 January 1987.
[7] *The Times*, 28 January 1987.

[8] *Financial Times*, 21 January 1987.

[9] *Financial Times*, 22 January 1987.

[10] It later emerged that Morgan Grenfell had asked the Bank of England for help in arranging loans from a group of commercial banks if there was a run on the bank's deposits in the wake of the resignations (*Standard*, 20 February 1987; *Financial Times*, 21 February 1987; *Daily Mail*, 21 February 1987; *Investors Chronicle*, 20 February 1987).

[11] *Sunday Telegraph*, 25 January 1987.

[12] *Financial Times*, 4 August 1987; *Observer*, 9 August 1987.

[13] *Private Eye*, 18 September 1987.

[14] *Guardian*, 7 September 1987; *The Independent*, 7 September 1987; *The Independent*, 28 April 1988.

[15] *Observer*, 16 August 1987; *The Times*, 17 August 1987; *Daily Telegraph*, 17 August 1987.

[16] *Sunday Times*, 6 September 1987.

[17] *The Times*, 19 October 1987.

[18] *Wall Street Journal*, 30 April 1987.

[19] *Daily Telegraph*, 7 September 1987.

[20] *The Times*, 24 September 1987; *Daily Express*, 24 September 1987.

[21] *Observer*, 16 August 1987.

[22] *The Independent*, 4 September 1987.

[23] *Wall Street Journal*, 30 April 1987.

[24] *Observer*, 25 January 1987.

[25] *The Economist*, 17 January 1987.

[26] *The Times*, 3 February 1987.

[27] *Financial Times*, 3 February 1987.

[28] *The Economist*, 17 January 1987.

[29] *The Observer Magazine*, 30 July 1989.

[30] *The Economist*, 5 February 1987.

[31] Nicholas Shakespeare, *Londoners*, Sidgwick & Jackson, 1986.

[32] Morgan Grenfell Group plc, Annual Report and Acounts, 1987.

[33] *Daily Telegraph*, 25 November 1986.

[34] *The Economist*, 15 February 1987.

[35] *Observer*, 26 April 1987.

[36] *Wall Street Journal*, 27 April 1987.

[37] *Sunday Times*, 26 April 1987; *Observer*, 26 April 1987.

[38] *Wall Street Journal*, 27 April 1987.

[39] *Sunday Telegraph*, 26 April 1987.

[40] *Observer*, 26 April 1987.

[41] Morgan Grenfell Group plc, Annual Report and Accounts, 1987.

[42] *Euromoney*, June 1988.

[43] *Financial Times*, 24 April 1987.

[44] *Financial Times*, 4 and 10 December 1986.

[45] *The Independent*, 10 December 1986.

[46] *Financial Weekly*, 16 April and 16 July 1987; *The Observer Magazine*, 30 July 1989.

[47] *Sunday Times*, 12 July 1987.

[48] *Global Finance*, February 1988.

[49] *Today*, 22 October 1986.

[50] *Australian Financial Review*, 29 January 1987; *Daily Telegraph*, 6 March 1987; *Daily Express*, 6 March 1987; *Today*, 6 March 1987.

[51] Vincent P. Carosso, *The Morgans: Private International Bankers, 1854–1913*, Harvard University Press, 1987.

[52] *Standard*, 23 October and 20 November 1986.

[53] *Sunday Times*, 1 February 1987.

[54] *Guardian*, 18 November 1986; *The Times*, 2 February 1987; *Guardian*, 11 February 1987.

[55] *The Scotsman*, 18 March 1987.

[56] *Observer*, 25 January 1987.

[57] *Guardian*, 29 April 1987; *Financial Times*, 29 April 1987; *The Independent*, 29 April 1987.

[58] *Standard*, 17 July 1987.

[59] *Financial Times*, 27 May 1987.

[60] *The Times*, 20 July 1987; *The Independent*, 20 July 1987.

[61] *Sunday Times*, 12 July 1987.

[62] *Observer*, 2 August 1987.

[63] *Sunday Telegraph*, 19 July 1987.

[64] *Standard*, 17 July 1987.

[65] *Observer*, 29 May 1988.

[66] *Observer*, 19 July 1987.

[67] *The Independent*, 17 August 1987.

[68] *Sunday Times*, 23 August 1987; *Observer* 23 August 1987; *Sunday Telegraph*, 23 August 1987.

[69] *Sunday Times*, 30 August 1987.

[70] *Sunday Times*, 18 October 1987.

[71] *Daily Telegraph*, 19 October 1987.

[72] *Financial Times*, 15 October 1987.

[73] *Daily Telegraph*, 1 April 1988.

[74] Ivan Fallon and James Srodes, *Takeovers*, Hamish Hamilton, 1987.

[75] *Financial Times*, 22 January 1987.

[76] *Euromoney*, June 1988.

[77] *Wall Street Journal*, 14 January 1987.

[78] *Financial Times*, 19 December 1987.
[79] Morgan Grenfell Group plc, Annual Reports and Accounts, 1986 and 1987.
[80] *Standard*, 6 February 1987.
[81] *Sunday Times*, 25 January 1987.
[82] *Acquisitions Monthly*, January 1988.
[83] *The Economist*, 5 February 1987.
[84] *Acquisitions Monthly*, March 1987.
[85] *Euromoney*, June 1988: *The Observer Magazine*, 30 July 1989.
[86] *The Times*, 9 May 1987; *Euromoney*, June 1988; *Australian Financial Review*, 7 May 1987.
[87] *Financial Times*, 12 May 1987.
[88] *Financial Times*, 18 September 1987.
[89] *The Economist*, 25 June 1988.

THIRTEEN

The Good, The Bad and The Ugly

As soon as **Big Bang** occurred on 27 October 1986 all gilt-edged dealerships, including Morgan Grenfell Government Securities, began to lose money.[1] This was hardly surprising. The trade in gilts for clients nearly doubled, from £1.25 billion a day to over £2 billion a day, and the total trade in gilts in London, both for clients and between market-makers, doubled to nearly £4 billion a day. Although turnover was substantially higher, the abolition of minimum commissions meant that profits were slim. Even before **Big Bang** abolished minimum commissions, commission income on long- and medium-dated gilts averaged only 0.09 per cent[2] or less, while commissions on short-dated securities, which were negotiable before **Big Bang**, reduced the overall average to 0.02 per cent after it.[3] After **Big Bang**, with 27 primary dealers and around £600 million of capital chasing business formerly handled by three principal jobbers with £80 million, commissions disappeared altogether.[4] Revenues then depended only on dealing 'spreads' – the difference between the price at which the gilts are bought and the price at which they are sold – but these too were squeezed. Average spreads halved from roughly 0.25 per cent to 0.125 per cent. Unlike share-dealers, gilt-dealers advertised not the price at which they would sell and the price at which they would buy, but an indicative 'middle' price, with the actual price fixed over the telephone. This squeezed spreads even further, to perhaps a tenth of the notional amount. That meant that on a £1 million trade the dealer made just £125, scarcely enough to pay the price of the telephone calls, let alone his salary or the space he occupied. The dealing cost of a £1 million trade fell by 60 per cent.[5] In the first year after **Big Bang**, the gilts market as a whole lost probably £60 million, or perhaps as much as £80–90 million. A similar amount was lost the following year too.[6] By the end of 1988 the cumulative losses amounted to £190 million.[7]

Morgan Grenfell Government Securities was a high-cost business in a low-margin market. Nor, with 26 other primary dealers already in business and the huge Japanese securities houses, Daiwa and Nomura, joining soon, was there any serious prospect of profitability in the near future. Before Big Bang the two top jobbers, Akroyd & Smithers and Wedd Durlacher, had controlled three-quarters of turnover in the gilt-edged market. After Big Bang, the market share of the top six primary dealers fluctuated between two-fifths and half of turnover, implying that most commanded market shares of only about 5 per cent.[8] From the outset it was clear that some of the participants would have to withdraw. Surprisingly, in view of the terms in which the debate about Big Bang had been conducted since 1983, a lot of capital and a large market share were not necessarily the keys to survival. Both Hardman and Buchanan had pressed for a lot of capital, because they anticipated heavy losses at the outset, but in fact Morgan Grenfell Government Securities was modestly capitalized, at about £25 million. Market share mattered less than most participants thought, because it could always be bought in exchange for some loss of capital. Indeed, the heaviest losses were incurred by those primary dealers that opted to buy market share. Profitability was the crucial test and, though views varied as to whether profits were sustainable without market share, it quickly became clear that less obvious advantages – confidence, camaraderie, teamwork, communication – probably counted for more in this respect than capital and market share. At Warburg's and BZW, the acquisition of the largest brokers and jobbers ensured that these virtues survived the trauma of restructuring, but at Morgan Grenfell Government Securities they were lost. Like other houses, Morgan Grenfell had formed a trading team, consisting largely of jobbers from Pinchin Denny, and a sales force, consisting largely of brokers from Pember & Boyle.

Though the old Pinchin Denny gilt-edged jobbers initially made profits, at least until overheads were taken into account,[9] they could not deal in the sizes which the former partners of Pember & Boyle were used to. With sales driven solely by price, the salesmen also complained that the market-makers were not giving them stock at competitive prices. By the spring of 1987 it was clear that Morgan Grenfell Government Securities was failing. Ten primary dealers controlled two-thirds of the market, and Morgan Grenfell was not among them. An assessment by Greenwich Associates of Morgan Grenfell's position in the market that spring placed the bank nineteenth, where it remained when the survey was repeated the following year. It was obvious to all in the City that the bank had failed to integrate and manage its purchases, and handicapped them in a crowded and ruinously competitive market with the Collier and Guinness scandals. As the failure of the enterprise became obvious, its management collapsed in a welter of recriminations.

Alistair Buchanan was the first victim. Among his friends in the City, it was well known that his relationship with Blaise Hardman was poor. He complained to them of Hardman's unwillingness to communicate, and considered it childish. In a manner typical of the chaos which followed Big Bang, Buchanan found himself with less and less to do, and eventually left at the end of May 1987.[10] Clients were astonished at the bewildering series of appointments which followed Buchanan's departure, and found it hard to know who was in charge. Jamie Dundas, John Forsyth and Geoff Munn, a former head of foreign-exchange dealing, traversed the company's accounts as heads of trading during those years.[11] After the closure of Morgan Grenfell Securities, City bars reverberated with anecdotes about the confusion which reigned in the wake of Buchanan's departure. One story said that Jamie Dundas, Buchanan's deputy, for a time measured success in trading positions, rather than realized gains and losses. Another said that he had requested his salesmen to abjure a cheery 'Hallo' in favour of sombre greetings like 'Morgan Grenfell Securities' or their full names when answering the telephone. As losses mounted, it was decided to cut costs. On Friday, 17 July 1987 – the day Robert Holmes à Court appeared publicly on the shareholder register for the first time – Morgan Grenfell Government Securities announced that it had sacked half its gilts sales force the previous day and 're-deployed' five others, citing excessive overheads as the cause of continuing losses. Morgan Grenfell sacked none of its own – all those dismissed had worked previously for Pember & Boyle and Pinchin Denny. They included three former partners of Pinchin Denny and one former partner of Pember & Boyle.[12] One of the juniors dismissed had turned down a job elsewhere just a month earlier after assurances from Martin Knight that his position was secure. It was, of course, the Morgan Grenfell staff who were 're-deployed'. With appalling insensitivity John Rawlings told the press that they had been useless anyway. 'When you buy a business you buy the good, the bad and the ugly,' he said.[13] The head of gilt sales, Francesca Edwards, was horrified at the manner of the dismissals. She resigned in disgust in early September.[14] Martin Knight left Morgan Grenfell in November 1987 to set up his own corporate-finance boutique, BKR.[15] Management responsibility for gilt-edged sales and trading was diffused. Tony Bohannon, originally hired by John Forsyth from Salomon Brothers as a Eurodollar bond-trader, assumed effective control of the rump, under the titular leadership of Munn. Morgan Grenfell Government Securities now employed just five traders and six salesmen. Its market share, hit by the ructions, slumped from $2\frac{1}{2}$ per cent to perhaps $\frac{1}{2}$–1 per cent, but by making suicidal spreads, the bank had increased its share of the non-professional market to 5–6 per cent by the time Morgan Grenfell Securities withdrew from the market altogether.[16] It was a commendable, if unprofitable, performance, but to thrive the bond business needed a regular supply of new Eurobond issues to sell and trade. Unfortunately, the bank was shortly to pull out of the Eurobond market altogether.[17]

*

In the Eurobond Department, the dispute that had simmered since the 1984 Citicorp disaster, between Keith Harris, who believed that Morgan Grenfell should compete aggressively in the Eurodollar bond market and John Rawlings, who favoured a less ambitious strategy, was still unresolved when Morgan Grenfell was overtaken by the Guinness scandal.[18] The bank led its last Eurodollar bond issue in 1985 and 14 of the 15 Eurobond issues it lead managed in 1986 were Eurosterling bonds.[19] Because between half and three-quarters of all Eurodollar bond issues were subsequently swapped,[20] it was impossible for Morgan Grenfell to re-enter the market without Eurodollar swaps experts and Eurodollar bond traders, who could make markets in the new issues Harris could bring from his clients in the United States. Harris had hired six dollar-swaps specialists from Chemical Bank in New York in May 1986.[21] All that was missing was experienced Eurodollar bond traders, but they were not hired.

Any hopes that Harris might have entertained of reversing the decision to withdraw permanently from the Eurodollar bond market were dashed by the dismissal of Jon Perry as head of the Eurobond Department in the management reshuffle which accompanied the departures of Roger Seelig, Christopher Reeves and Graham Walsh. Perry, Harris's closest ally in London, swapped jobs with Christopher Whittington, then group director of overseas companies. Whittington, who had once run the International Banking Division, was close to John Rawlings, an alumnus of the Division, and secured his elevation to the Group Executive Committee formed by Sir Peter Carey after the submission of the Catto committee report in February 1987.[22] From February 1987 Rawlings – who remained opposed to an open-ended commitment to the Eurodollar bond market – effectively began to run Debt Securities and Banking.[23] Harris's hopes of persuading the bank to return in force to the Eurodollar bond market faded commensurately, and he returned disconsolately to New York. His hopes were finally extinguished with the appointment of John Craven, who despised Eurobonds as a 'commodity business' in

which price alone won business and relationships counted for
nothing.[24] 'We have no ambition to be a major multinational
distributor of debt securities in all currencies,' he said, flatly.[25]
Keith Harris resigned in December 1987, taking with him to
Drexel Burnham Lambert in New York four members of his
team at Morgan Grenfell Inc. Harris had learned, like Philip
Chappell, the perils of absence from the metropolis. 'I felt that
an ability to issue debt securities was an essential part of being
an international investment bank,' he lamented.[26] He was
replaced temporarily by his former mentor, Jon Perry, in his
new and lesser guise as head of overseas operations.[27] In his
last major executive decision for Morgan Grenfell, Perry
replaced himself with Martin Wade from Shearson Lehman.[28]

The view of John Rawlings and John Craven that the
Eurodollar bond market was too unprofitable to merit a serious
commitment was confirmed by a crisis of confidence in the
market stemming almost entirely from suicidal competition for
business. Prices weakened first in the perpetual Floating Rate
Note market. Like other Floating Rate Notes, perpetuals are
intended never to depart very far from their par value, because the
interest they pay is adjusted every few months in line with interest
rates generally. Competition to underwrite new issues had
squeezed interest rates on all Floating Rate Notes to the point
where it was no longer economic for other banks, who were the
biggest buyers, to own them. They turned instead to money-
market instruments like Eurocommercial paper, where the
returns were better and liquidity was still intact. This hit the
perpetual Floating Rate Note market especially hard, since the
only way investors can realize their investment is by selling in
a liquid market. On one day in December 1986, prices of
perpetual bonds fell by 5 per cent, destroying the faith of
market-makers in the ability of perpetual Floating Rate Notes to
hold their value. Morgan Grenfell Securities, which had only
recently started to make markets in Floating Rate Notes, lost
£4 million. By March 1987 the perpetual market was dead.
The crisis of confidence spread to the fixed-rate Eurodollar
bond market, where banks had also competed for new-issue

business by underwriting bonds at unrealistic rates of interest, depressing prices by flooding the market with unsaleable bonds.

This added momentum to Rawlings's decision to quit the bond markets and confine the Eurobond Department to banking activities where Morgan Grenfell could 'add value' with its intellectual input. Swaps were just such an area, and the swap specialists stuck rigidly to selling only swaps in sterling, the bank's natural currency, or 'structured interest-rate and currency swaps to hedge complex cash flows'.[29] Domestic banking had been added to the bank's Eurobond operations in 1985, in recognition of the increased 'securitization' of straightforward lending. In fact, the Eurobond Department had been renamed the Banking and Capital Markets Division at the close of that year.[30] After the Guinness affair, international banking – the export and project-finance teams that had transformed the bank's reputation in the 1970s – and staid businesses like leasing and local-authority finance, all of which generated dependable profits, were tacked on as well.[31] It was felt – *pace* the Credits for Export bond issue – that some exports and projects might now be financed in the Eurobond market. Hardman's division of bond-trading and underwriting between Morgan Grenfell Securities and Morgan Grenfell was undone simultaneously. Though made on impeccably logical grounds – to take advantage of the lighter capital requirements imposed by the Bank of England on bond trading as opposed to bank lending – the decision was widely seen by the City as ill-advised. The trading of gilts, Eurobonds and money-market securities like sterling commercial paper and certificates of deposit needed to be managed closely with the new-issue, swaps and treasury activities.[32] The split had made it hard, for example, to hedge new Eurobond issues in the gilt-edged market. It also made it hard for new-issue executives to follow the market. Fittingly, the division was renamed Banking and Fixed Income.[33]

Though the bank made public its continuing commitment to the Eurosterling convertible bond market,[34] Jon Perry's dream of establishing Morgan Grenfell as a great Eurobond issuing house was over. In common with other banks, Rawlings authorized the use of swaps as a means of selling the mispriced fixed-rate Eurobonds which accumulated in the market once liquidity collapsed. A swaps trader was assigned to developing asset swaps, or buying packages of outstanding fixed-rate bonds and swapping them into floating-rate loans for sale to commercial banks. Another sold complex forward-currency agreements and interest-rate options and futures.[35] Export and project finance and swapping defaulted Third World debt into equity also yielded satisfactorily to intellectual repackaging. All of these 'products', as bankers had begun to call them, commanded higher margins than those available in the moribund Eurodollar bond market, which was increasingly dominated by a handful of houses with sufficient capital to trade bonds in large volumes. Morgan Grenfell was not alone in its decision to retrench in the Eurobond market – its example was preceded or followed by Orion Royal Bank, once a market leader, Chemical Bank, Paine Webber and a host of others – but its exit bore the hallmarks of a weak and divided organization. It had failed to capitalize on the Corporate Finance Department's unrivalled contacts in corporate Britain, to diversify from a profitable niche in Eurosterling bonds or to buy a broker of sufficient standing to secure a loyal group of domestic investors in its bonds. Nearly two years before Morgan Grenfell Securities succumbed to a combination of excessive costs, cutthroat competition and illiquidity in the equity markets, the bank had limped out of the first and greatest of the deregulated markets almost completely unnoticed.

'Our burning ambition is for the UK securities side to catch up with the market share and standing of our corporate finance division,' said John Craven, who emphasized his own commitment to equity securities by exchanging the wood-panelled luxury of the Partners' Room for the proletarian visibility of a glass-panelled office in 20 Finsbury Circus.[36] In June he displaced Blaise Hardman as chairman of Morgan

Grenfell Securities.[37] But by failing to buy an equity broker with an established list of clients in London, let alone New York or Tokyo, Morgan Grenfell Securities had set itself a formidable task. As John Holmes admitted before either the Guinness or the Collier affairs added to his difficulties, building up market share from zero in the deregulated London equity markets was close to impossible:

It took Wood Mackenzie 18 years to achieve a five or six per cent market share – something we aim to do in two years.[38]

The propensity of institutional investors to deal with Morgan Grenfell's salesmen and market-makers, never stronger than a willingness to give them an equal chance, was not increased by the Collier and Guinness revelations. The organization's ability to outperform its rivals was further weakened not just by the manner, but by the fact, of Geoffrey Collier's departure. Without him, the fledgling operation was deprived of its most astute and authoritative trader within less than a fortnight of Big Bang. Unlike the jobbers of Pinchin Denny, Collier had experience of screen-based trading, and the visibility and aggression it requires. Unlike John Holmes, whose principal gift was salesmanship, Collier also understood that profitability was preferable to market share, and that good settlements staff mattered just as much as salesmen. Unfortunately, he was not replaced.

Charles Peel, who joined Morgan Grenfell Securities as head of sales after Collier's departure, was an old-fashioned agency broker who did not believe in the new dispensation. He regretted the passing of the old City and seems never to have believed that Morgan Grenfell Securities was a viable business, and derided its prospects openly outside the bank. Ruddy-faced, tall, and Etonian, Peel is descended from the Prime Minister who split the Tory Party in 1846, and like Sir Robert, lacked the gift of blurring differences or shrinking from conflict. Yet he came with a formidable reputation, forged before Big Bang at the stockbroker, Fielding Newson-Smith, which was bought by County Bank, the merchant-banking subsidiary of the National Westminster Bank, in July 1984. The incompetence, bureaucracy and politicking which characterized County's muddled approach to the Big Bang made him cynical about the changes and nostalgic for the past. However, he was not able to work in London for a year, because County held him to a clause in his contract forbidding him from working for a competitor for twelve months.[39] County proved immovable on the issue and he spent his first year with Morgan Grenfell working in New York, where their writ did not run.[40]

In the merger and aquisition markets Big Bang had not sundered old loyalties to the extent anticipated. Clients were unwilling to abandon established broking relationships, and there was no incentive to ask them to buy and sell shares through a bank's broking subsidiary. Having traded for years off prestige alone, merchant bankers never appreciated that an illustrious reputation counted for little in the securities markets. Similarly, fund managers, obliged by the rules of their trade to find the keenest prices in the market, were free to place business with whomsoever they chose, and the unseen promptings of 'Chinese Walls' always held that it was safer to deal with outside brokers and market makers. These problems were apparent at Morgan Grenfell, and John Craven frequently made public his belief that Morgan Grenfell Securities' gravest weakness was its inability to find investors to whom it could sell the shares generated by the Corporate Finance and Asset Management Departments.

These weaknesses were severely tested as soon as Big Bang occurred, on 27 October 1986. 'We're as ready as we possibly could be. Maybe some of us aren't ready in a psychological sense but if that doesn't change they won't be here. We'll either make it or end up being owned by someone else,' said John Holmes on the eve of the great event.[41] In the days following the Big Bang the effects of the greater capital and competition being brought to bear were felt instantaneously by massive increases in turnover. By September 1987, the month before the crash, the average value of share-dealing for customers was running at over £1.1 billion a day, nearly twice the pre-Big Bang level. With thirty-five market-makers replacing thirteen jobbers, business between market-makers also soared, generating an additional £0.8 billion of turnover a day.[42] At its peak, in July 1987, daily turnover averaged £2.2 billion, more than half of it between market-makers.[43] Turnover in London in international shares also boomed, with forty-five market-makers trading some 700 foreign shares worth over £500 million a day at their peak before the crash. At one point shares were changing hands so fast that firms were unable to effect exchanges quickly enough to keep up, and the Stock Exchange contemplated closing the market to allow them to clear the backlog.

Trading methods changed radically too. Instead of brokers strolling on to the floor of the Stock Exchange to look a jobber in the eye and ask a price, the competing market-makers stayed in their offices and advertised the prices at which they would buy and sell on an electronic screen system. SEAQ, or SEAQ International for foreign shares. Buyers merely looked for the cheapest price on the screen in the size they wanted and then telephoned their order. The increased capital benefited investors, who found they could buy and sell large numbers of shares without the price being marked up or down to accommodate them. The cost of dealing also halved, as they paid less in tax and commissions, especially for large orders.[44] The biggest investors, like the Prudential, often paid no commission at all, leaving the market-maker to squeeze a profit out of buying the shares more cheaply than he sold them, or vice versa. This was not at first disastrous because rising share prices and increased turnover allowed commission income to rise although commission rates were falling. Even without commission, the average 'touch' – the gap between the most attractive buying and selling prices advertised on SEAQ – left room for profit, changing little between Big Bang and the crash and still widening comfortably to absorb large orders.[45] It took the crash, with its sudden collapse in turnover, to cause casualties.

In this bracing environment, Morgan Grenfell Securities'

distribution weaknesses mattered much more than was immediately obvious. The bank's overall strategy in the securities markets was, like Warburg's or BZW's, based on the 'synergies' derived from 'vertical integration'. That meant underwriting, trading, researching and selling share issues within a single organization, and collecting a profit or a fee at every juncture on a share's journey from the seller to the buyer. Clearly, the buy and sell recommendations to institutional investors from the research analysts competed with the advice and services offered by other houses, and so were unlikely to generate sufficient turnover to fully occupy the 450 staff gathered at 20 Finsbury Circus. To generate additional turnover, Morgan Grenfell Securities, like all integrated houses, had to capitalize on the strengths of other parts of the bank. The Corporate Finance Department's ability to generate shares for sale and trading, through company flotations, takeovers, and rights issues, was as good as any in the City. Similarly, the Asset Management Department managed funds from around the world worth £14.5 billion in 1986, generating an enormous potential turnover for Morgan Grenfell Securities.[46] This was especially attractive where large portfolios of securities were offered for sale, which the broking arm could 'buy' for onward sale without involving other underwriters, and so collect both a profit and any underwriting fees. Yet it was Morgan Grenfell Securities' ability to sell shares that was most in doubt. It was a false economy not to buy an equity broker with established sales contacts. Theoretically, the weakness could be easily rectified by recruitment; in practice, this was difficult. John Holmes and Geoffrey Collier had imagined that prominent salesmen, lured by the bank's formidable reputation in other areas, would defect to them for the opportunity alone. In the event, they had to pay very substantial 'golden hallos' and guaranteed bonuses to attract sales staff, including payments of £100–150,000 a head to a three-man sales team hired from Kleinwort Grieveson in April 1986.[47] Few were very senior, and virtually none were partners, lumbering the business with heavy costs but denying it the ballast of experience. Though

Holmes had a remarkable gift for inspiring loyalty and affection, and the bank suffered fewer defections than some houses, faces continued to come and go after Big Bang, making it hard to create and sustain any sort of *esprit de corps*. At the time of the flotation, Morgan Grenfell Securities employed just ten salesmen, some from elsewhere in the bank. Holmes had wanted another ten to fifteen 'in the thirty to forty age bracket'.[48] When he failed to get them, the bank began to toy with more drastic solutions, starting in New York and Tokyo.

At the time of Big Bang the New York office, though it employed 60 people, was still limited to corporate-finance and fund-management advice.[49] With shares and bonds criss-crossing the Atlantic in increasing numbers, it was essential to the bank's international and 'integrated' pretensions that Morgan Grenfell Securities had an outlet in New York. In December 1986 the bank bought Cyrus J. Lawrence Inc., a New York securities broker. The lesson of Big Bang – that cheap acquisitions are a waste of money – had been learned. The bank paid $70 million for an organization of just 220 people with net assets of $26 million. 'We have paid a fair price although a considerable proportion of it was for goodwill,' admitted Holmes.[50] C. J. Lawrence was an old-fashioned partnership, with about 1,500 US institutional investors as clients, to whom it sold new issues of shares and bonds it had underwritten and made markets in unlisted shares. It also managed the investment of around $450 million on their behalf. But its greatest strength was in research. Seven of its twenty-two equity research analysts had appeared in the 1986 *Institutional Investor* rankings, a league table compiled by a trade magazine from a straw poll of fund managers in New York. In theory, Morgan Grenfell Securities could sell obscure American shares in London on the back of their research.

This fitted the overall plan: to use C. J. Lawrence to sell European shares in the United States and Morgan Grenfell Securities to sell American shares in Europe. Sales teams were swapped immediately for this very purpose but, being a partnership, C. J. Lawrence rewarded its salesmen partly through a percentage of their commission income, which made them reluctant to introduce their clients to Morgan Grenfell. Charles Peel, whose misgivings about the bank were well known, became ambassador to its newest outlet. C. J. Lawrence's clients gossiped to the newspapers that the backer had assured them the essential character of the firm was unaltered by its new pact. The acquisition also added little to the bank's corporate finance capabilities in New York and, in deference to the cultural tensions evident in London, it was judged unwise to merge C. J. Lawrence with Morgan Grenfell Inc. immediately, and the two firms continued to occupy separate offices until the summer of 1989. Tokyo, where the bank felt markedly less self-assured, was developed along more traditional lines, though the strategy – selling European and American shares to Japanese investors – was much the same.[51] It was held up pending the award of a licence to do so from the Japanese authorities, which was finally received in December 1986. Morgan Grenfell Japan opened for business as a securities firm four months later. It employed nearly 70 people, either hired in Japan or transferred from London to sell the bonds and shares supplied from London and New York.[52] The weakness of the theory behind the moves in both New York and Tokyo – that an essentially bull-market phenomenon, the global trading of shares and bonds, would continue indefinitely – was ruthlessly exposed by the after-effects of the crash.

Craven shared Holmes's belief that in the long run Morgan Grenfell Securities could survive only if the Corporate Finance Department ensured it a regular supply of new stock to sell:

A client carrying out a takeover may need finance from a bond issue or a bank loan, or it may issue equity ... this is what integrated investment banking means.[53]

For a time he favoured merging the two departments. Craven forecast the demise of the traditional separation of underwriting and broking in the London merger markets and the migration from the United States (and the Eurobond market) of the 'bought deal', whereby a single bank buys batches of shares for onward sale, taking a turn as it does so:

The whole practice is going to change and I don't think people here realize it yet. Groups like us are going to have to bear more risk.[54]

This difference of opinion explained Craven's concern, often voiced in public, that Morgan Grenfell Securities was incapable of selling the securities the bank underwrote. He scoured the market for an acquisition which would rectify the bank's weakness in sales. He looked first at Wood Mackenzie, the Edinburgh stockbroker owned by the troubled Hill Samuel, and likely to be disgorged by any new parent. Craven is believed to have approached Union Bank of Switzerland in July 1987 to express an interest in buying Wood Mackenzie at the time that Union Bank was negotiating with Hill Samuel.[55] Critics found this odd, believing that Wood Mackenzie's principal strength was in research rather than sales but, although the firm was in decline, it still commanded a 5–6 per cent market share. In the event, nothing came of the discussions.

Craven's dealings with Hoare Govett, a London stockbroker with a formidable reputation for sales, were altogether more substantial. In August and September 1987 he twice met executives from Security Pacific, the West Coast bank which owned four-fifths of Hoare Govett. On one occasion he flew to Los Angeles to meet David Lovejoy, the executive vice-president in charge of merchant banking. They discussed a possible acquisition by Morgan Grenfell of the major interest in Hoare Govett, with Security Pacific retaining a minority stake.[56] Though Security Pacific had been the first to take a stake in a London stockbroker, its attitude to the London securities markets had always been ambivalent. It was first attracted to Hoare Govett in June 1982 by its Far Eastern business rather than its London operations. Two Hoare Govett alumni – John Holmes and Basil Postan – were in senior positions with Morgan Grenfell Securities, and they were familiar with their old firm's strengths in research and sales, and its relative weakness in corporate finance. Senior figures at Hoare Govett, like the chief executive, Anthony Greayer, were keen on the merger as a means of ridding themselves of Security Pacific, and Greayer is believed to have approached Morgan Grenfell with the idea first.[57] Almost everyone at Morgan Grenfell Securities agreed that the two firms would have made a good fit, but the talks foundered on Security Pacific's unwillingness to sanction a minority shareholding. The regulatory position in the United States was also unclear. The Glass-Steagall Act still forbade commercial banks to own securities operations in the United States, making C. J. Lawrence an obstacle to the retention by Security Pacific of a minority stake. Because the Act was then considered likely to lapse, one option discussed was that Security Pacific should take its stake in preference shares, convertible into ordinary shares once the Act was repealed.[58] Security Pacific eventually bought the balance of Hoare Govett instead, taking advantage of their right to do so under the terms of the original deal. Though these talks were later dismissed by Craven as 'merely conceptual, covering the potential regulatory and commercial fit', Greayer's enthusiasm for mergers led to him leaving the firm and their failure was a serious, and ultimately fatal, blow to Morgan Grenfell Securities.[59]

The talks were serious enough for Willis Faber to be alarmed by the possibility of another rights issue to pay for the acquisition. Willis Faber was never especially supportive of the bank's decision to endorse the Big Bang, and the talks with Wood Mackenzie and Hoare Govett suggested that its unwelcome exposure to the securities markets could increase, rather than diminish. Willis Faber appointed Lazard's to advise on the disposal of its 20.7 per cent stake. David Palmer, Willis Faber's then chairman, conceded that it was considering a sale:

We are loyal shareholders but with the change that is going on we have to keep our options open. Our relationship has elements of instability because they want to make fundamental changes that affect us and our shareholders. We would not be an unwilling seller if an acceptable offer came along.[60]

These talks dragged on desultorily after the crash too, suggesting wider implications. When a report appeared in *The Economist* that Morgan Grenfell was discussing a merger with Deutsche Bank, coupled with the suggestion that John Craven might welcome relinquishing his responsibilities to a caring parent, Sir Peter Carey threatened the magazine with defamation proceedings.[61] The following week, the magazine recorded that Morgan Grenfell had issued a press release denying that any talks had taken place.[62]

News of David Palmer's doubts about Willis Faber's relationship with Morgan Grenfell surfaced publicly on 19 October 1987, a date now etched in City memories as 'Black Monday', and the day on which the value of his company's stake in Morgan Grenfell was cut almost in half. On Black Monday share prices on Wall Street fell 23 per cent, spreading panic across the world's stock markets. The same day market-makers in London absorbed £250 million of shares sold by panicking investors.[63] Though Morgan Grenfell, in common with most market-makers during the long bull market of the 1980s, already owned or had agreed to buy rather more shares than it had agreed to sell (the bank was, in the jargon, 'long' rather than 'short') its lack of success in the underwriting of new issues contained the immediate losses that resulted from the crash. It lost only £1.5 million on its share of the underwriting of the government's £7 billion sale of shares in BP, which coincided with the crash. Rivals County Bank, underwriting an £837 million share sale for Blue Arrow, lost at least £49 million on its underwriting of that issue alone. Within a fortnight of the crash, Morgan Grenfell had written off only £5 million in London, in addition to its losses on BP. In the immediate vicinity of the crash, at least, the edifice of Morgan Grenfell Securities was shaken, but it was still standing.

Unfortunately, the crash was not over in a fortnight. The crisis was the supreme test of trading skill, and it exposed the weaknesses of the Pinchin Denny market-makers. Rival traders who took the initiative, like Smith New Court, boasted how they had aggressively outwitted Morgan Grenfell Securities.

By the end of the year the crash and its aftermath had neatly transformed a profit of £10 million at the end of September into a £10 million loss at the end of December. This loss, of £20 million, was described in the bank's annual report as 'a satisfactory outcome'.[64]

Abroad, the bank's preference for delegation and local autonomy had dreadful consequences during the crash. Morgan Grenfell had composed no strategy for central direction of the bank's global exposure in the event of a disaster. The arbitrage business in New York, of course, was especially vulnerable to a radical realignment of stock-market values. After reports circulated that Mitchell Sahn, Morgan Grenfell Inc.'s leading arbitrageur in New York, had lost $25 million,[65] the bank issued a statement admitting to having lost only $14 million.[66] In fact the loss was probably $18 million, or very nearly half the $40 million book run by Sahn, once the $10 million profit it showed ahead of the crash was taken into account. The bank eventually admitted that a profit of $12 million had been transformed into a loss of $12 million.[67] It was a very substantial loss, rather exceeding the £20 million forgone in London, and prompted the merger of Morgan Grenfell Inc. with C. J. Lawrence, to create an 'integrated' business along the lines of Morgan Grenfell Securities in London. Keith Harris resigned and Jim Moltz, the former chairman and chief executive of C. J. Lawrence, became head of the merged companies, a radical departure from the usual policy of using Morgan Grenfell placemen to run overseas offices.[68] The losses at Morgan Grenfell Australia, where the fall in the stock market was the sharpest and steepest of all, were equally horrific, and led eventually to a complete withdrawal from the Australian securities business when the Stock Market failed to recover.[69] In Singapore, Morgan Grenfell Asia was left with most of a rights issue for the marine engineering group, Van der Horst.[70] In both Australia and Singapore the bank had only just entered stockbroking through the acquisition of local firms. The purchase of the Australian brokers, Hordern, Utz & Bode and Barnes, Tolhurst & Milner and the acquisition of a half-share in the Singapore broker, Su F-Min, were completed in 1987, just in time for the crash to make them look exceptionally foolish.[71] The overall losses incurred by Morgan Grenfell Securities around the world during the crash was estimated by analysts to have totalled more than £40 million.

The crash precipitated a malaise across all of Morgan Grenfell's businesses, shaving £30 million from the profit it had expected to make in 1987 and reversing an upward growth in profits which stretched back to 1979, the year that Christopher Reeves took office. The crash, by making it harder and more expensive to pay for companies with shares rather than cash, prolonged the hostility towards major takeover bids. The Corporate Finance Department advised in bids worth less than half (£7.3 billion) those in 1986 (£15.2 billion). The contribution to profits of Morgan Grenfell Asset Management, whose advisory fees were linked to share prices much reduced by the crash, remained virtually static, at £15.8 million against £15.6 million in 1986, despite increasing the number of funds under management. Students of corporate camouflage noted that a wholly forgivable decline in their fees' value was obscured by quoting them in dollars for the first time, underlining the cost of the equipment needed to remain competitive.[72] Overall, Morgan Grenfell's pre-tax profits slipped from £82 million in 1986 to only £60 million in 1987. They were propped up by a £26 million capital gain from selling the bank's 19.9 per cent interest in Target Group plc to the Trustee Savings Bank, of which only £5.7 million was treated as extraordinary.[73] Coupled with losses of £8.7 million on the sale of Third World debt, these oddities meant that all but £5.2 million of profits were earned in the first half of 1987.[74]

The crash also put an end to any speculation that Morgan Grenfell would buy a broker, though the subsequent weakness of the share price revived speculation that the bank itself might be taken over in the spring and summer of 1988. The weak price of the stock made it hard for the bank to use its shares as a takeover currency even if a further foray into the traumatized securities markets was considered advisable, which it was not. Craven put a brave face on his disappointment:

A year ago, there were one or two pockets of feeling that, if a good offer came along, it would be as well to take it. Now, the managers' tails are up, and we are all dedicated to remaining independent.[75]

Both Willis Faber and Morgan Grenfell began to deny that Willis Faber's stake had ever been for sale and for the first time John Craven began to ponder less exhilarating solutions to Morgan Grenfell's shortcomings. In January 1988 the senior management was replaced.

The detail of the changes was excessive, but the significant shifts were obvious enough. Blaise Hardman, Jon Perry, Charles Rawlinson and Sir John Sparrow, all of whom had prospered greatly under Reeves, lost their executive status. Sparrow conceded gracefully that he had fallen to a management coup of exactly the type his own generation had plotted, but Perry felt humiliated, only learning of his dismissal from a leak in the *Sunday Telegraph*, which he read on board a plane returning from New York. Of those most closely associated with Christopher Reeves, only Christopher Whittington survived, in a guise (deputy chairman) which took him a step closer to the dreaded 'departure lounge'. Under Reeves, directors of the bank had spent more time on management responsibilities than cultivating clients. Craven now charged nine of them, including George Magan, with a roving brief to drum up business.[76] The idea of salvaging the equity business by merging the Corporate Finance Department with Morgan Grenfell Securities was shelved temporarily. Directors were told that they would have to encourage co-operation between divisions of the bank and all staff were told that they would have to switch divisions periodically.[77] The Group Executive Committee formed by Sir Peter Carey a year earlier was renamed the Group Management Committee, and the main administrative jobs on it given wholeheartedly to the 'Young Turks' for the first time. Guy Dawson, just thiry-five, became head of Corporate Finance. Robert Binyon, the thirty-eight-

year-old head of Morgan Grenfell Japan, also joined the committee, whose average age plunged to forty-one. Michael Dobson,
unknown a year before and still only thiry-five, became deputy
chief executive. Cynics attributed his elevation to the increasing
use of videos to sell the bank, on which his telegenic good looks
captivated staff and clients. The City rumour mill also suggested that he had thwarted a management buy-out at Morgan
Grenfell Asset Management, for which the profit-starved
Craven was duly grateful.[78]

The Group Management Committee was charged with for-
mulating a strategy for the future. In July 1988 it delivered a
business plan which envisaged a full merger of the Corporate
Finance Department and Morgan Grenfell Securities within
three years. It also predicted a £20 million loss if trading
conditions did not improve. As the committee deliberated, an
awareness of costs crept into the bank's calculations for the first
time. 'It is our intention to protect the employment of staff as
far as possible,' was Craven's Christmas message in 1987.[79]
Yet the day after the Morgan Grenfell Securities Christmas
party at the Hippodrome fourteen mainly junior staff in MGSI
were sacked by Basil Postan, and another ten or so were
released elsewhere in Morgan Grenfell Securities.[80] Pay rises
and Christmas bonuses were still paid to those who kept their
jobs, but the next pay round was deferred for 15 months,
rather than the usual 12. Nervous traders noted that it gave
the bank leeway to sack them at their old salaries. The free,
interest-bearing bank accounts offered to staff were closed, and
newspaper and telephone allowances curtailed. In the prelude
to Big Bang, Morgan Grenfell had gorged itself on screen-
based share-, bond- and foreign-exchange-dealing equipment
and personal computers. The market-makers were nevertheless
unhappy with their equipment. It had to be upgraded in 1987,
after 'Fast-trade' – the most sophisticated system, which allows
up to fifteen different stocks to be displayed on the screen
simultaneously – was rejected as being too expensive. After the
crash an information-technology manager, Joseph de Fayo,
was hired from Goldman Sachs to make changes. His major

reform – sacking sixteen members of the staff and splitting his department into four teams, each assigned to one business activity – was designed principally to improve cost accounting and sensitivity.[81]

Craven told staff that natural wastage would trim the payroll sufficiently to avoid the spectacular mass sackings which came at County Bank, Greenwell Montagu, Scrimgeour Vickers, Chemical Bank and others in the wake of the crash. He preferred imperceptible extinction in unprofitable markets rather than self-immolation. Euromarket rivals noticed that the firm was withdrawing from the Eurobond market. The private-client stockbroking department was given quietly to Svenska & Co. in March 1988.[82] Twenty-three staff were fired by Morgan Grenfell Securities in June 1988, denting morale severely for the first time. George Nissen, the former senior partner of Pember & Boyle, left the Group Board at Christmas 1987, although he remained a consultant, working in the Compliance Department. Other partners had departed earlier in the year, and more were to go, the early redemption of their 'golden handcuffs' more of a burden to their employer than to them. By Christmas a year later only four were left.[83] The convulsions in the City which followed the crash allowed John Holmes to recruit some senior equity salesmen at last. Once his two-year agreement with his old firm not to poach their staff was up, Holmes hired four salesmen from Hoare Govett, where many had been unsettled by the crash and the aggressive management style of Security Pacific. Four joined Morgan Grenfell Securities, including Alistair Kerr and Brian Rawson, who had held senior positions at Hoare Govett.[84] Though their salaries were reputedly enormous, their arrival boosted morale and there was talk of a 4 per cent market share at the beginning of 1988.

Throughout 1988 John Craven's public commitment to Morgan Grenfell Securities hardly wavered, though he spent much of 1987 and 1988 asking clients if an integrated investment bank was crucial to their requirements, and found that for many of them it was not.[85] Thereafter, the bank was no longer shaped by strategic vision; rather, it was a creature of events. Publicly, at least, Craven insisted that the totems of the Reeves regime – an integrated securities business and international growth – were still worshipped in the Partners' Room, whence he returned in the spring of 1988. He argued to journalists that the conventional wisdom of Big Bang – that a bank had either to be large enough to be everywhere or small enough to be somewhere – could be defied. He talked of a 'cluster' of profitable businesses grouped around the core businesses of corporate finance, investment management and banking, including reliable workhorses like export and project finance. Rather than seek to match BZW or Warburg's by making markets in every conceivable security, he confined the bank's ambitions to making markets in British and some French and German equities; broking American and European shares through C. J. Lawrence; and issuing and trading only gilts and those Eurobonds convertible into equities.[86]

Unlike most other merchant banks, Craven ditched plans to make markets in American Treasury bonds in New York and spurned a seat on the Tokyo Stock Exchange. C. J. Lawrence, he felt, lacked a sufficiently serious presence in the New York bond markets. In New York, risk arbitrage was also closed. The securities dealing, investment management and Eurobond operations in Australia, ruined by the crash, were closed and many of the staff sacked. Hordern, Utz & Bode, the private-client stockbroker, was sold to ANZ McCaughan Dyson. Barnes, Tolhurst & Milner, the Adelaide broker, was sold back to its partners.[87] Though only one of the four corporate-finance stars who came with Geoff Hill in 1982 remained, Morgan Grenfell's Australian ambitions were now limited to corporate-finance advisory work.[88] The New Zealand office was sold to its staff and the Hong Kong trust operation abandoned.[89] Morgan Grenfell Switzerland S.A., the bond-underwriting and -trading subsidiary in Geneva, was sold to Compagnie de Banque et d'Investissements. The profitable private-client banking operation, Banque Morgan Grenfell en Suisse, was retained. Across all countries and markets Morgan

443

Grenfell was in headlong retreat, for the first time in its history.

In reality, Craven's 'cluster' strategy was not a strategy at all, but merely made a virtue of necessity. The retrenchments and retentions mirrored exactly where Morgan Grenfell had succeeded or failed. There was little evidence of new thinking, barring a tardy decision to enter the £37 billion unit-trust market, the last major merchant bank to do so. Until 1988 Morgan Grenfell Asset Management was the unsung success of the bank. It had increased the funds it managed eightfold since 1979, from £1.7 billion to £13.5 billion in 1986. Despite this success, from the death of Henry Gorell Barnes in 1983 until the emergence of Michael Dobson as deputy group chief executive in 1988, the division lacked a powerful voice in the highest counsels of the bank. Sir John Sparrow, appointed head of the department after the death of Gorell Barnes, was not respected by younger directors like Piotr Poloniecki, who had failed to convince him of the need for the bank to tackle the unit-trust market years earlier. 'Chinese Walls' had isolated the department's activities from the mainstream of the bank, and there was talk of a management buy-out or even a sale. S. G. Warburg had floated a proportion of its fund-management business on the Stock Exchange, underlining how few of the vaunted 'synergies' of an integrated bank were derived from this quarter. But after the Guinness affair and the crash, Morgan Grenfell could not afford to lose such a stable and relatively successful part of its business. After research suggested that the Collier and Guinness affairs had not sullied the bank's reputation in the eyes of the public, Dobson argued successfully for entry into the retail unit-trust market, recruiting Tony Fraher from Allied Irish Bank as managing director of the new company, Morgan Grenfell Unit Trust Managers.[90]

Dobson's target was to attract £200 million within two years.[91] Morgan Grenfell had ignored the unit-trust market since 1975, when it sold £6.5 million of funds to Gartmore.[92] This previous experience, which dated back to 1969, was forgotten during the £1 million press and television advertising campaign to sell four new unit trusts, which boasted of a 'new way into Morgan Grenfell Asset Management skills'.[93] Reminded of it by an anonymous former member of staff, Janet McCurrie, the Group legal adviser, effected changes in the advertisements.[94] The timing, in the wake of the crash, was inauspicious. The £18 million eventually raised by the four funds in the spring of 1988 compared badly with the £56 million raised by Marks & Spencer in the autumn and the launch costs, at £2 million, were a large proportion of the monies raised.[95] Three new trusts scheduled for launch in May were duly postponed. In October the Morgan Grenfell Tracker Trust – an indexed unit trust, whose performance matches as closely as possible the performance of the *Financial Times* All-Share index – prompted criticism as misleading, since once administration costs were subtracted from the results, under-performance was guaranteed. It drew in just £8 million.[96] But the Tracker Trust's mascot, a lovable bloodhound called Cherry, became a familiar sight on the financial pages and in December the *Sunday Telegraph* voted Morgan Grenfell its Smaller Unit Trust Group of the Year. Plans were also prepared to offer a high-interest bank account, join a cash-dispenser network and market a gold credit card. It was a long way from the time when Roger Seelig and George Magan seemed to be reshaping the industrial destiny of Britain.[97]

Meanwhile, the losses at Morgan Grenfell Securities grew steadily worse. It lost £5 million in the first half of 1988.[98] As turnover dwindled in the wake of the crash, the competition for the available business intensified, eventually precipitating a vicious price war. Though conflict between market-makers simmered for much of 1988, the war did not break out in earnest until the end of August 1988, when the balance of payments figure for July was published by the government. The figure was a poor one, prompting fears of a rise in interest rates to curb consumer spending, and the market fell accordingly. As prices tumbled, two of the larger market-makers, Phillips & Drew and Citicorp Scrimgeour Vickers, cut their spreads (reduced the gap between the price at which they would buy shares and the price at which they would sell them) and reduced the number of shares they would buy or sell at the prices they advertised on SEAQ. They were quickly joined by BZW and others were forced to follow suit. The Stock Exchange reported that the average 'touch' narrowed from 2 per cent at the time of the crash to 0.80 per cent a year later. At the time, the Stock Exchange insisted that market-makers should deal without exception at the prices and in the amounts they advertised on SEAQ, to ensure a 'visible' market. By narrowing spreads and cutting dealing size, Phillips & Drew and Citicorp Scrimgeour Vickers increased the pressure on smaller market-makers like Morgan Grenfell Securities, which had hitherto relied on the larger houses to buy the shares they did not want or could not sell. The smaller houses also lost touch with the price at which large transactions were effected, since this was increasingly fixed privately over the telephone, without appearing immediately on SEAQ. They were thus forced to narrow their spreads further, which reduced their income from trading. The profit margin disappeared altogether in Alpha stocks, the largest and most liquid shares, which made up three-quarters of turnover. Because the larger market-makers no longer advertised the price for bigger deals, the prices advertised on SEAQ by the smaller houses drifted out of line, and they lost business to the larger houses.

Morgan Grenfell Securities lost market share almost immediately. Its share of equity turnover in London had climbed to 4 per cent by the end of June, but during the price war it slipped below 2 per cent again. It also failed to contain its losses as prices fell on publication of the poor balance of payments figure, and its £20 million 'long' position that day cost it dear. This coincided with losses in other areas, notably in Switzerland, by MGSI in Europe and in Alex Catto's convertible bond department, where an issue for Centerparcs, a European leisure company, sold conspicuously poorly. Perhaps another £5 million was lost in August alone. Yet it was the loss of market share, rather than any specific loss, which finally persuaded the senior management at Morgan Grenfell

Securities that the position was irrecoverable, and that its market share would never attain the coveted 5 per cent at which they judged a reasonable profit might be generated. Outsiders confirmed their own gloomy assessment. Stock Exchange surveys revealed that four-fifths of market-making was controlled by ten houses, which excluded Morgan Grenfell. In one survey of 126 investment institutions Morgan Grenfell Securities was absent from the ratings altogether.[99] Short of real orders and lacking sufficient market share to make a profit out of spreads alone Morgan Grenfell Securities was living on borrowed time from August 1988 onwards. Sir Peter Carey, with his customary insouciance, described the £5 million loss in the first half of the year as 'containable'.[100] One news service transcribed his comment as 'continuable', which seemed more likely. But before the end Morgan Grenfell Securities had one final agony to endure.

After lunch on Wednesday 3 August 1988, David Gray, the £50,000-a-year pharmaceuticals salesman Morgan Grenfell Securities had hired from Quilter Goodison in 1986, was telephoned by Cathy Rowlands, his girlfriend, who worked in the Corporate Finance Department at Samuel Montagu. She told Gray to wait while she called back from a 'phone where the walls are more friendly'. A few minutes later she called back and told Gray, 'The event which we expected to happen is going to happen tomorrow.' Gray replied that he thought it was going to be 'a *pleasurable* event'. Rowlands said 'Yes'. 'I had better have a drink with Bill,' said Gray. 'That would be a good idea,' said Rowlands.[102] In this coded manner Cathy Rowlands told David Gray that the following day Mecca Leisure, advised by Samuel Montagu, would launch a £600 million takeover bid for Pleasurama, another leisure company. Gray then called Bill Liggins, a fund manager at Lazard's whom he had worked with at the jobber Wedd Durlacher before joining Quilter, and told him of the bid. He suggested that Liggins should buy 15,000 shares in Pleasurama through a provincial stockbroker, with the profits split between the three of them. Liggins later called Gray back to tell him that it had been done. Gray then called Mark Riding, a fund manager at the Co-operative Insurance Society in Manchester, and repeated the advice, apparently referring to a 'dickie bird'. In active trading the day before Mecca's bid, Pleasurama's shares rose 30p; on the announcement of the bid they rose another 30p, netting Rowlands, Gray and Liggins a profit of about £9,000. Unknown to them, the contact at the Co-op was already under internal investigation for insider dealing and his suspiciously frequent dealings with Gray had been referred to managers at Morgan Grenfell Securities. When a purchase of shares in Pleasurama the day before the Mecca bid was uncovered, two members of the Morgan Grenfell compliance team, Nick Tatman and John Goddard, were alerted. They were not surprised at the implication of Gray, whom they had been monitoring for months.[102]

Tatman was once Pember & Boyle's only equity salesman, but had become an administrator at Morgan Grenfell Securities. Goddard had been an administrative partner at Pember & Boyle, the 'man of business' who ensured that the partnership kept its accounts and paid its taxes. Goddard, an accountant, had become senior compliance officer under George Law, the cadaverous former partner at Slaughter & May and sometime head of Corporate Finance, who finished his career as the group compliance director. In order to police the various 'Chinese Walls', all Morgan Grenfell staff were obliged to deal in shares only through the bank's own dealers. So Tatman and Goddard first checked Gray's staff dealing forms – the slips of paper that record all personal share-dealings by members of staff – but found that they were all legitimate. Then they checked the tape recordings of all his conversations in recent weeks. Morgan Grenfell Securities, in common with other securities firms, recorded all the telephone calls made and received by its salesmen and market-makers, not to spy on staff but to settle disagreements on the price of transactions agreed over the telephone. On the Thursday afternoon they finally discovered the calls from Rowlands to Gray and from Gray to Liggins.

They were not surprised at the involvement of Rowlands, whose relationship with Gray was known to them. They then called the Stock Exchange to check whether or not Liggins had actually bought the Pleasurama shares, to discover that the Exchange was not only probing already the suspicious upward lurch in the Pleasurama share price the day before the bid, but had been looking into unusual personal-account dealings by Gray for some time, following an anonymous telephone tip-off.[103] Mike Feltham of the Stock Exchange's surveillance department came to Finsbury Circus to listen to the tapes; back at the Exchange, his computer systems rapidly unveiled the illicit transaction. Goddard and Tatman also told George Law and Alan Bartlett, then head of sales and trading, of what they had discovered. To avoid collusion, Law insisted that Gray, Liggins and Rowlands were confronted simultaneously with the discoveries at a pre-set time. On Thursday night, Morgan Grenfell staff removed Gray's diary and address book from his desk, made copies and returned them. Gray was confronted by Tatman and Bartlett at 10.30 a.m. on Friday 12 August; he confessed and was escorted from the premises without being allowed to return to his desk. Rowlands, who also confessed, and Liggins, were sacked at the same time.[104] Mark Riding was initially suspended, but later sacked.[105] They are likely to be prosecuted under the 1985 Insider Dealing Act.

The Gray insider-dealing incident inflicted little further damage on Morgan Grenfell. Indeed, it was handled with some aplomb, at least by comparison with the clumsy methods employed by County Bank to deal with two contemporaneous dismissals for breaches of compliance rules. The accompanying publicity, far from suggesting that the bank's Compliance Department was lazy and inefficient, emphasized its probity and alertness. This was true; a workable paranoia had set in after the Collier affair. At the announcement of the interim results in September 1988, John Craven's assurances that he had prepared detailed strategic plans for each business alarmed, rather than comforted, the staff and shareholders.[106]

The longer that turnover languished and the price war continued, the more questionable Morgan Grenfell's commitment to integrated investment banking became. At the end of September John Craven reassured the staff of Morgan Grenfell Securities that the bank was still committed to the securities markets. As Craven put it:

We began to feel the cold draught on our necks in September and October and we started to ponder whether we could remain in the business or re-position it in a way that it would no longer be a major drain on resources.[107]

At the beginning of November the bank told Rosehaugh Stanhope, the developers of the Broadgate office complex, that it would not occupy the 380,000 square feet of space that had been reserved for it. Craven explained that the move would have cost 'an enormous amount of money' (£17 million a year in rent alone) and it also marked the abandonment of his cherished ambition to improve communication within the bank by moving all its employees into a single building.[107] More ominously, on the day the Broadgate decision appeared in the press, Craven invited David Ewart, the group finance director, and Charles Benson, the finance director of Morgan Grenfell Asset Management, to work with John Holmes on a detailed review of the mounting losses of Morgan Grenfell Securities.[108] Ewart became chairman of Morgan Grenfell Securities, Benson finance director. Anthony Richmond-Watson also joined the board of Morgan Grenfell Securities, to represent the interests of the Corporate Finance Department in any restructuring that took place.[110] They found that the management of Morgan Grenfell Securities was already moving towards the closure of the business.

With Morgan Grenfell Securities in obvious trouble, predators gathered. The Australian businessman, Alan Bond, had acquired control of the shares once held by Robert Holmes à Court, giving him a holding of over 8 per cent.[111] Though nobody thought he would buy the bank himself, unlike Willis Faber he would not much care who did. Willis itself had revived speculation that its 20 per cent shareholding was for sale again, and Deutsche Bank was reported to be the most likely buyer. Willis admitted that it would consider offers to buy it.[112] It had tired of the costs of the adventure in the securities markets, and the restlessness of the bank's largest shareholder was one of many influences that impelled the closure of Morgan Grenfell Securities. Closure heightened the attractions of the bank for predators too. At one point Swiss Bank Corporation was rumoured to be building a stake in the bank and Hong Kong & Shanghai was reported to be in talks with Craven.[113] Mitsubishi and the large American financial group, Travellers Insurance, also appeared on the share register for the first time.[114] Whatever the fate of Morgan Grenfell Securities, there were those outside the bank at least who doubted that Morgan Grenfell had an independent future any longer, and none of them were likely to be interested in sustaining the bank's most costly subsidiary, Morgan Grenfell Securities.

NOTES

[1] Morgan Grenfell Government Securities made an operating loss of £1.872 million in 1986 and of £1.928 million in 1987 (Morgan Grenfell Government Securities Limited, Accounts, 1986 and 1987).
[2] Pre-Big Bang commissions on long gilts were 0.125 per cent and on medium-dated gilts about half of that, or an average of 0.09375 per cent. Margaret Reid (in *All-Change in the City*, Macmillan, 1988) suggests they averaged 0.05 per cent.
[3] Reid, *op. cit.*
[4] The Bank of England has estimated that the capital deployed in the gilt-edged market before Big Bang amounted to £80 million. This had risen to £595 million at Big Bang. Subsequent withdrawals reduced this by £70 million, but additional capital of £85 million was injected, raising it to £610 million. Withdrawals of £170 million since the crash in October 1987 have reduced it to £420 million (*Bank of England Quarterly Bulletin*, February 1989).
[5] *ibid.*

[6] Reid, *op. cit.* The bulk of the losses in the gilt-edged market were incurred in the summer of 1987 and the last three quarters of 1988. The Bank of England estimated that losses in the gilt-edged market averaged £4 million a week in the summer of 1987 and £2 million a week in the last three quarters of 1988, suggesting losses in 1987 may have totalled £80–90 million and perhaps another £80 million in the last three quarters of 1988. This, coupled with smaller but continuing losses at other times is consistent with the Bank's estimate of cumulative losses of £190 million (*Bank of England Quarterly Bulletin*, February 1989).

[7] *ibid.*, cited in *The Independent*, 9 February 1989. The figure excludes, of course, the opportunity cost of capital which might have been deployed in more profitable activities.

[8] *Bank of England Quarterly Bulletin*, February 1989.

[9] Gross profits of £761,000 in 1986 and of £5.078 million in 1987 were erased by administrative costs of £2.633 million in 1986 and of £7.006 million in 1987 (Morgan Grenfell Government Securities Limited, Accounts, 1987).

[10] Morgan Grenfell Government Securities Limited, Accounts, 1987.

[11] *ibid.*

[12] *The Times*, 20 July 1987.

[13] *Financial Times*, 17 July 1987.

[14] *Daily Telegraph*, 9 September 1987.

[15] *The Economist*, 12 November 1987; *The Independent*, 18 April 1988.

[16] *Financial Times*, 12 December 1988.

[17] *The Economist*, 7 November 1987.

[18] *ibid.*

[19] Morgan Grenfell Group plc, Annual Report and Accounts, 1986.

[20] *ibid.*

[21] *Forbes Magazine*, 2 June 1986.

[22] *The Economist*, 5 February 1987.

[23] *The Economist*, 12 November 1987.

[24] *The Economist*, 25 June 1988.

[25] *Euromoney*, June 1988.

[26] *ibid.*

[27] *The Times*, 28 and 29 October 1987.

[28] *Financial Times*, 16 December 1987.

[29] Morgan Grenfell Group plc, Annual Report and Accounts, 1986.

[30] Morgan Grenfell Holdings Limited, Annual Report and Accounts, 1985.
[31] Morgan Grenfell Group plc, Annual Report and Accounts, 1986.
[32] *The Economist*, 5 February 1987
[33] Morgan Grenfell Group plc, Annual Report and Accounts, 1987.
[34] *The Economist*, 30 January 1988.
[35] Morgan Grenfell Group plc, Annual Report and Accounts, 1986 and 1987.
[36] *Sunday Times*, 30 August 1987; *Euromoney*, June 1988.
[37] *Glasgow Herald*, 4 September 1987.
[38] *The Times*, 23 June 1986.
[39] *Financial Times*, 17 January 1987.
[40] *Financial Times*, 29 January 1987.
[41] *Wall Street Journal*, 24 October 1986.
[42] Reid, *op. cit.*
[43] Morgan Grenfell Securities, *UK Equity Market Turnover Analysis, 1987 Year Book*, by Christopher Chaitow and Jane Shattock.
[44] *Bank of England Quarterly Bulletin*, February 1987.
[45] The Stock Exchange, *Quality of Markets Quarterly*, Summer 1987.
[46] Morgan Grenfell Group plc, Annual Report and Accounts, 1986.
[47] *Sunday Times*, 23 March 1986.
[48] *Financial Times*, 19 June 1986.
[49] *Financial Times*, 13 December 1986.
[50] *The Times*, 13 December 1986.
[51] Morgan Grenfell Group plc, Annual Report and Accounts, 1987.
[52] *Daily Telegraph*, 20 December 1986.
[53] *The Economist*, 30 January 1988.
[54] *Financial Times*, 4 September 1987.
[55] *Sunday Times*, 11 October 1987.
[56] *Standard*, 24 August 1987; *The Scotsman*, 25 August 1987; *Euromoney*, June 1988; *Sunday Times*, 11 October 1987; *Glasgow Herald*, 21 October 1987.
[57] *Sunday Times*, 6 March 1988.
[58] *The Economist*, 12 November 1987.
[59] *Sunday Times*, 6 March 1988.
[60] *Daily Telegraph*, 19 October 1987.
[61] *The Economist*, 14 November 1987.
[62] *The Economist*, 21 November 1987.
[63] The Stock Exchange, *Quality of Markets Quarterly*, Winter 1987.

[64] *The Independent*, 18 March 1988; Morgan Grenfell Group plc, Annual Report and Accounts, 1987.

[65] *The Times*, 28 October 1987; *Standard*, 28 October 1987.

[66] *Financial Times*, 29 October 1987; *The Economist*, 7 November 1987.

[67] *The Independent*, 18 March 1988.

[68] *Financial Times*, 8 January 1988.

[69] *Financial Times*, 1 December 1988.

[70] *Lloyd's List*, 8 December 1987.

[71] Morgan Grenfell Group plc, Annual Report and Accounts, 1987.

[72] *Financial Times*, 18 March 1988; Morgan Grenfell Group plc, Annual Report and Accounts, 1987.

[73] *ibid.*

[74] *Daily Telegraph*, 18 March 1988; Morgan Grenfell Group plc, Annual Report and Accounts, 1986 and 1987.

[75] *Euromoney*, June 1988.

[76] *The Economist*, 30 January 1988.

[77] *ibid.*

[78] *The Independent*, 26 January 1988; *Financial Times*, 26 January 1988; *Guardian*, 26 January 1988; *The Economist*, 30 January 1988.

[79] *Observer*, 30 July 1989; *The Times*, 22 December 1987.

[80] *The Independent*, 19 and 21 December 1987; *The Times*, 22 December 1987.

[81] *The Economist*, 25 June 1988; *Daily Telegraph*, 16 May and 13 June 1988.

[82] *Sunday Telegraph*, 27 March 1988.

[83] *Observer*, 3 January 1988.

[84] *Sunday Telegraph*, 29 January 1988; *The Times*, 2 August 1988.

[85] *Sunday Times*, 11 December 1988.

[86] *The Economist*, 30 January 1988.

[87] *Financial Times*, 1 December 1988.

[88] *Australian Financial Review*, 11 December 1987.

[89] *The Economist*, 25 June 1988.

[90] *Financial Times*, 16 December 1987.

[91] *The Independent*, 25 January 1988.

[92] *Standard*, 10 December 1975.

[93] *The Times*, 3 February 1969.

[94] Janet McCurrie was the first woman to serve on the board of Morgan Grenfell.

[95] *The Independent*, 9 September 1988.

[96] *The Mail on Sunday*, 13 November 1988.

[97] *Daily Telegraph*, 1 February 1988; *The Independent*, 18 May and 8 October 1988; *Sunday Telegraph*, 9 October 1988; *Financial Times*, 4 November 1988 and 16 January 1989.

[98] *The Independent*, 7 December 1988.

[99] Greenwich Associates Survey, *Financial Times*, 20 October 1988.

[100] *Financial Times*, 9 September 1988.

[101] *The Independent*, 15 August 1988.

[102] Morgan Grenfell leaked the transcripts of the taped conversation between Gray and Rowlands to the press, and they appeared first in the *Sunday Times* of 21 August 1988. A second version of the conversation was given to the *Observer Magazine* of the 30 July 1989. It runs as follows:

Rowlands: 'Remember the stock and don't mention any names
that I have just got stuffed in.'
Gray   : 'Yes.'
Rowlands: 'Well tomorrow is the day.'
Gray   : 'OK, what a pleasurable thing to have occurred.'
Rowlands: 'Lovely day.'
Gray   : 'It's very pleasing to see things like that.'
Rowlands: 'It's my day for having a drink with Bill, but I get
very busy.'
Gray   : 'I think I will. Pleasing news. OK.'

The first version reads more plausibly, so it has been preferred.

[103] *Financial Times*, 17 August 1988.

[104] *Financial Times*, 16 August 1988; *Sunday Times*, 21 August 1988; *Observer*, 21 August 1988.

[105] *Sunday Telegraph*, 28 August 1988.

[106] *Guardian*, 9 September 1988; *Financial Times*, 9 September 1988; *The Independent*, 9 September 1988.

[107] *Sunday Times*, 11 December 1988.

[108] *Daily Telegraph*, 3 November 1988; *The Independent*, 4 November 1988.

[109] *Sunday Times*, 11 December 1988.

[110] *Financial Times*, 4 November 1988.

[111] *The Times*, 24 May and 26 October 1988; *The Independent*, 26 October 1988.

[112] *The Independent*, 14 September and 3 November 1988.

[113] *The Independent*, 7 June 1988; *The Times*, 7, 8 and 14 June 1988; *Standard*, 29 November 1988.

[114] *Sunday Times*, 16 October 1988.

FOURTEEN

Nemesis

Early on the morning of Tuesday 6 December 1988, those members of Morgan Grenfell Securities who read the *Daily Telegraph* pointed out to their colleagues a story in the financial pages whose headline read confidently enough to suggest that it was well-informed: 'Morgan Grenfell to quit stock market.'[1] News of the story spread quickly throughout 20 Finsbury Circus, paralysing most of the 450 or so staff who occupied its six floors. Though the gilts dealers carried on trading for an hour or so and the SEAQ equity screens initially showed just red prices, indicating only that Morgan Grenfell Securities was not making a market, a flash across the screen at 9 a.m. confirmed that they would never do so again. Some staff were more surprised than others. Charles Peel, who had flown to New York before the weekend to attend the C. J. Lawrence Christmas party, had been telephoned by Holmes with confirmation of the news on Friday afternoon, and had discussed it more or less openly at the party in New York that night. It is likely that the leak to the *Telegraph* was made by someone he spoke to. The joint heads of market-making, Richard Harris and Steve Davies, were told of the plan on Monday, but few other staff came to work on Tuesday expecting the sack. Rumours and counter-rumours had traversed the building for weeks, but few had given them much credit. The recent introduction of new contracts, gearing notice periods to length of service, coupled with reminders that the payment of Christmas bonuses had been deferred until April, induced a sense of anxiety but at least referred to the future.[2] Only secretaries, who were put on one-month contracts, cheapening substantially the cost of mass dismissals, had reasonable cause to feel alarmed.

Details of the decision to close the department were leaked to journalists. Peel had been convinced of the need to close for some time, and Bartlett since at least September. On Monday John Craven, Guy Dawson and Michael Dobson voted two to one in favour of closure, Dawson demurring. He had grown fond of Morgan Grenfell Securities as a window on the market and a valuable source of research (for which the Corporate Finance Department paid) even if he gave it little of his business, and had retained his faith in the concept of integration. Ewart and Benson had earlier reported to both groups their conclusion that Morgan Grenfell Securities could not be 're-positioned' successfully, which they had reached only after an exhaustive study of every alternative. Morgan Grenfell had just 2.5 per cent of equity turnover (perhaps only 2 per cent of client turnover) and a meagre 5 per cent of turnover in gilts.[3] Any retrenchment short of full-scale closure still necessitated a large investment in fixed costs like floorspace and computer dealing and settlement systems. In the first eleven months of 1988 Morgan Grenfell Securities had lost £18 million in share-dealing and a further £4.5 million trading in gilts. Given that the bank lost only £5 million on share-dealing in the first six months of the year, the rate of loss had doubled since the price war broke out in equities in August.[4] On the Friday, John Craven, who had planned to stay at home in Chelsea after cancelling a day's shooting because of a sore throat, came into work to plan the timing and the terms of 450 redundancies.[5] A meeting of the group board was convened on the following Monday morning to approve the decision.

Craven claims that he originally planned to announce the shut-down at the close of business on Thursday 8 December. The uproar which followed the leak in Tuesday's *Telegraph* obliged him to act immediately, and he appeared pesonally on the trading floor at 20 Finsbury Circus to confirm the story at 8.00 a.m.[6] The logistics were depressing. A list of the 450 victims was posted in the reception area at 20 Finsbury Circus, directing each member of staff to a room somewhere in the building where, at 4.00 p.m., they were addressed by senior directors, including Richard Webb and Michael Dobson. In his address to the trading floor, Craven apologized for the manner in which the staff had learned of their demise. He said that the bank had allocated £10 million for redundancy payments and advised staff to go home while the bank worked out the terms of each package. He asked them not to talk to the press, a request accepted naturally enough by people who had lost their jobs and were now fearful of losing their redundancy payments if they did talk: when the ITN news team walked into The Pavilion, a wine bar in the middle of Finsbury Circus popular with Morgan Grenfell staff, most of the customers crept out.[7] Charles Peel, back from New York, repeated the message to the analysts on the second floor, adding that some of them would be retained as the core of a small agency-only brokerage business headed by himself, to match in London the service offered in New York by C. J. Lawrence.

Michael Dobson addressed a collection of junior executives and secretaries drawn from around the building. Though he had once boasted of his prowess in sacking people – 'I wouldn't hesitate to sack someone. Their cost to the company is two and a half times their salary. And it's very much my arse that's on the line'[8] – he was woefully underbriefed. His explanation that the bank's overall performance would improve without the burden on the payroll of those that he was sacking testified to it. Angry staff, who had read about the sack in a daily newspaper, were tired of managers who, in Norman Tebbit's phrase, were strangled by their old school ties. They asked for the terms of their redundancy packages and whether or not it was true that Morgan Grenfell Securities in London was carrying the can for momentous losses in the securities markets in Tokyo. (In the year to September 1988 Morgan Grenfell Japan lost £3.9 million.[9]) When he could not answer, they sent him away to find out. The settlement staff were offered 'deferred redundancy', which allowed the bank to sack them with a month's notice but permitted them to sack the bank only with six months' notice. The bank hoped in this way to hang on to sufficient settlement staff to unwind or complete all the transactions left by its hasty withdrawal from the market. Elsewhere, the 120 sacked computer staff were shadowed by security men as they cleared their desks, the management fearing that one of them might plant a vengeful 'virus' in the bank's computer systems.[10] Even the 40 sacking-hardened counsellors from Sanders & Sidney, the outplacement consultancy retained by the bank to help redundant staff get new jobs, thought Morgan Grenfell had handled the dismissals with crass insensitivity.

Amid the chaos, Charles Peel tried vainly to enthuse others with his plan for the creation of a small agency broker, akin to C. J. Lawrence in New York. Around a dozen analysts, especially those who had worked well with Corporate Finance, and half a dozen salesmen were invited to stay on. Jim Moltz, the head of C. J. Lawrence, flew to London on 9 December to explain his firm's success. Craven and Dobson offered the qualified support of the bank, guaranteeing it a three-year trial, subject to losses. The concept was treated with justifiable derision by those left out as a feeble propaganda ploy, designed for external consumption only, or as a scheme to avoid massive redundancy payments to top-rated analysts by offering them an option to buy back any business they created within two years.[11] There was a splendidly surreal aspect to the discovery that a memorandum listing the 20-odd lucky survivors was circulating within the bank – unwanted news for an audience that had departed, leaving an empty building. 'The integrated concept is not dead,' said Craven, but it was.[12] Though the Corporate Finance Department was supportive, Asset Management was not. Of those invited to stay, only two junior salesmen voted to do so. The senior analysts worried that their ratings would decline, and the better salesmen feared for their future without market-makers to execute their orders, and opted to leave. Craven rejected their offer to stay at higher salaries to compensate them for the risk and the loss of their redundancy payments.[13] The closure itself cost £52.4 million before tax. The bank paid £22.3 million in redundancy costs, £22.9 million in equipment write-offs and another £7.2 million in overseas closure costs in addition to market-making and distribution losses of £21 million.[14] In an ironic rebuke to everything that Christopher Reeves had created, the share price rose on the news of the closure of Morgan Grenfell Securities. Dealers calculated that, shorn of its loss-making securities arm, Morgan Grenfell was a more tempting target for the gathering predators. For John Holmes, the decision rubbed out everything he had done in the last three years. As he addressed the sales, market-making and research teams which he had welded painstakingly out of nothing, he was close to tears. A late convert to the closure plan, he explained how he had fought to persuade the bank to remain committed to the equity markets. There is no doubt that his staff nursed a genuine affection for Holmes – many had joined almost solely to work for him. 'The best years of my life,' said one of them, the property analyst, Alec Pelmore.[15] At the end of his speech they burst into spontaneous applause. That night John Holmes gave an envelope to the tea lady, who had brought him tea and coffee twice on every working day but now would do so no more. When she got home she discovered it contained £200 in cash.

In July 1986, nearly a year before he became chief executive at Morgan Grenfell, John Craven reviewed a book for *Business* magazine. The book was *Greed and Glory on Wall Street* by Ken Auletta, which tells the story of how the oldest surviving investment-banking partnership on Wall Street, Lehman Brothers, was destroyed in the years after America's own Big Bang – May Day 1975 – by internecine strife between an Ivy League banker called Peter Peterson and a red-blooded trader called Lew Glucksman. Eventually, the business of Lehman Brothers suffered so much that it was taken over by the Shearson division of American Express. The parallels between what happened at Lehman Brothers and what happened at Morgan Grenfell are suggestive rather than exact, but Craven's assessment then must surely have surfaced again in his mind at Christmas 1988:

The politics and intrigue, the greed and cowardice that came to the surface make fascinating reading. The story is also revolting in the true sense of the word, given that the struggle was about money, of which there was more than enough to go round – the amounts boggle the imagination of the ordinary mortal.

Glucksman had bad luck in that his assumption of power was followed by a period of difficult trading markets. Profits turned into losses and capital began to evaporate. Panic set in and fear overcame greed as the dominant motivation of the partnership. The manoeuvring that resulted in the sale of the firm to Shearson as a means of enabling the partners to extract a premium capital sum from the business is on its own an absorbing story.

The story has a moral. The fundamental weakness of Lehman Brothers was the absence of leadership, a leadership that could promote the community of economic interest needed to bind the partnership together. Instead, the pursuit of personal interest and publicity prevailed over the common good. The seeds of this must have been sown many years before the final dénouement. As a former partner of Lehman Brothers said, 'The ground was well prepared for the poison ivy to take root.'[16]

In deciding to close Morgan Grenfell Securities John Craven was, in his own words, facing up to the consequences of the poor decisions made by Christopher Reeves and Blaise Hardman in 1984.[17] They had, he said,

implemented their decision in a way which I would hardly say was ideal. To take a zero market share and build a meaningful business was frankly a hell of an uphill task which I don't think that anybody could have achieved.[18]

He could have gone further than this. John Craven has abandoned most of the markets by which the men of the Reeves regime gauged their success – Eurobonds, gilts, shares, Australia, Switzerland – and returned to where it all started in 1979: corporate finance, fund management and banking. He has even added unit trusts and venture capital, which Reeves rejected as insufficiently profitable.[19] The remaining businesses

461

are bigger, and wiser, for the journey of the last decade, and the men running them know now their limitations, but it cost the shareholders of the bank about £120 million for them to find out these things.

A ghoulish search for culprits follows most disasters in the modern world, as if men are shocked, rather than humbled, by their own imperfections. It is not a tendency much imitated in the City of London, where the penalties for error and incompetence are more usually measured in thousands of pounds than thousands of curses. But the temptation to say 'There but for the grace of God go I', or that the strategic mistakes have become obvious only with hindsight, common enough in a closed world like the City, is in the end unjust to the shareholders and staff who are the victims of management error. Big Bang, Geoffrey Collier, the Guinness affair, the crash, even the price war in London did not cause the death of Morgan Grenfell Securities; they merely hastened it. The 450 people who lost their jobs on 6 December 1988 paid the price for the mistakes of the men who managed the response of the bank to the events unleashed by Big Bang. They were not, of course, alone in making them. The greed, caution, panic, incompetence, pride, arrogance, cowardice and foolishness that disfigured their tenureship were all too common in the City of London in the 1980s but others, rather than they, have paid the price for that.

None of those unseated by the Guinness affair is short of money or work, save Ernest Saunders. On the afternoon of 7 January 1988, early editions of the *Evening Standard* were advertised by an intriguingly daring bill proclaiming 'Bank blocks £1 million City cheat's job'. It sold a lot of copies before the telephone began to ring and it transpired that the sign-writer had misheard 'cheat' for 'chief'.[20] It referred to Christopher Reeves and a rumour that his appointment to Merrill Lynch Europe, John Craven's old job, had been vetoed by the Bank of England because of his association with the Guinness affair.[20] The rumour was denied by Merrill Lynch, and Reeves continued to work for them as a consultant until in January

1989 the Bank cleared his appointment as vice-chairman.[22] He has not spoken to the press since he was sacked by Morgan Grenfell. Roger Seelig is still awaiting trial on the charges arising from his involvement in the Guinness affair, but is working as hard and living as comfortably as ever. In 1987 he helped sell Stockley, the property-development company he started with Elliott Bernerd and Jacob Rothschild, to Tony Clegg's Mountleigh Group. He also advised his old friend, Sir Terence Conran, on how Storehouse could repel bidders. In October 1988 he persuaded George Davies of Next to sell over 400 shops to Gerald Ratner, of Ratner's the jewellers, where the finance director is a former colleague from the Corporate Finance Department at Morgan Grenfell.[23] Graham Walsh joined Bankers Trust of New York in June 1988, to advise on their European merchant-banking activities. The inspectors were much amused by a letter sent to him in 1982 by Sir Gordon Richardson, then governor of the Bank of England, thanking him for his work as director-general of the Takeover Panel. For some reason, Richardson had signed it 'Graham Walsh'.[24] His appointment at Bankers Trust was eventually cleared with the Bank of England, which initially precluded a managerial role.[25]

Patrick Spens is still awaiting trial too, but runs a successful corporate-finance 'boutique' off Oxford Street called Castlecrest Investments. He has chosen to conduct his own defence in the forthcoming trial.[26] Elliott Bernerd now runs a substantial private-property company, Chelsfield, from a plush Mayfair office where he employs former staff of Morgan Grenfell. His recent deals have included the sale of the former *Times* building in Gray's Inn Road, the repurchase of Stockley Park from Mountleigh and the purchase of an interest in Wentworth Golf Club at Virginia Water in Surrey from Benlox, which is now chaired by a former colleague from Morgan Grenfell Laurie and whose biggest but most ambiguous shareholder is Dr Ashraf Marwan. Bernerd has also been advised by George Magan, who left Morgan Grenfell in February 1988 to set up a small corporate-finance house with Rupert Hambro, the former chairman of Hambro's Bank.[27] Magan left with Morgan Grenfell's best wishes, littering his path with promises not to take any of its staff or clients with him.[28] His departure was 'rather a bore' said Craven.[29] 'We will mobilize finance, which is the historic role of merchant banks,' said Magan.[30] One of Hambro Magan's recent deals – advising Carless against a bid from Kelt Energy – pitched him against Patrick Spens, helping his old friend Ashraf Marwan buy into Kelt.[31] Spens's client in the battle for Bell's, Raymond Miquel, lost his job as chief executive at Belhaven Brewery in September 1988 after a boardroom row, but collected £390,000 in compensation.[32] David Mayhew is still working at Cazenove, his position in City society strained by his association with the Guinness affair.

Philip Chappell is now an adviser to the Association of Investment Trust Companies in London, and reflects that he 'got out at just the right time'.[33] Blaise Hardman has an advisory job with the Tokai Bank, Morgan Grenfell's oldest friend among the Japanese banks. Jon Perry had a similar assignment at Deutsche Bank, but is now a consultant on the securities industry. Charles Rawlinson is more or less retired, but remains a 'senior adviser' to Morgan Grenfell.[34] Geoffrey Collier has spent much of the time after his trial in New York, attempting to rebuild a career in the securities industry after being banned for life by the London Stock Exchange. In July 1988, the US Securities and Exchange Commission settled a civil insider-trading suit against him arising from the AE and Cadbury purchases, freeing him to work there again but he is now working in London, outside the securities industry.[35] Ernest Saunders is out of work and owes his lawyers £662,000. He has been granted legal aid to defend himself at his trial, the postponement of which he has described as an affront to human rights, but his solicitors resigned the assignment on the grounds that he had been granted insufficient aid for them to perform adequately.[36] His son, James, has published an account of his father's career. James Gulliver left Argyll Foods to his deputy, Alistair Grant, resurfacing later as leader of the consortium which bought Sir Phil Harris's Harris Queensway carpets business. Bay Green, the adviser to Distillers, is now at Hill Samuel, trying to revive its demoralized Corporate Finance Department.

Most of those sacked by Morgan Grenfell Securities in December 1988 have found new jobs, but a few have left the City altogether. John Holmes has joined Morgan Stanley as managing director of United Kingdom and European equities.[37] Basil Postan is a managing director at Dillon Read, an American investment bank.[38] Lord Catto is still the president of Morgan Grenfell though his son, Alex, is now with Lazard's. Sir Peter Carey retired as chairman of Morgan Grenfell in October 1989. In September 1988 he ordered the suppression of a 'full and frank' history of Morgan Grenfell, commissioned in happier days as part of the celebrations of the 150th anniversary of the foundation of the bank at 31 Moorgate in 1838, though he eventually relented and agreed to publish the story up to 1981.[39] A month later he gave £500,000 on behalf of the bank to the Tower Hamlets Centre for Small Business in Brick Lane, near the site of the first Peabody Buildings in Spitalfields.[40] After all the tumult and venality of the previous years, the bank has rediscovered George Peabody's 'higher pleasure and a greater happiness than making money – that of giving it away for good purposes'.

NOTES

[1] *Daily Telegraph*, 6 December 1988.
[2] *The Times*, 7 December 1988.
[3] *Financial Times*, 7 December 1988.
[4] *The Independent*, 7 December 1988.
[5] *Sunday Times*, 11 December 1988.
[6] The *Observer Magazine*, 30 July 1989.
[7] *Guardian*, 7 December 1988.
[8] Nicholas Shakespeare, *Londoners*, Sidgwick & Jackson, 1986.
[9] *The Independent*, 13 and 14 January 1989.

[10] *The Times*, 7 December 1988.
[11] *Daily Telegraph*, 10 December 1988
[12] *Financial Times*, 7 December 1988.
[13] *The Independent*, 5 January 1989.
[14] Morgan Grenfell Group plc, Annual Report and Accounts, 1988.
[15] *The Times*, 8 December 1988.
[16] *Business*, July 1988.
[17] *The Times*, 7 December 1988.
[18] *Daily Telegraph*, 7 December 1988.
[19] *Financial Times*, 24 April 1989.
[20] *The Times*, 8 January 1988.
[21] *The Independent*, 8 January 1988.
[22] *Financial Times*, 10 January 1989.
[23] *Mail on Sunday*, 30 October 1988.
[24] *The Times*, 9 November 1988.
[25] *Financial Times*, 15 June 1988; *The Independent*, 15 June 1988
[26] *The Times*, 29 April 1989.
[27] *The Times*, 9 March 1988; *Sunday Times*, 15 May and 10 July 1988; *Sunday Telegraph*, 16 October 1988; *The Times*, 5 January 1989.
[28] *Financial Times*, 23 February 1988.
[29] *The Times*, 23 February 1988.
[30] *The Independent*, 23 February 1988.
[31] *Financial Times*, 2 November 1988.
[32] *The Independent*, 25 October 1988.
[33] *Planned Savings*, July 1988.
[34] Morgan Grenfell Group plc, Annual Report and Acounts, 1988.
[35] *Financial Times*, 27 July 1988.
[36] *The Times*, 27 September, 13 December 1988 and 28 April 1989; *Financial Times*, 14 December 1988.
[37] *Euroweek*, 10 February 1989.
[38] *The Times*, 22 February 1989.
[39] *Financial Times*, 19 September 1988.
[40] *Financial Times*, 4 October 1988; *The Times*, 6 October 1988.

Index

Accepting Houses Committee, 65–6
AE Ltd and G. Collier, 300ff
Akroyd & Smithers – Jobbers, 199, 206
Alexander, Robert (Collier's counsel), 309–11
Allied Lyons, 334–5
'Aluminium War' (1958), 98–102
American Tobacco Co. and Gallaher's shares, 115–22`
Ansbacher, J. Henry: and P. Spens, 325–6, 332, 365–8, 377; and Guinness dividend, 373, 392, 403
Argentina, Morgan's involvement, 43–5, 51–2, 65
Argyll Ltd: Distillers bid, 282, 334–6, 342, 344–50, 354, 358 379–80; Boesky, 362
ARIEL (Automated Real Time Investments Exchange Ltd), 201
Asprey & Co.: bought by Morgan Grenfell, 178–9
Astley & Pearce (Exco's moneybrokers), 283–4

Bain and Co.: and E. Saunders, 323; 'Bainies', 361; and Sir Jack Lyons, 387–8
Bank for International Settlements, 70
Bank Leu: and Guinness, 358–9, 364
Bank of England: and Peabody loan, 19; Baring's crisis, 43; gold standard, 47, 66–8; Vivian

Smith (Bicester), 50; Edward Grenfell, 51, 56–7; Lord Cunliffe, 60; Montagu Norman, 64; Accepting Houses Committee, 65; nationalized, 79, 85; Argentinian debts, 43–4; Gallaher's sale, 118–21; secondary banks, 137; ICL crisis, 167; A. Buchanan, 253; Morgan Grenfell and Exco, 281; Stock Exchange, 346–7; changes at Morgan Grenfell, 400–2
Bank Rate Tribunal: evidence by Lord Kindersley, 88
Banque Morgan Grenfell en Suisse, 443
Barclays de Zoete Wedd: and Big Bang, 213, 422
Baring Brothers: and banking, 10; Boston, 15; Samuel Ward, 16; Europe, 21, 25; Baltimore & Ohio Railroad, 26; Lord Revelstoke, 45, 48–9, 52; Argentinian crisis, 43–5, 51–2; Boer War, 47–8; post-World War I, 65; and ICI bid for Courtauld's, 106–7; and AEI defence against GEC, 108–9
Barnes, Tolhurst & Milner, stockbrokers, Adelaide, 261, 438
Barrington, Sir Kenneth: Morgan Grenfell 1929–76, 105, 122, 124, 140, 160
Bartlett, Alan: Morgan Grenfell head of sales and trading, 264, 449, 457

467

150; Europe, 152; replaced by Mackworth-Young, 157; chairman, 161, 277; Big Bang, 206; Hong Kong, 214; Chappell's resignation, 275; shareholding, 290; Ernest Saunders, 320; Guinness, 374–5; resignations of Reeves and Walsh, 377, 400; president, 408, 465

Catto, Thomas Sivewright, 1st Baron Catto: 74–5; and Yule & Co., 74; Great Crash, 78; director of Morgan Grenfell, 80; introduces corporate advice, 81, 84; in WWII, 82–3; Governor of Bank of England, 83; death, 83

Cazenove & Co.: and Gallahers, 115–19; Tillings, 180; Morgan Grenfell flotation, 287; Big Bang, 293; Distillers, 340, 356, 358, 363; DTI inspectors, 369; Schenley, 370

Chambers, Sir Paul: ICI chairman, 106

Channon, Paul: and Collier, 305–6; UB-Imperial merger, 337; Guinness, 376; BTR bid for Pilkington, 414–15

Chappell, Philip: joins Morgan Grenfell, 106; *News of the World* bid, 125; 'Project Triangle', 141; Willis Faber flotation, 156; biography, 159–60; dismissed as ICL chairman, 167; corporate finance policy, 173; Australia, 175–6; Ladbroke, 176; Big Bang, 208; resigns, 275–7, 426; Association of Investment Trust Companies, 465

Chiene, John: Wood Mackenzie, 361

'Chinese Walls': at Morgan Grenfell, 255, 299–300, 430, 449

Churchill, Winston: as Chancellor, 64, 68; Prime Minister, 83

CIFCO: and S. W. Berisford, 384–6

Citicorp Scrimgeour Vickers: brokers, 300–1, 445

Civil War, US, 21–2, 27–8, 33n

Clore, Charles: and Watney bid, 98, 102; Hill Samuel, 166

Collier, Geoffrey: and Vickers da Costa, 250–1; career, 250–1, 308–9; at Morgan Grenfell, 260, 262–3, 429; salary, 265; portfolio trading, 294–5; insider dealing, 300–12; Press coverage, 303–6; sentenced, 310–11; Schroder Wagg, 369; banned by Stock Exchange, 464

Collins, J. E. H. ('Tim'): at Morgan Grenfell, 83; vice-chairman, 113; leasing, 111–12; film financing, 135; chairman of Holdings board, 150–1; and Labour Government, 151, 155; retirement, 161

Combe, S. H., Watney Mann chairman: and Charles Clore 98

Commune, Paris, 24

Compliance: and conflicts of interest, 256; Morgan Grenfell brochure, 311–12; Mecca bid, 448–50

Connell, John: Distillers chairman, 334, 340, 361

Conran, Sir Terence: and Seelig, 271, 318, 415, 463

Cook, Robin: Labour MP, 310; on Collier sentence, 310; on Distillers bid, 369

Coolidge, President Calvin: and WWI debts, 63

Cort, Roger: and Patrick Spens, 326, 332

Cotton, Jack: and Hill Samuel, 166

Courtauld's: bid by ICI, 106–7

County Bank: and Charles Peel, 429; redundancies, 442

Crash, the Great Crash, 1929, 71, 76–7, 78–9, 81

Grenfell in Australia, 175–6;
gilt-edged trading, 257–8, 423
Durham, Sir Kenneth: Morgan
Grenfell director, 277

Eagle Star Insurance: and Allianz
bid, 183–9; purchase by BAT,
337
ECGD (Export Credit Guarantee
Department): and Morgan
Grenfell, 143–4, 159; and
exports to Brazil, 241
Economist, The: opinion of Morgan
Grenfell, 298; and Collier, 303–
4; and Deutsche Bank, 437
Edwards, Francesca: head of
Morgan Grenfell gilts sales, 424
Edwardes, Sir Michael: and
Dunlop rescue, 221–4
Elliott, Pat: and Morgan Grenfell
Australia, 262
England, Bank of: see Bank of
England
Erskine, Sir George: joins Morgan
Grenfell, 83; and steel
denationalization, 86, 105
Eurobonds: introduced, 63; and
Warburg's, 102; origins, 103;
and Morgan Grenfell, 170–2;
neglected, 200, 204; changes in
market, 232–46; swaps, 238–9;
trading staff, 242; Morgan
Grenfell Perpetual Floating Rate
Notes, 287, 426–7; after Big
Bang, 292–4, 298; Morgan
Grenfell leaves market, 424–9,
442; and convertible bond losses,
447
European Community; British
membership, 152
Evans, Philip: Morgan Grenfell
corporate finance department,
300; and Bell's shares, 323, 402
Ewart, David: Morgan Grenfell
group finance director, 450
Exco: and Morgan Grenfell
takeover plan, 280–5

Faber, Julian: joins Morgan
Grenfell board, 168
Fallon, Ivan: *Sunday Times*, 321,
362
'Fan Clubs', 354, 364, 403
Feltham, Mike: Stock Exchange
surveillance department, 449
Fenhalls, Richard: chief executive,
Ansbacher's, 365, 373; and
Guinness, 376–7
Fielding Newson-Smith: brokers,
356
Fisk, Jim, 26
Fleet, Kenneth (*The Times*): and
Distillers, 340; and banking
ethics, 401
Fleming, Ian: and Morgan
Grenfell, 82
Fleming, Robert & Co., Ltd: and
Imperial group, 115
Fletcher, Alex: Argyll adviser, 342
Forbes, Anthony: Cazenove's; and
Guinness, 319ff, 360
Forrest, Bill: Distillers director,
340
Forsyth, John: Morgan Grenfell
director; and Eurobonds, 170;
Big Bang, 208; gilt-edged
trading, 257, 423; strategic
planning, 441
Fraher, Tony: manager Morgan
Grenfell Unit Trust Managers,
444
Franco-Prussian war of 1870, 23–4
Franklin, John: Morgan Grenfell
Inc., 260
Fraser, Charles: Morgan Grenfell
and United Biscuits, 341; and
Sir Thomas Risk, 362
Fraser, Ian: Lazard's chairman,
292
Freshfields: Guinness solicitors,
379. (See also D. Napley, H.
Smith.)
Fulton, Charles: moneybroker, 283
Furer, Dr Arthur: Bank Leu, 358,
364; and Guinness, 378